ENGLISH
FOR EVERYONE
COURSE BOOK
LEVEL 1 BEGINNER

FREE AUDIO
website and app
www.dkefe.com

Author

Rachel Harding has a background in English-language teaching and is now a full-time author of English-language learning materials. She has written for major English-language publishers including Oxford University Press.

Course consultant

Tim Bowen has taught English and trained teachers in more than 30 countries worldwide. He is the co-author of works on pronunciation teaching and language-teaching methodology, and author of numerous books for English-language teachers. He is currently a freelance materials writer, editor, and translator. He is a member of the Chartered Institute of Linguists.

Language consultant

Professor Susan Barduhn is an experienced English-language teacher, teacher trainer, and author, who has contributed to numerous publications. In addition to directing English-language courses in at least four different continents, she has been President of the International Association of Teachers of English as a Foreign Language, and an adviser to the British Council and the US State Department. She is currently a Professor at the School for International Training in Vermont, USA.

ENGLISH FOR EVERYONE

COURSE BOOK

LEVEL 1 BEGINNER

SECOND EDITION
Senior Editor Ankita Awasthi Tröger
Editor Elizabeth Blakemore
Art Editor Amy Child
Managing Editor Carine Tracanelli
Managing Art Editor Anna Hall
Production Editor Gillian Reid
Senior Production Controller Meskerem Berhane
Jacket Designer Surabhi Wadhwa-Gandhi
Jacket Design Development Manager Sophia MTT
Publisher Andrew Macintyre
Managing Director, DK Learning Hilary Fine

DK INDIA
Senior Jackets Coordinator Priyanka Sharma Saddi
DTP Designer Rakesh Kumar

FIRST EDITION
US Editors Allison Singer, Jenny Siklos
Editors Gareth Clark, Lisa Gillespie, Andrew Kerr-Jarrett
Art Editors Chrissy Barnard, Ray Bryant
Senior Art Editor Sharon Spencer
Editorial Assistants Jessica Cawthra, Sarah Edwards
Illustrators Edwood Burn, Denise Joos, Michael Parkin, Jemma Westing
Audio Producer Liz Hammond
Managing Editor Daniel Mills
Managing Art Editor Anna Hall
Project Manager Christine Stroyan
Producer, Pre-Production Luca Frassinetti
Producer Mary Slater
Jacket Designer Natalie Godwin
Jacket Editor Claire Gell
Jacket Design Development Manager Sophia MTT
Publisher Andrew Macintyre
Art Director Karen Self
Publishing Director Jonathan Metcalf

DK INDIA
Jacket Designer Surabhi Wadhwa
Managing Jackets Editor Saloni Singh
Senior DTP Designer Harish Aggarwal

This American Box Set Edition, 2024
First American Edition, 2016
Published in the United States by DK Publishing,
a division of Penguin Random House LLC
1745 Broadway, 20th Floor, New York, NY 10019

25 26 27 28 10 9 8 7 6 5 4 3
003–342958–Sep/2024

Published in Great Britain by Dorling Kindersley Limited

A catalog record for this book is available from the Library of Congress.
Box Set ISBN 978-0-5938-4961-3
ISBN 978-0-7440-9856-3

Printed and bound in China

www.dk.com

Contents

How the course works

English for Everyone is designed for people who want to teach themselves the English language. Like all language courses, it covers the core skills: grammar, vocabulary, pronunciation, listening, speaking, reading, and writing. Unlike in other courses, the skills are taught and practiced as visually as possible, using images and graphics to help you understand and remember. The best way to learn is to work through the book in order, making full use of the audio available on the website and app. Turn to the practice book at the end of each unit to reinforce your learning with additional exercises.

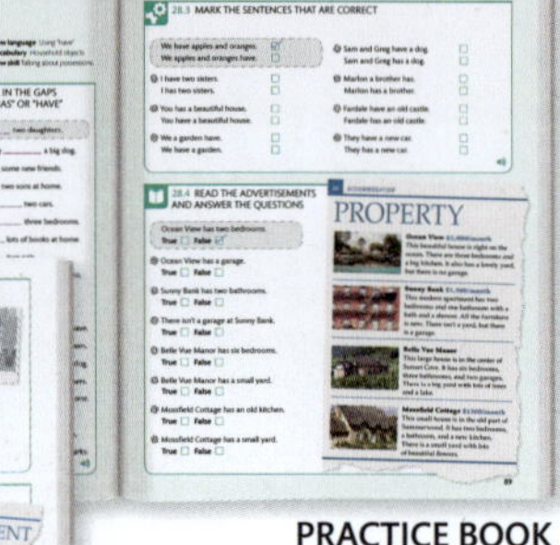

PRACTICE BOOK

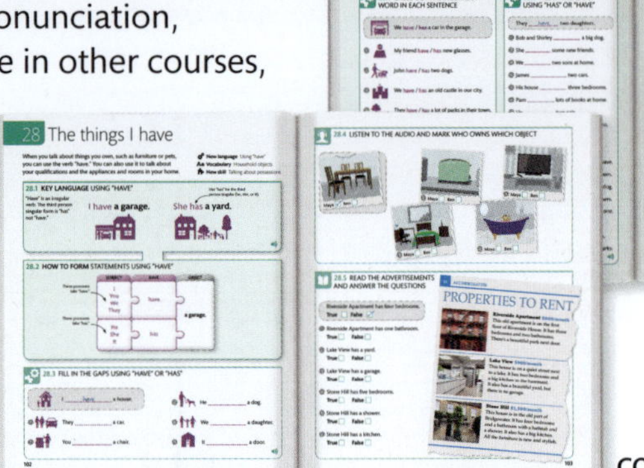

COURSE BOOK

Unit number The book is divided into units. The unit number helps you keep track of your progress.

Learning points Every unit begins with a summary of the key learning points.

Modules Each unit is broken down into modules, which should be done in order. You can take a break from learning after completing any module.

Language learning Modules with colored backgrounds teach new vocabulary and grammar. Study these carefully before moving on to the exercises.

10 Talking about your job

You can use the verb "to be" to describe your job. The verb "to work" can give more information about where you work and who you work with.

New language Using "I am" for your job
Vocabulary Jobs and workplaces
New skill Describing your job

10.1 KEY LANGUAGE YOUR JOB

Use "to be" before the job noun.
Use "a" before a noun beginning with a consonant.
I am / I'm a police officer.
You can use contractions for these statements.
Use "an" before a noun beginning with a vowel.
He is an engineer.
There is no article before a plural.
They are scientists.

10.2 FILL IN THE GAPS WITH THE CORRECT VERB AND ARTICLE

I am an engineer.
1 You ___ doctor.
2 She ___ farmer.
3 They ___ teachers.
4 We ___ nurses.
5 I ___ actor.
6 She ___ chef.

10.3 CROSS OUT THE INCORRECT WORDS

They are / is farmers.
1 You are / is a driver.
2 I am / is a mechanic.
3 He is / are a vet.
4 We am / are sales assistants.
5 They is / are businesswomen.
6 She is / are a waitress.
7 We is / are receptionists.
8 She is / are a gardener.

38

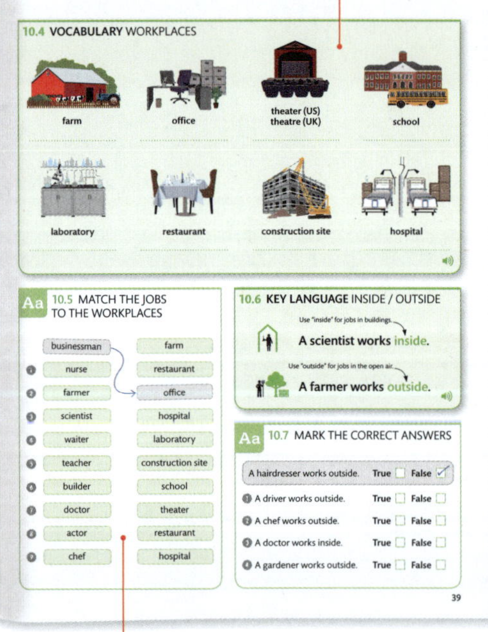

Audio support Most modules have supporting audio recordings of native English speakers to help you improve your speaking and listening skills.

Exercises Modules with white backgrounds contain exercises that help you practice your new skills to reinforce learning.

FREE AUDIO
website and app
www.dkefe.com

Language modules

New language points are taught in carefully graded stages, starting with a simple explanation of when they are used, then offering further examples of common usage, and a detailed breakdown of how key constructions are formed.

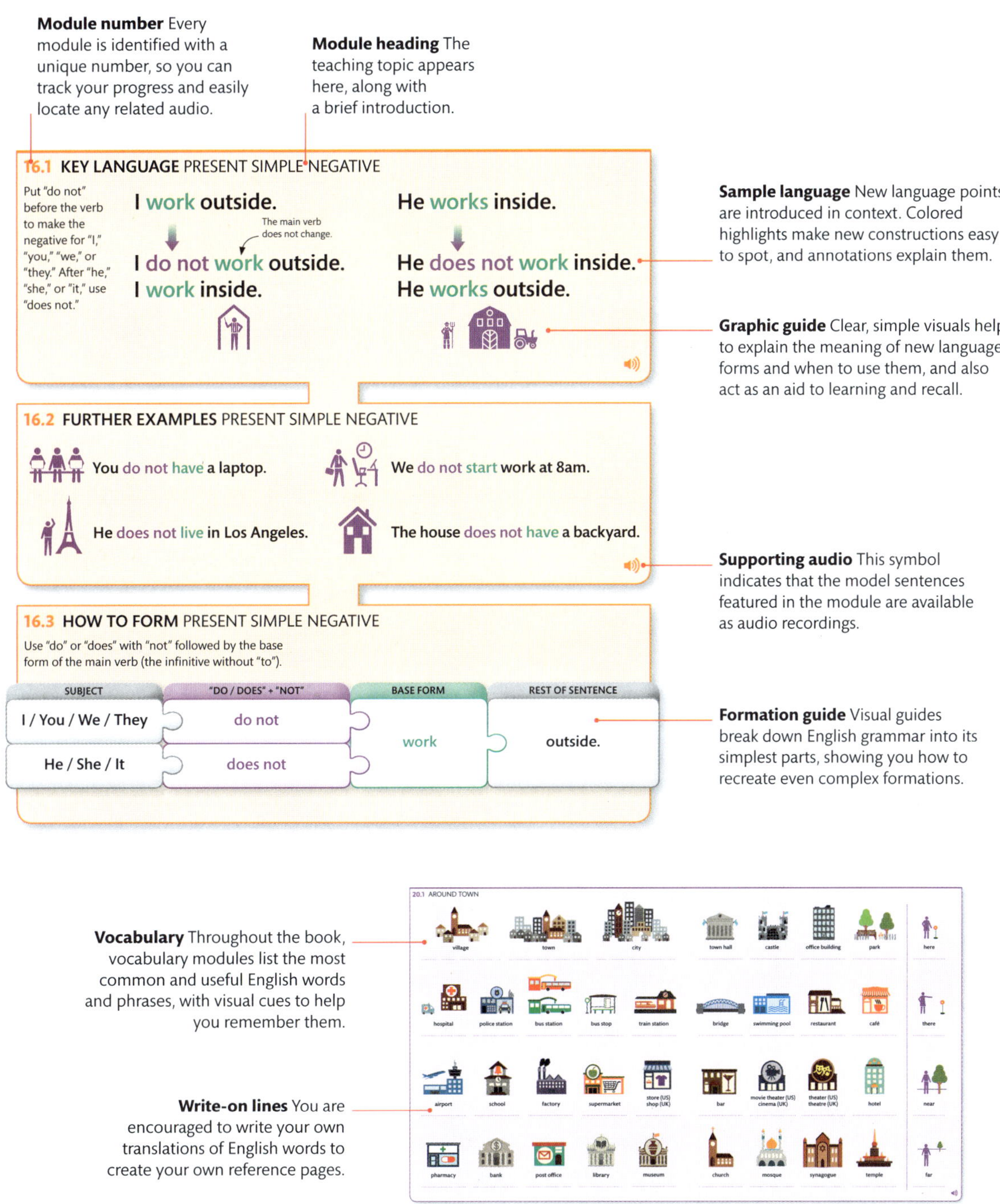

Practice modules

Each exercise is carefully graded to drill and test the language taught in the corresponding course book units. Working through the exercises alongside the course book will help you remember what you have learned and become more fluent. Every exercise is introduced with a symbol to indicate which skill is being practiced.

GRAMMAR
Apply new language rules in different contexts.

VOCABULARY
Cement your understanding of key vocabulary.

READING
Examine target language in real-life English contexts.

SPEAKING
Compare your spoken English to model audio recordings.

LISTENING
Test your understanding of spoken English.

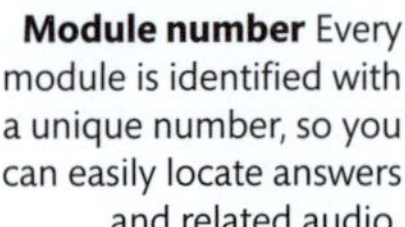

Module number Every module is identified with a unique number, so you can easily locate answers and related audio.

Exercise instruction Every exercise is introduced with a brief instruction, telling you what you need to do.

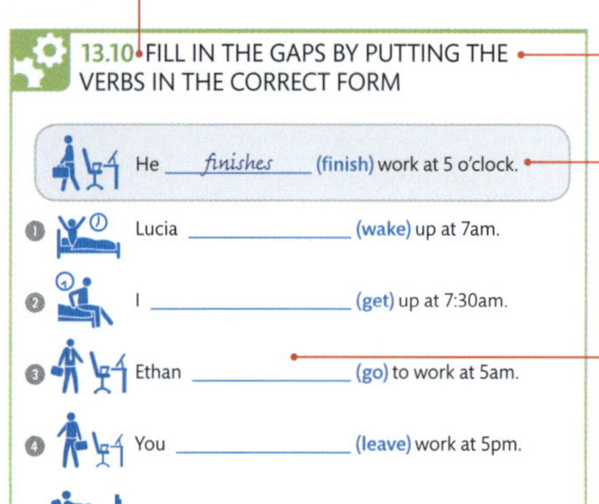

Sample answer The first question of each exercise is answered for you, to help make the task easy to understand.

Space for writing You are encouraged to write your answers in the book for future reference.

Supporting graphics Visual cues are given to help you understand the exercises.

Supporting audio This symbol shows that the answers to the exercise are available as audio tracks. Listen to them after completing the exercise.

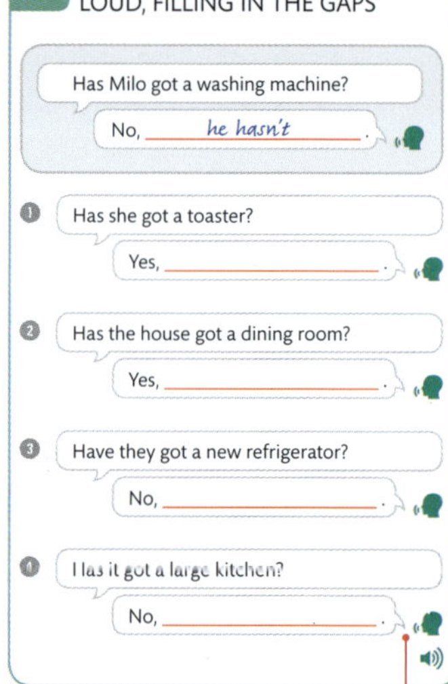

Listening exercise This symbol indicates that you should listen to an audio track in order to answer the questions in the exercise.

Speaking exercise This symbol indicates that you should say your answers out loud, then compare them to model recordings included in your audio files.

Audio

English for Everyone features extensive supporting audio materials. You are encouraged to use them as much as you can, to improve your understanding of spoken English, and to make your own accent and pronunciation more natural. Each file can be played, paused, and repeated as often as you like, until you are confident you understand what has been said.

LISTENING EXERCISES
This symbol indicates that you should listen to an audio track in order to answer the questions in the exercise.

SUPPORTING AUDIO
This symbol indicates that extra audio material is available for you to listen to after completing the module.

Track your progress

The course is designed to make it easy to monitor your progress, with regular summary and review modules. Answers are provided for every exercise, so you can see how well you have understood each teaching point.

Checklists Every unit ends with a checklist, where you can check off the new skills you have learned.

08 CHECKLIST

"These" and "those" ☐ | Aa Possessions ☐ | Using determiners and pronouns ☐

Review modules At the end of a group of units, you will find a more detailed review module, summarizing the language you have learned.

Check boxes Use these boxes to mark the skills you feel comfortable with. Go back and review anything you feel you need to practice further.

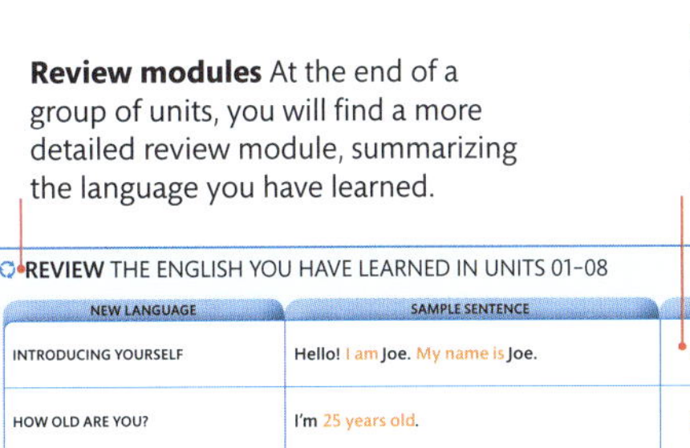

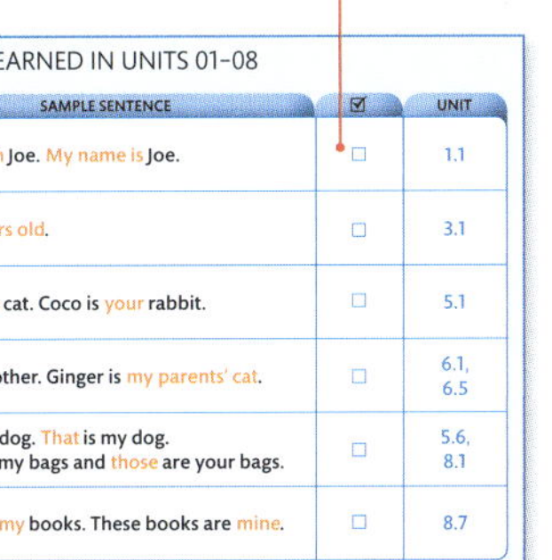

REVIEW THE ENGLISH YOU HAVE LEARNED IN UNITS 01–08

NEW LANGUAGE	SAMPLE SENTENCE	☑	UNIT
INTRODUCING YOURSELF	Hello! I am Joe. My name is Joe.	☐	1.1
HOW OLD ARE YOU?	I'm 25 years old.	☐	3.1
POSSESSIVE ADJECTIVES	Felix is my cat. Coco is your rabbit.	☐	5.1
APOSTROPHE WITH "S"	Lizzie's mother. Ginger is my parents' cat.	☐	6.1, 6.5
"THIS," "THAT," "THESE," AND "THOSE"	This is my dog. That is my dog. These are my bags and those are your bags.	☐	5.6, 8.1
DETERMINERS AND PRONOUNS	These are my books. These books are mine.	☐	8.7

35

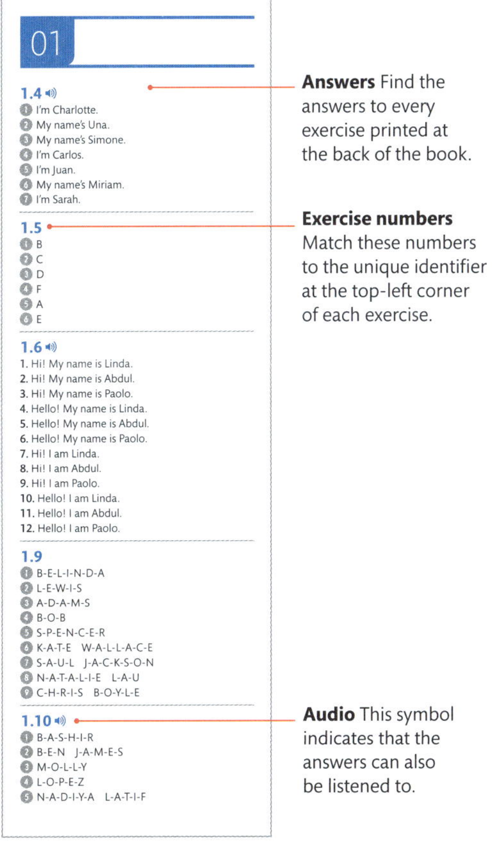

01

1.4
1 I'm Charlotte.
2 My name's Una.
3 My name's Simone.
4 I'm Carlos.
5 I'm Juan.
6 My name's Miriam.
7 I'm Sarah.

1.5
1 B
2 C
3 D
4 F
5 A
6 E

1.6
1. Hi! My name is Linda.
2. Hi! My name is Abdul.
3. Hi! My name is Paolo.
4. Hello! My name is Linda.
5. Hello! My name is Abdul.
6. Hello! My name is Paolo.
7. Hi! I am Linda.
8. Hi! I am Abdul.
9. Hi! I am Paolo.
10. Hello! I am Linda.
11. Hello! I am Abdul.
12. Hello! I am Paolo.

1.9
1 B-E-L-I-N-D-A
2 L-E-W-I-S
3 A-D-A-M-S
4 B-O-B
5 S-P-E-N-C-E-R
6 K-A-T-E W-A-L-L-A-C-E
7 S-A-U-L J-A-C-K-S-O-N
8 N-A-T-A-L-I-E L-A-U
9 C-H-R-I-S B-O-Y-L-E

1.10
1 B-A-S-H-I-R
2 B-E-N J-A-M-E-S
3 M-O-L-L-Y
4 L-O-P-E-Z
5 N-A-D-I-Y-A L-A-T-I-F

Answers Find the answers to every exercise printed at the back of the book.

Exercise numbers Match these numbers to the unique identifier at the top-left corner of each exercise.

Audio This symbol indicates that the answers can also be listened to.

01 Introducing yourself

You can greet people by saying "Hello!" or "Hi!" Introduce yourself using "I am." You may also need to spell out the letters of your name.

New language Using "to be" with names
Aa Vocabulary Names and letters
New skill Saying your name

1.1 KEY LANGUAGE SAYING YOUR NAME

There are different ways of greeting someone and introducing yourself.

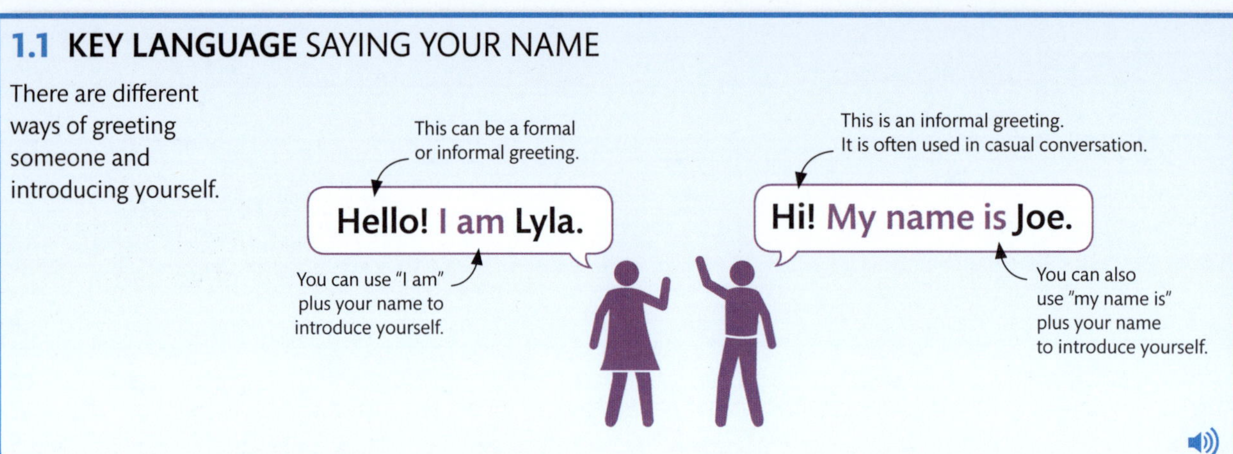

1.2 OTHER WAYS TO SAY YOUR NAME

In conversational English, speakers often use contractions. These are shortened versions of pairs of words.

I am Lyla. → I'm Lyla.

My name is Joe. → My name's Joe.

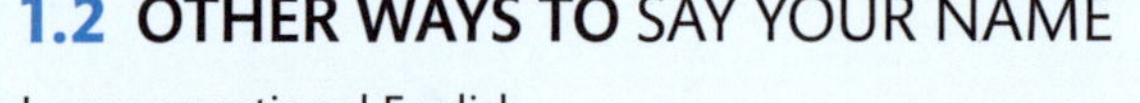

1.3 HOW TO FORM SAYING YOUR NAME

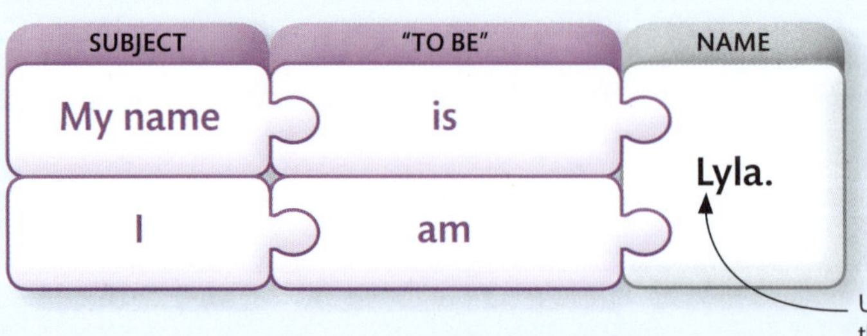

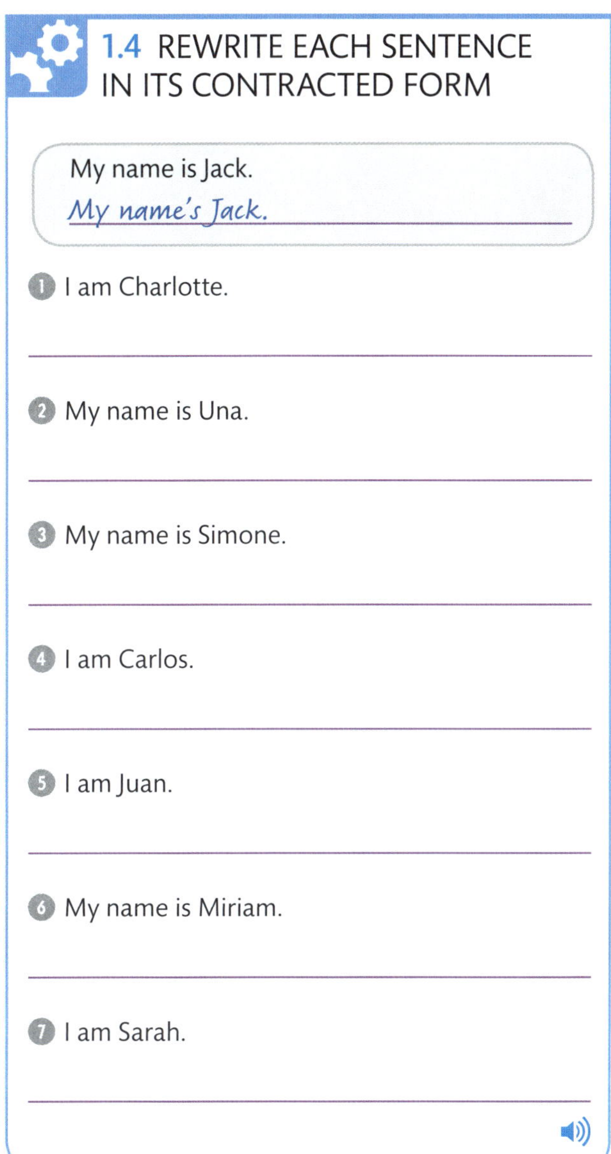

1.4 REWRITE EACH SENTENCE IN ITS CONTRACTED FORM

My name is Jack.
My name's Jack.

1. I am Charlotte.
2. My name is Una.
3. My name is Simone.
4. I am Carlos.
5. I am Juan.
6. My name is Miriam.
7. I am Sarah.

1.5 LISTEN TO THE AUDIO, THEN NUMBER THE PEOPLE IN THE ORDER IN WHICH THEY SPEAK

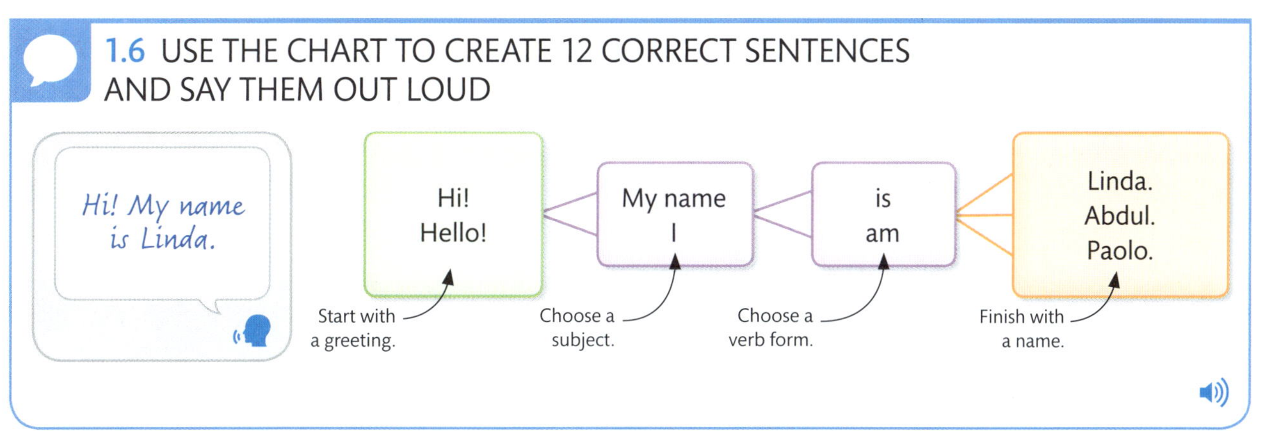

1.6 USE THE CHART TO CREATE 12 CORRECT SENTENCES AND SAY THEM OUT LOUD

1.7 KEY LANGUAGE SPELLING YOUR NAME

How do you spell your first name?

This is how you ask someone to spell their first name.

My name's Jacob, J-A-C-O-B.

You say each letter.

How do you spell your last name?

This is how you ask someone to spell their last name.

Williams, W-I-L-L-I-A-M-S.

How do you spell your full name?

This is your first name and your last name.

J-A-C-O-B W-I-L-L-I-A-M-S.

1.8 PRONUNCIATION THE ALPHABET

Listen to how the letters of the alphabet are pronounced in English.

Aa Bb Cc Dd Ee Ff Gg Hh Ii

Jj Kk Ll Mm Nn Oo Pp Qq

Rr Ss Tt Uu Vv Ww Xx Yy Zz

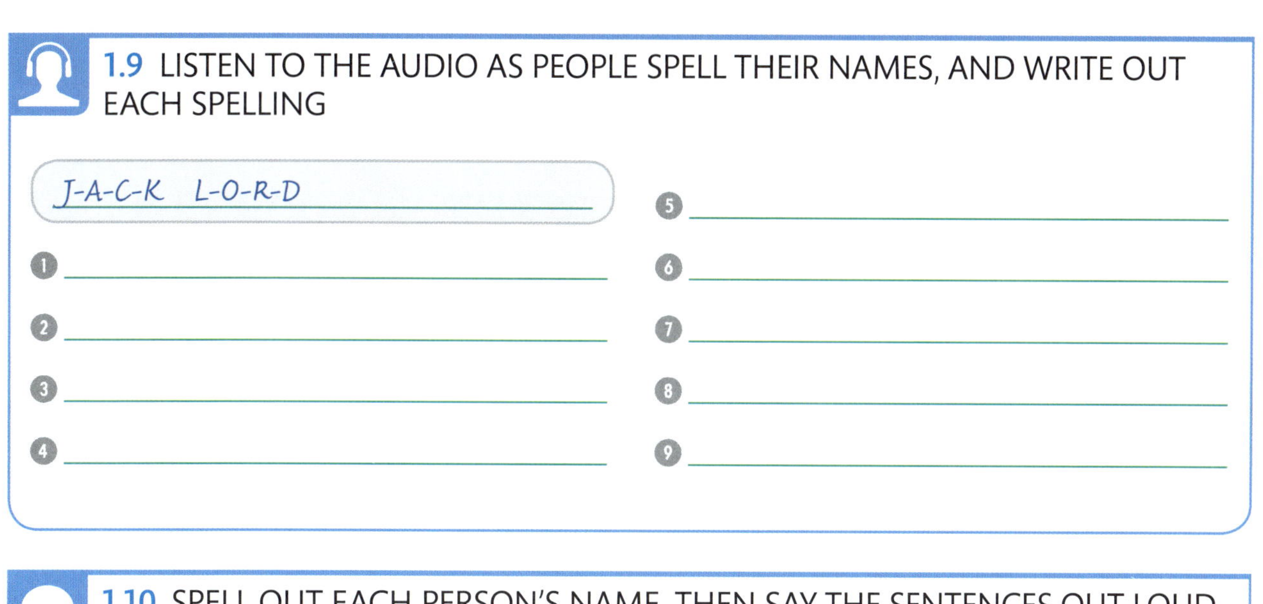

1.10 SPELL OUT EACH PERSON'S NAME, THEN SAY THE SENTENCES OUT LOUD

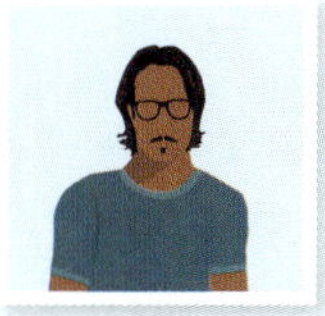

My name is Gabriel, *G-A-B-R-I-E-L.*

1. 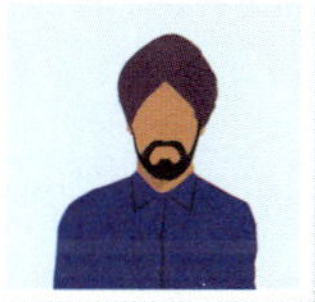 My last name is Bashir, ______________

2. 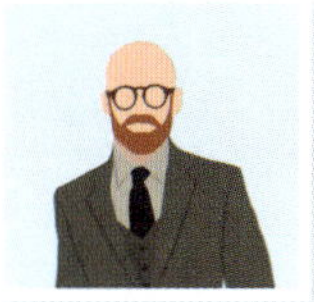 I am Ben James, ______________

3. 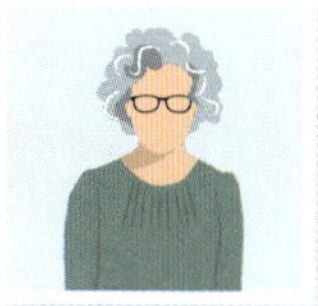 My name's Molly, ______________

4. 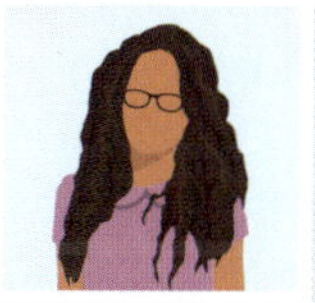 My last name's Lopez, ______________

5. 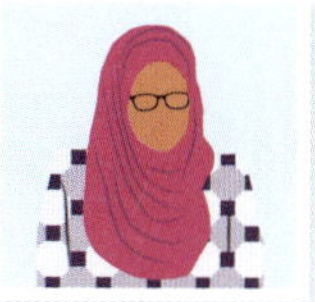 I'm Nadiya Latif, ______________

02 Vocabulary

2.1 COUNTRIES

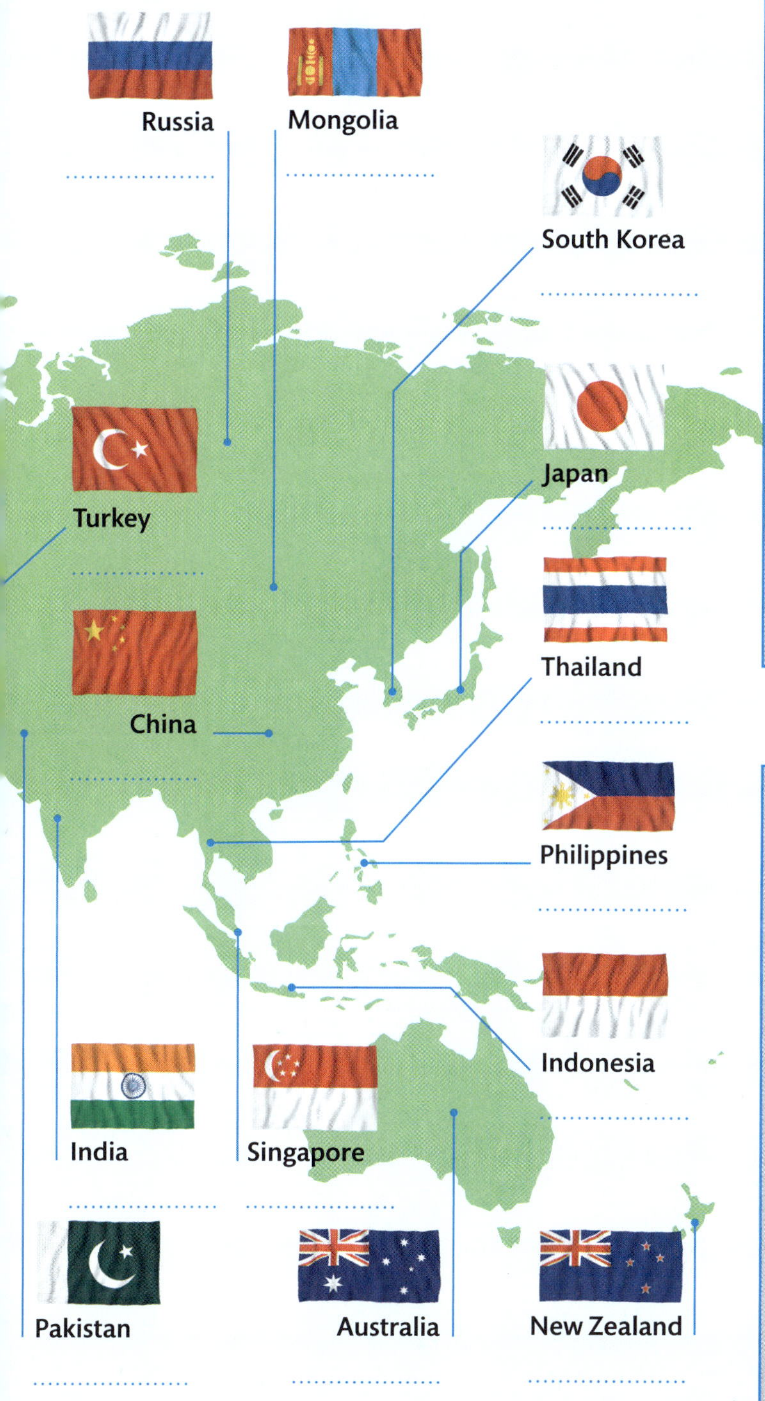

Russia

Mongolia

South Korea

Turkey

Japan

China

Thailand

Philippines

Indonesia

India

Singapore

Pakistan

Australia

New Zealand

2.2 NATIONALITIES

Country	Nationality
USA	American
Canada	Canadian
Mexico	Mexican
Brazil	Brazilian
Argentina	Argentinian
UK	British
France	French
Russia	Russian
Spain	Spanish
Portugal	Portuguese
Poland	Polish
Greece	Greek
Turkey	Turkish
Egypt	Egyptian
China	Chinese
Japan	Japanese
India	Indian
Pakistan	Pakistani
Mongolia	Mongolian
Australia	Australian
Germany	German
Switzerland	Swiss
Austria	Austrian

03 Talking about yourself

It's useful to know how to say your age and where you come from. You can use the verb "to be" to talk about these topics.

New language "To be" with ages and nationalities
Vocabulary Numbers and nationalities
New skill Talking about yourself

3.1 KEY LANGUAGE SAYING YOUR AGE

Use the verb "to be" to talk about your age.

How old are you?

I am 25 years old.

The verb "to be" changes with the subject.

3.2 FURTHER EXAMPLES SAYING YOUR AGE

Ruby is seven years old.

Izzy and Chloe are 13.

I'm 44 today.

My grandma is 92 years old.

3.3 HOW TO FORM SAYING YOUR AGE

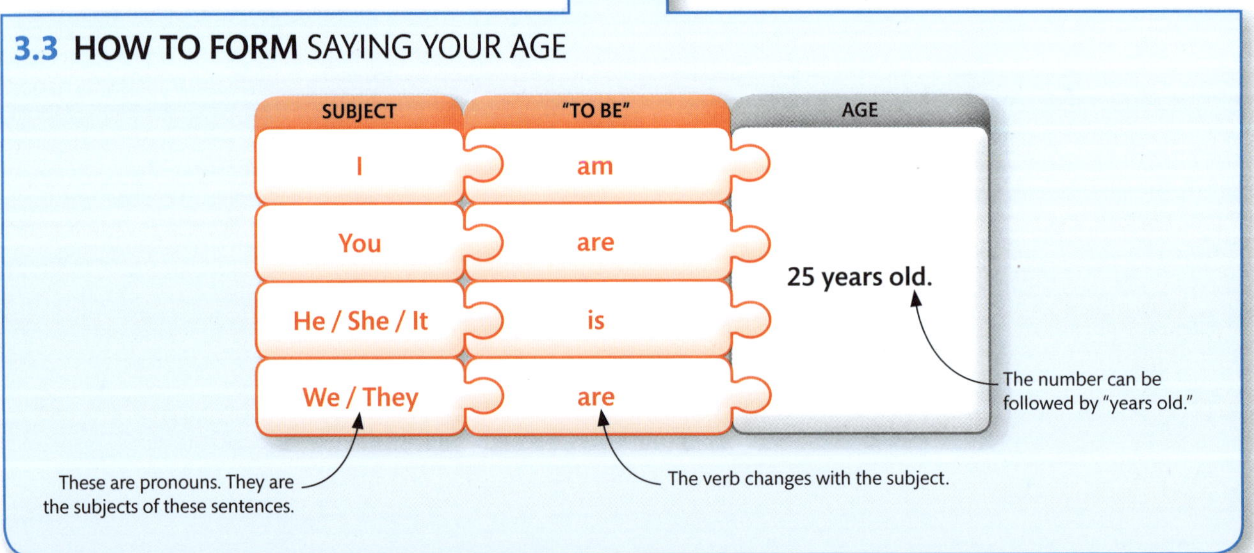

SUBJECT	"TO BE"	AGE
I	am	25 years old.
You	are	
He / She / It	is	
We / They	are	

These are pronouns. They are the subjects of these sentences.

The verb changes with the subject.

The number can be followed by "years old."

3.4 VOCABULARY NUMBERS

1 one	2 two	3 three	4 four	5 five	6 six
7 seven	8 eight	9 nine	10 ten	11 eleven	12 twelve
13 thirteen	14 fourteen	15 fifteen	16 sixteen	17 seventeen	18 eighteen
19 nineteen	20 twenty	21 twenty-one	22 twenty-two	30 thirty	40 forty
50 fifty	60 sixty	70 seventy	80 eighty	90 ninety	100 one hundred

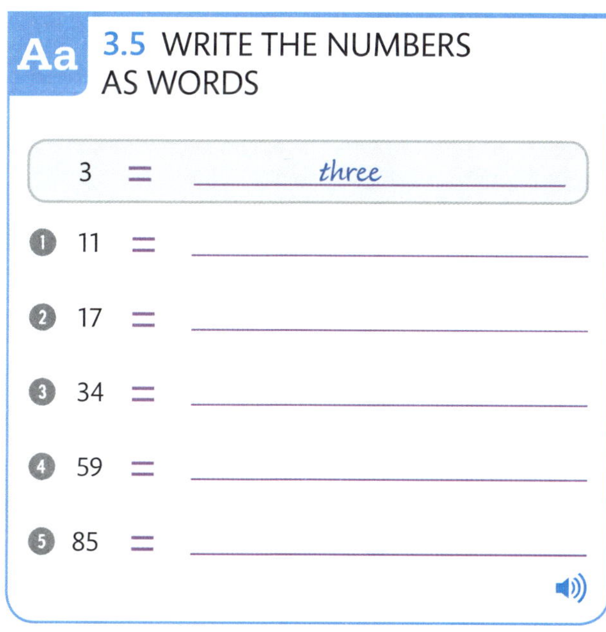

3.5 WRITE THE NUMBERS AS WORDS

3 = *three*

1. 11 = ____
2. 17 = ____
3. 34 = ____
4. 59 = ____
5. 85 = ____

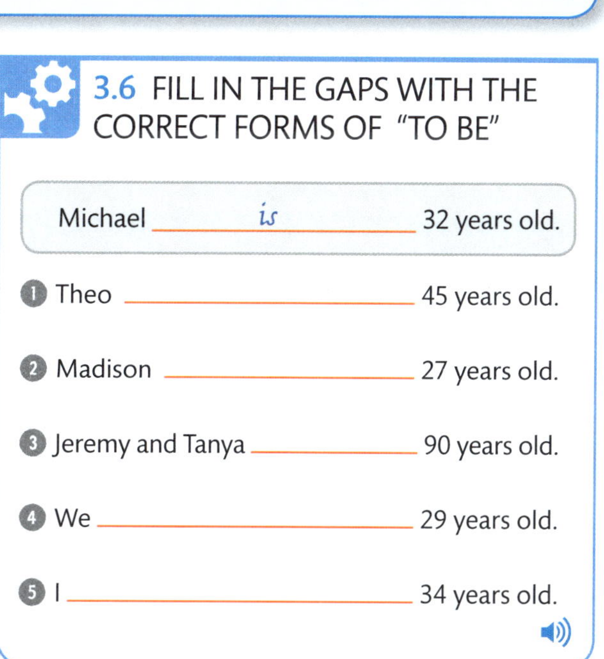

3.6 FILL IN THE GAPS WITH THE CORRECT FORMS OF "TO BE"

Michael *is* 32 years old.

1. Theo ____ 45 years old.
2. Madison ____ 27 years old.
3. Jeremy and Tanya ____ 90 years old.
4. We ____ 29 years old.
5. I ____ 34 years old.

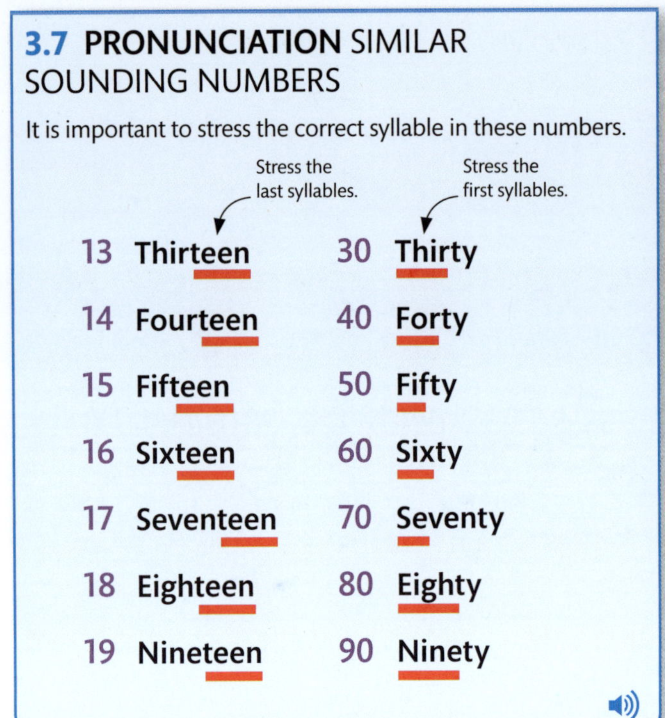

3.7 PRONUNCIATION SIMILAR SOUNDING NUMBERS

It is important to stress the correct syllable in these numbers.

Stress the last syllables. / Stress the first syllables.

13	Thirteen	30	Thirty
14	Fourteen	40	Forty
15	Fifteen	50	Fifty
16	Sixteen	60	Sixty
17	Seventeen	70	Seventy
18	Eighteen	80	Eighty
19	Nineteen	90	Ninety

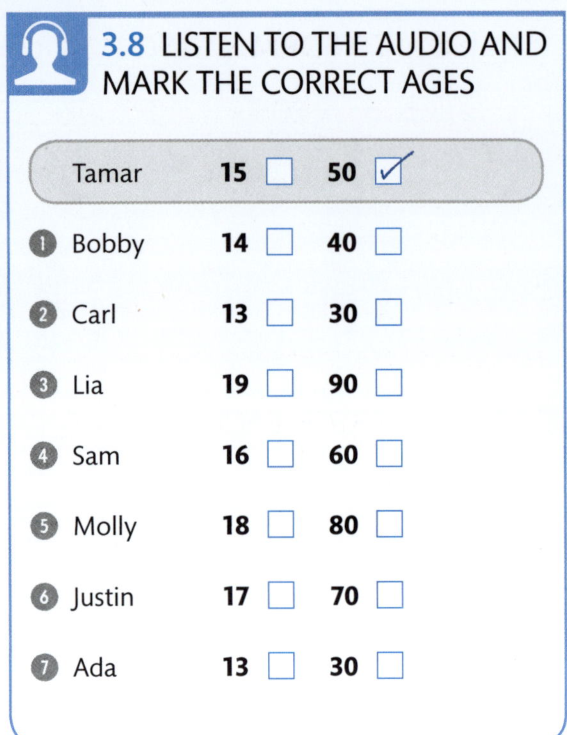

3.8 LISTEN TO THE AUDIO AND MARK THE CORRECT AGES

Tamar	15	☐	50	☑
1 Bobby	14	☐	40	☐
2 Carl	13	☐	30	☐
3 Lia	19	☐	90	☐
4 Sam	16	☐	60	☐
5 Molly	18	☐	80	☐
6 Justin	17	☐	70	☐
7 Ada	13	☐	30	☐

3.9 KEY LANGUAGE SAYING WHERE YOU'RE FROM

There are different ways of saying where you are from.

"Where" is the question word for place.

Where are you from?

Remember, "to be" changes with the subject.

I am from Spain.

This describes the country that you belong to.

What nationality are you?

You use an adjective to talk about nationality.

I'm Spanish.

3.10 FURTHER EXAMPLES SAYING WHERE YOU'RE FROM

I am Dutch.

We are Italian.

I'm from Switzerland.

3.11 HOW TO FORM SAYING WHERE YOU'RE FROM

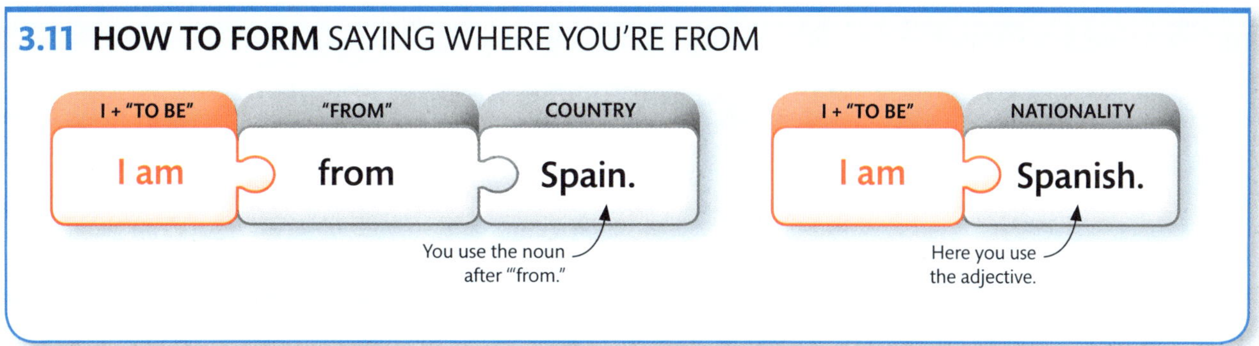

3.12 MATCH EACH FLAG TO ITS COUNTRY

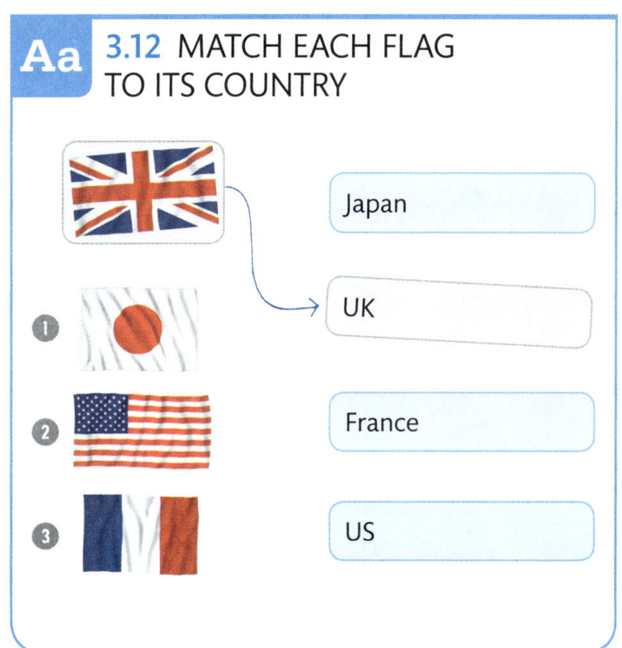

3.13 WRITE THE NATIONALITY FOR EACH COUNTRY

3.14 USE THE CHART TO CREATE 12 CORRECT SENTENCES AND SAY THEM OUT LOUD

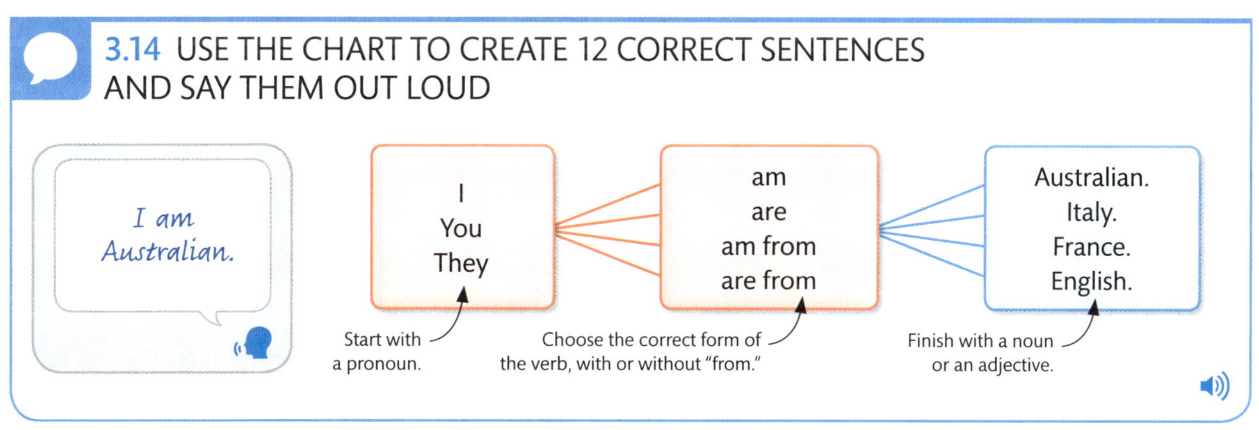

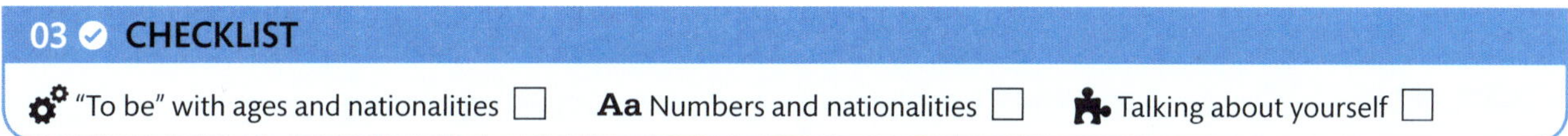

04 Vocabulary

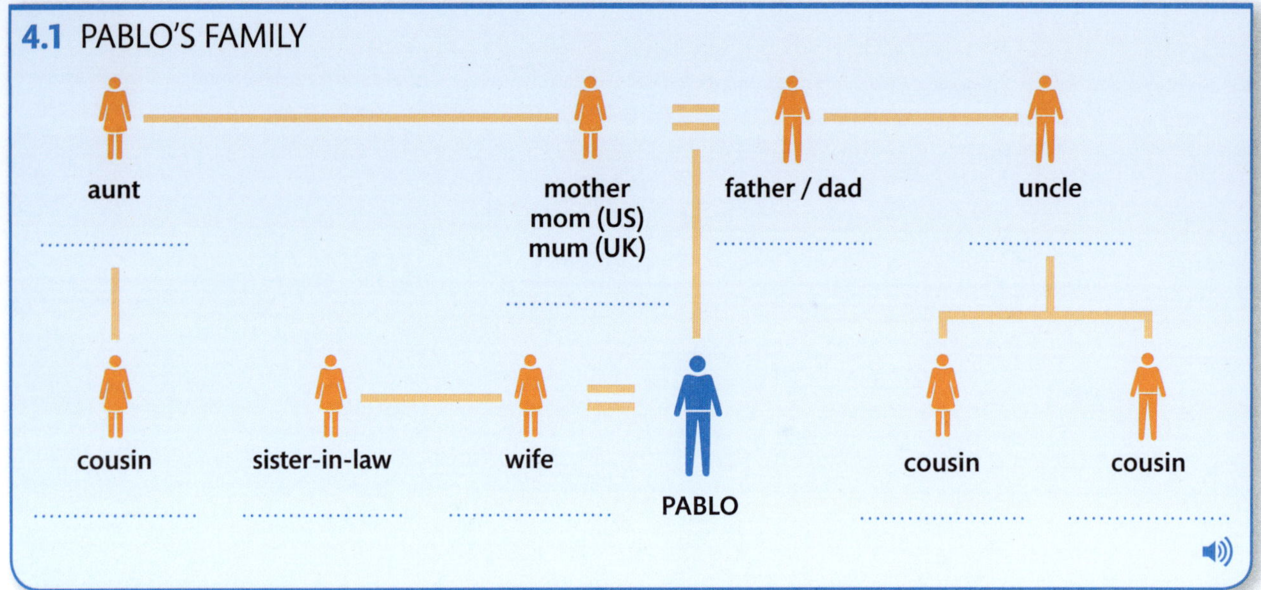

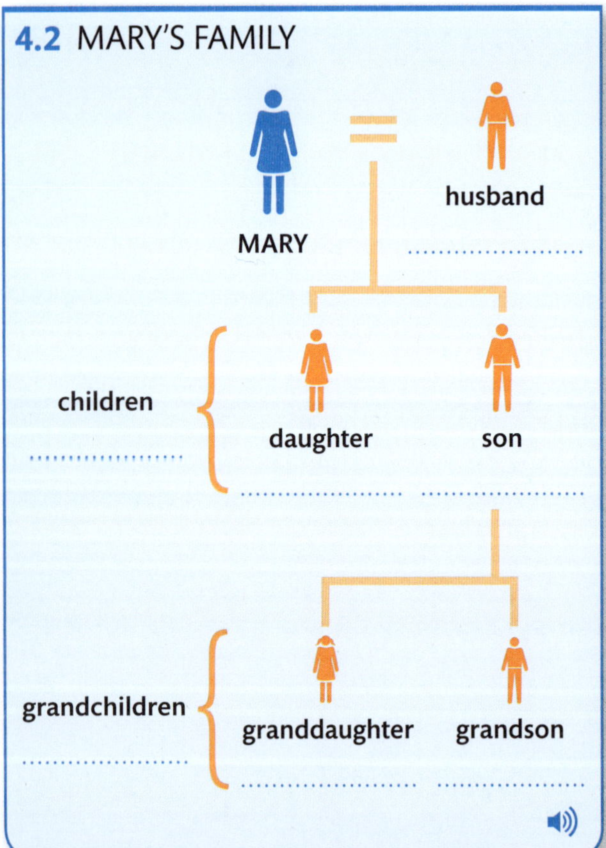

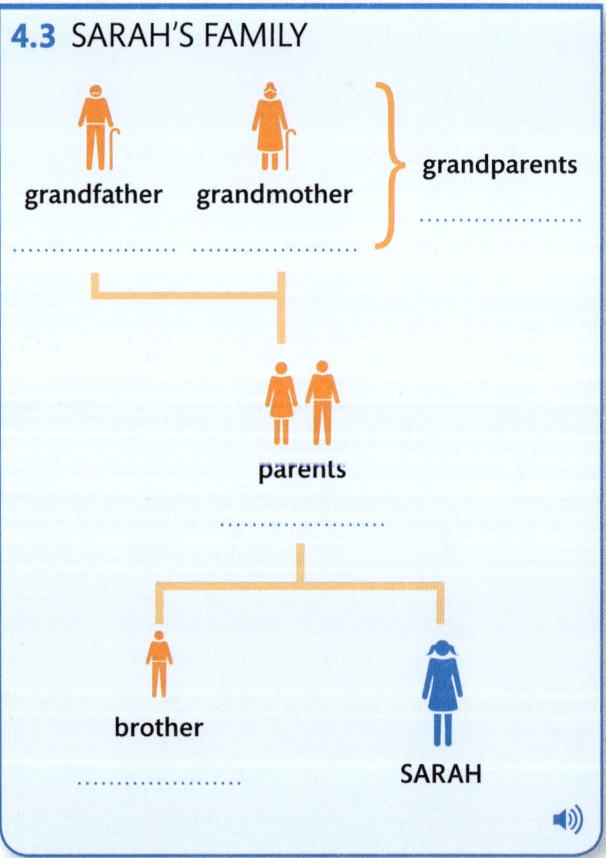

4.4 DAN'S FAMILY

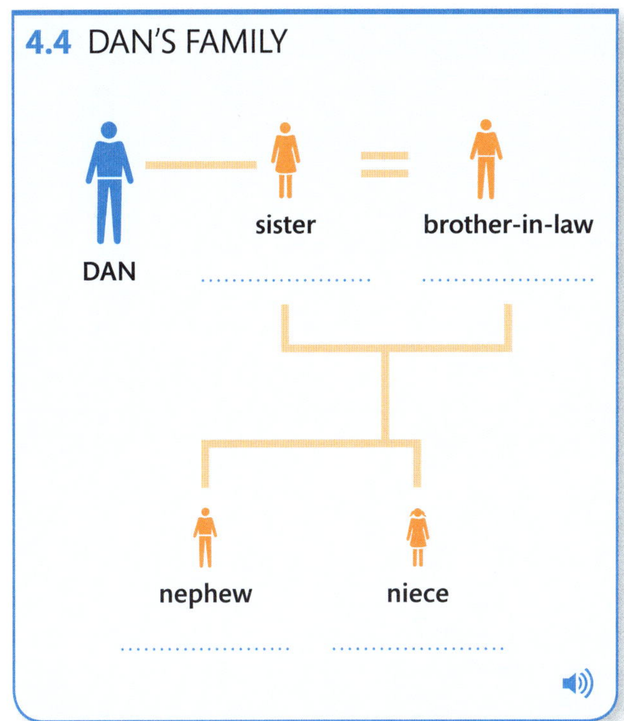

4.5 HARRY'S FAMILY

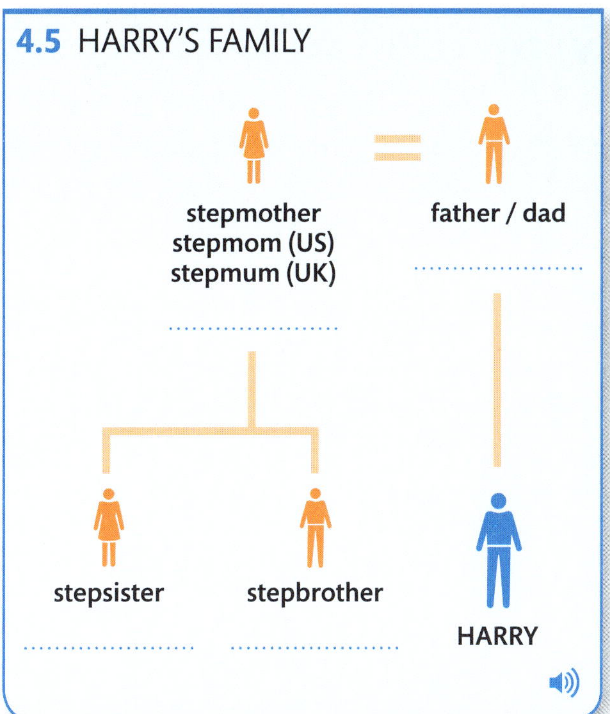

4.6 PETS AND DOMESTIC ANIMALS

cat

dog

rabbit

hamster

guinea pig

fish

parrot

tortoise

snake

donkey

pig

chicken

sheep

horse

cow

05 Things you have

Possessive adjectives tell you who something (such as a pet) belongs to. "This" and "that" are determiners. They point out a specific object or person.

New language Possessive adjectives; "this" and "that"
Aa Vocabulary Animals and family
New skill Talking about who things belong to

5.1 KEY LANGUAGE POSSESSIVE ADJECTIVES

Possessive adjectives are used before the noun. They change depending on whether the owner is singular, plural, male or female, the person you are talking to, or yourself.

Felix is my cat.

I own the cat.

Coco is your rabbit.

The rabbit belongs to you.

Buster is her dog.

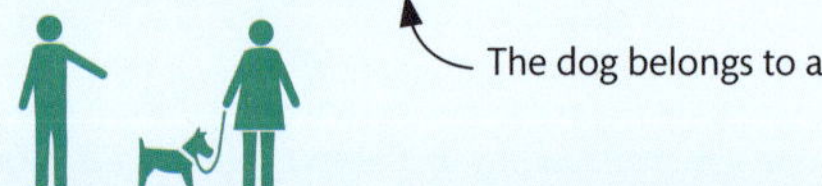

The dog belongs to a woman.

Polly is his parrot.

The parrot belongs to a man.

Rachel is our daughter.

We are her parents.

John is their son.

They are his parents.

5.2 HOW TO FORM POSSESSIVE ADJECTIVES

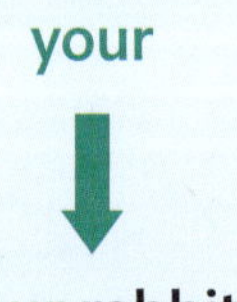
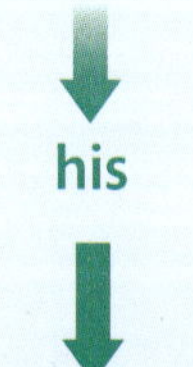
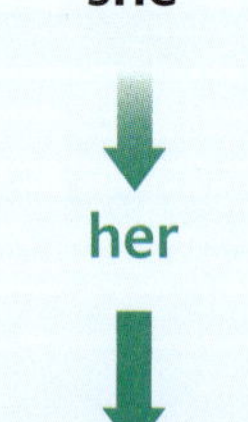

I	you	he	she	it	we	they
my	your	his	her	its	our	their
my cat	your rabbit	his wife	her sister	its ball	our horse	their son

Aa 5.3 MATCH THE PICTURES TO THE PHRASES

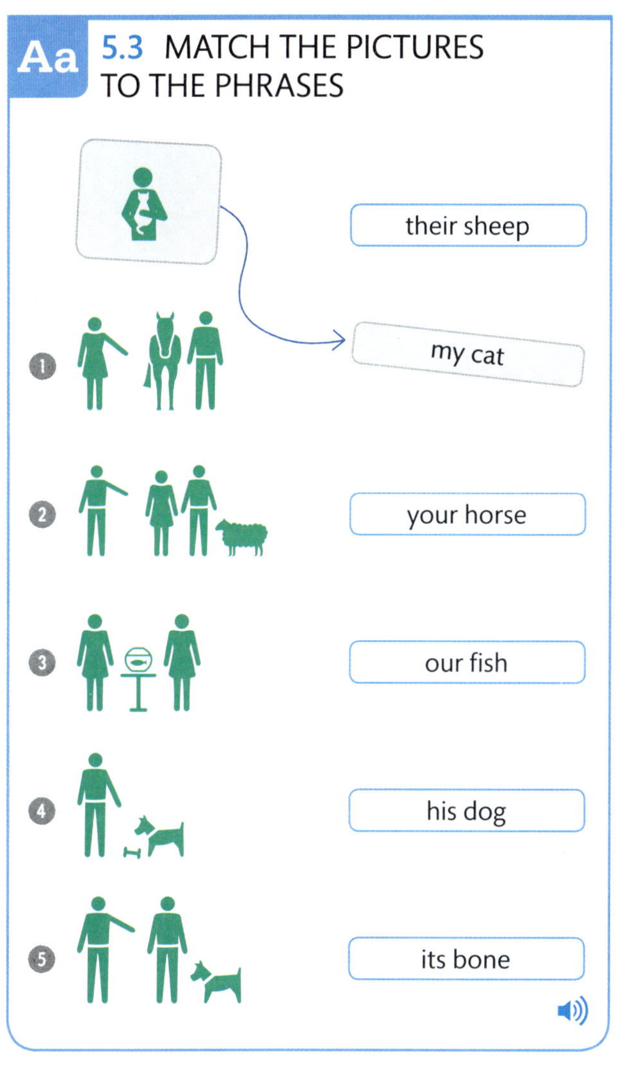

5.4 FILL IN THE GAPS USING THE CORRECT POSSESSIVE ADJECTIVES

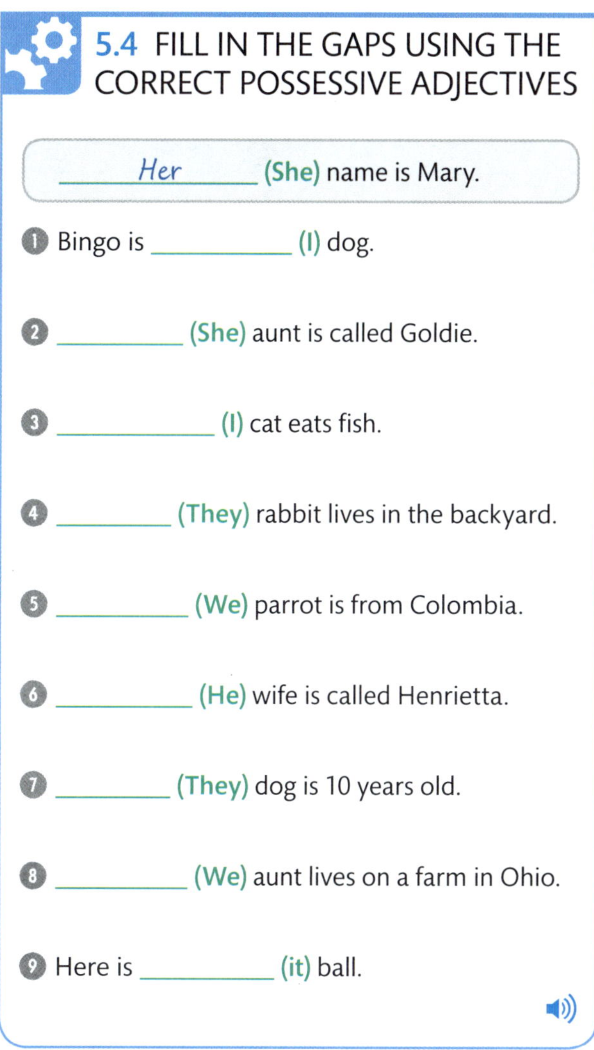

Her (She) name is Mary.

1. Bingo is ________ (I) dog.
2. ________ (She) aunt is called Goldie.
3. ________ (I) cat eats fish.
4. ________ (They) rabbit lives in the backyard.
5. ________ (We) parrot is from Colombia.
6. ________ (He) wife is called Henrietta.
7. ________ (They) dog is 10 years old.
8. ________ (We) aunt lives on a farm in Ohio.
9. Here is ________ (it) ball.

5.5 REWRITE THE SENTENCES, CORRECTING THE ERRORS

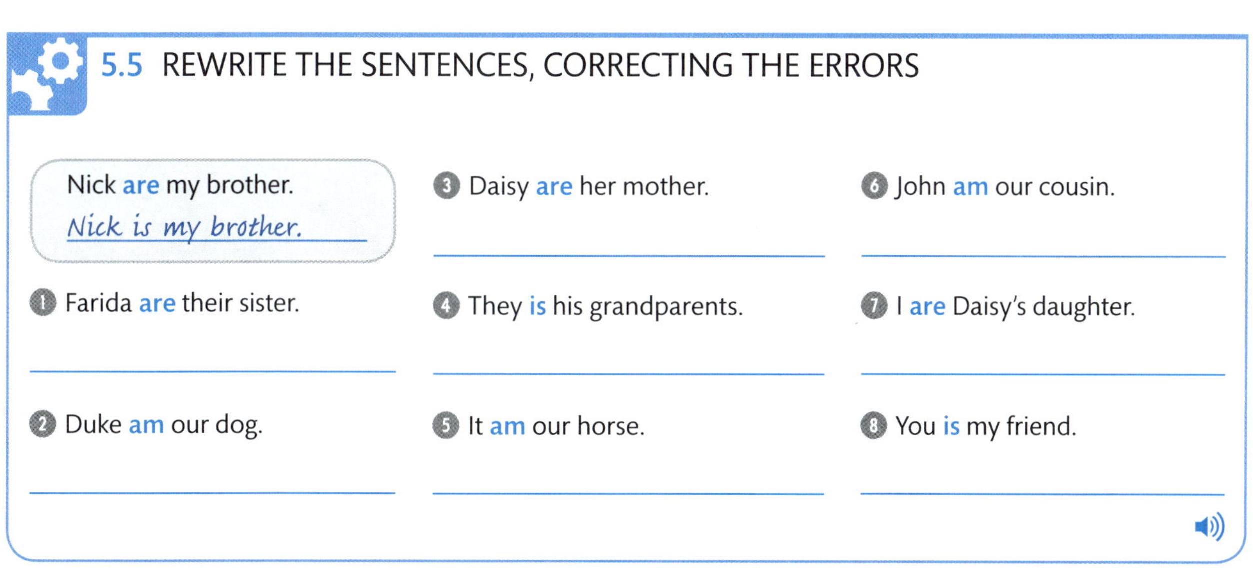

Nick are my brother.
Nick is my brother.

1. Farida are their sister.
2. Duke am our dog.
3. Daisy are her mother.
4. They is his grandparents.
5. It am our horse.
6. John am our cousin.
7. I are Daisy's daughter.
8. You is my friend.

5.6 KEY LANGUAGE "THIS" AND "THAT"

"This" and "that" are called determiners. They point out a specific object you want to talk about. Use "this" for something close to you. Use "that" for something farther away.

This is my dog.

The dog is close to you.

That is my dog.

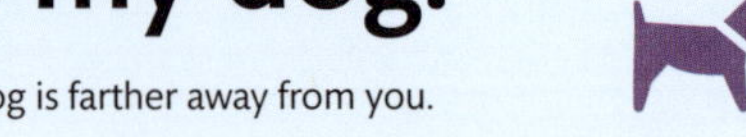

The dog is farther away from you.

5.7 FURTHER EXAMPLES "THIS" AND "THAT"

This is your rabbit.

This is her horse.

This is its bed.

That is your rabbit.

That is her horse.

That is its bed.

5.8 FILL IN THE GAPS WITH "THIS" OR "THAT"

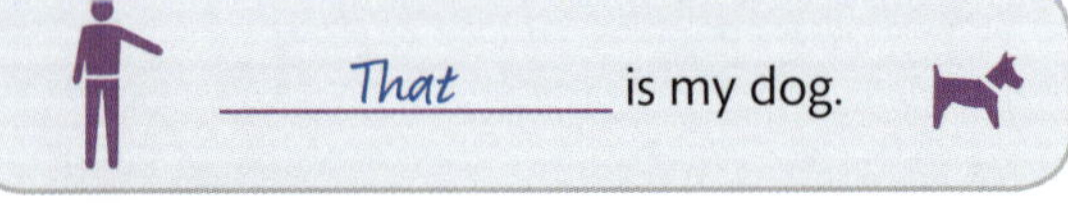

That is my dog.

1  ________ is her horse.

2  ________ is our rabbit.

3  ________ is their pig.

4   ________ is his cow.

5  ________ is your fish.

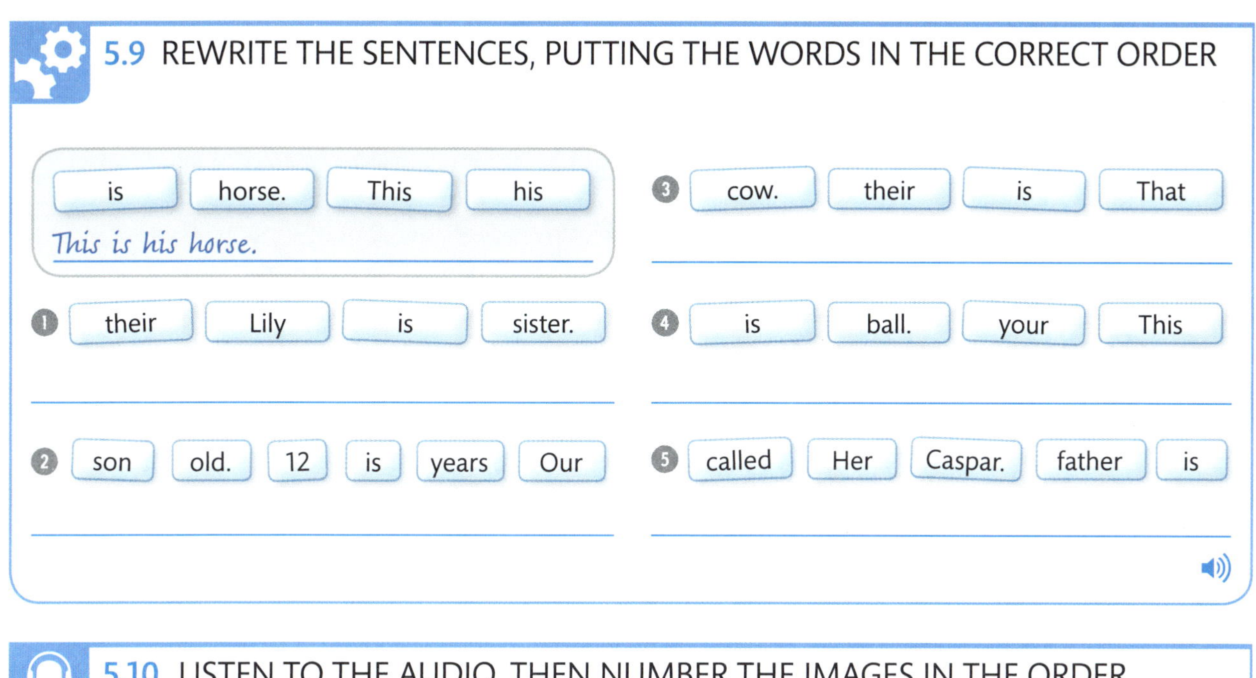

5.9 REWRITE THE SENTENCES, PUTTING THE WORDS IN THE CORRECT ORDER

is | horse. | This | his

This is his horse.

1. their | Lily | is | sister.
2. son | old. | 12 | is | years | Our
3. cow. | their | is | That
4. is | ball. | your | This
5. called | Her | Caspar. | father | is

5.10 LISTEN TO THE AUDIO, THEN NUMBER THE IMAGES IN THE ORDER THEY ARE DESCRIBED

A ☐ B *1* C ☐ D ☐ E ☐

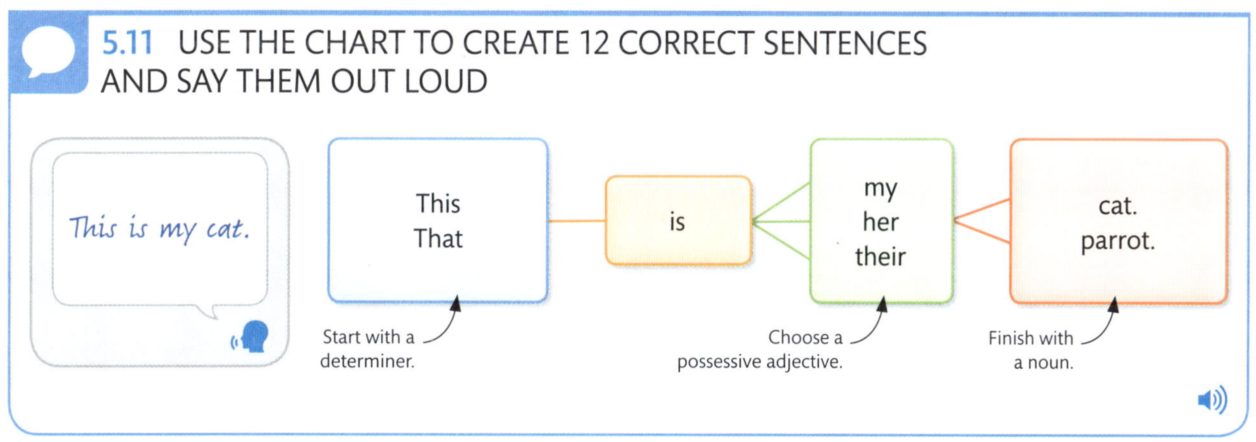

5.11 USE THE CHART TO CREATE 12 CORRECT SENTENCES AND SAY THEM OUT LOUD

This is my cat.

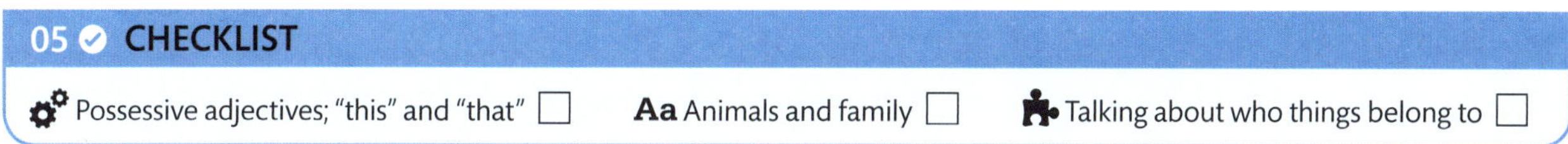

05 CHECKLIST

Possessive adjectives; "this" and "that" ☐ **Aa** Animals and family ☐ Talking about who things belong to ☐

06 Using apostrophes

In English, you can use apostrophes (') to show belonging. You can use them to show who owns something, such as a pet, and to talk about your family.

New language Possessive apostrophe
Vocabulary Family and pets
New skill Talking about belonging

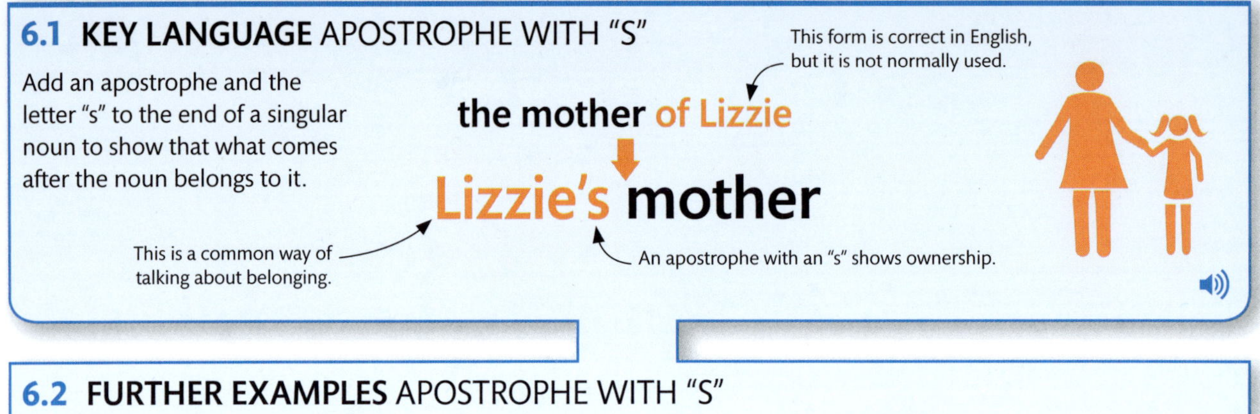

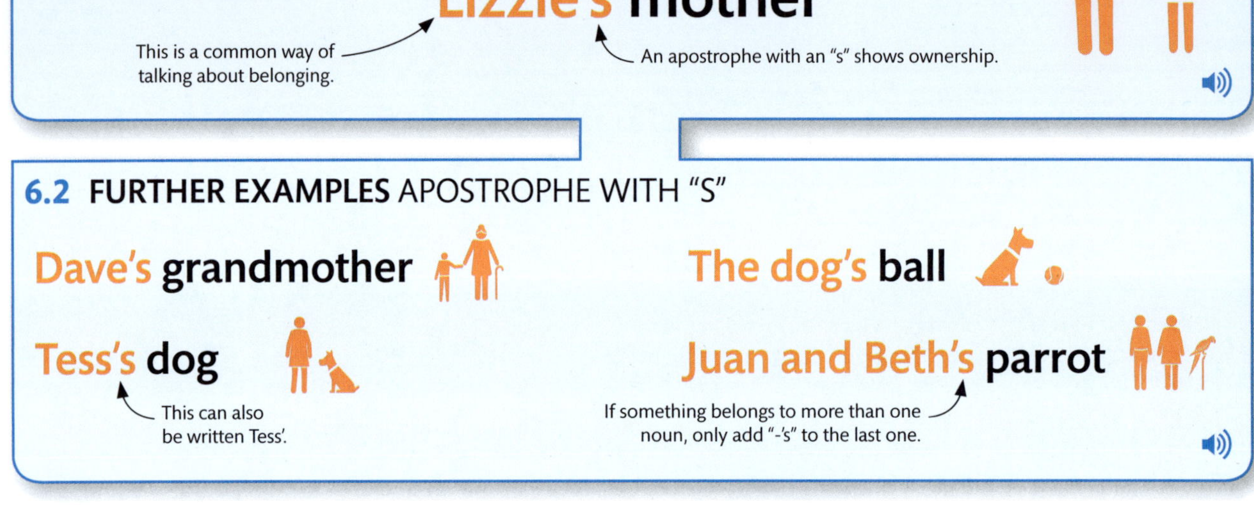

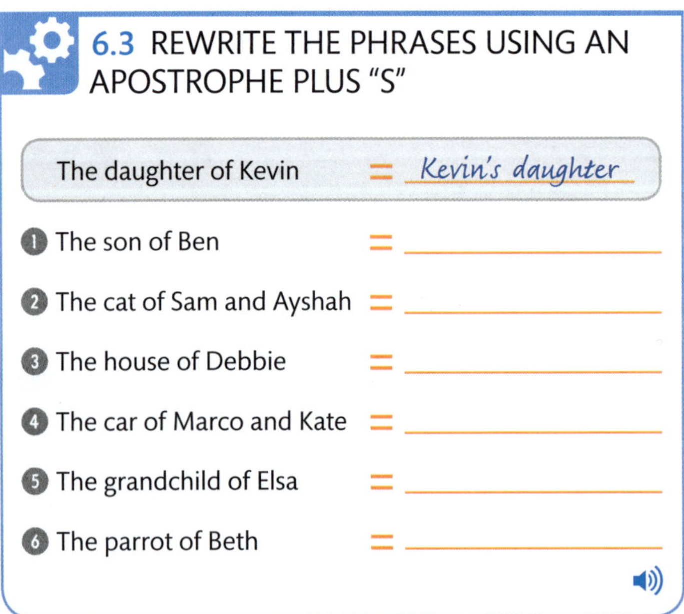

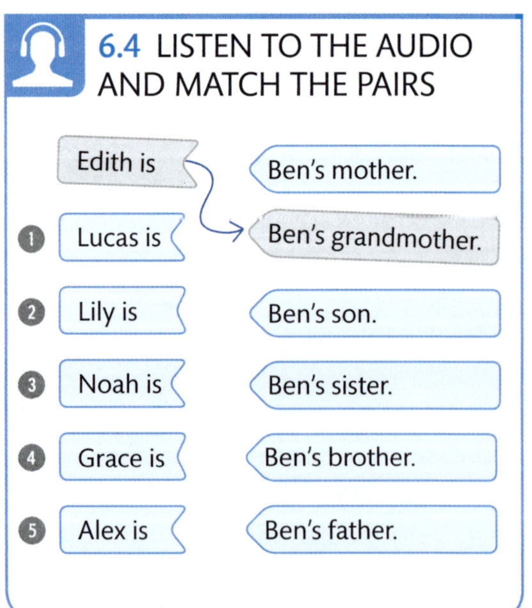

6.5 KEY LANGUAGE APOSTROPHES AND PLURAL NOUNS

To show belonging with a plural noun, just add an apostrophe with no "s."

Ginger is my parents' cat.

Plural nouns use an apostrophe with no "s."

6.6 FURTHER EXAMPLES APOSTROPHES AND PLURAL NOUNS

This is my cousins' rabbit.

That is his grandparents' house.

Rex is her brothers' dog.

Polly is our children's parrot.

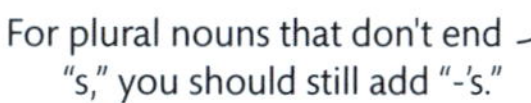

For plural nouns that don't end "s," you should still add "-'s."

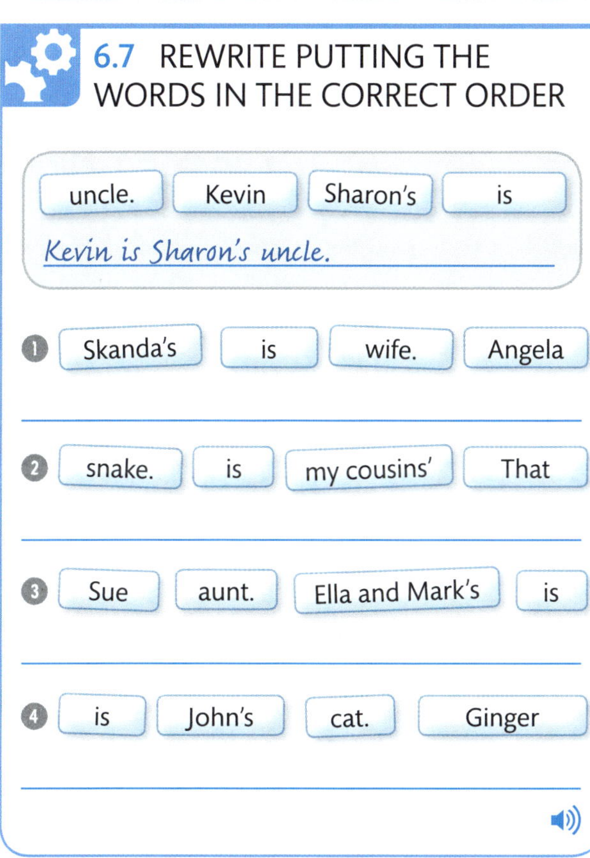

6.7 REWRITE PUTTING THE WORDS IN THE CORRECT ORDER

uncle. | Kevin | Sharon's | is

Kevin is Sharon's uncle.

1. Skanda's | is | wife. | Angela

2. snake. | is | my cousins' | That

3. Sue | aunt. | Ella and Mark's | is

4. is | John's | cat. | Ginger

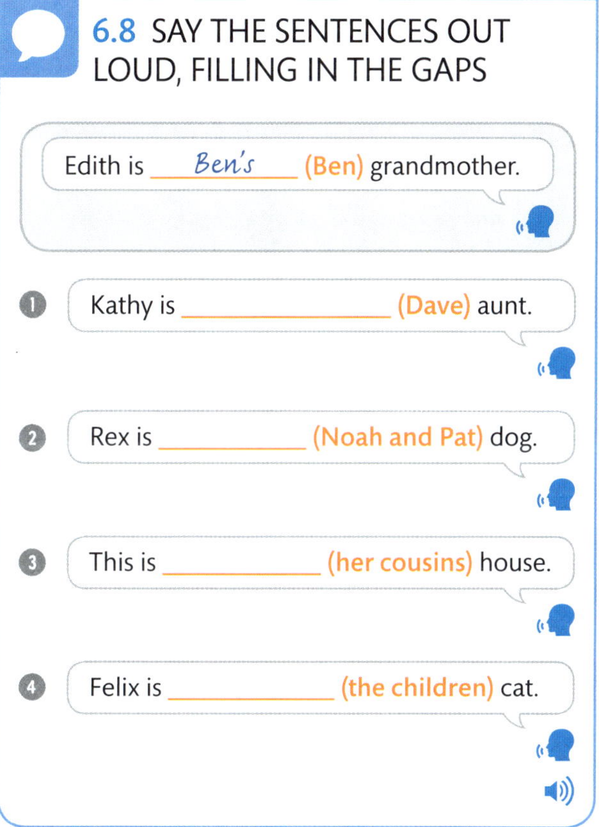

6.8 SAY THE SENTENCES OUT LOUD, FILLING IN THE GAPS

Edith is *Ben's* (Ben) grandmother.

1. Kathy is ________ (Dave) aunt.

2. Rex is ________ (Noah and Pat) dog.

3. This is ________ (her cousins) house.

4. Felix is ________ (the children) cat.

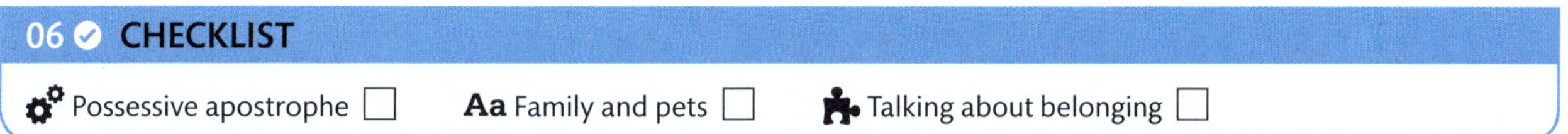

06 CHECKLIST

Possessive apostrophe ☐ **Aa** Family and pets ☐ Talking about belonging ☐

07 Vocabulary

7.1 EVERYDAY THINGS

wallet (US)
purse (UK)

wallet

coins

keys

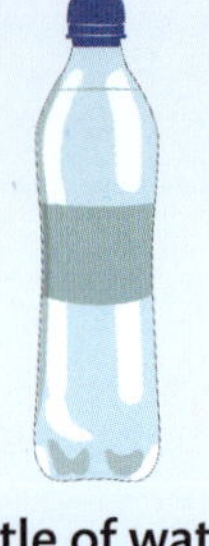
bottle of water

apple

sandwich

cell phone (US)
mobile phone (UK)

camera

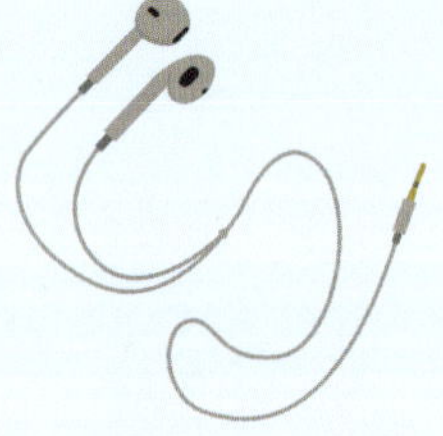
earphones

tablet

laptop

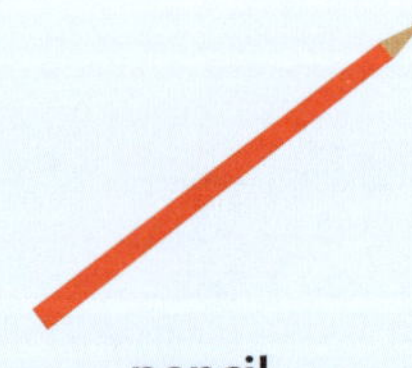
pencil

pen

notebook

letter

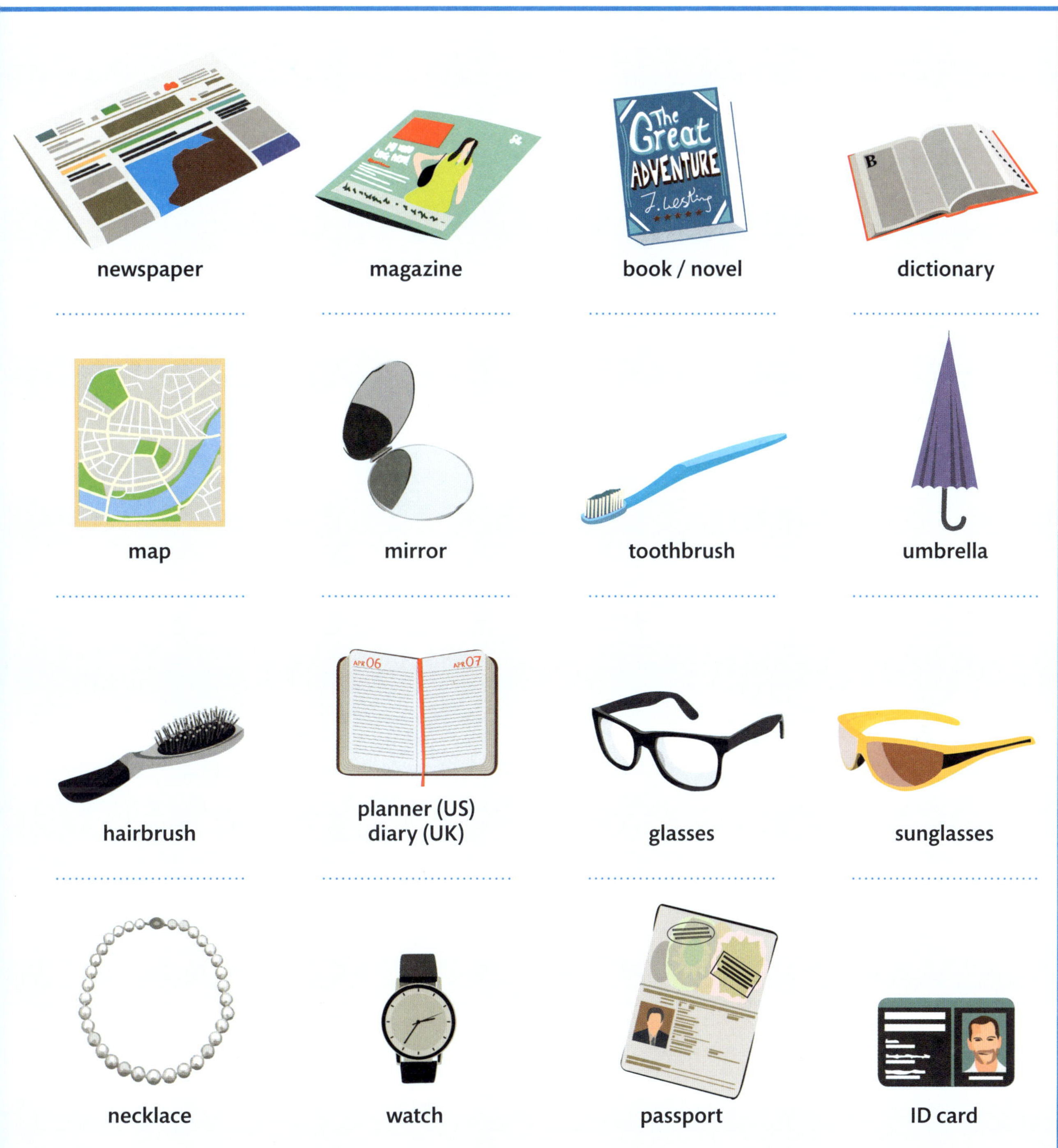

The Great ADVENTURE
newspaper
magazine
book / novel
B
dictionary
map
mirror
toothbrush
umbrella
APR 06
APR 07
hairbrush
planner (US)
diary (UK)
glasses
sunglasses
necklace
watch
passport
ID card

08 Talking about your things

You use "these" and "those" when you are referring to more than one thing. To show who owns a thing, you can use determiners or possessive pronouns.

New language "These" and "those"
Aa Vocabulary Possessions
New skill Using determiners and pronouns

8.1 KEY LANGUAGE USING "THESE" AND "THOSE"

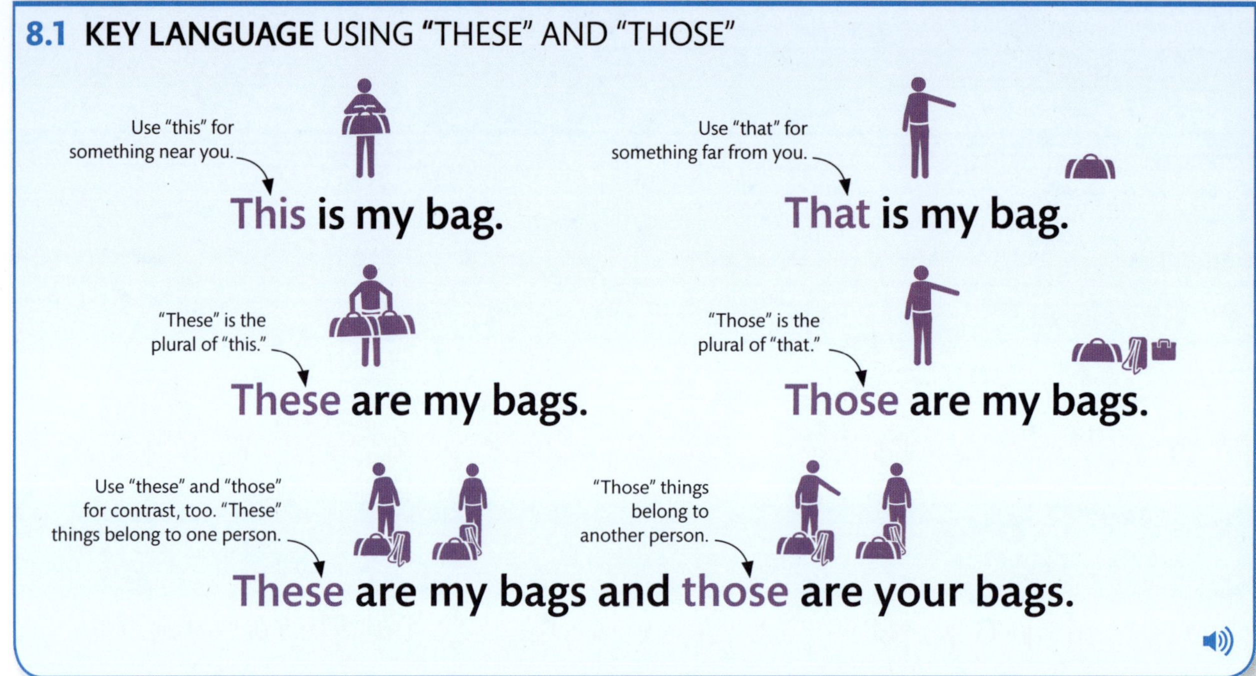

8.2 CROSS OUT THE INCORRECT WORD IN EACH SENTENCE

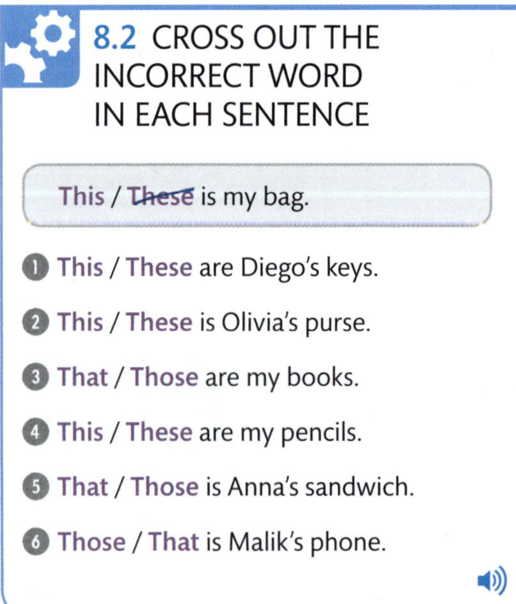

This / ~~These~~ is my bag.

1. This / These are Diego's keys.
2. This / These is Olivia's purse.
3. That / Those are my books.
4. This / These are my pencils.
5. That / Those is Anna's sandwich.
6. Those / That is Malik's phone.

8.3 WRITE EACH SENTENCE IN ITS OTHER FORM

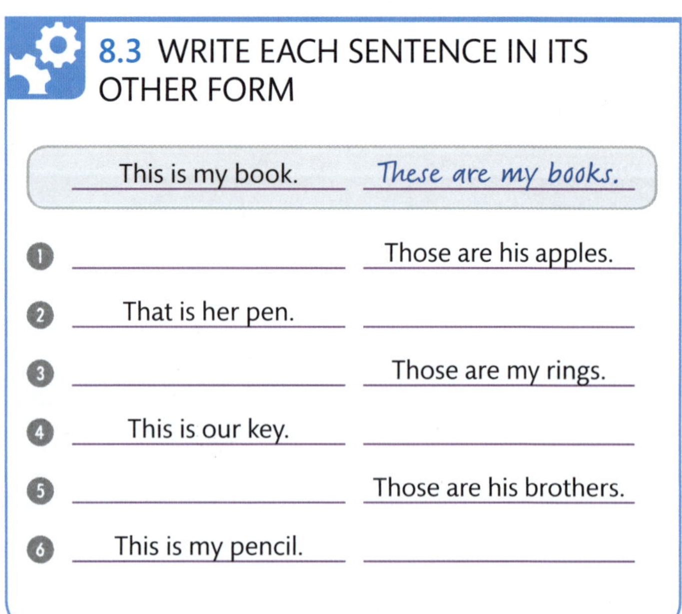

	This is my book.	*These are my books.*
1	______	Those are his apples.
2	That is her pen.	______
3	______	Those are my rings.
4	This is our key.	______
5	______	Those are his brothers.
6	This is my pencil.	______

8.4 **VOCABULARY** SPELLING RULES FOR PLURALS

For most nouns, to make the plural you add "s."

book

books

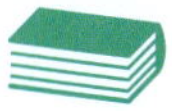

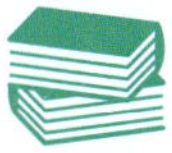

For nouns ending in "x," "ch," and "sh," you add "es."

watch → **watches**

brush → **brushes**

box → **boxes**

For nouns ending in a consonant followed by a "y," drop the "y" and add "ies."

dictionary → **dictionaries**

Aa 8.5 FIND EIGHT PLURALS IN THE GRID AND WRITE THEM IN GROUPS

W	A	T	C	H	E	S	O	B	W	O	A	D
A	B	P	X	E	I	N	G	A	Q	E	P	I
N	D	E	M	B	R	U	S	H	E	S	P	A
N	E	C	K	L	A	C	E	S	A	C	L	R
S	A	N	D	W	I	C	H	E	S	I	E	I
D	I	C	T	I	O	N	A	R	I	E	S	E
B	O	T	T	L	E	S	Z	I	S	R	E	S
P	Q	I	W	T	I	O	S	Y	U	R	D	S
T	L	E	L	L	S	H	B	N	E	Y	S	I

"S" PLURALS:	"ES" PLURALS:	"IES" PLURALS:
1 *apples*	4 ______	7 ______
2 ______	5 ______	8 ______
3 ______	6 ______	

Aa 8.6 WRITE A PLURAL TO DESCRIBE EACH PICTURE

 pencils

1 ______

2 ______

3 ______

4 ______

5 ______

6 ______

7 ______

8 ______

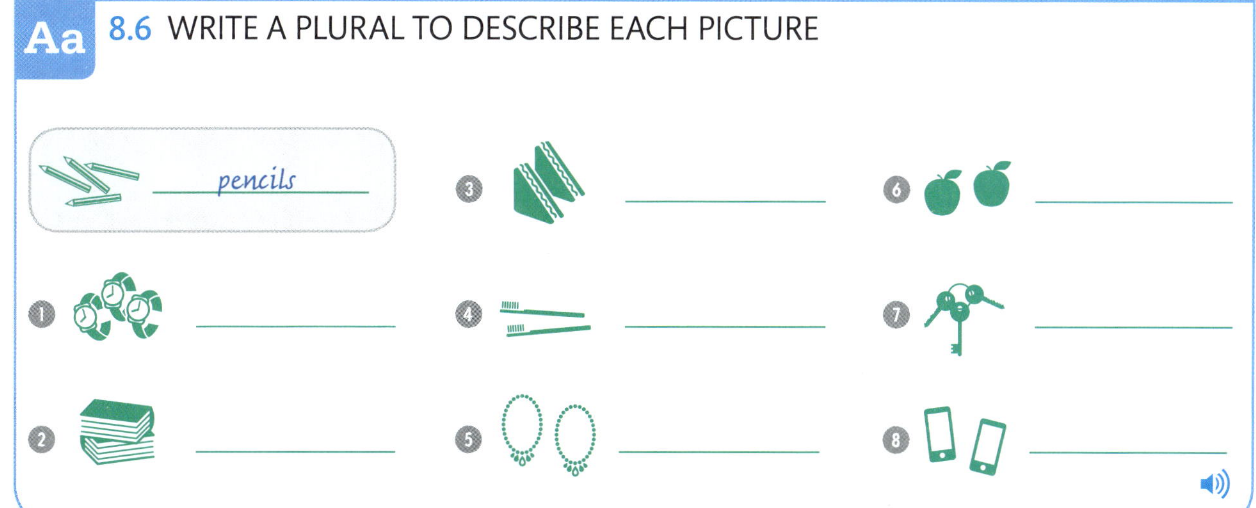

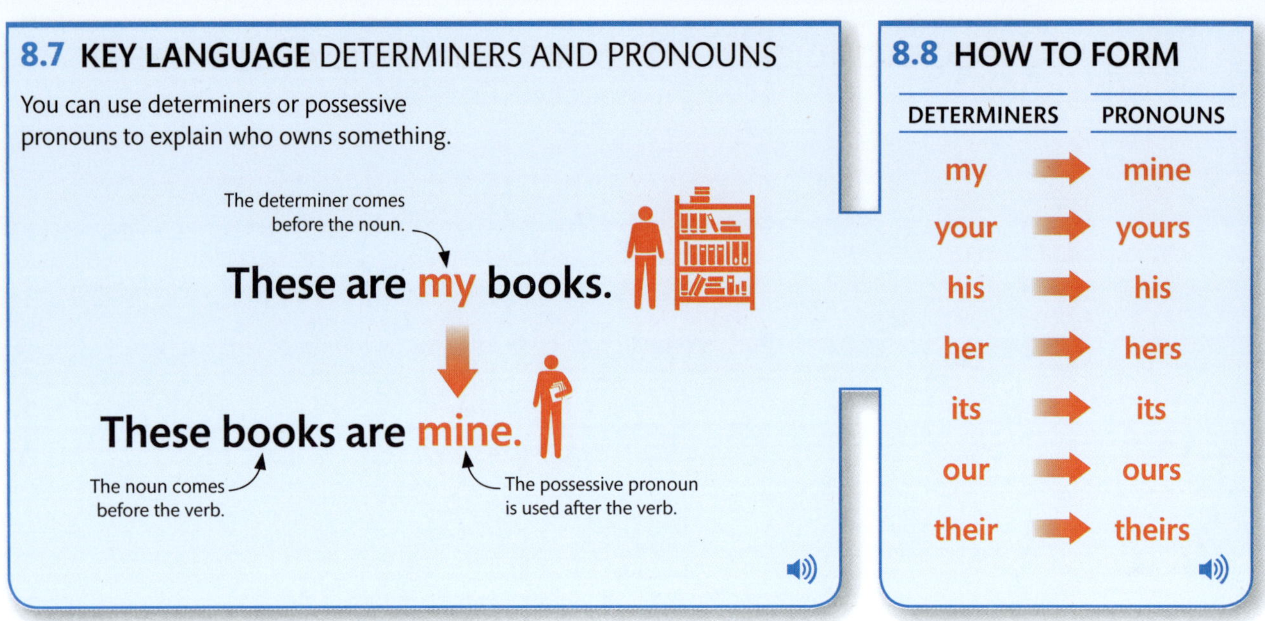

8.7 KEY LANGUAGE DETERMINERS AND PRONOUNS

You can use determiners or possessive pronouns to explain who owns something.

8.8 HOW TO FORM

DETERMINERS	PRONOUNS
my	mine
your	yours
his	his
her	hers
its	its
our	ours
their	theirs

8.9 FILL IN THE GAPS TO WRITE EACH SENTENCE TWO OTHER WAYS

These are Aman's books.	*These are his books.*	*These books are his.*
1. This is Leesa's laptop.		
2. Those are Una and Ben's keys.		
3. These are Jo's and my passports.		
4. That is John's brush.		

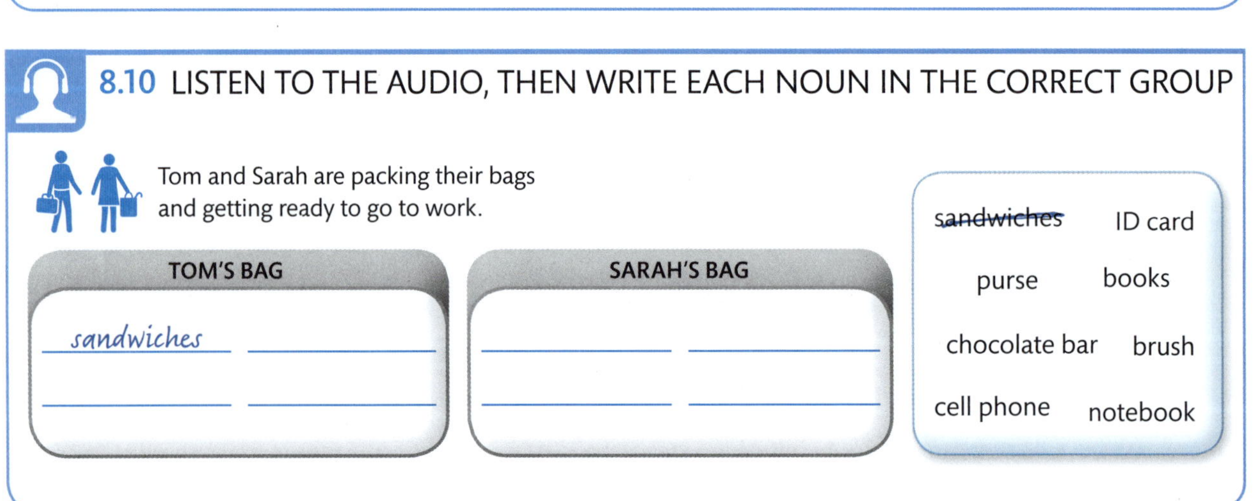

8.10 LISTEN TO THE AUDIO, THEN WRITE EACH NOUN IN THE CORRECT GROUP

Tom and Sarah are packing their bags and getting ready to go to work.

TOM'S BAG	SARAH'S BAG
sandwiches	

~~sandwiches~~ ID card purse books chocolate bar brush cell phone notebook

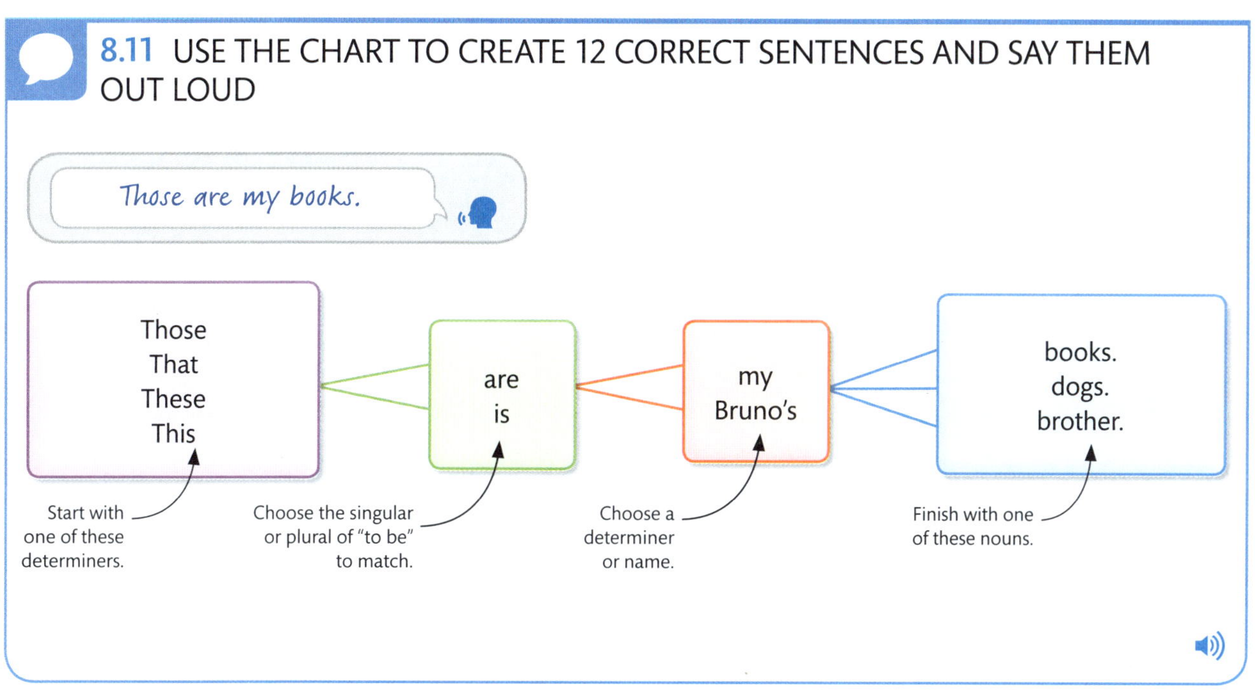

08 CHECKLIST

"These" and "those" ☐ **Aa** Possessions ☐ Using determiners and pronouns ☐

REVIEW THE ENGLISH YOU HAVE LEARNED IN UNITS 01–08

NEW LANGUAGE	SAMPLE SENTENCE	☑	UNIT
INTRODUCING YOURSELF	Hello! I am Joe. My name is Joe.	☐	1.1
HOW OLD ARE YOU?	I'm 25 years old.	☐	3.1
POSSESSIVE ADJECTIVES	Felix is my cat. Coco is your rabbit.	☐	5.1
APOSTROPHE WITH "S"	Lizzie's mother. Ginger is my parents' cat.	☐	6.1, 6.5
"THIS," "THAT," "THESE," AND "THOSE"	This is my dog. That is my dog. These are my bags and those are your bags.	☐	5.6, 8.1
DETERMINERS AND PRONOUNS	These are my books. These books are mine.	☐	8.7

09 Vocabulary

9.1 JOBS

cleaner

driver

sales assistant

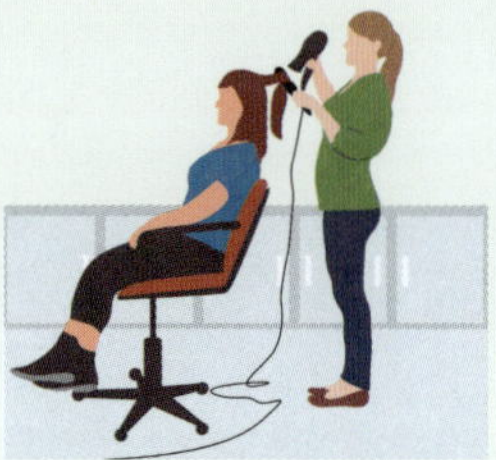
hairdresser

chef

gardener

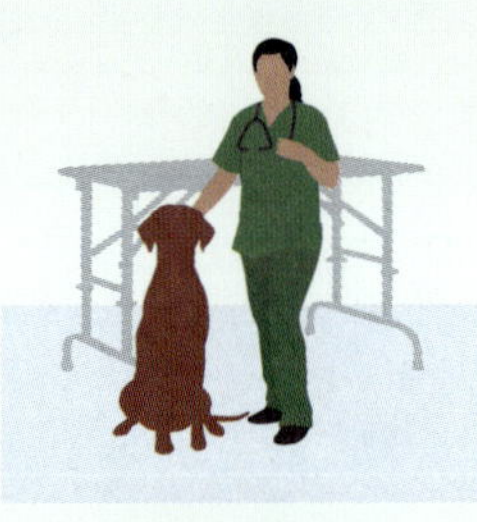
vet

actor

doctor

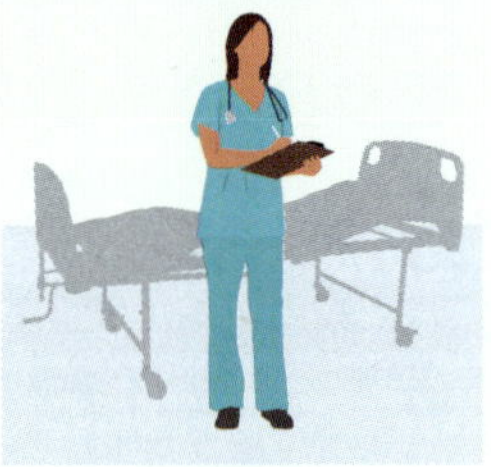
nurse

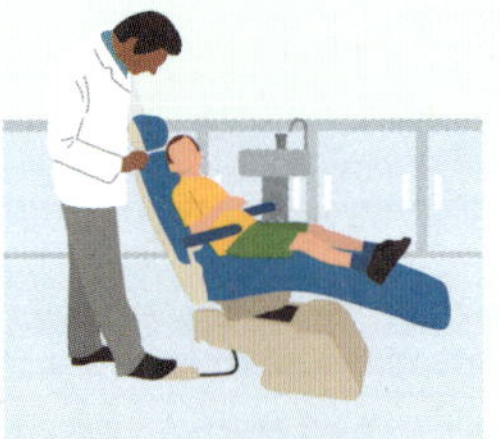
dentist

police officer

fire fighter

farmer

construction worker (US)
builder (UK)

artist

receptionist

mechanic

engineer

scientist

teacher

businesswoman

businessman

waiter

waitress

electrician

pilot

judge

9.2 PLURALS

Most nouns about people and jobs are made plural in the usual way by adding "-s" or "-es".

driver → drivers

waitress → waitresses

Nouns that end in "man" change to end in "men" in the plural.

man → men

woman → women

businessman → businessmen

businesswoman → businesswomen

For nouns made up of two words, the second word is made plural.

police officer → police officers

10 Talking about your job

You can use the verb "to be" to describe your job. The verb "to work" can give more information about where you work and who you work with.

New language Using "I am" for your job
Aa Vocabulary Jobs and workplaces
New skill Describing your job

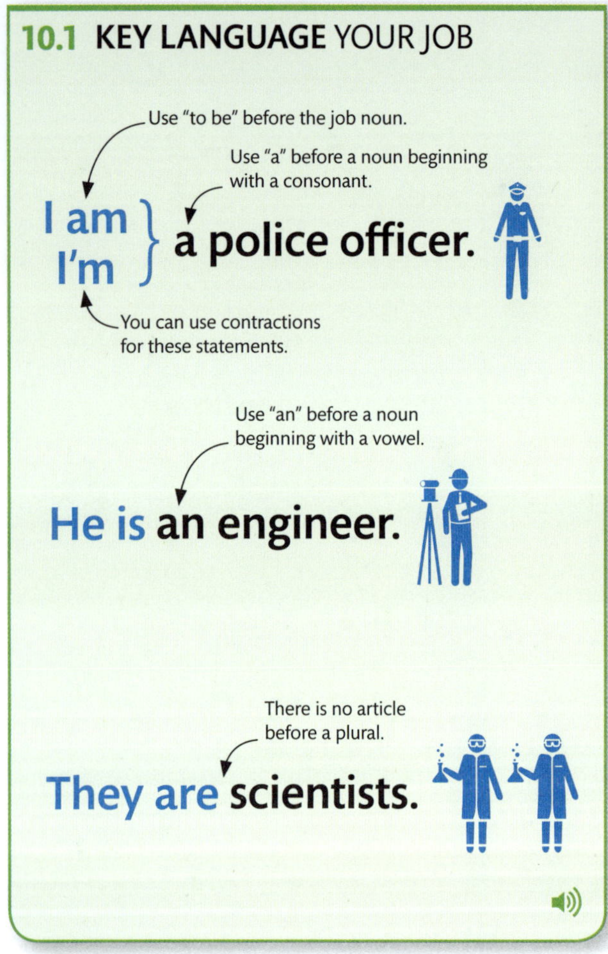

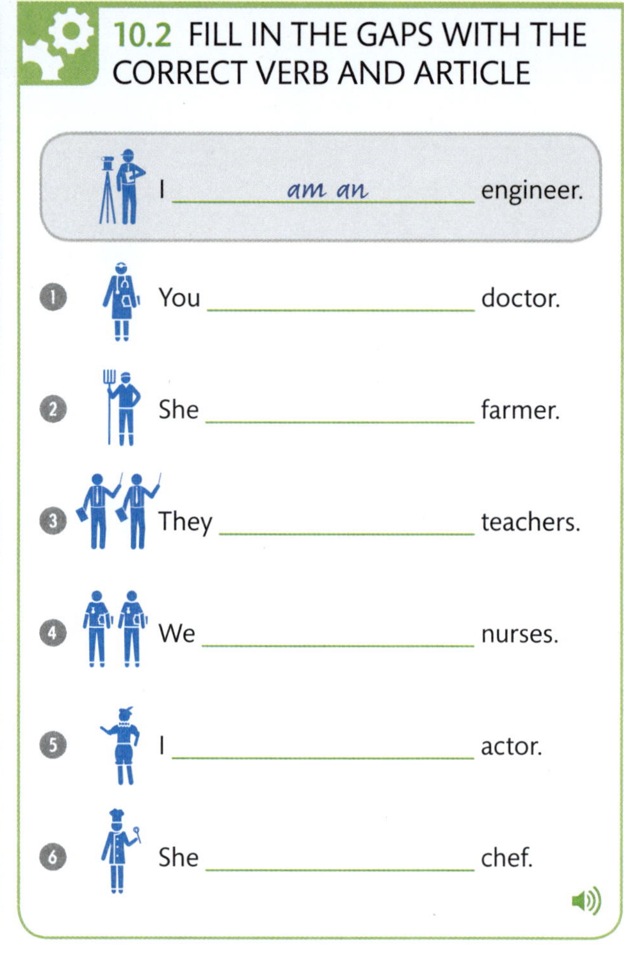

10.3 CROSS OUT THE INCORRECT WORD IN EACH SENTENCE

They are / ~~is~~ farmers.

1. You are / is a driver.
2. I am / is a mechanic.
3. He is / are a vet.
4. We am / are sales assistants.
5. They is / are businesswomen.
6. She is / are a waitress.
7. We is / are receptionists.
8. She is / are a gardener.

10.4 VOCABULARY WORKPLACES

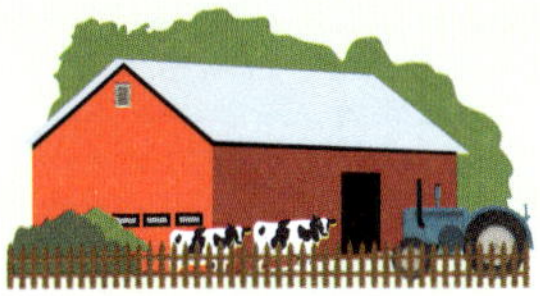

farm

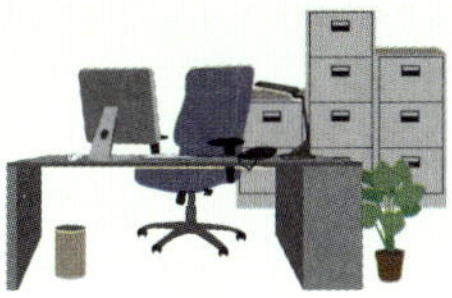

office

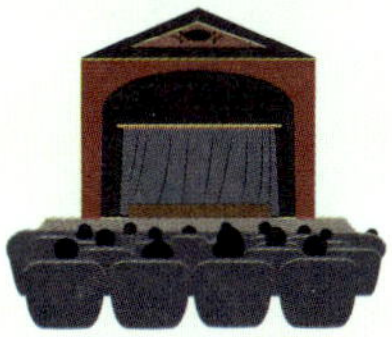

theater (US)
theatre (UK)

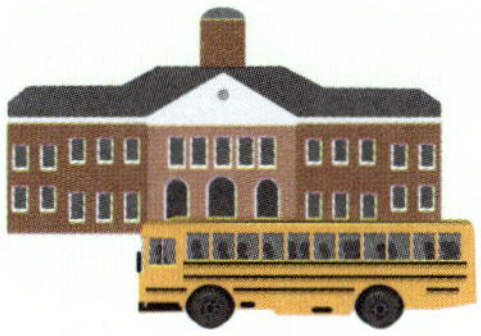

school

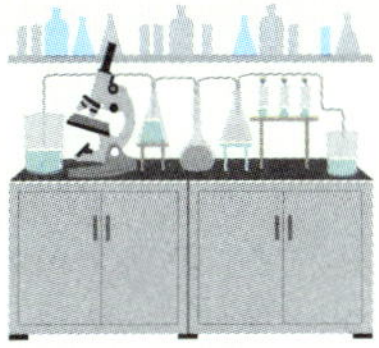

laboratory

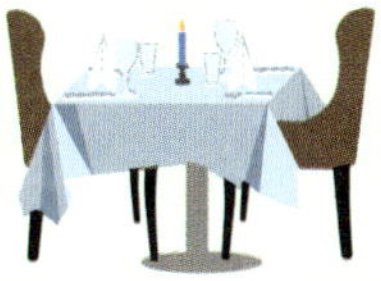

restaurant

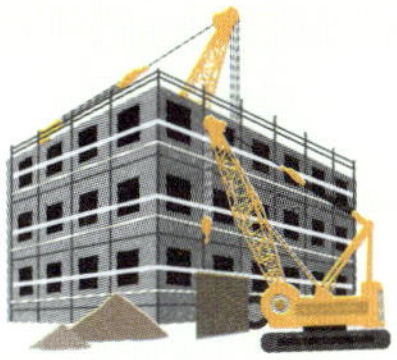

construction site

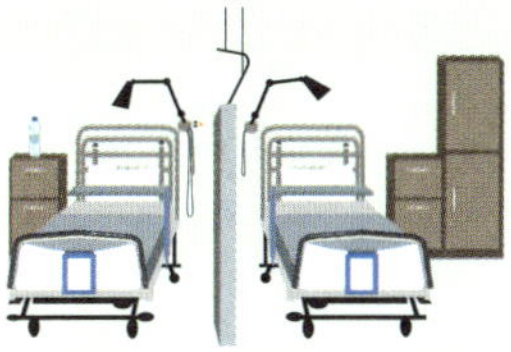

hospital

Aa 10.5 MATCH THE JOBS TO THE WORKPLACES

businessman → office	farm
1 nurse	restaurant
2 farmer	office
3 scientist	hospital
4 waiter	laboratory
5 teacher	construction site
6 builder	school
7 doctor	theater
8 actor	restaurant
9 chef	hospital

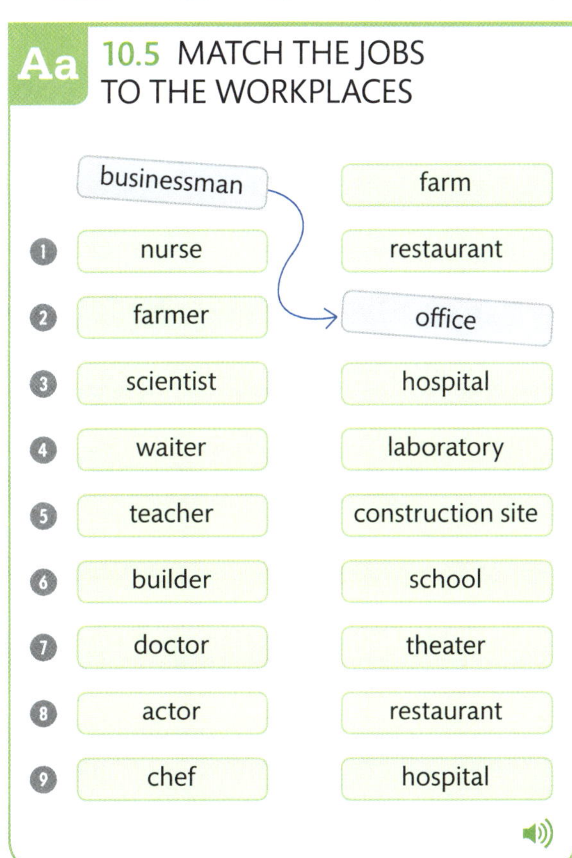

10.6 KEY LANGUAGE INSIDE / OUTSIDE

Use "inside" for jobs in buildings.

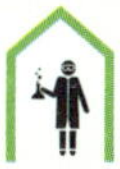

A scientist works inside.

Use "outside" for jobs in the open air.

A farmer works outside.

Aa 10.7 MARK THE CORRECT ANSWERS

A hairdresser works outside. **True** ☐ **False** ☑

1 A driver works outside. **True** ☐ **False** ☐

2 A chef works outside. **True** ☐ **False** ☐

3 A doctor works inside. **True** ☐ **False** ☐

4 A gardener works outside. **True** ☐ **False** ☐

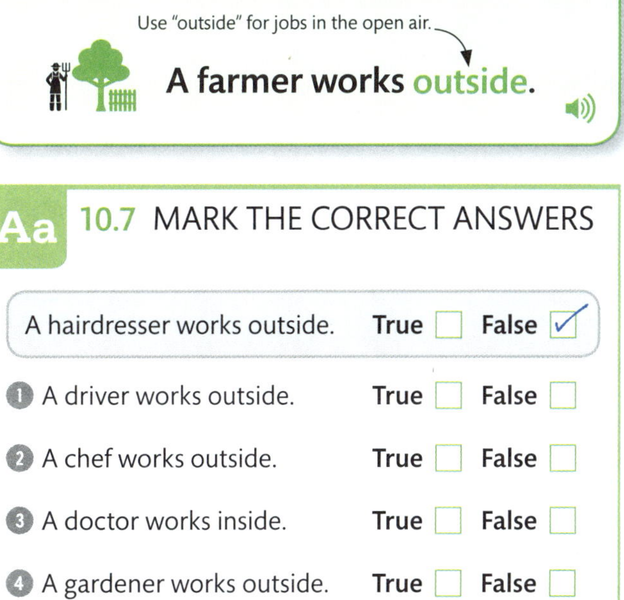

10.8 KEY LANGUAGE USING "WORK IN" AND "WORK ON"

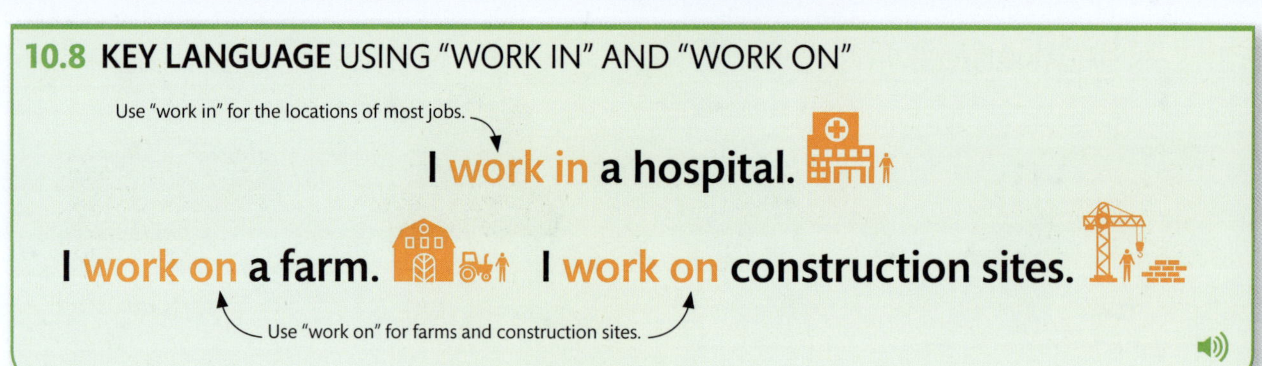

10.9 LISTEN TO THE AUDIO AND NUMBER THE IMAGES IN THE ORDER THEY ARE DESCRIBED

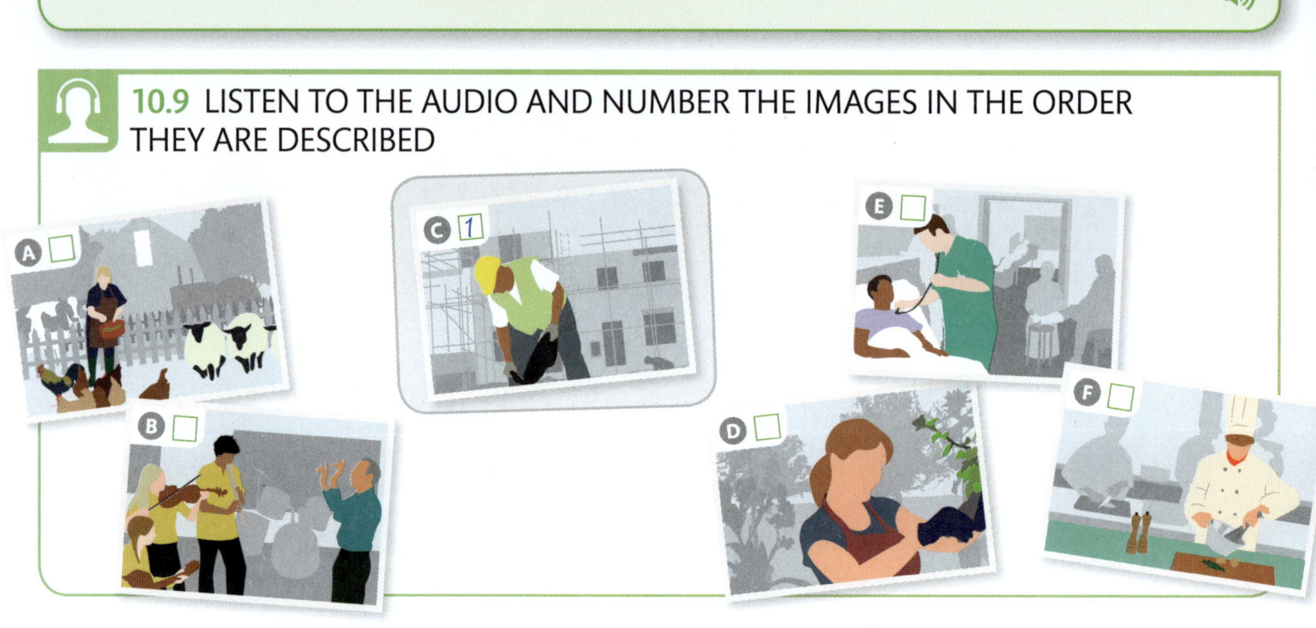

10.10 WRITE TWO SENTENCES TO DESCRIBE EACH PICTURE

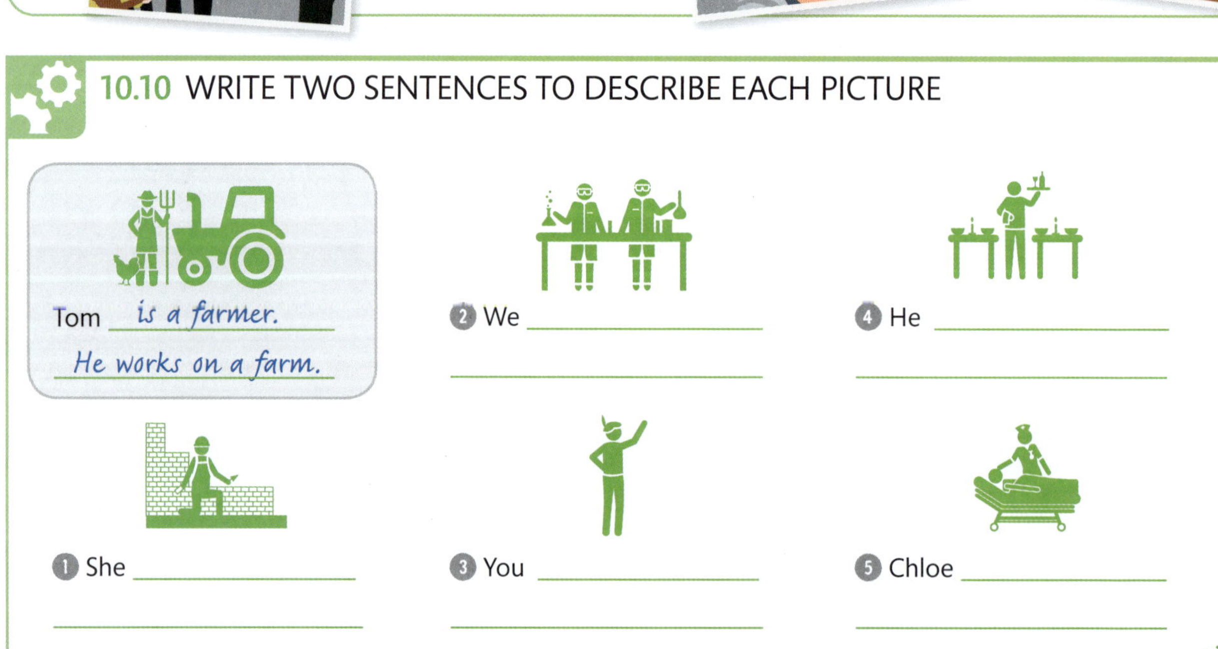

Tom *is a farmer.*
He works on a farm.

1. She ______
______

2. We ______
______

3. You ______
______

4. He ______
______

5. Chloe ______
______

10.11 KEY LANGUAGE "WORK WITH"

Use "work with" followed by a noun that relates to your job.

I work with animals.

10.12 VOCABULARY "WORK WITH"

animals ....

children ....

patients ....

plants ....

food ....

people ....

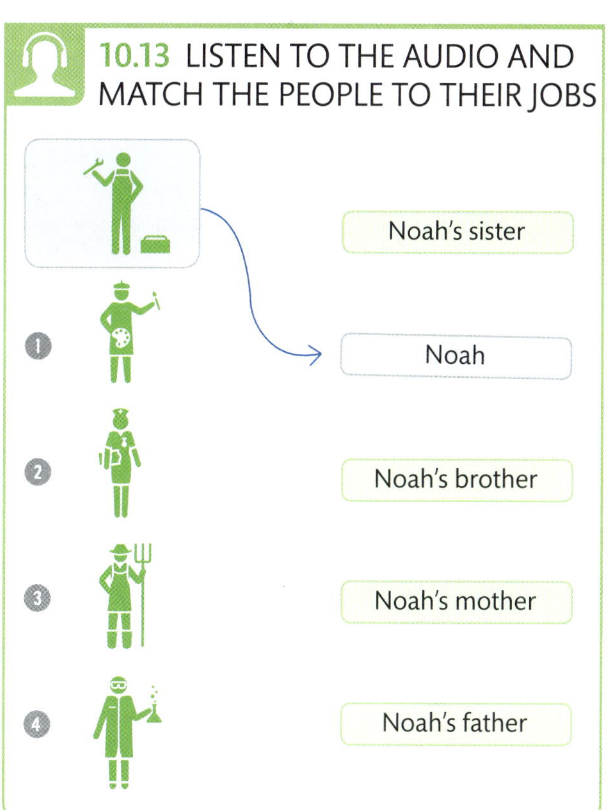

10.13 LISTEN TO THE AUDIO AND MATCH THE PEOPLE TO THEIR JOBS

1

2

3

4

Noah's sister

Noah

Noah's brother

Noah's mother

Noah's father

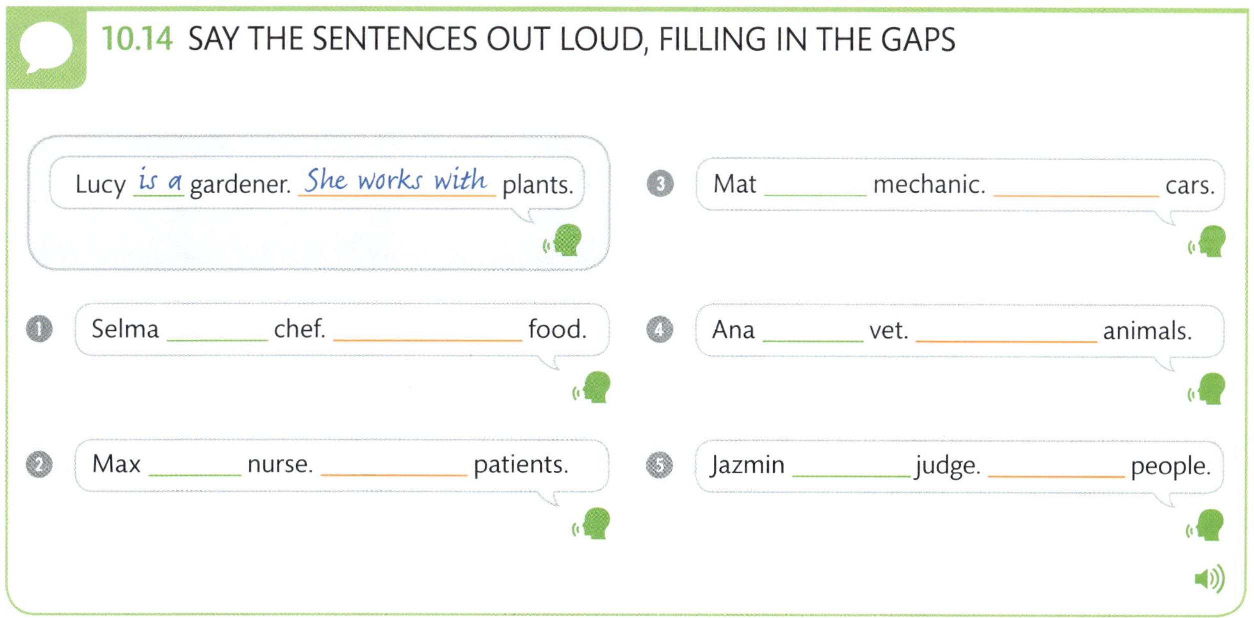

10.14 SAY THE SENTENCES OUT LOUD, FILLING IN THE GAPS

Lucy *is a* gardener. *She works with* plants.

1 Selma ________ chef. ________________ food.

2 Max ________ nurse. ________________ patients.

3 Mat ________ mechanic. ________________ cars.

4 Ana ________ vet. ________________ animals.

5 Jazmin ________ judge. ________________ people.

10 CHECKLIST

Using "I am" for your job ☐ Aa Jobs and workplaces ☐ Describing your job ☐

11 Telling the time

There are two ways of saying the time in English. You can use hours and minutes, or you can say the minutes first and state their relation to the hour.

New language Times of day
Aa Vocabulary Words for time
New skill Saying what the time is

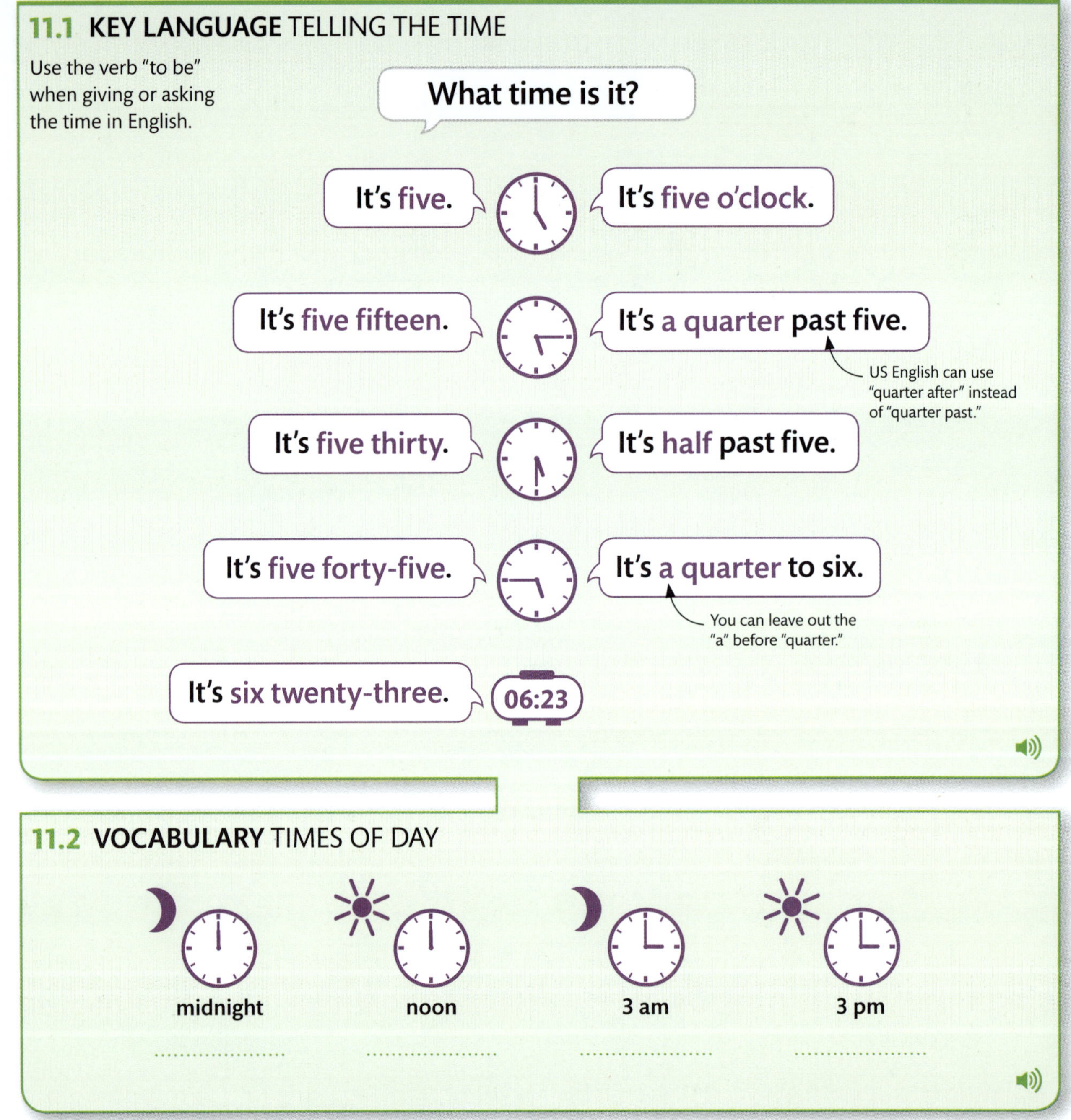

11.3 MATCH THE CLOCKS TO THE TIME PHRASES

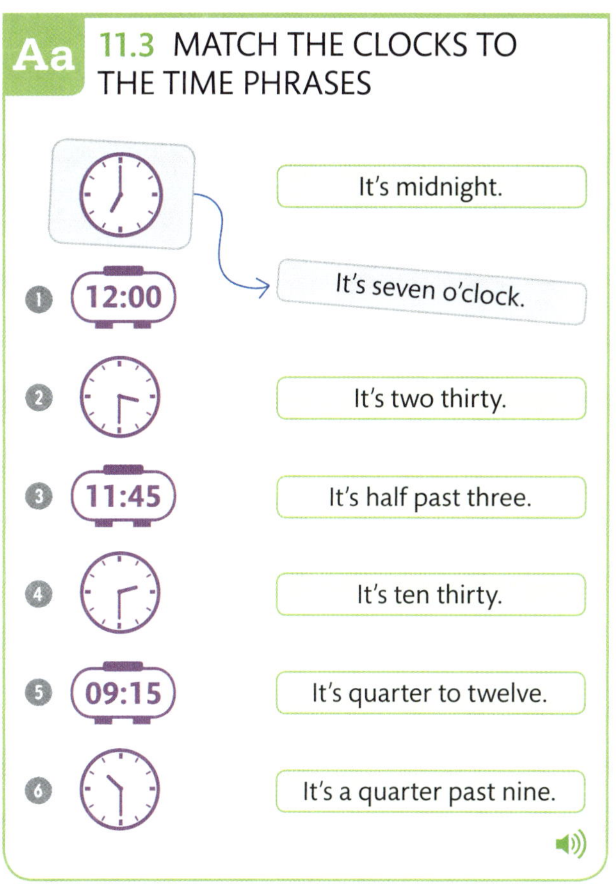

11.4 LISTEN TO THE AUDIO AND MARK THE TIMES YOU HEAR

11.5 WRITE THE TIMES IN FIGURES

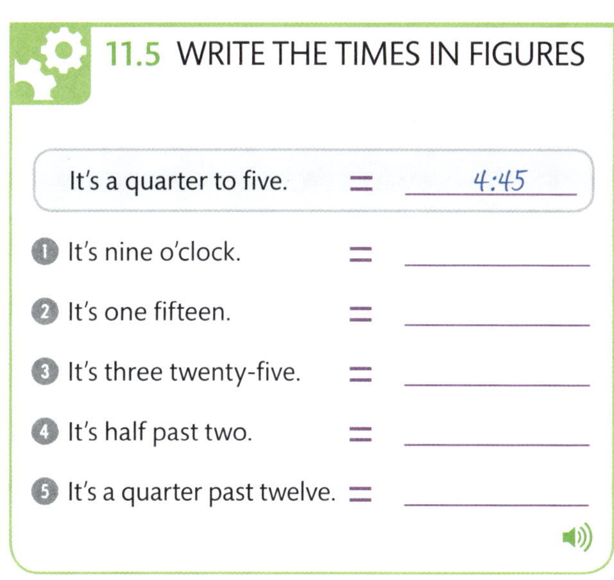

11.6 WRITE DOWN THE TIMES, THEN SAY THEM OUT LOUD

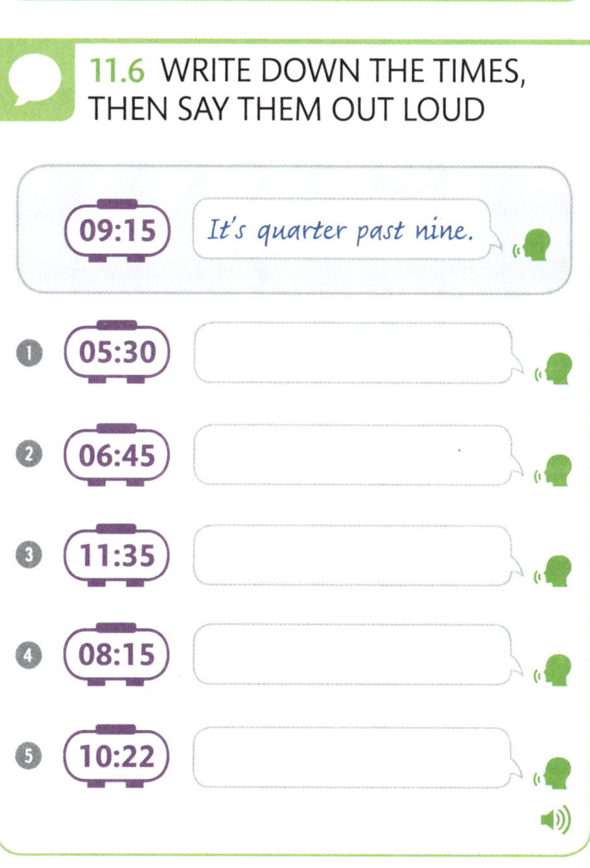

11 CHECKLIST

Times of day ☐ Words for time ☐ Saying what the time is ☐

12 Vocabulary

12.1 DAILY ROUTINES

wake up

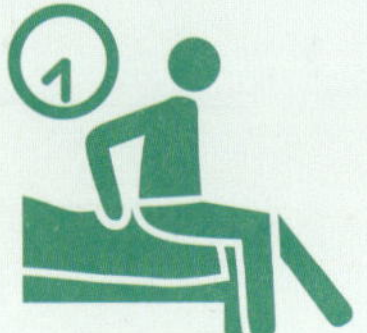
get up

take a shower (US)
have a shower (UK)

take a bath (US)
have a bath (UK)

brush your hair

have breakfast / eat breakfast

go to work

go to school

buy groceries

go home

cook dinner

have dinner / eat dinner

12.2 TIMES OF THE DAY

day

night

dawn

morning

iron a shirt

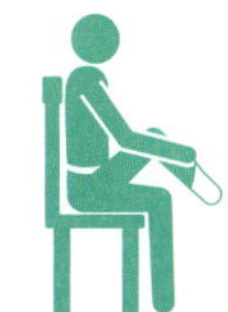
get dressed

brush your teeth

wash your face

start work

have lunch / eat lunch

finish work

leave work

clear the table

do the dishes (US)
wash the dishes (UK)

walk the dog

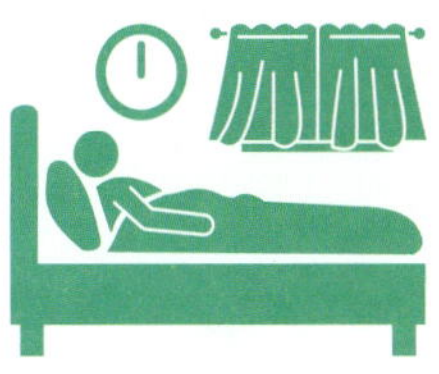
go to bed

afternoon

dusk

evening

late evening

13 Describing your day

Use the present simple tense to talk about the things you do regularly: for example, when you normally go to work or eat lunch.

New language The present simple
Aa Vocabulary Routine activities
New skill Talking about your daily routine

13.1 KEY LANGUAGE THE PRESENT SIMPLE

To make the present simple, use the base form of the verb (the infinitive without "to").

The base form of the verb "to eat."

I eat lunch at noon every day.

She eats lunch at 2pm every day.

With he, she, and it, add "s" to the base form.

13.2 FURTHER EXAMPLES THE PRESENT SIMPLE

You **get** up at 7 o'clock. 

She **gets** up at 5:30am. 

We **start** work at 9 o'clock. 

He **starts** work at 11am. 

They **leave** work at 5pm. 

Rob **leaves** work at 7pm. 

13.3 HOW TO FORM THE PRESENT SIMPLE

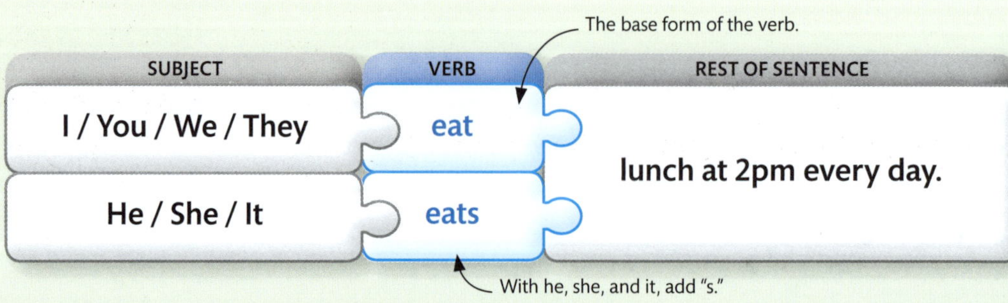

13.4 CROSS OUT THE INCORRECT WORD IN EACH SENTENCE

She ~~eat~~ / eats dinner in the evening.

1. He wake up / wakes up at 7 o'clock.
2. You leave / leaves home at 8:30am.
3. I start / starts work at 10am.
4. Ellen get / gets up at 5 o'clock.
5. My wife take / takes a shower in the evening.
6. I take / takes a shower in the morning.
7. My parents eat / eats lunch at 2pm.
8. We leave / leaves work at 4pm.
9. My brother work / works with animals.

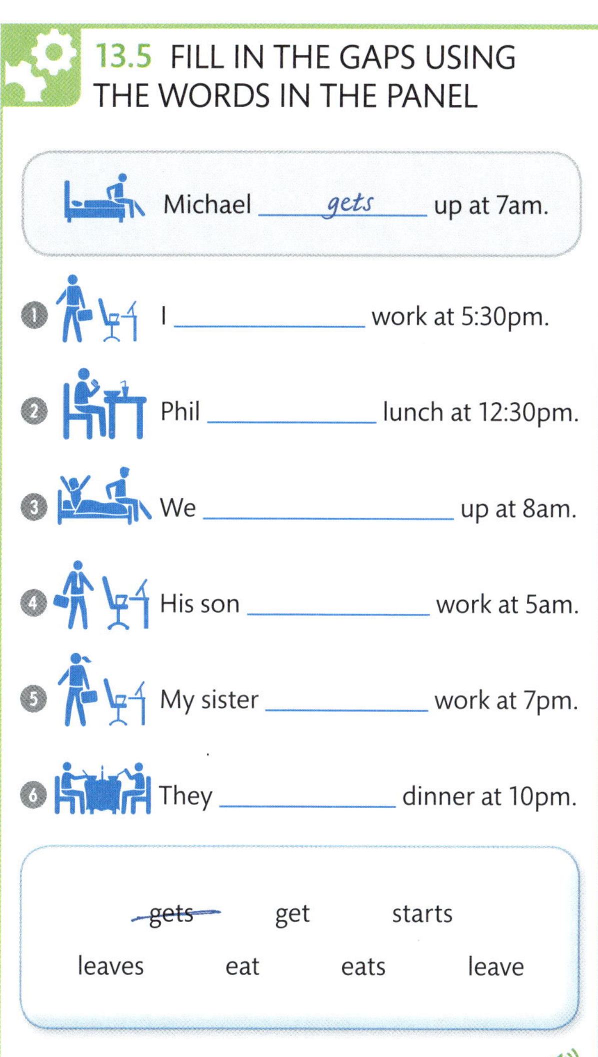

13.5 FILL IN THE GAPS USING THE WORDS IN THE PANEL

Michael ___gets___ up at 7am.

1. I __________ work at 5:30pm.
2. Phil __________ lunch at 12:30pm.
3. We __________ up at 8am.
4. His son __________ work at 5am.
5. My sister __________ work at 7pm.
6. They __________ dinner at 10pm.

~~gets~~ get starts leaves eat eats leave

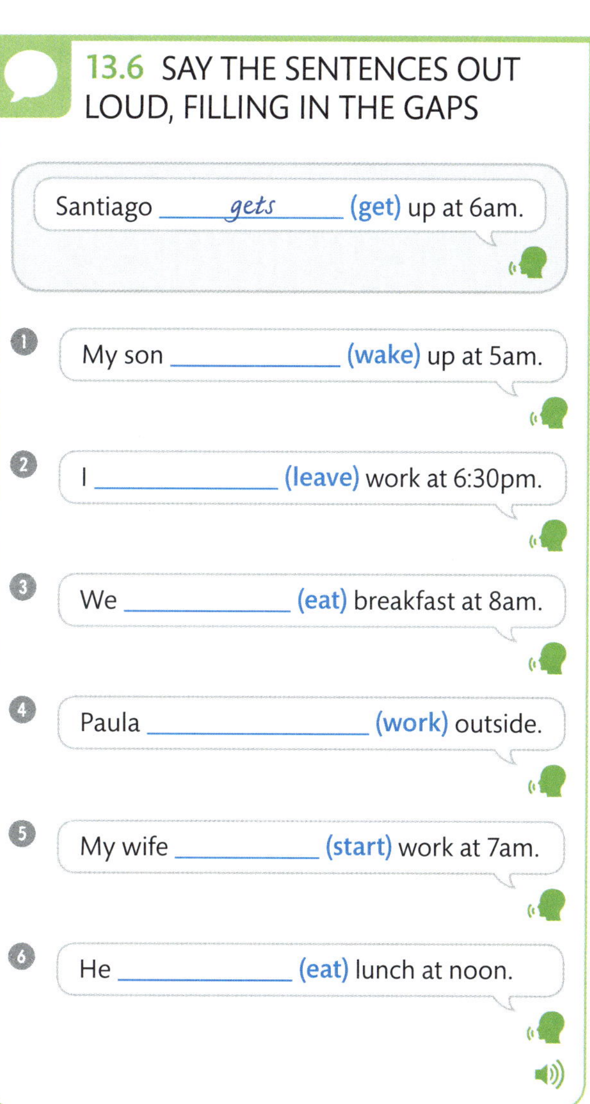

13.6 SAY THE SENTENCES OUT LOUD, FILLING IN THE GAPS

Santiago ___gets___ (get) up at 6am.

1. My son __________ (wake) up at 5am.
2. I __________ (leave) work at 6:30pm.
3. We __________ (eat) breakfast at 8am.
4. Paula __________ (work) outside.
5. My wife __________ (start) work at 7am.
6. He __________ (eat) lunch at noon.

13.7 KEY LANGUAGE "S" AND "ES" ENDINGS

With some verbs you add "es" for he, she, and it. These include verbs ending "sh," "ch," "o," "ss," "x," and "z."

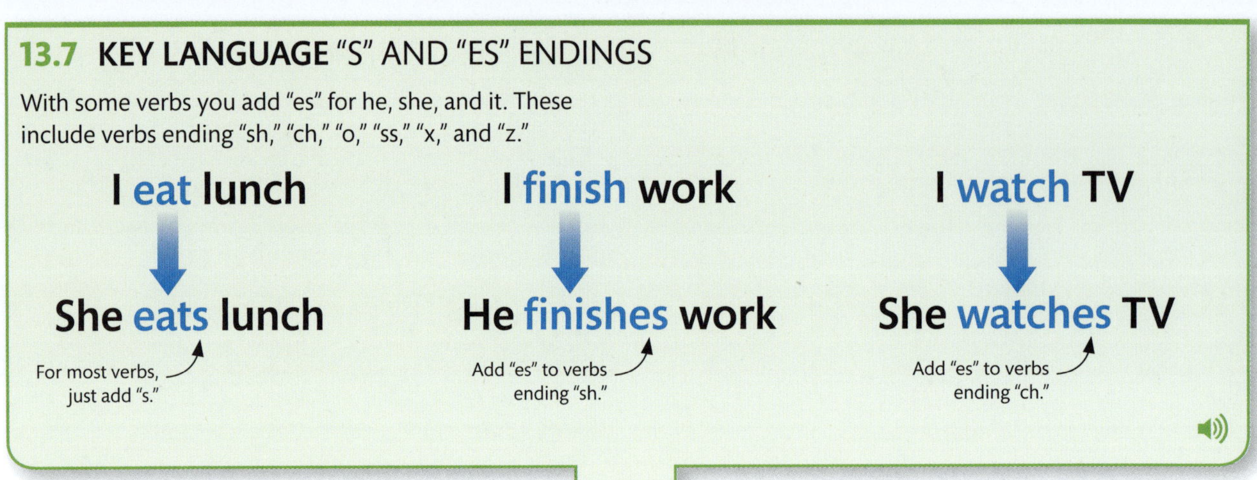

13.8 PRONUNCIATION SAYING "S" AND "ES"

The "-s" endings are pronounced different ways. Listen to the difference.

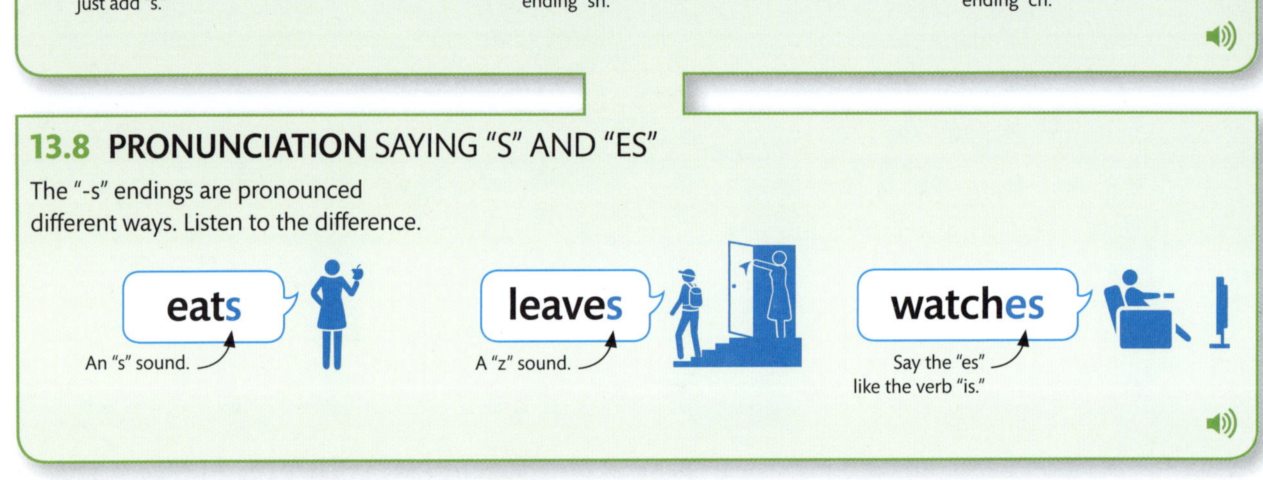

13.9 SAY THE WORDS OUT LOUD

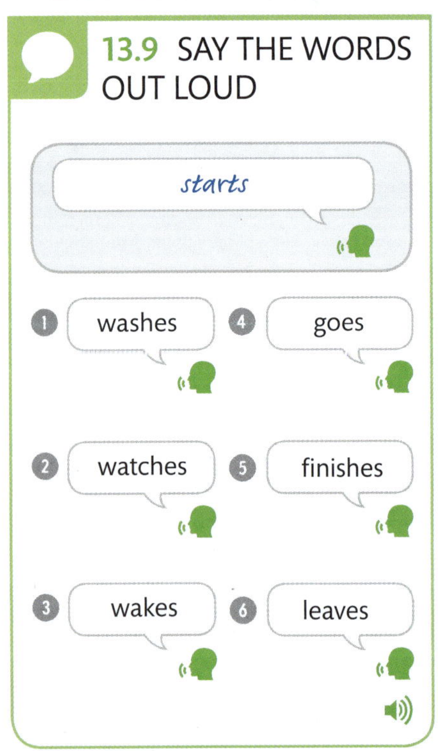

13.10 FILL IN THE GAPS BY PUTTING THE VERBS IN THE CORRECT FORM

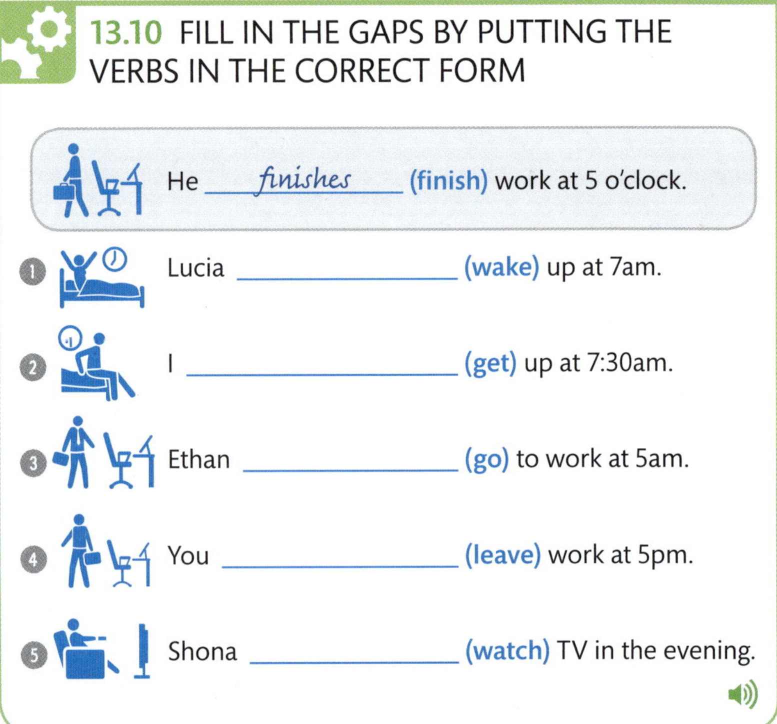

He *finishes* (finish) work at 5 o'clock.

1. Lucia ______ (wake) up at 7am.
2. I ______ (get) up at 7:30am.
3. Ethan ______ (go) to work at 5am.
4. You ______ (leave) work at 5pm.
5. Shona ______ (watch) TV in the evening.

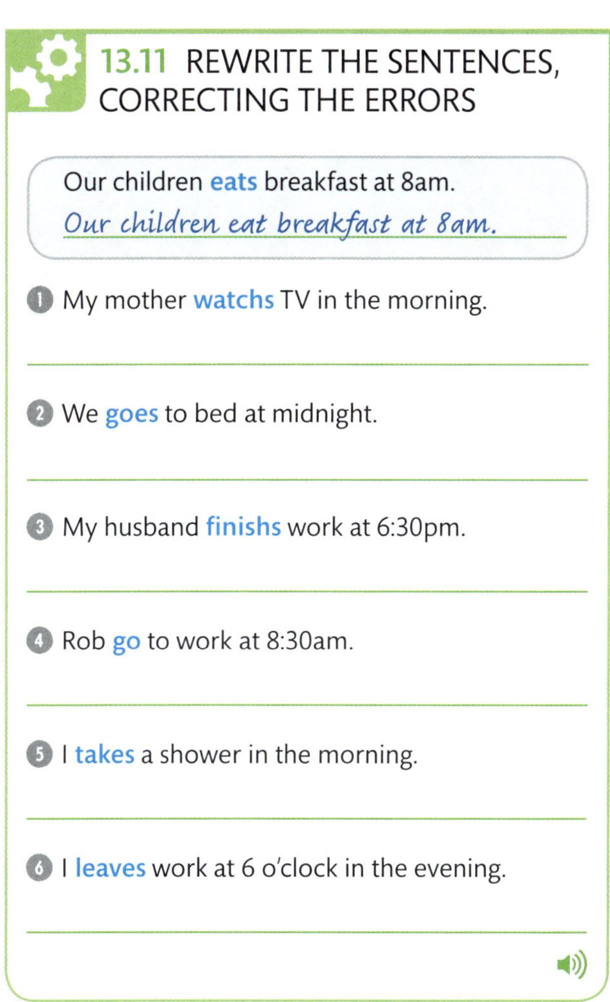

13.11 REWRITE THE SENTENCES, CORRECTING THE ERRORS

Our children **eats** breakfast at 8am.

Our children eat breakfast at 8am.

1. My mother **watchs** TV in the morning.
2. We **goes** to bed at midnight.
3. My husband **finishs** work at 6:30pm.
4. Rob **go** to work at 8:30am.
5. I **takes** a shower in the morning.
6. I **leaves** work at 6 o'clock in the evening.

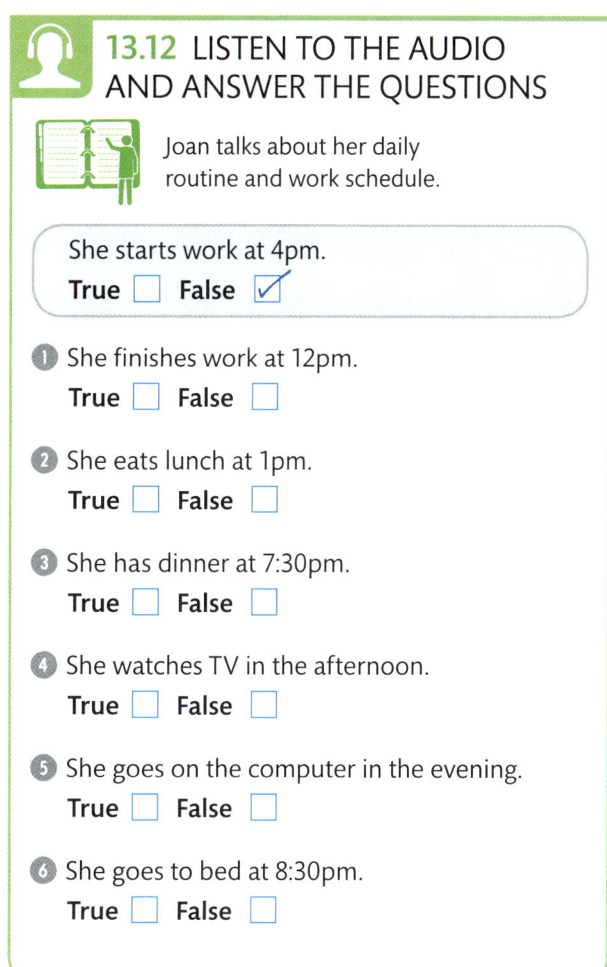

13.12 LISTEN TO THE AUDIO AND ANSWER THE QUESTIONS

Joan talks about her daily routine and work schedule.

She starts work at 4pm.
True ☐ **False** ☑

1. She finishes work at 12pm.
   True ☐ **False** ☐
2. She eats lunch at 1pm.
   True ☐ **False** ☐
3. She has dinner at 7:30pm.
   True ☐ **False** ☐
4. She watches TV in the afternoon.
   True ☐ **False** ☐
5. She goes on the computer in the evening.
   True ☐ **False** ☐
6. She goes to bed at 8:30pm.
   True ☐ **False** ☐

13.13 USE THE CHART TO CREATE 12 CORRECT SENTENCES AND SAY THEM OUT LOUD

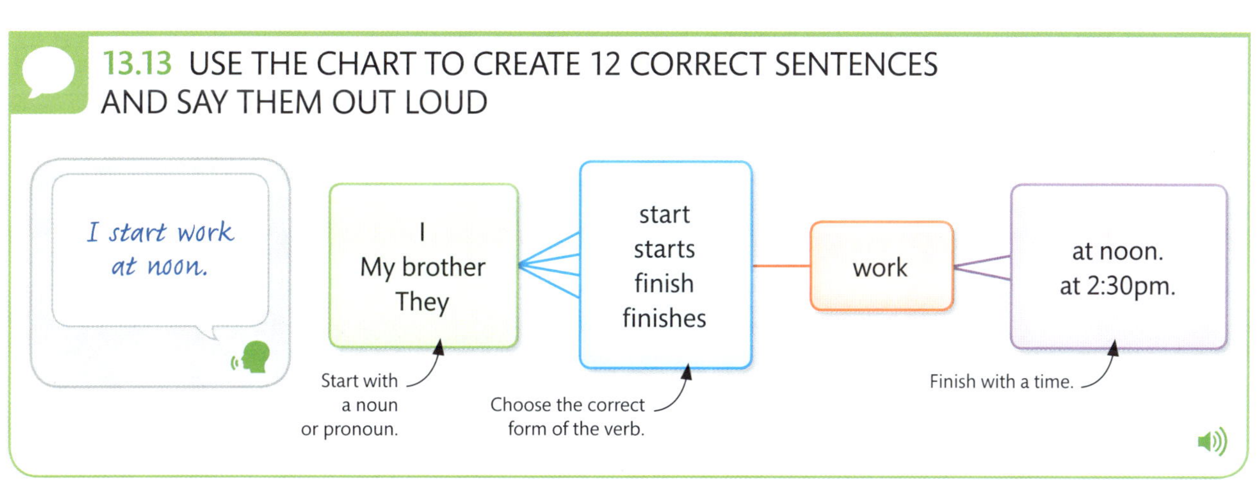

13 CHECKLIST

The present simple ☐ **Aa** Routine activities ☐ Talking about your daily routine ☐

14 Describing your week

You can talk about your usual weekly activities using the present simple with time phrases. Time phrases are often formed using prepositions and days of the week.

New language Days and prepositions
Aa Vocabulary Days of the week
New skill Talking about your weekly routine

14.1 VOCABULARY DAYS OF THE WEEK

weekend

Monday | Tuesday | Wednesday | Thursday | Friday | Saturday | Sunday

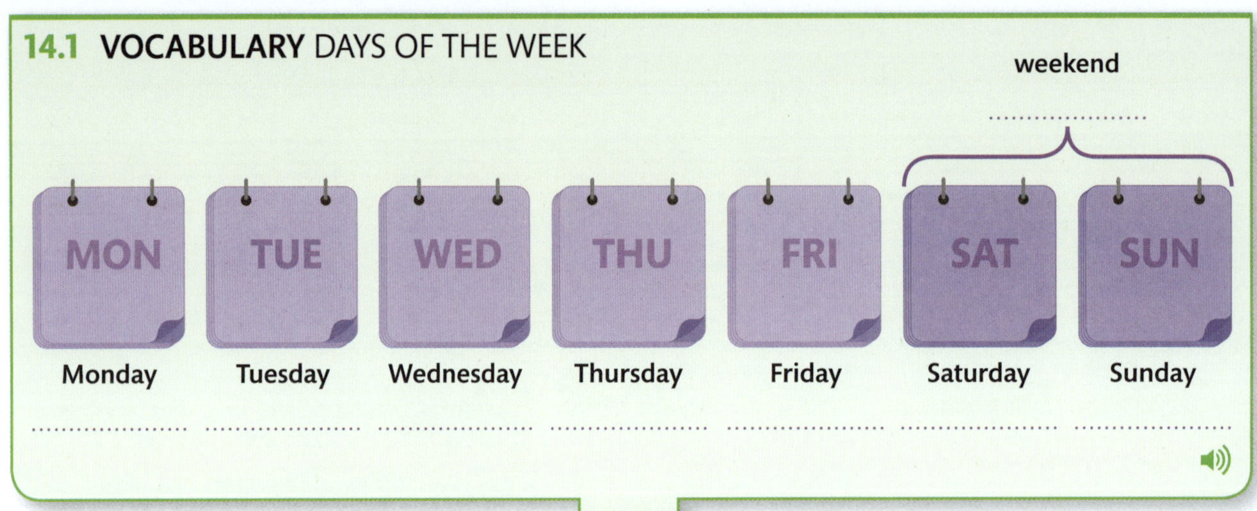

14.2 KEY LANGUAGE PREPOSITIONS AND DAYS OF THE WEEK

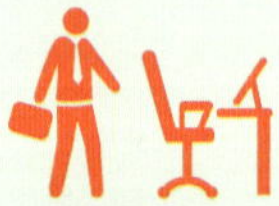

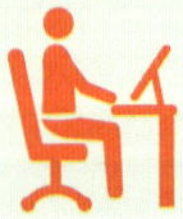

I go to work on Mondays.

Use "on" before the day of the week to say the day you do something.

You can add "-s" to the day of the week to show that the thing happens regularly on that day.

I work from Monday to Friday.

Use "from" to say the day you start doing something.

Use "to" to say the day you finish doing something.

TIP
In US English, you can also leave out "go to" and the preposition when saying what day you work: "I work Mondays."

I watch TV {on / at} the weekend.

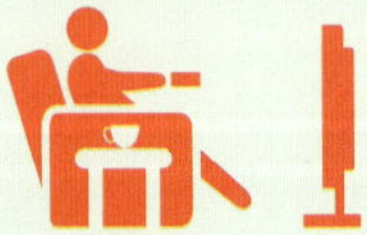

"On the weekend" is more common in the US.

"At the weekend" is more common in the UK.

14.3 FILL IN THE GAPS TO COMPLETE THE SENTENCES

Sharon wakes up at 5am ___on___ Mondays.

1. We eat lunch at 3pm ________ the weekend.
2. She goes to bed at 1am ________ the weekend.
3. I go to work _____ Monday _____ Wednesday.
4. They eat dinner at 9pm ________ the weekend.
5. We finish work at 3pm ________ Fridays.
6. I eat breakfast at work ________ Mondays.

14.4 VOCABULARY ACTIVITIES

go to the gym

go swimming

play tennis

play soccer

read the newspaper

take a bath

14.5 FILL IN THE GAPS TO COMPLETE THE SENTENCES

 She ___plays tennis___ on Mondays.

1.  He ________________ on Tuesdays and Fridays.
2.  They ________________ on Thursdays.
3.  He ________________ on Wednesdays.
4.  I ________________ on the weekend.
5.  You ________________ on Saturdays.

14.6 SAY THE SENTENCES OUT LOUD, FILLING IN THE GAPS

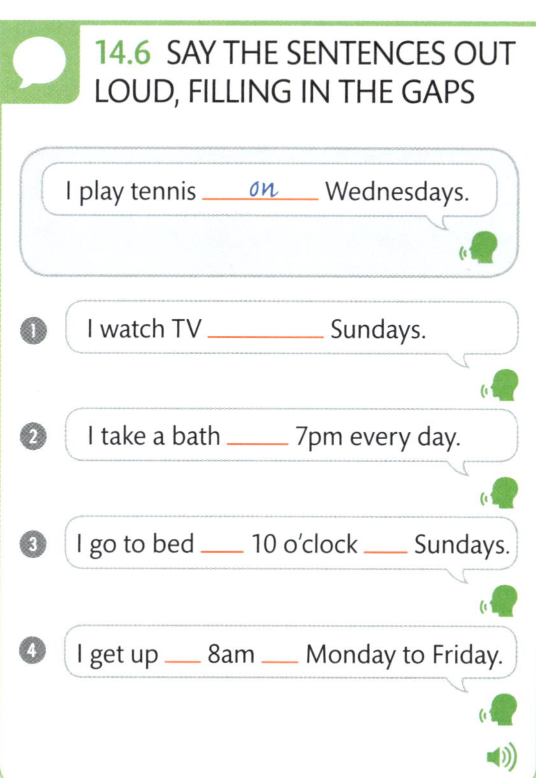

I play tennis ___on___ Wednesdays.

1. I watch TV ________ Sundays.
2. I take a bath _____ 7pm every day.
3. I go to bed _____ 10 o'clock _____ Sundays.
4. I get up _____ 8am _____ Monday to Friday.

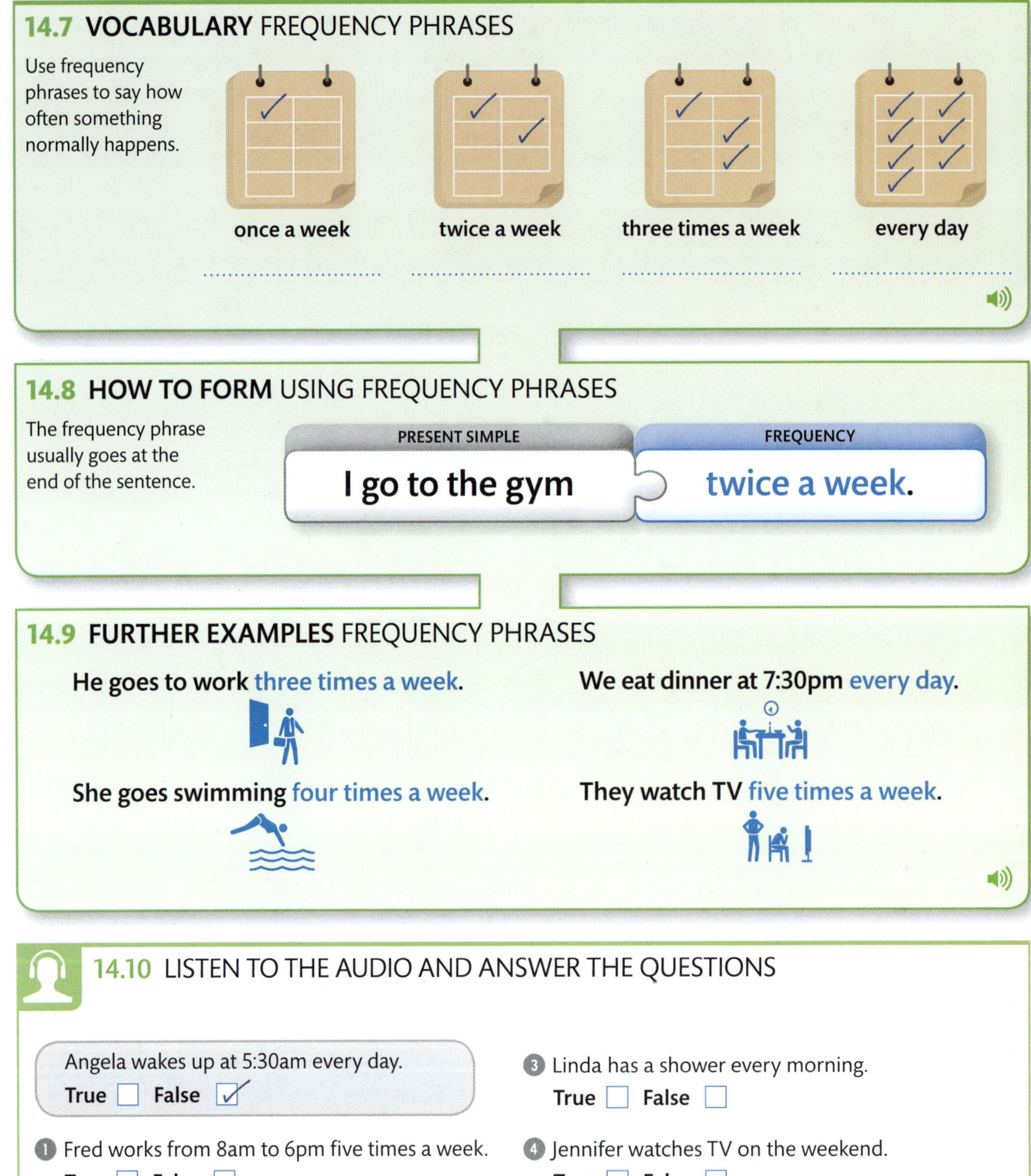

14.7 VOCABULARY FREQUENCY PHRASES

Use frequency phrases to say how often something normally happens.

once a week ....

twice a week ....

three times a week ....

every day ....

14.8 HOW TO FORM USING FREQUENCY PHRASES

The frequency phrase usually goes at the end of the sentence.

PRESENT SIMPLE	FREQUENCY
I go to the gym	twice a week.

14.9 FURTHER EXAMPLES FREQUENCY PHRASES

He goes to work **three times a week**.

We eat dinner at 7:30pm **every day**.

She goes swimming **four times a week**.

They watch TV **five times a week**.

14.10 LISTEN TO THE AUDIO AND ANSWER THE QUESTIONS

Angela wakes up at 5:30am every day.
True ☐ False ☑

1. Fred works from 8am to 6pm five times a week.
True ☐ False ☐

2. Scott has dinner at 6am.
True ☐ False ☐

3. Linda has a shower every morning.
True ☐ False ☐

4. Jennifer watches TV on the weekend.
True ☐ False ☐

5. Tim's daughter goes to bed at 7:30pm on Sundays.
True ☐ False ☐

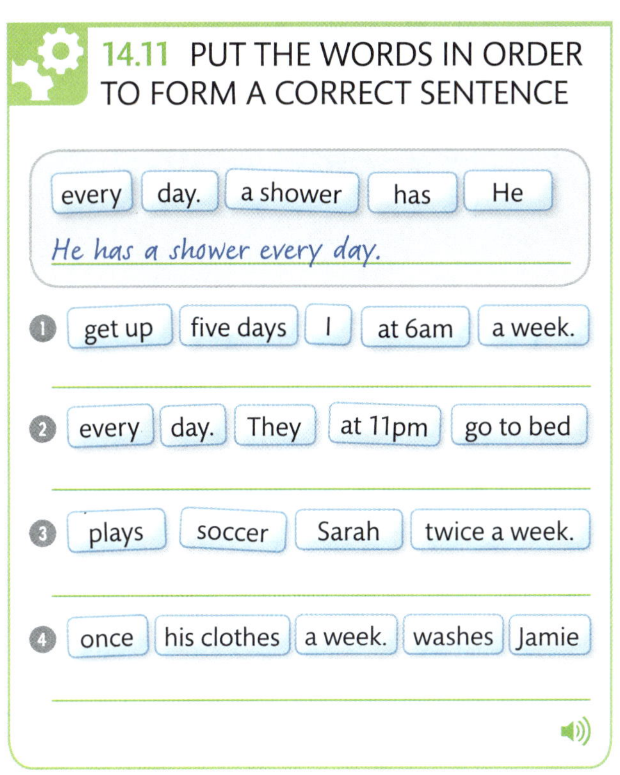

14.11 PUT THE WORDS IN ORDER TO FORM A CORRECT SENTENCE

every | day. | a shower | has | He

He has a shower every day.

1. get up | five days | I | at 6am | a week.

2. every | day. | They | at 11pm | go to bed

3. plays | soccer | Sarah | twice a week.

4. once | his clothes | a week. | washes | Jamie

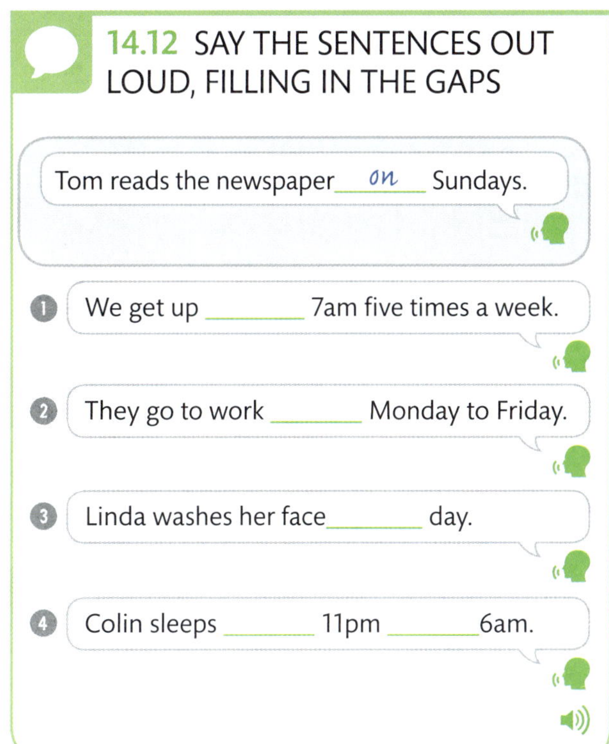

14.12 SAY THE SENTENCES OUT LOUD, FILLING IN THE GAPS

Tom reads the newspaper *on* Sundays.

1. We get up ______ 7am five times a week.

2. They go to work ______ Monday to Friday.

3. Linda washes her face ______ day.

4. Colin sleeps ______ 11pm ______ 6am.

14 CHECKLIST

Days and prepositions ☐ **Aa** Days of the week ☐ Talking about your weekly routine ☐

REVIEW THE ENGLISH YOU HAVE LEARNED IN UNITS 10-14

NEW LANGUAGE	SAMPLE SENTENCE	☑	UNIT
TALKING ABOUT JOBS	I am a police officer. He is an engineer.	☐	10.1
USING "WORK IN," "WORK ON," AND "WORK WITH"	I work in a hospital. I work on a farm. I work with animals.	☐	10.8, 10.11
TELLING THE TIME	It's five. It's five o'clock.	☐	11.1, 11.2
THE PRESENT SIMPLE	I eat lunch at noon every day. She eats lunch at 2pm every day.	☐	13.1
PREPOSITIONS AND DAYS OF THE WEEK	I work on Mondays. I work from Monday to Friday.	☐	14.2
FREQUENCY PHRASES	I go to the gym twice a week.	☐	14.8, 14.9

15 Negatives with "to be"

You make a sentence negative by using "not" or its short form "n't." Negative sentences with the verb "to be" have different rules than negatives with other verbs.

New language Negatives with "to be"
Aa Vocabulary "Not"
New skill Saying what things are not

15.1 KEY LANGUAGE NEGATIVES WITH THE VERB "TO BE"

Add "not" after "to be" to make the sentence negative.

I am a farmer. I am not a doctor.

"Not" is added to make the sentence negative.

15.2 FURTHER EXAMPLES NEGATIVES WITH THE VERB "TO BE"

He is not an adult.

It is not 5 o'clock.

They are not engineers.

This is not a pig.

We are not actors.

That is not my bag.

15.3 HOW TO FORM NEGATIVES WITH THE VERB "TO BE"

The verb "to be" takes the same form in positive and negative sentences. The only difference is adding "not."

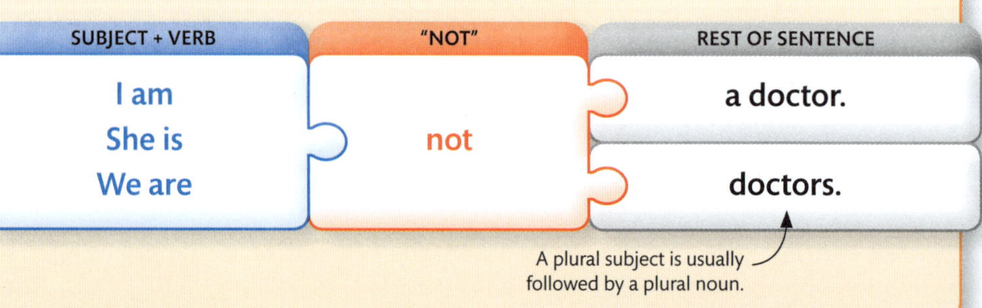

15.4 REWRITE THE SENTENCES, PUTTING THE WORDS IN THE CORRECT ORDER

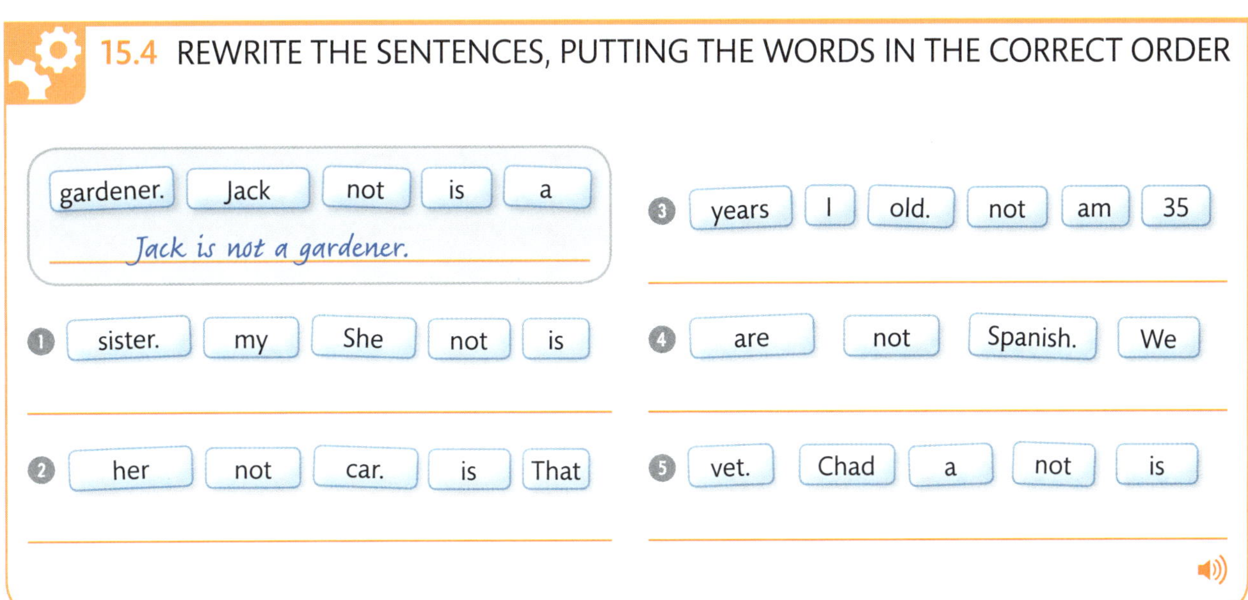

gardener. | Jack | not | is | a

Jack is not a gardener.

1. sister. | my | She | not | is
2. her | not | car. | is | That
3. years | I | old. | not | am | 35
4. are | not | Spanish. | We
5. vet. | Chad | a | not | is

15.5 FILL IN THE GAPS TO MAKE NEGATIVE SENTENCES

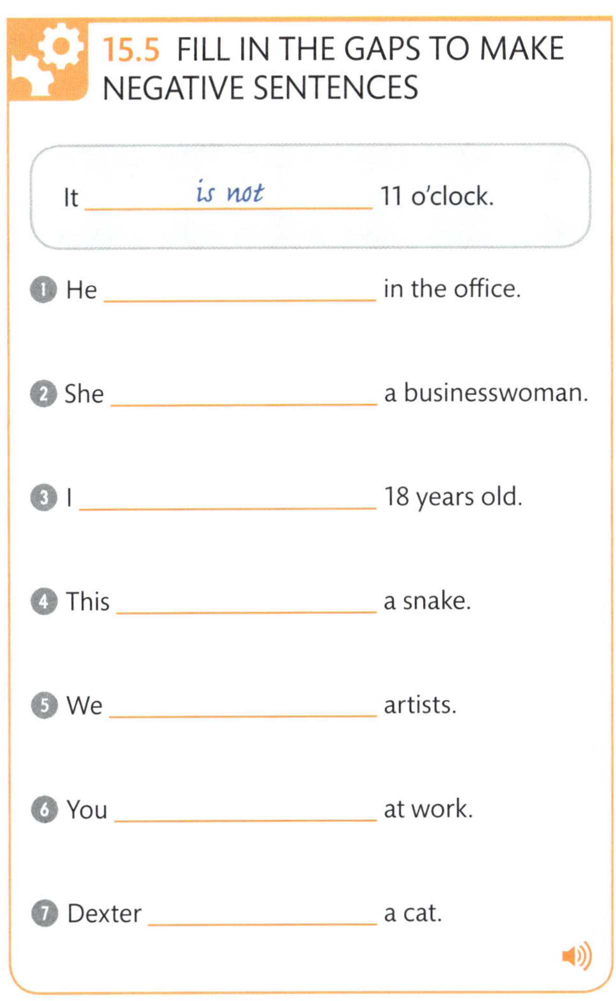

It *is not* 11 o'clock.

1. He ______ in the office.
2. She ______ a businesswoman.
3. I ______ 18 years old.
4. This ______ a snake.
5. We ______ artists.
6. You ______ at work.
7. Dexter ______ a cat.

15.6 LISTEN TO THE AUDIO, THEN NUMBER THE IMAGES IN THE ORDER THEY ARE DESCRIBED

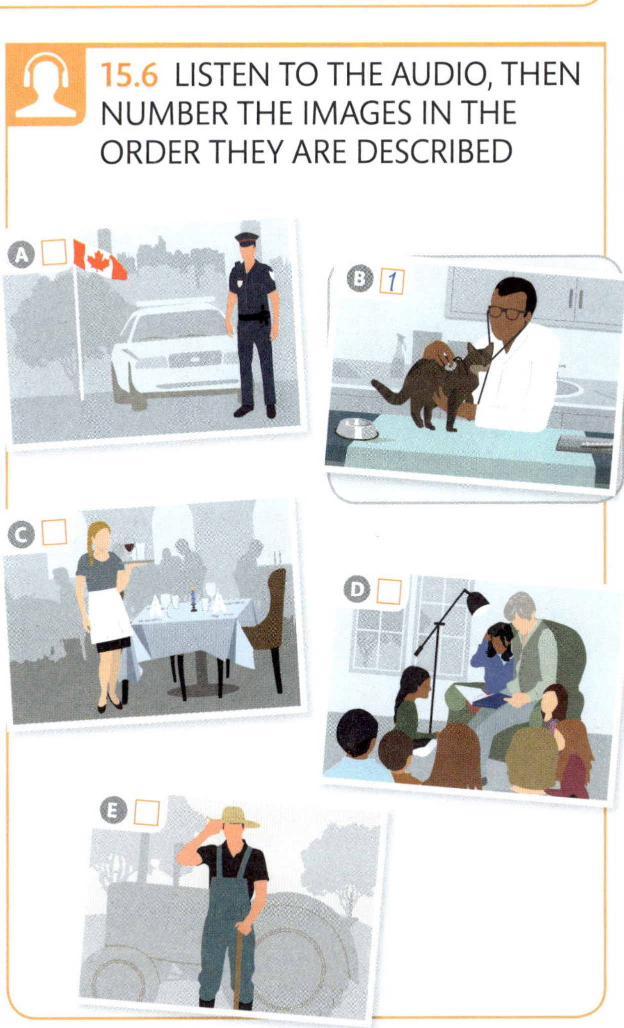

15.7 KEY LANGUAGE NEGATIVE SHORT FORMS

You can contract "you are not" in two ways. You can contract the subject and verb, or you can contract the verb and "not."

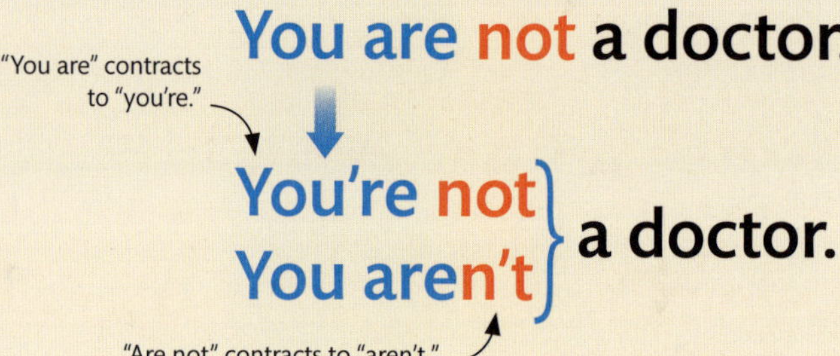

You are not a doctor.

"You are" contracts to "you're."

You're not / You aren't a doctor.

"Are not" contracts to "aren't."

15.8 FURTHER EXAMPLES NEGATIVE SHORT FORMS

I am not a teacher.

I'm not a teacher.

You cannot say "I amn't."

He is not a farmer.

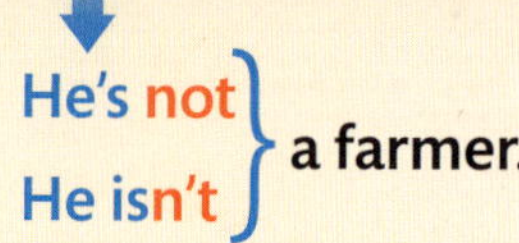

He's not / He isn't a farmer.

She is not American.

She's not / She isn't American.

It is not a pencil.

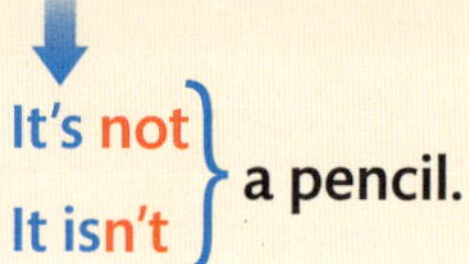

It's not / It isn't a pencil.

We are not waiters.

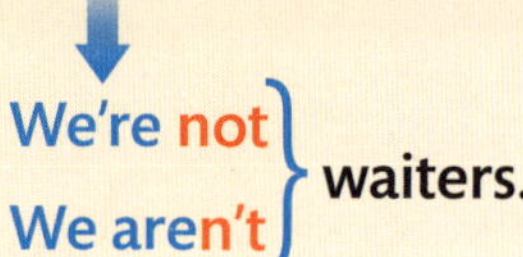

We're not / We aren't waiters.

They are not British.

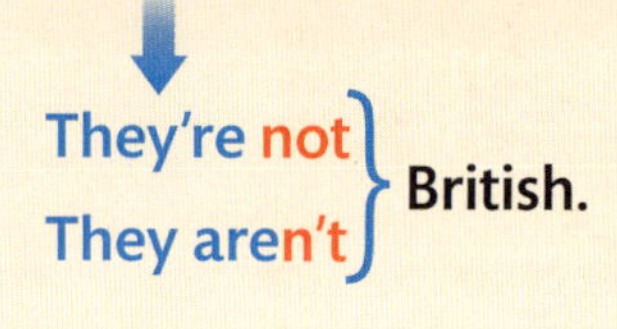

They're not / They aren't British.

15.9 REWRITE THE SENTENCES, CORRECTING THE ERRORS

Louis aren't Hayley's uncle.
Louis isn't Hayley's uncle.

1. It am not 10 o'clock in the morning.

2. You isn't 35 years old.

3. I aren't Australian.

4. My brother aren't married.

5. Tom and Angela isn't construction workers.

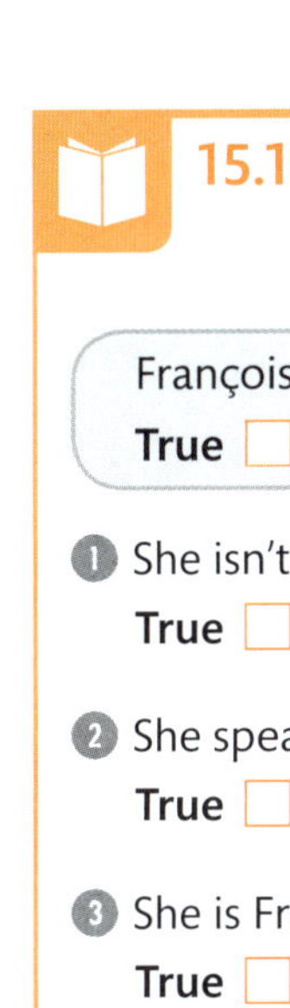

15.10 READ THE BLOG AND ANSWER THE QUESTIONS

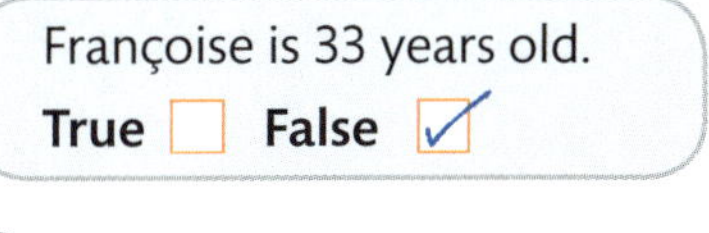

Françoise is 33 years old.
True ☐ False ☑

1. She isn't from the USA.
True ☐ False ☐

2. She speaks French.
True ☐ False ☐

3. She is French.
True ☐ False ☐

4. Her husband speaks English.
True ☐ False ☐

5. Her husband is British.
True ☐ False ☐

6. They live in the USA.
True ☐ False ☐

7. Her husband isn't a student.
True ☐ False ☐

15.11 USE THE CHART TO CREATE 12 CORRECT SENTENCES AND SAY THEM OUT LOUD

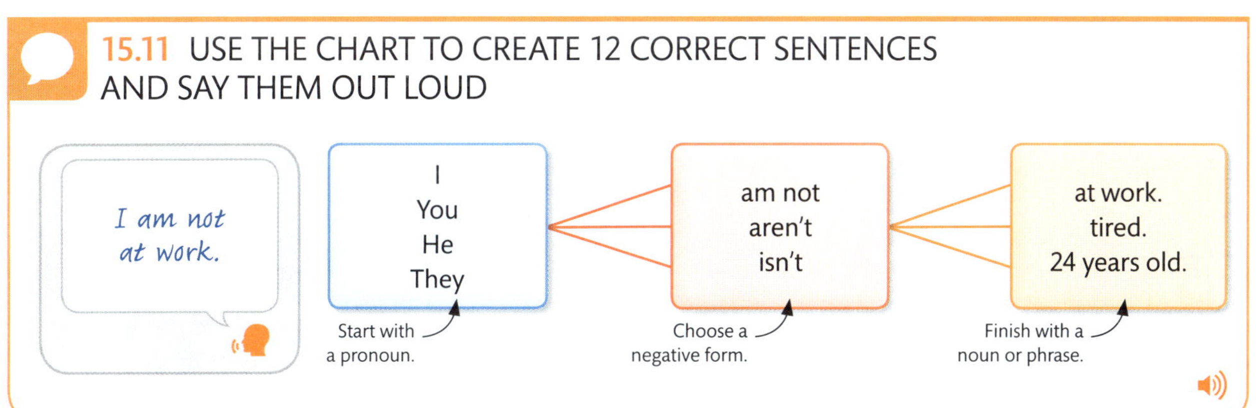

15 CHECKLIST

Negatives with "to be" ☐ Aa "Not" ☐ Saying what things are not ☐

16 More negatives

Add "do not" or "does not" before most verbs in English to make them negative. This is often shortened to "don't" or "doesn't."

New language Present simple negative
Vocabulary Daily activities
New skill Saying what you don't do

16.1 KEY LANGUAGE PRESENT SIMPLE NEGATIVE

Put "do not" before the verb to make the negative for "I," "you," "we," or "they." After "he," "she," or "it," use "does not."

I work outside.

The main verb does not change.

I do not work outside.
I work inside.

He works inside.

He does not work inside.
He works outside.

16.2 FURTHER EXAMPLES PRESENT SIMPLE NEGATIVE

You do not have a laptop.

We do not start work at 8am.

He does not live in Los Angeles.

The house does not have a backyard.

16.3 HOW TO FORM PRESENT SIMPLE NEGATIVE

Use "do" or "does" with "not" followed by the base form of the main verb (the infinitive without "to").

SUBJECT	"DO / DOES" + "NOT"	BASE FORM	REST OF SENTENCE
I / You / We / They	do not	work	outside.
He / She / It	does not		

16.4 FILL IN THE GAPS USING "DO NOT" OR "DOES NOT"

She *does not* go to the gym on Thursdays.

1. I ____________ read the papers on Saturday.
2. The dog ____________ eat fish.
3. They ____________ go to the theater often.
4. Ben and I ____________ live on a farm now.
5. Theo ____________ cycle to work.
6. You ____________ work at Fabio's café.
7. Claire ____________ watch TV in the evening.
8. We ____________ play football at home.
9. Pierre ____________ wake up before noon.

16.5 LISTEN TO THE AUDIO AND ANSWER THE QUESTIONS

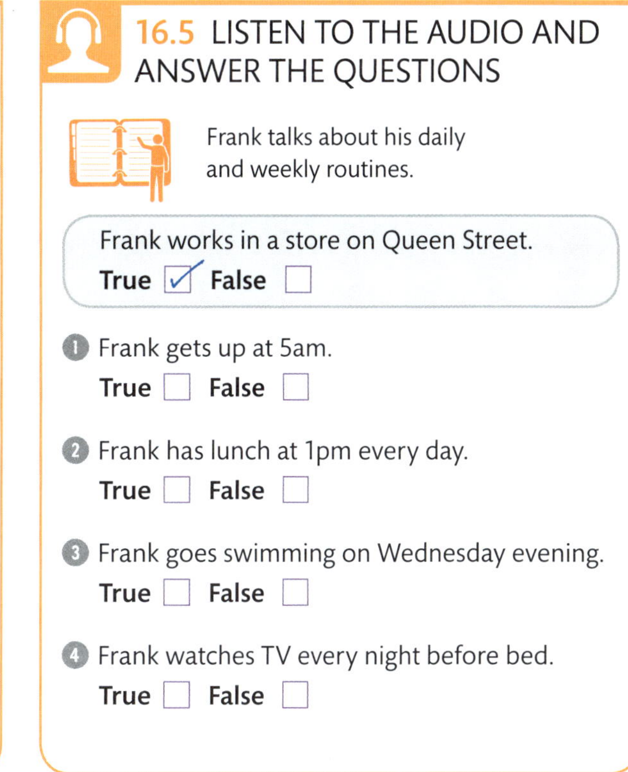

Frank talks about his daily and weekly routines.

Frank works in a store on Queen Street.
True ☑ False ☐

1. Frank gets up at 5am.
   True ☐ False ☐
2. Frank has lunch at 1pm every day.
   True ☐ False ☐
3. Frank goes swimming on Wednesday evening.
   True ☐ False ☐
4. Frank watches TV every night before bed.
   True ☐ False ☐

16.6 KEY LANGUAGE CONTRACTED NEGATIVES

In English, "do not" and "does not" are often contracted to "don't" and "doesn't."

I do not work outside. → I don't work outside.

He does not work outside. → He doesn't work outside.

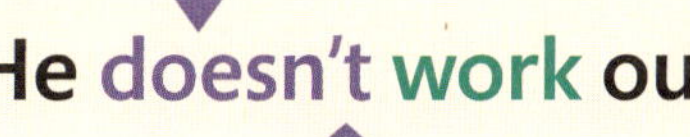

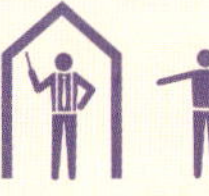

16.7 FURTHER EXAMPLES PRESENT SIMPLE NEGATIVE: SHORT FORMS

You don't play soccer.

She doesn't speak English.

We don't want that cake.

He doesn't live near here.

16.8 FILL IN THE GAPS TO WRITE EACH SENTENCE THREE DIFFERENT WAYS

	I get up at 7am.	*I do not get up at 7am.*	*I don't get up at 7am.*
1	________	________	We don't go to work every day.
2	________	He does not watch TV in the evening.	________
3	You work in an office.	________	________
4	________	________	They don't play tennis.
5	________	She does not work with children.	________

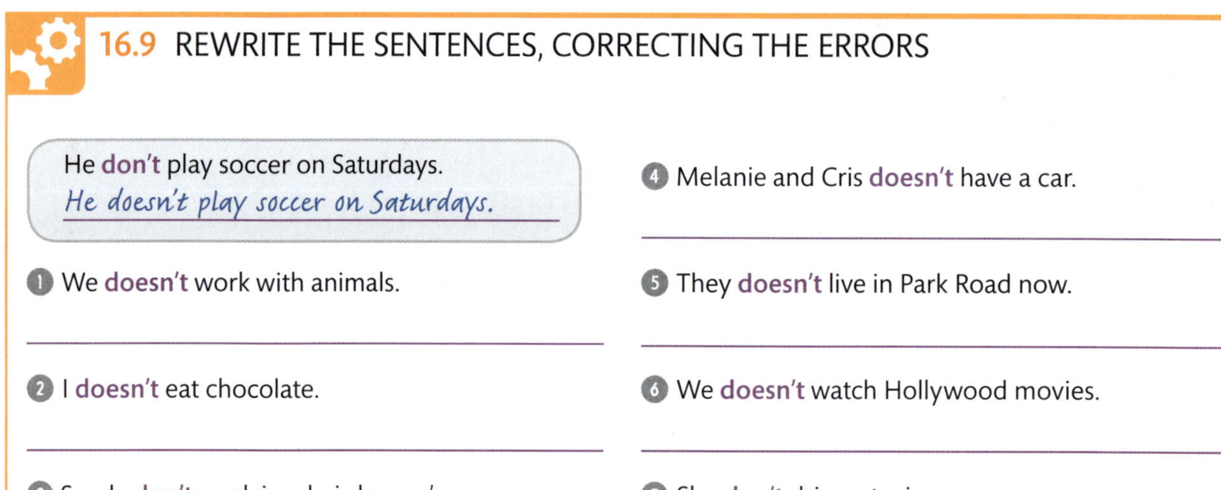

16.9 REWRITE THE SENTENCES, CORRECTING THE ERRORS

He **don't** play soccer on Saturdays.
He doesn't play soccer on Saturdays.

1. We **doesn't** work with animals.
____

2. I **doesn't** eat chocolate.
____

3. Sandy **don't** work in a hairdresser's.
____

4. Melanie and Cris **doesn't** have a car.
____

5. They **doesn't** live in Park Road now.
____

6. We **doesn't** watch Hollywood movies.
____

7. She **don't** drive a taxi.
____

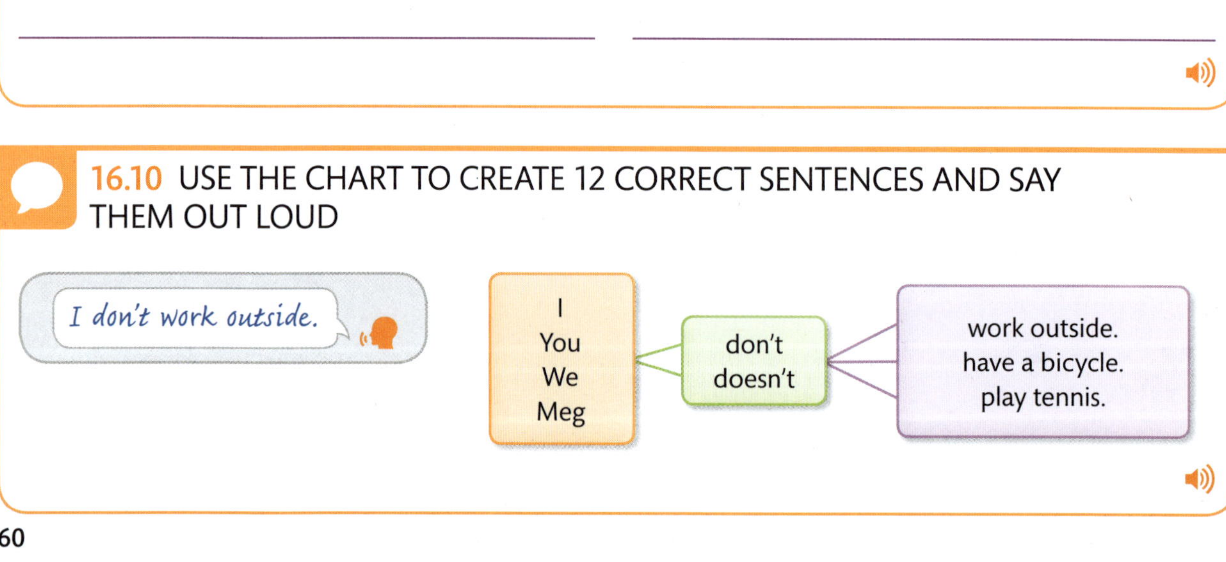

16.10 USE THE CHART TO CREATE 12 CORRECT SENTENCES AND SAY THEM OUT LOUD

I don't work outside.

16.11 READ THE ARTICLE AND ANSWER THE QUESTIONS

WORKERS FROM AROUND THE WORLD

Maria

I live in an apartment in the city and I cycle to work every day. I work from Monday to Friday in an office, so I don't go outside much during the day. I always eat breakfast and lunch. I go to the gym after work because I don't move a lot in my job.

Chiyo

I'm an actress and I live in Tokyo. I'm in a TV show called *Different People*. I work inside, in a TV studio, and I always have lunch at noon. I work for 15 hours on Mondays and Tuesdays, but I don't work from Wednesday to Sunday. My show is on TV on Fridays.

Kim

I live in the countryside and I drive to work every day. I'm a gardener, so I work outside. I usually have a sandwich for lunch. I go swimming once or twice a week. I sometimes swim in rivers and lakes near my house. The water is cold, but it's a lot of fun.

Selma

I'm a chef and I work in the kitchen of a restaurant in New York. I live above the restaurant. I start work at 2pm and I work until midnight. I don't eat lunch, but I always eat dinner at 6pm before the customers arrive. I work six days a week from Tuesday to Sunday.

Who doesn't live in a city?
Maria ☐ **Kim** ☑ **Chiyo** ☐ **Selma** ☐

1. Who works outside?
Maria ☐ **Kim** ☐ **Chiyo** ☐ **Selma** ☐

2. Who doesn't eat lunch?
Maria ☐ **Kim** ☐ **Chiyo** ☐ **Selma** ☐

3. Who doesn't work on Thursday?
Maria ☐ **Kim** ☐ **Chiyo** ☐ **Selma** ☐

4. Who goes to the gym?
Maria ☐ **Kim** ☐ **Chiyo** ☐ **Selma** ☐

5. Who doesn't work in the morning?
Maria ☐ **Kim** ☐ **Chiyo** ☐ **Selma** ☐

16 ✓ CHECKLIST

Present simple negative ☐ **Aa** Daily activities ☐ Saying what you don't do ☐

17 Simple questions

To form simple questions with the verb "to be," you change the order of the subject and verb. The answer to a simple question usually starts with "yes" or "no."

New language Simple questions
Vocabulary Jobs and routine activities
New skill Asking simple questions

17.1 KEY LANGUAGE QUESTIONS WITH "TO BE"

To make a question using the verb "to be," put the verb before the subject.

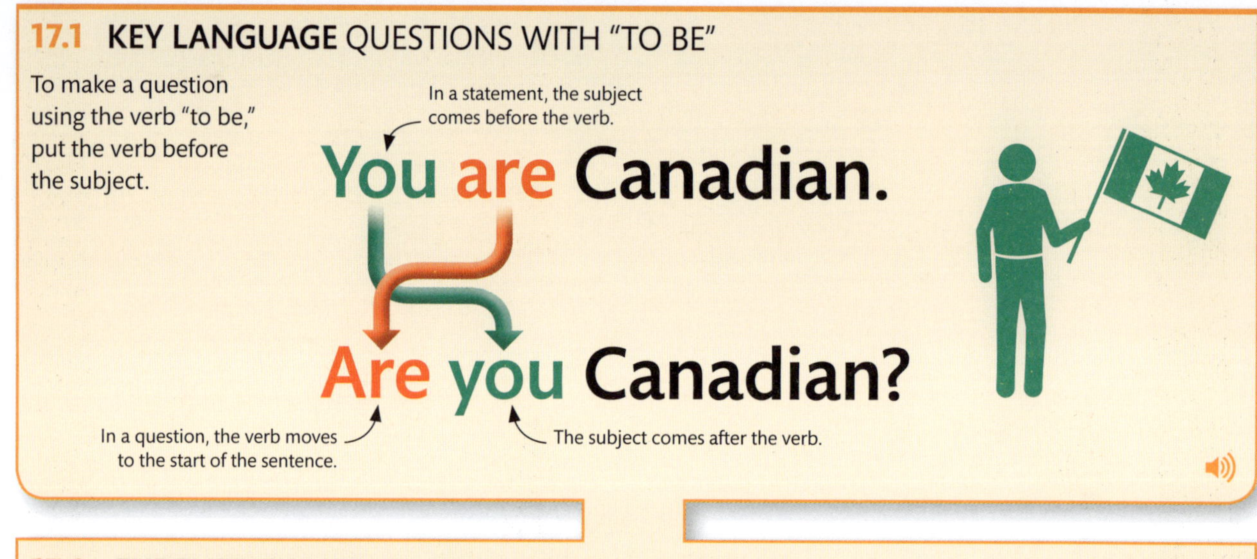

17.2 FURTHER EXAMPLES QUESTIONS WITH "TO BE"

Is Judi an actor?

Are they engineers?

Is he French?

Are you a student?

17.3 HOW TO FORM QUESTIONS WITH "TO BE"

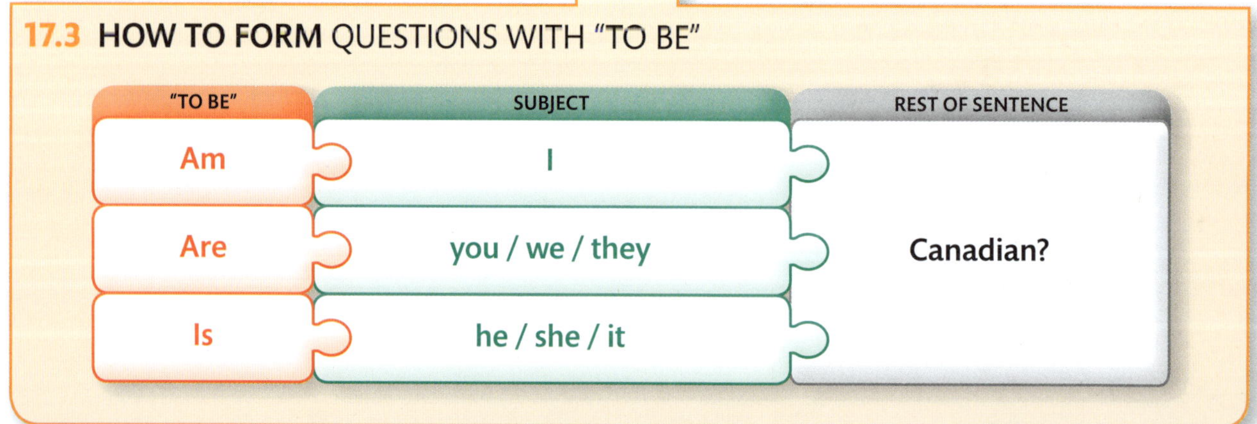

"TO BE"	SUBJECT	REST OF SENTENCE
Am	I	Canadian?
Are	you / we / they	
Is	he / she / it	

17.4 REWRITE THE SENTENCES AS QUESTIONS

She is a gardener.
Is she a gardener?

1. Brad is a nurse.
   ____
2. These are my keys.
   ____
3. Ruby and Farid are actors.
   ____
4. This is his laptop.
   ____
5. Valeria is his sister.
   ____

17.5 LISTEN TO THE AUDIO AND CIRCLE THE CORRECT ANSWER TO EACH QUESTION

1. 

2. 

3. 

4. 

5. 

6. 

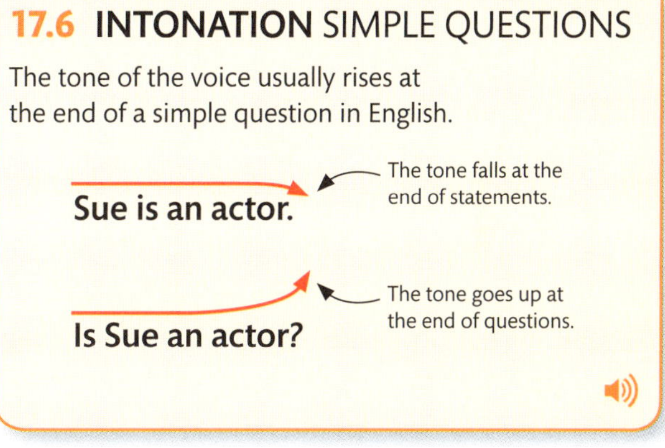

17.6 INTONATION SIMPLE QUESTIONS

The tone of the voice usually rises at the end of a simple question in English.

Sue is an actor. — The tone falls at the end of statements.

Is Sue an actor? — The tone goes up at the end of questions.

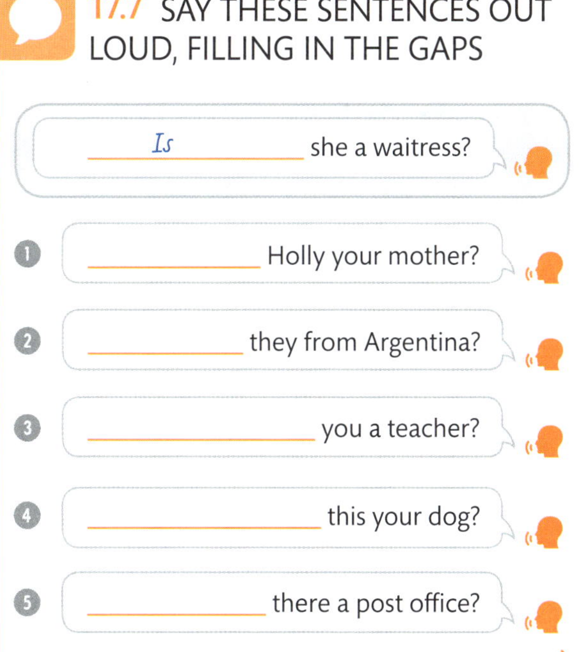

17.7 SAY THESE SENTENCES OUT LOUD, FILLING IN THE GAPS

Is she a waitress?

1. ______________ Holly your mother?
2. ______________ they from Argentina?
3. ______________ you a teacher?
4. ______________ this your dog?
5. ______________ there a post office?

17.8 KEY LANGUAGE QUESTIONS WITH "DO" AND "DOES"

For questions without the verb "to be," start the question with "do" or "does."

You work in an office. → **Do you work in an office?**

Add "do" to questions with "I," "you," "we," and "they."

She works in a school. → **Does she work in a school?**

Add "does" to questions with "he," "she," and "it."

The main verb is in its base form (the infinitive without "to").

17.9 FURTHER EXAMPLES QUESTIONS WITH "DO" AND "DOES"

Do they live in Paris?

Does Tom get up at 6am?

Do you finish work at 4pm today?

Does the party start at 7pm?

17.10 HOW TO FORM QUESTIONS WITH "DO" AND "DOES"

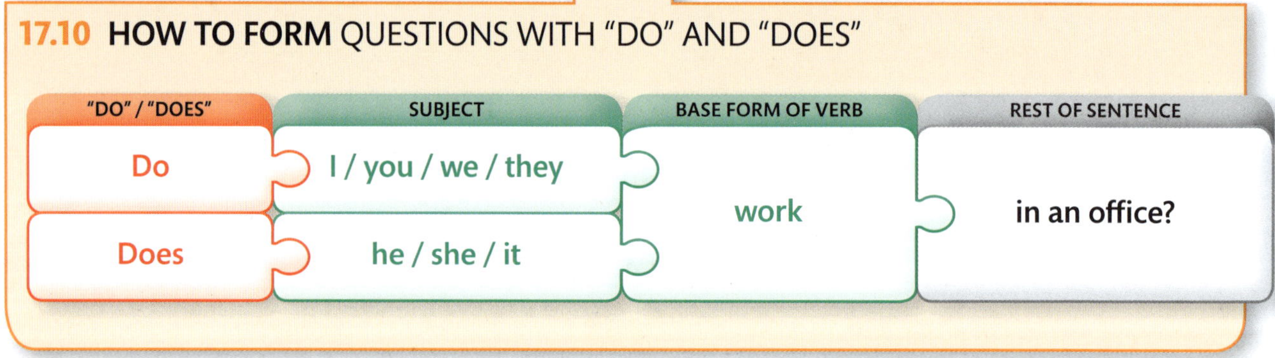

"DO" / "DOES"	SUBJECT	BASE FORM OF VERB	REST OF SENTENCE
Do	I / you / we / they	work	in an office?
Does	he / she / it		

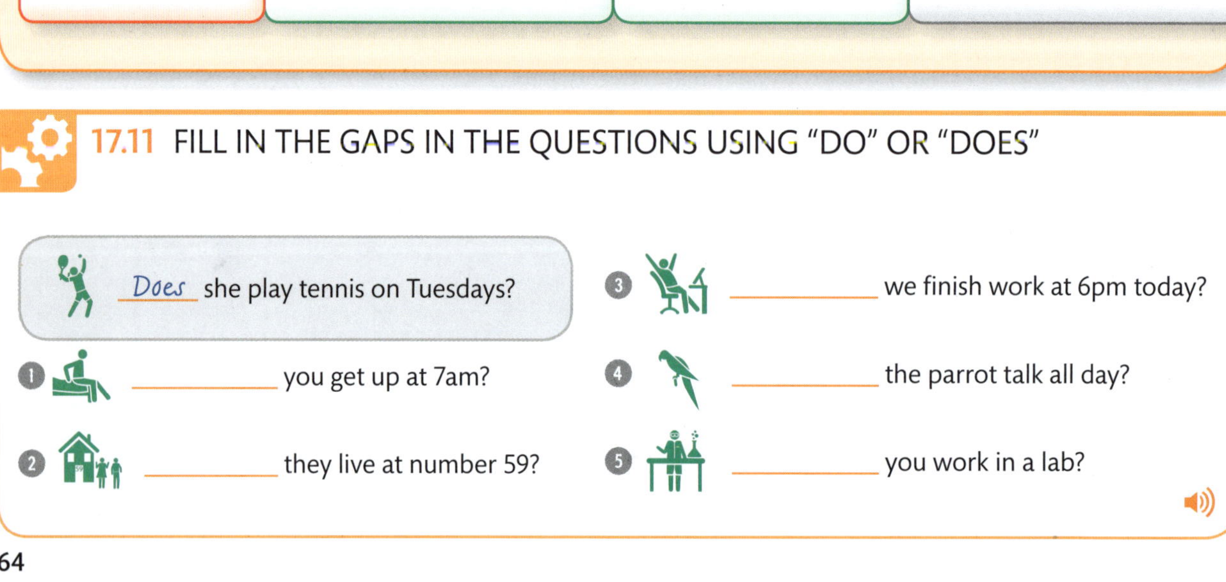

17.11 FILL IN THE GAPS IN THE QUESTIONS USING "DO" OR "DOES"

Does she play tennis on Tuesdays?

1 ________ you get up at 7am?

2 ________ they live at number 59?

3 ________ we finish work at 6pm today?

4 ________ the parrot talk all day?

5 ________ you work in a lab?

17.12 REWRITE THE QUESTIONS, PUTTING THE WORDS IN THE CORRECT ORDER

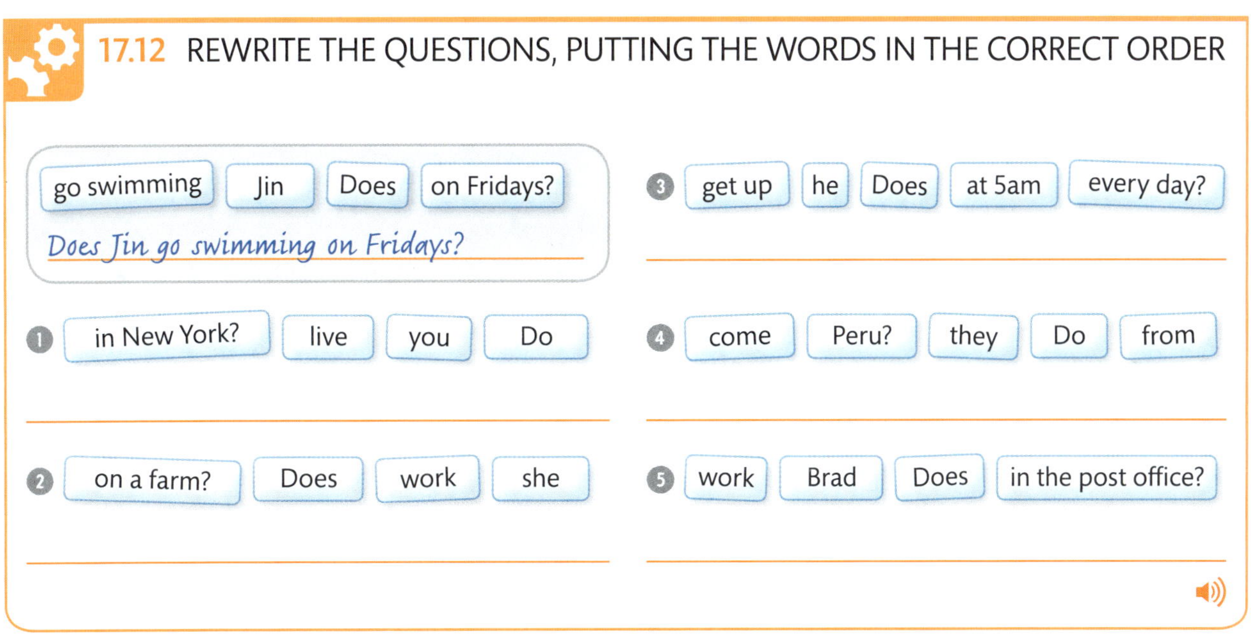

go swimming / Jin / Does / on Fridays?

Does Jin go swimming on Fridays?

1 in New York? / live / you / Do

2 on a farm? / Does / work / she

3 get up / he / Does / at 5am / every day?

4 come / Peru? / they / Do / from

5 work / Brad / Does / in the post office?

17.13 REWRITE THE SENTENCES AS QUESTIONS

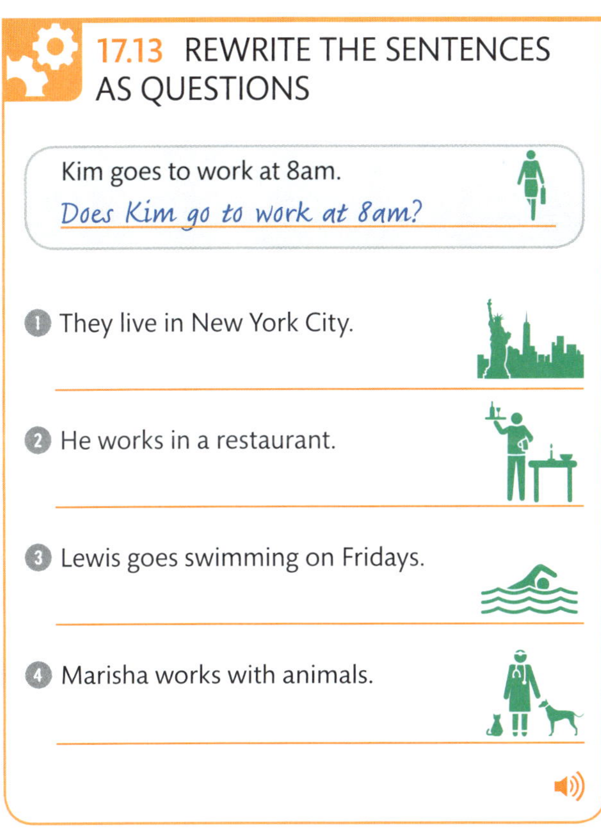

Kim goes to work at 8am.

Does Kim go to work at 8am?

1 They live in New York City.

2 He works in a restaurant.

3 Lewis goes swimming on Fridays.

4 Marisha works with animals.

17.14 SAY THE SENTENCES OUT LOUD, FILLING IN THE GAPS

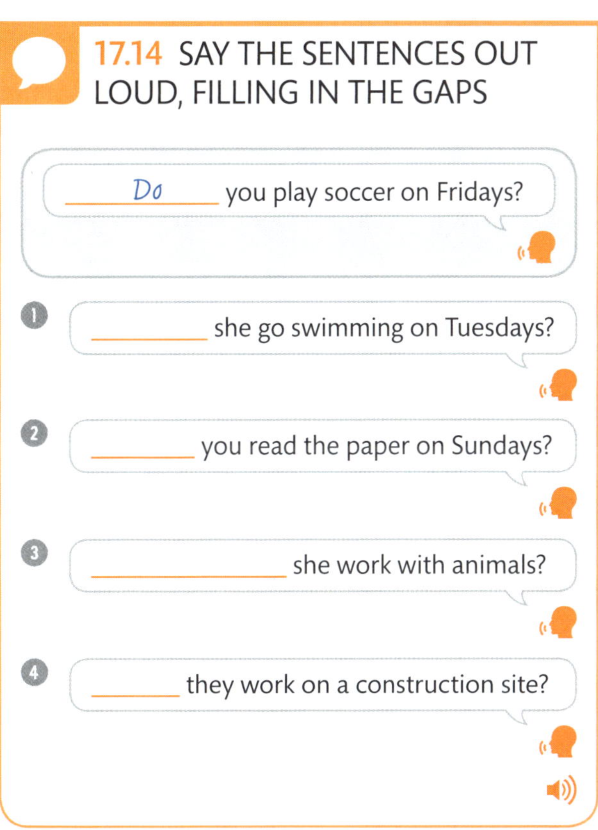

Do you play soccer on Fridays?

1 ______ she go swimming on Tuesdays?

2 ______ you read the paper on Sundays?

3 ______ she work with animals?

4 ______ they work on a construction site?

17 CHECKLIST

Simple questions ☐ **Aa** Jobs and routine activities ☐ Asking simple questions ☐

18 Answering questions

When answering questions in English, you can often leave out words to shorten your response. These short answers are often used in spoken English.

New language Short answers
Vocabulary Jobs and routines
New skill Answering spoken questions

18.1 KEY LANGUAGE SHORT ANSWERS

When the question uses the verb "to be," use "to be" in the short answer. If the question uses "do" or "does," so does the short answer.

Question uses "to be."

Are you a doctor?
Yes, I am.
No, I'm not.

You don't need to repeat "a doctor" in your answer.

Do you work in an office?
Yes, I do.
No, I don't.

Question uses "do."

The rest of the sentence is implied.

18.2 FURTHER EXAMPLES SHORT ANSWERS

Does he live here? — **Yes, he does.** / **No, he doesn't.**

Question uses "does."

Is your name Sophie? — **Yes, it is.** / **No, it isn't.**

Do they live in Delhi? — **Yes, they do.** / **No, they don't.**

Are you Chinese? — **Yes, I am.** / **No, I'm not.**

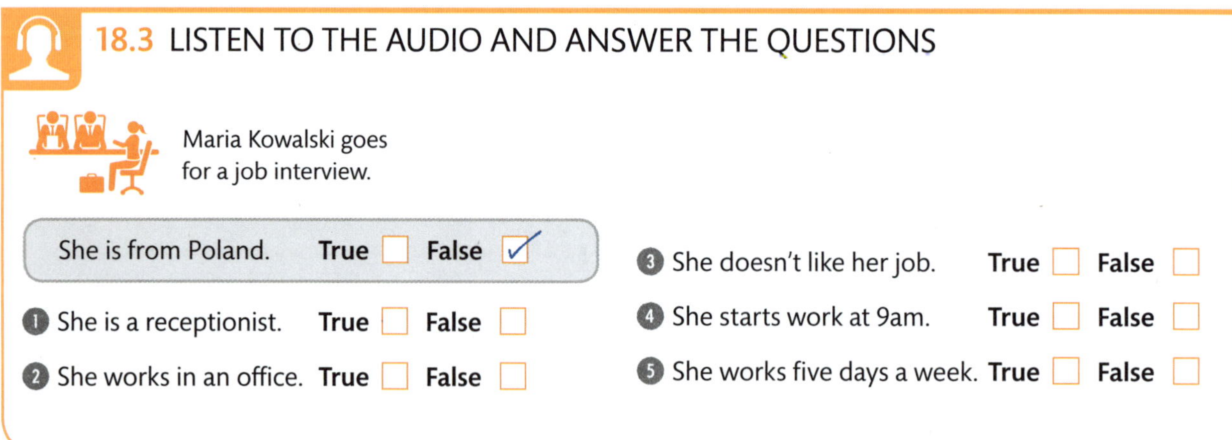

18.3 LISTEN TO THE AUDIO AND ANSWER THE QUESTIONS

Maria Kowalski goes for a job interview.

She is from Poland. **True** ☐ **False** ☑

1. She is a receptionist. **True** ☐ **False** ☐
2. She works in an office. **True** ☐ **False** ☐
3. She doesn't like her job. **True** ☐ **False** ☐
4. She starts work at 9am. **True** ☐ **False** ☐
5. She works five days a week. **True** ☐ **False** ☐

18.4 MARK THE CORRECT REPLY TO EACH QUESTION

Are you American? 
Yes, I am. ☑
Yes, I do. ☐

1. Is your name Maisy? 
No, it isn't. ☐
No, it doesn't. ☐

2. Is this your laptop? 
Yes, it is. ☐
Yes, it does. ☐

3. Does she work in your office? 
Yes, she is. ☐
Yes, she does. ☐

4. Do you eat a big breakfast? 
No, I'm not. ☐
No, I don't. ☐

5. Is that your cat? 
No, it isn't. ☐
No, it doesn't. ☐

18.5 ANSWER THE QUESTIONS, SPEAKING OUT LOUD

Does Joe watch TV?
Yes, he does.

1. Are you a student?
No, ________________.

2. Do they speak English?
Yes, ________________.

3. Is that your house?
No, ________________.

4. Does she play tennis?
Yes, ________________.

5. Is Miranda your aunt?
No, ________________.

6. Do they work in a hospital?
Yes, ________________.

7. Is he your grandfather?
No, ________________.

18 CHECKLIST

Short answers ☐ **Aa** Jobs and routines ☐ Answering spoken questions ☐

19 Asking questions

Use question words such as "what," "who," "when," and "where" to ask open questions that can't be answered with "yes" or "no."

New language Open questions
Aa Vocabulary Question words
New skill Asking for details

19.1 KEY LANGUAGE OPEN QUESTIONS WITH THE VERB "TO BE"

The question word goes at the beginning of the question. It is usually followed by the verb "to be."

My name is Sarah.
What is your name?

The question word goes at the beginning.

The question is "open" because it can't be answered "yes" or "no."

19.2 FURTHER EXAMPLES OPEN QUESTIONS WITH THE VERB "TO BE"

What is Ruby's job? 

What is the time? 

What is in the bag? 

What are we here for? 

What is this thing? 

What are Elliot's sisters called? 

19.3 CROSS OUT THE INCORRECT WORDS IN EACH SENTENCE

What is / ~~are~~ / ~~am~~ the capital of France?

1. What is / are / am their names?
2. What is / are / am the time?
3. What is / are / am my favorite colors?
4. What is / are / am the hotel next to?
5. What is / are / am they?
6. What is / are / am your uncle's name?
7. What is / are / am my name?

19.4 VOCABULARY QUESTION WORDS

19.6 MATCH THE QUESTIONS TO THE CORRECT ANSWERS

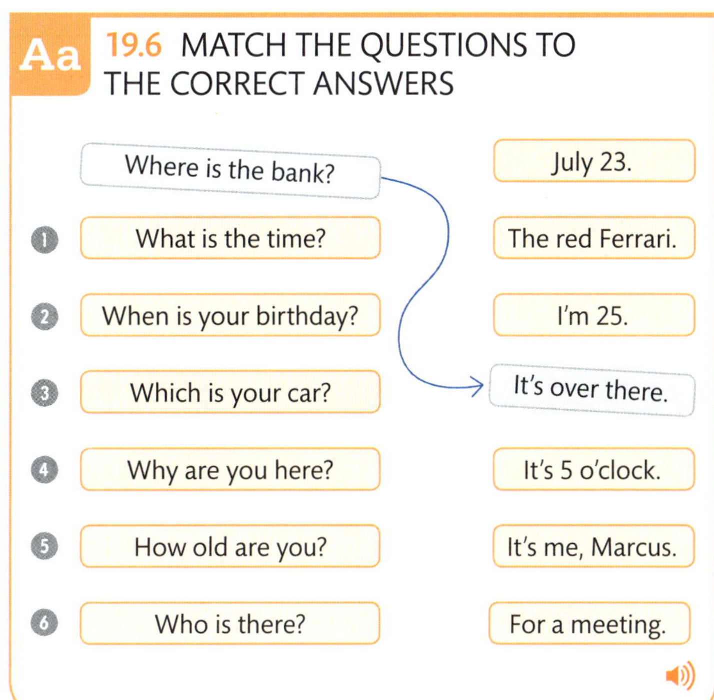

19.5 FURTHER EXAMPLES QUESTION WORDS

19.7 FILL IN THE GAPS USING THE WORDS IN THE PANEL

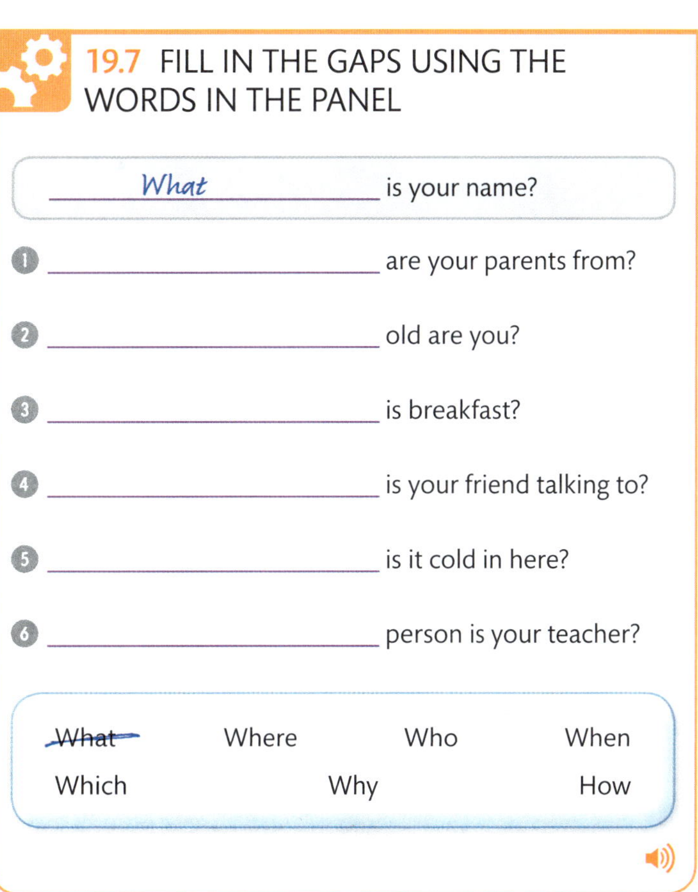

19.8 KEY LANGUAGE OPEN QUESTIONS USING "DO" AND "DOES"

With most verbs other than "to be" you use the question word followed by "do" or "does" to make a question.

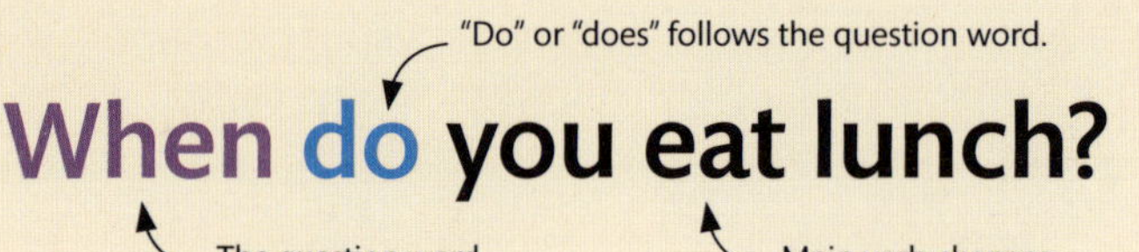

19.9 HOW TO FORM OPEN QUESTIONS USING "DO" AND "DOES"

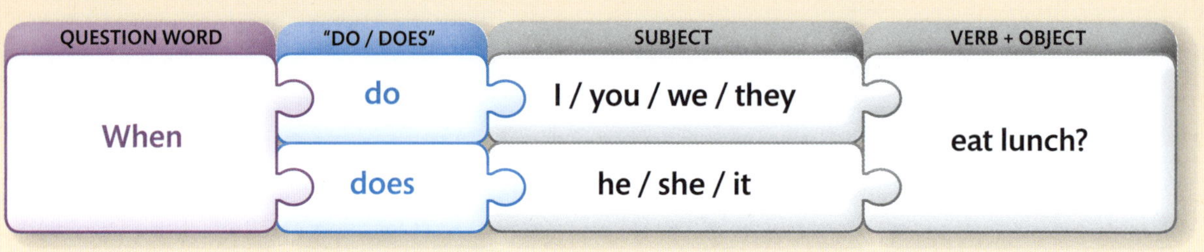

QUESTION WORD	"DO / DOES"	SUBJECT	VERB + OBJECT
When	do	I / you / we / they	eat lunch?
	does	he / she / it	

19.10 FURTHER EXAMPLES OPEN QUESTIONS USING "DO" AND "DOES"

Where do you go swimming? 

When does he finish work? 

What does she do on the weekend? 

Which car do you drive to work? 

19.11 FILL IN THE GAPS TO COMPLETE THE QUESTIONS

When ___do___ they start work?

1. When ________ she eat lunch?
2. Where ________ they live?
3. Which bag ________ you want?
4. Where ________ he come from?
5. When ________ the movie end?

19.12 REWRITE THE SENTENCES, PUTTING THE WORDS IN THE CORRECT ORDER

eat | do | When | breakfast? | you

When do you eat breakfast?

1. does | play | he | football? | Where

2. you | When | clean | do | car? | the

3. the | start? | What | party | does | time

4. tennis? | Which | do | days | play | you

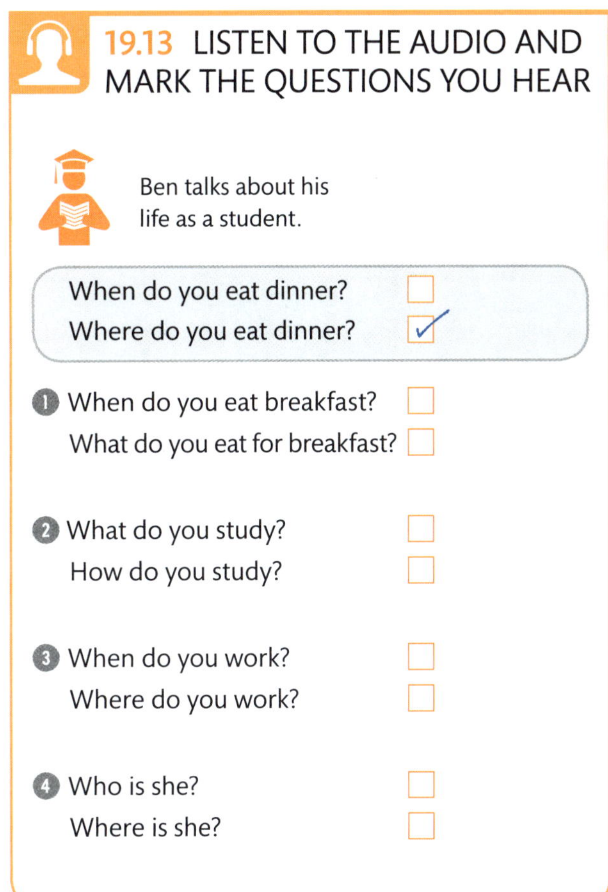

19.13 LISTEN TO THE AUDIO AND MARK THE QUESTIONS YOU HEAR

Ben talks about his life as a student.

When do you eat dinner? ☐
Where do you eat dinner? ☑

1. When do you eat breakfast? ☐
   What do you eat for breakfast? ☐

2. What do you study? ☐
   How do you study? ☐

3. When do you work? ☐
   Where do you work? ☐

4. Who is she? ☐
   Where is she? ☐

19.14 SAY THE QUESTIONS OUT LOUD, FILLING IN THE GAPS USING THE WORDS IN THE PANEL

What do you do for a living?

1. ________ do you work in the city?

2. ________ do you start work?

3. ________ time does it open?

4. ________ many people do you work with?

5. ________ do you work with?

When | How | ~~What~~ | What | Where | Who

19.15 READ THE EMAIL AND ANSWER THE QUESTIONS

Which village is Bernadette in?
Torremolinos ☐
Mijas ☑

1. Who is Bernadette on vacation with?
Her brother ☐
Her sister ☐

2. How many swimming pools does the hotel have?
Two ☐
Three ☐

3. What time does Bernadette get up?
At 7am ☐
At 7:30am ☐

4. What does Bernadette do in the morning?
Goes to the gym ☐
Goes swimming ☐

5. Where does Bernadette have breakfast?
In her room ☐
By the pool ☐

6. When is the flamenco dancing?
Tonight ☐
Tomorrow ☐

To: Mary Jones

Subject: Vacation in Spain

Hi Mary.

We're in Spain, in a village called Mijas, near Torremolinos. My sister is at work this week, so I'm here with my brother, John. Our hotel is next to some apartments. It's in a complex and has two swimming pools and a gym. Breakfast is from 7:30am until 9 every morning, so I get up at 7am and have a swim before I eat. John stays in his room and we meet later for breakfast. The restaurant is by the pool. We have our breakfast there every day. There's also dancing at night. There's salsa dancing tonight, and tomorrow it's flamenco.

See you soon,

Bernadette

19.16 USE THE CHART TO CREATE 12 CORRECT SENTENCES AND SAY THEM OUT LOUD

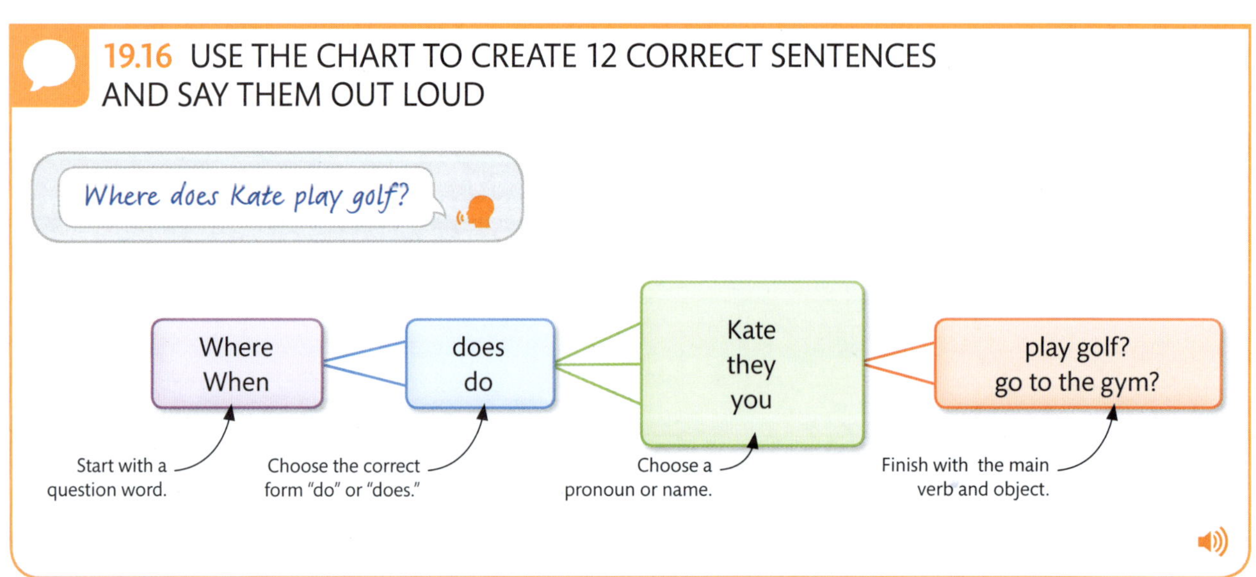

19.17 REWRITE THE SENTENCES, CORRECTING THE ERRORS

Where are my laptop?
Where is my laptop?

1. How often does they play tennis?

2. Which office do he work in?

3. Where are the party?

4. What does you do?

19.18 FILL IN THE GAPS TO COMPLETE THE QUESTIONS

When *does Russell go to the gym?*
Russell goes to the gym on Tuesdays.

1. What ______________________?
Her cat is called Ginger.

2. Who ______________________?
My English teacher is Mrs. Price.

3. Where ______________________?
Ben works in a hospital.

4. How ______________________?
My grandmother is fine, thanks.

19 CHECKLIST

Open questions ☐ **Aa** Question words ☐ Asking for details ☐

REVIEW THE ENGLISH YOU HAVE LEARNED IN UNITS 15-19

NEW LANGUAGE	SAMPLE SENTENCE	☑	UNIT
NEGATIVES WITH "TO BE"	I am a farmer. I am not a doctor. You're not a doctor. You aren't a doctor.	☐	15.1, 15.3, 15.7
PRESENT SIMPLE NEGATIVE	He does not work inside. He works outside. I work outside. I do not work inside.	☐	16.1, 16.3, 16.6
SIMPLE QUESTIONS	Are you Canadian? Do you work in an office? Does she work in a school?	☐	17.1, 17.8
SHORT ANSWERS	Are you a doctor? Yes, I am. Do you work in an office? No, I don't.	☐	18.1, 18.2
OPEN QUESTIONS WITH "TO BE"	My name is Sarah. What is your name?	☐	19.1, 19.2
OPEN QUESTIONS USING "DO" AND "DOES"	When do you eat lunch? When does she eat lunch?	☐	19.8, 19.9

20 Vocabulary

20.1 AROUND TOWN

village

town

city

hospital

police station

bus station

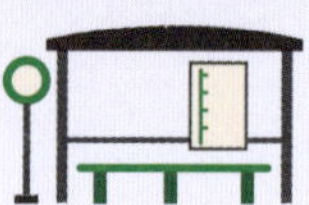
bus stop

train station

airport

school

factory

supermarket

store (US)
shop (UK)

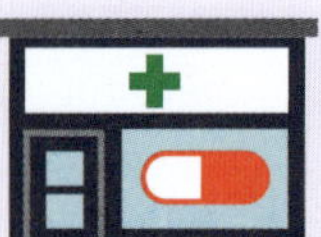
pharmacy

bank

post office

library

museum

town hall

castle

office building

park

here

bridge

swimming pool

restaurant

café

there

bar

movie theater (US)
cinema (UK)

theater (US)
theatre (UK)

hotel

near

church

mosque

synagogue

temple

far

21 Talking about your town

When you talk about things, you can use "there is" for one and "there are" for more than one. "There isn't" and "there aren't" are the negatives.

New language "There is" and "there are"
Vocabulary Towns and buildings
New skill Describing a town

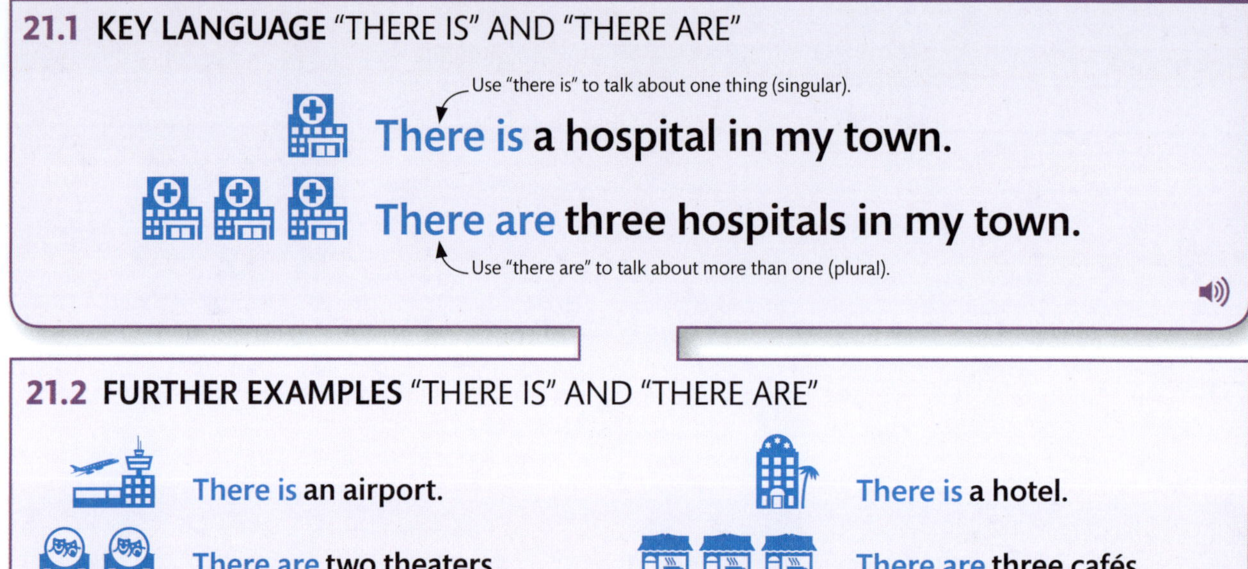

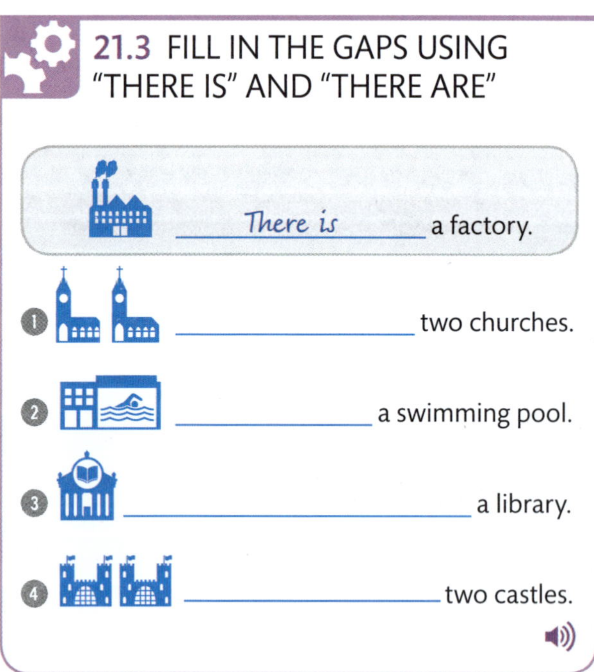

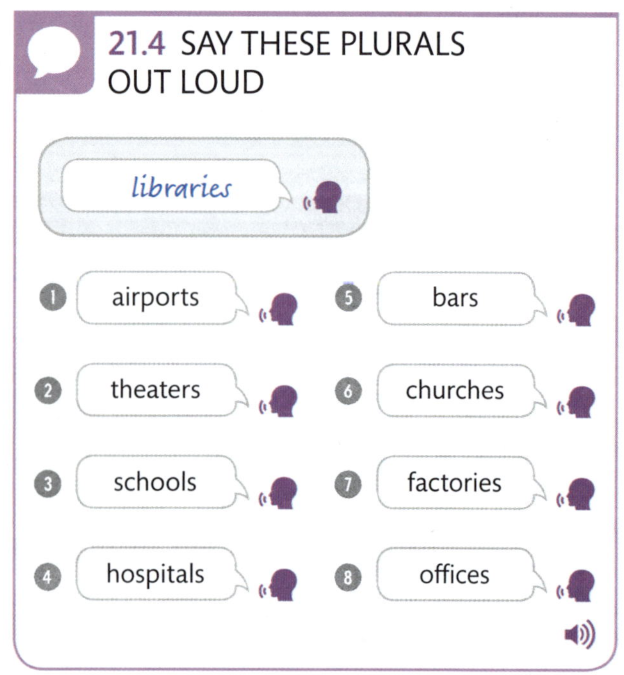

21.5 LOOK AT THE PICTURES AND FILL IN THE GAPS TO COMPLETE THE SENTENCES

There is a *town hall*.

1 There are ______________.

2 There are ______________.

3 There is a ______________.

4 There is a ______________.

5 There are ______________.

21.6 KEY LANGUAGE "THERE IS NOT" AND "THERE ARE NOT ANY"

Add "not" to make a singular sentence negative.

There is not a school.

There isn't a school.

You can shorten "is not" to "isn't."

Add "not any" to make a plural sentence negative.

There are not any schools.

There aren't any schools.

You can shorten "are not" to "aren't."

21.7 CROSS OUT THE INCORRECT WORD IN EACH SENTENCE

There isn't / ~~aren't~~ a castle.

1 There isn't / aren't a theater.

2 There isn't / aren't any factories.

3 There isn't / aren't a bus station.

4 There isn't / aren't any airports.

5 There isn't / aren't any churches.

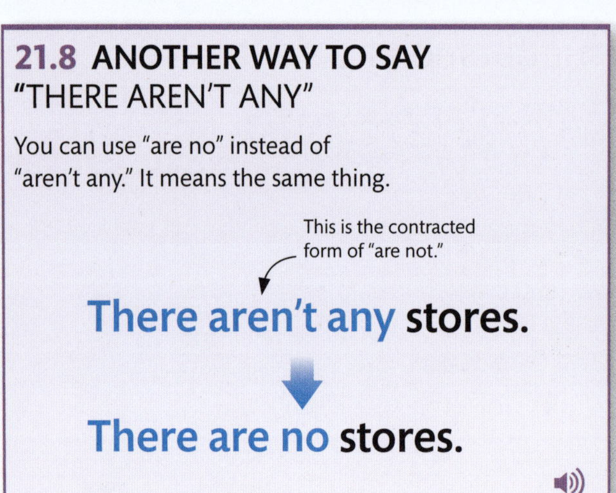

21.8 ANOTHER WAY TO SAY "THERE AREN'T ANY"

You can use "are no" instead of "aren't any." It means the same thing.

This is the contracted form of "are not."

There aren't any stores.

There are no stores.

21.9 FURTHER EXAMPLES "ARE NO"

There are no libraries in Oldtown.

There are no factories in Newport.

There are no schools in our village.

21.10 FILL IN THE GAPS USING "ARE" AND "AREN'T"

There *aren't* any theaters.

1. There ______________ no castles.
2. There ______________ any factories.
3. There ______________ no hospitals.
4. There ______________ any churches.
5. There ______________ no swimming pools.
6. There ______________ no airports.

21.11 LISTEN TO THE AUDIO, THEN NUMBER THE PICTURES IN THE ORDER THEY ARE DESCRIBED

A ☐

B *1*

C ☐

D ☐

21.12 READ THE EMAIL AND ANSWER THE QUESTIONS

There are two schools.
True ☐ False ☑

1. There is a supermarket.
True ☐ False ☐

2. There is a theater.
True ☐ False ☐

3. There are four movie theaters.
True ☐ False ☐

4. There are three restaurants.
True ☐ False ☐

To: Matt

Subject: Our new place

Hi Matt,

We're in our new house in Littleton and it's great! There are three schools in the town, so that's good for the children. There's also a big swimming pool and Joanne goes there every evening. I work in an office above the supermarket. It's near our house.

There are lots of things to do on the weekend. There isn't a theater, but there are two movie theaters, three restaurants, and a library. There's also a great museum. We go there every weekend because the children love it!

Come and see us soon. It's easy to get here. There isn't an airport or a train station, but there's a bus station.

See you soon! Jamal

21.13 LOOK AT THE PICTURE, THEN SAY EACH SENTENCE OUT LOUD, FILLING IN THE GAPS

There is a supermarket.

1. ______ a park.
2. ______ a hotel.
3. ______ no cafés.
4. ______ an airport.
5. ______ stores.
6. ______ a train station.
7. ______ theaters.

21 CHECKLIST

"There is" and "there are" ☐ | **Aa** Towns and buildings ☐ | Describing a town ☐

22 Using "a" and "the"

Use the definite article ("the") or indefinite article ("a," "an") to talk about things in specific or general terms. Use "some" to talk about more than one thing.

New language Definite and indefinite articles
Aa Vocabulary Places in town
New skill Using articles

22.1 KEY LANGUAGE "A / AN / THE"

Use "a" to talk about a thing in general. Use "the" to talk about a place, person, or thing that you and the listener both know about.

Use "a" because you are talking about your work in general, not the specific place where you work.

I work in a library.

I work in the library on Main Street.

Use "the" because you are talking about the specific building where you work.

22.2 FURTHER EXAMPLES "A / AN / THE"

Use "a / an" to talk about jobs.

Jim is an artist.

Use "an" before words that start with a vowel.

Is there a bank near here?

Use "a" with "is there" and "there is."

Use "the" to talk about a particular doctor.

The doctor at my hospital is good.

I go to the bank on Broad Street.

Use "the" to talk about a particular bank.

22.3 CROSS OUT THE INCORRECT WORDS IN EACH SENTENCE

Charlotte is ~~a~~ / an / ~~the~~ actress.

1. A / An / The new teacher is called Miss Jones.
2. There is a / an / the good café in the park.
3. I work at a / an / the hotel next to the library.
4. There is a / an / the swimming pool near my office.
5. It is a / an / the dog's favorite toy.
6. Janie is a / an / the artist at the gallery.
7. See you at a / an / the café at the bus station.

22.4 KEY LANGUAGE "A / SOME"

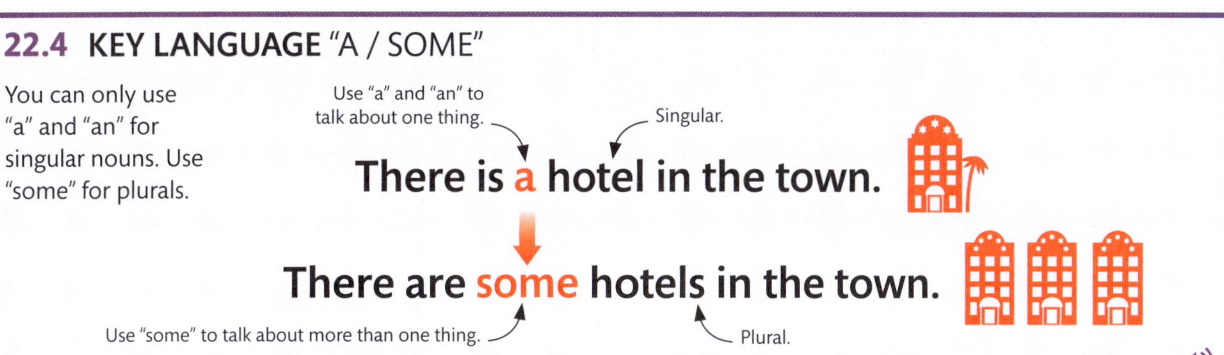

22.5 FURTHER EXAMPLES "A / SOME"

There is **a** bank on Main Street.

There are **some** banks on Main Street.

There is **a** waiter over there.

There are **some** children in the park.

22.6 FILL IN THE GAPS WITH "A" OR "SOME"

There is ___a___ restaurant in the park.

1. There are ________ stores on Broad Street.
2. There is ________ café next to the castle.
3. There are ________ cakes on the table.
4. There is ________ phone here.
5. There are ________ factories downtown.

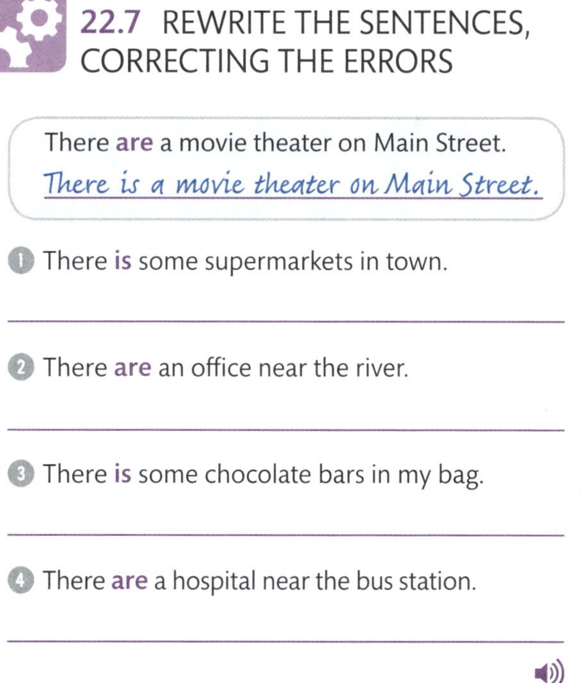

22.7 REWRITE THE SENTENCES, CORRECTING THE ERRORS

There **are** a movie theater on Main Street.
There is a movie theater on Main Street.

1. There **is** some supermarkets in town.
____
2. There **are** an office near the river.
____
3. There **is** some chocolate bars in my bag.
____
4. There **are** a hospital near the bus station.
____

22.8 **KEY LANGUAGE** QUESTIONS WITH "A / ANY"

There is a hotel in the town.

Is there a hotel in the town?

Use "a" to find out if there is one of something.

There are some hotels in the town.

Are there any hotels in the town?

Use "any" to find out if there is one or more of something.

22.9 **FURTHER EXAMPLES** QUESTIONS WITH "A / ANY"

Is there a restaurant?

Is there a hospital?

Are there any factories?

Are there any theaters?

22.10 CROSS OUT THE INCORRECT WORDS IN EACH QUESTION

Is there a / ~~an~~ / ~~any~~ hospital in the town?

1. Are there a / an / any stores on your street?
2. Is there a / an / any airport near Littleton?
3. Are there a / an / any mosques in the city?
4. Is there a / an / any swimming pool downtown?
5. Are there a / an / any offices in that building?

22.11 REWRITE THE SENTENCES, PUTTING THE WORDS IN THE CORRECT ORDER

any | in | town? | Are | your | factories | there

Are there any factories in your town?

1. there | here? | a | Is | supermarket | near

____

2. on | there | any | Elm Road? | Are | cafés

____

3. Are | your house? | there | any | near | hotels

____

4. a | café | office? | there | near | Is | your

____

5. the | there | a bar | next to | Is | bank?

____

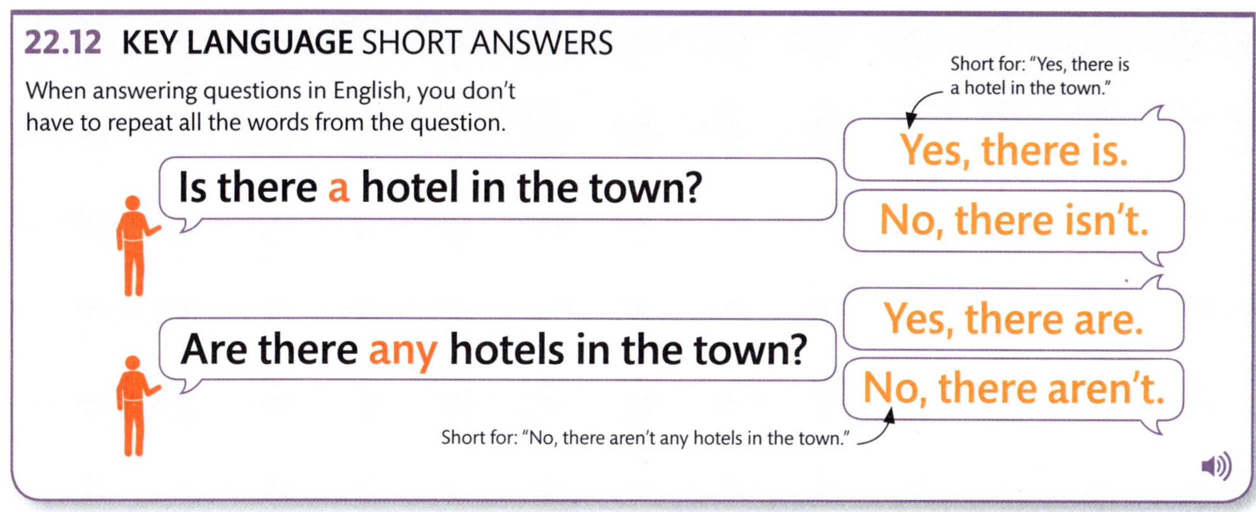

22.12 KEY LANGUAGE SHORT ANSWERS

When answering questions in English, you don't have to repeat all the words from the question.

Is there a hotel in the town?

Yes, there is. (Short for: "Yes, there is a hotel in the town.")

No, there isn't.

Are there any hotels in the town?

Yes, there are.

No, there aren't. (Short for: "No, there aren't any hotels in the town.")

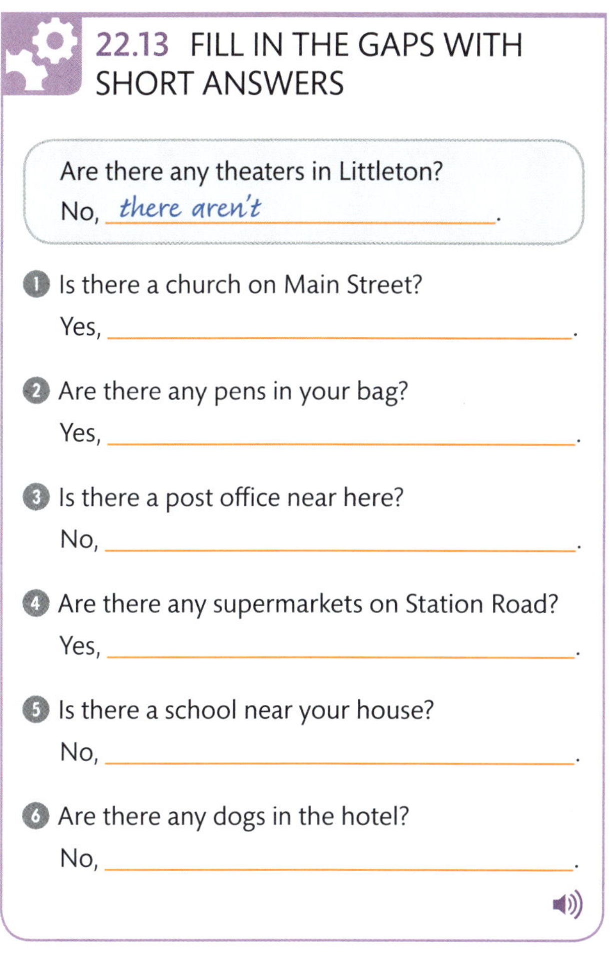

22.13 FILL IN THE GAPS WITH SHORT ANSWERS

Are there any theaters in Littleton?
No, *there aren't*.

1. Is there a church on Main Street?
   Yes, __________.
2. Are there any pens in your bag?
   Yes, __________.
3. Is there a post office near here?
   No, __________.
4. Are there any supermarkets on Station Road?
   Yes, __________.
5. Is there a school near your house?
   No, __________.
6. Are there any dogs in the hotel?
   No, __________.

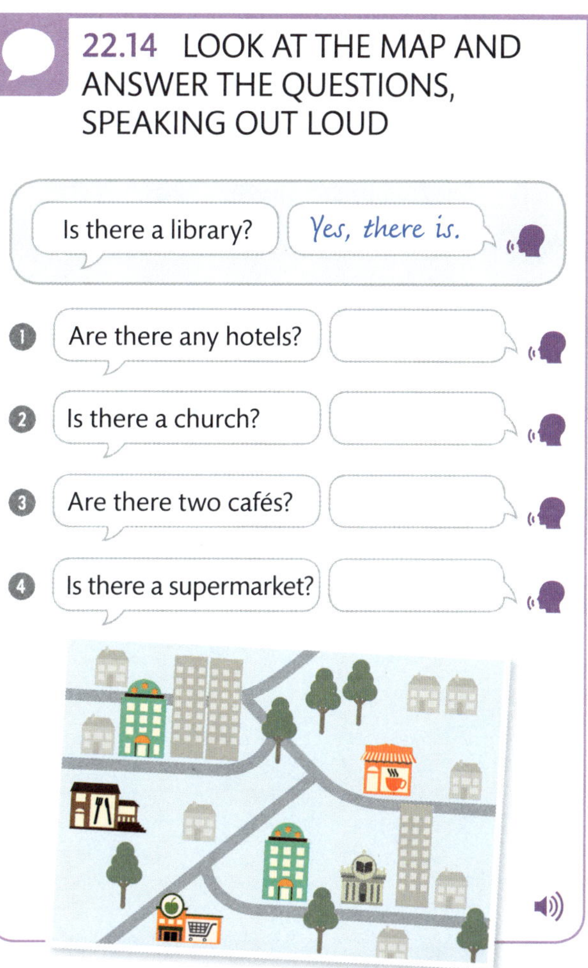

22.14 LOOK AT THE MAP AND ANSWER THE QUESTIONS, SPEAKING OUT LOUD

Is there a library? *Yes, there is.*

1. Are there any hotels?
2. Is there a church?
3. Are there two cafés?
4. Is there a supermarket?

22 CHECKLIST

Definite and indefinite articles ☐ **Aa** Places in town ☐ Using articles ☐

23 Orders and directions

Use imperatives to tell someone to do something. They are also useful to give a warning, or to give directions to someone.

New language Imperatives
Aa Vocabulary Directions
New skill Finding your way

23.1 KEY LANGUAGE IMPERATIVES

To make the imperative, use the base form of the verb (the infinitive without "to").

The base form of the verb "to stop."

23.2 FURTHER EXAMPLES IMPERATIVES

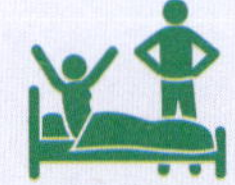
Get up.

Eat your breakfast.

Give that to me.

Be careful!

Help!

Read this book.

23.3 REWRITE THE INFINITIVES AS IMPERATIVES

to go = Go

1. to wake up = ______
2. to do = ______
3. to start = ______
4. to have = ______
5. to wait = ______
6. to stop = ______
7. to work = ______

23.4 KEY LANGUAGE GIVING DIRECTIONS

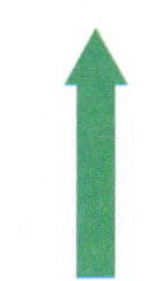

go straight ahead

turn left

turn right

go past

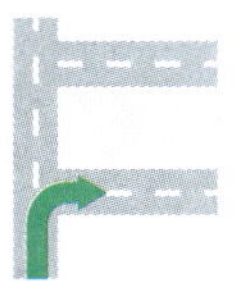

take the first right

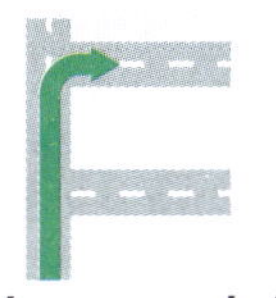

take the second right

23.5 MARK THE DIRECTIONS THAT LEAD YOU TO THE CORRECT PLACES ON THE MAP

For the Bridge Café:

Take the first right. The café is on the left. ☑

Take the first left. The café is on the right. ☐

1. For the train station:
   - **Take the second left. The station is on the right.** ☐
   - **Take the second right. The station is on the left.** ☐

2. For the Elm Tree Restaurant:
   - **Take the first left, then turn right. The restaurant is on the right.** ☐
   - **Take the second left, then turn right. The restaurant is on the left.** ☐

3. For the hospital:
   - **Take the second right, and the hospital is on the left.** ☐
   - **Take the second left, and the hospital is on the right.** ☐

4. For the Supreme Hotel:
   - **Take the first left, then go straight ahead. The hotel is on the right.** ☐
   - **Take the first right, then go straight ahead. The hotel is on the left.** ☐

5. For the castle:
   - **Take the first left, then turn right. The castle is on the left.** ☐
   - **Take the first left, then turn left. The castle is on the right.** ☐

23.6 **VOCABULARY** DIRECTIONS

next to

opposite

between

on the corner

behind

in front of

on the right

on the left

intersection (US)
crossroads (UK)

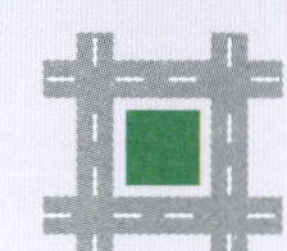

block

Aa 23.7 FILL IN THE GAPS USING DIRECTIONS

The Rathbone Theater is *opposite* the park.

1. The supermarket is ________ the post office.

2. The museum is ________ the café.

3. The station is ________ the church.

4. The cinema is on the ________ of the intersection.

5. The post office is ________ the café and the supermarket.

23.8 KEY LANGUAGE NEGATIVE IMPERATIVE

Add "don't" or "do not" before the verb to make an imperative negative.

Do not / Don't } turn right.

23.9 FURTHER EXAMPLES NEGATIVE IMPERATIVE

Don't eat that cake.

Don't sit there.

23.10 REWRITE THE SENTENCES AS NEGATIVE IMPERATIVES

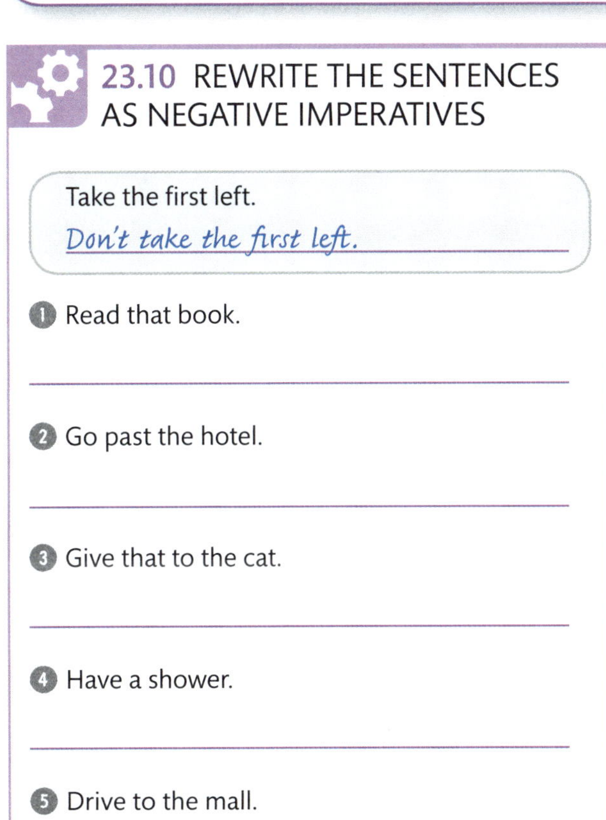

Take the first left.
Don't take the first left.

1. Read that book.
2. Go past the hotel.
3. Give that to the cat.
4. Have a shower.
5. Drive to the mall.

23.11 LISTEN AND MATCH THE DIRECTIONS TO THE PLACES

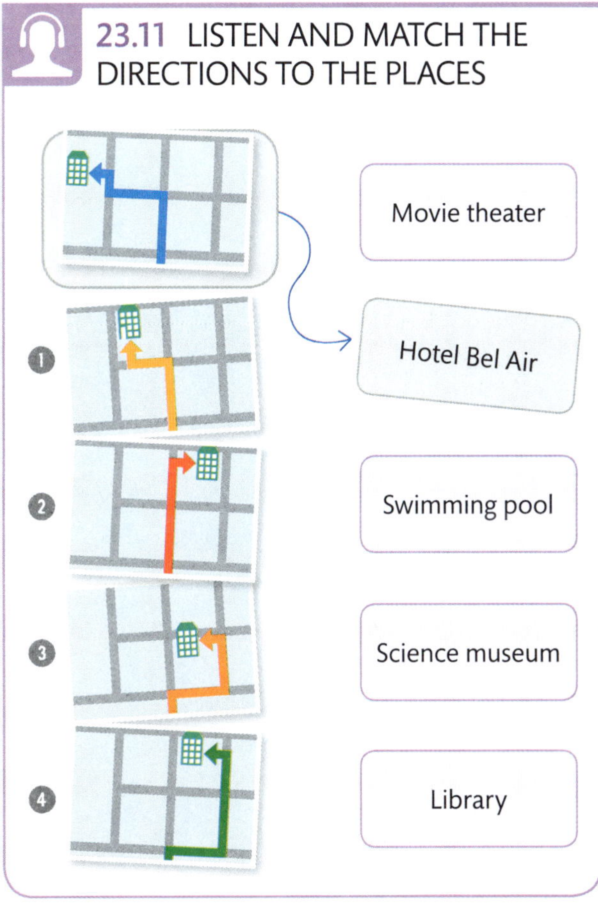

Movie theater

Hotel Bel Air

Swimming pool

Science museum

Library

23 CHECKLIST

Imperatives ☐ Aa Directions ☐ Finding your way ☐

24 Joining sentences

"And" and "but" are conjunctions: words that join statements together. "And" adds things to a sentence or links sentences together. "But" introduces a contrast to a sentence.

New language Using "and" and "but"
Aa Vocabulary Town, jobs, and family
New skill Joining sentences

24.1 KEY LANGUAGE USING "AND" TO JOIN SENTENCES

Use "and" to join two sentences together.

"There's" is the same as "There is."

There's a library. There's a restaurant.

There's a library and a restaurant.

You can drop the second "there's" when you join sentences using "and."

24.2 FURTHER EXAMPLES USING "AND" TO JOIN SENTENCES

Jazmin's sister lives and works in Paris.

My father and brother are both engineers.

Simon plays video games and watches TV every night.

24.3 REWRITE THESE STATEMENTS AS SINGLE SENTENCES USING "AND"

I get up. I have a shower.
I get up and have a shower.

1. There are two hotels. There are three shops.

____

2. Hilda works in a school. She works in a theater.

____

3. My uncle is a scientist. My aunt is a doctor.

____

4. Sue watches TV. She reads books.

____

5. The store opens at night. Jan starts work.

____

24.4 LISTEN TO THE AUDIO AND MATCH THE PLACES MENTIONED IN EACH "AND" STATEMENT

1

2

3

4

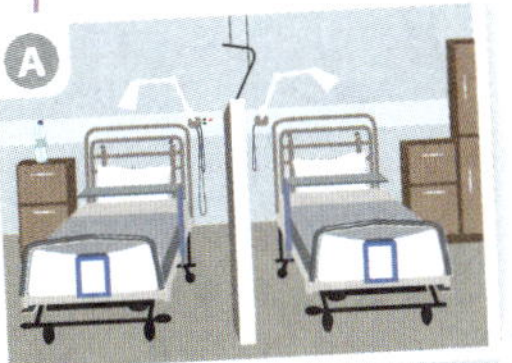

A

B

C

D

E

24.5 **KEY LANGUAGE** USING A COMMA INSTEAD OF "AND"

For lists of more than two items, you can use commas instead of "and."

You can use a comma to replace "and" in a list.

Use another comma before the "and."

There's a library, a store, and a café.

Keep the "and" between the final two nouns.

24.6 MARK THE SENTENCES THAT USE COMMAS AND "AND" CORRECTLY

I am a wife, a mother, and a daughter. ☑
I am a wife, and a mother, a daughter. ☐

1. There are hotels and bars and stores. ☐
   There are hotels, bars, and stores. ☐
2. Sam eats, breakfast lunch and dinner. ☐
   Sam eats breakfast, lunch, and dinner. ☐
3. I play tennis, soccer, and chess. ☐
   I play tennis, and soccer, and chess. ☐
4. Teo plays with his car and his train and his bus. ☐
   Teo plays with his car, train, and bus. ☐
5. There is a pencil, a bag and, a cell phone. ☐
   There is a pencil, a bag, and a cell phone. ☐
6. My friends, girlfriend, and aunt are here. ☐
   My friends, and, girlfriend and aunt are here. ☐
7. Ling works on Monday, Thursday, and Friday. ☐
   Ling works on Monday, and Thursday, Friday. ☐

24.7 **KEY LANGUAGE** USING "BUT" TO JOIN SENTENCES

Use "but" to join a positive and a negative statement.

There's a hotel. There isn't a store.

There's a hotel, but there isn't a store.

You can use "but" to add something negative to a positive sentence.

There isn't a store here, but there is a hotel.

You can use "but" to add something positive to a negative sentence.

24.8 MATCH THE BEGINNINGS OF THE SENTENCES TO THE CORRECT ENDINGS

There is a mosque, but	these aren't my car keys.
1 This is my car, but	it doesn't have a bathtub.
2 We eat a small breakfast, but	not on the weekend.
3 I work from Monday to Friday, but	there isn't a church.
4 The bathroom has a shower, but	we eat a big lunch.

24.9 REWRITE EACH PAIR OF STATEMENTS AS A SINGLE SENTENCE

There is a post office. There isn't a bank.
There is a post office, but there isn't a bank.

1 There isn't a bathtub. There is a shower.

____

2 There isn't a bar. There is a café.

____

3 This bag is Maya's. That laptop isn't hers.

____

4 Si doesn't have any dogs. He has two cats.

____

5 Sally reads books. She never watches TV.

____

24.10 CROSS OUT THE INCORRECT WORD IN EACH SENTENCE

I am a father and / ~~but~~ a son.

1. Lu reads books and / but magazines.
2. I work every weekday, and / but not on weekends.
3. Jim is a husband and / but a father.
4. There is a cinema, and / but no theater.
5. There isn't a gym, and / but there is a pool.

24.11 LOOK AT THE TABLE, THEN SAY "AND" AND "BUT" SENTENCES OUT LOUD

There is *a mosque and a church,* *but there isn't a factory*.

1. There is ______________________________.
2. There is ______________________________.
3. There is ______________________________.
4. There is ______________________________.

24 CHECKLIST

Using "and" and "but" ☐ **Aa** Town, jobs, and family ☐ Joining sentences ☐

25 Describing places

Use adjectives to give more information about nouns, for example to describe a person, building, or place.

New language Adjectives
Aa Vocabulary Place adjectives and nouns
New skill Describing places

25.1 KEY LANGUAGE USING ADJECTIVES

Adjectives are usually placed before the noun they describe.

She is a busy woman. 

He is a busy man. 

Adjectives are the same for male and female nouns.

It is a busy town. 

These are busy streets. 

Adjectives are the same for singular and plural nouns.

25.2 VOCABULARY ADJECTIVES

old

new

beautiful

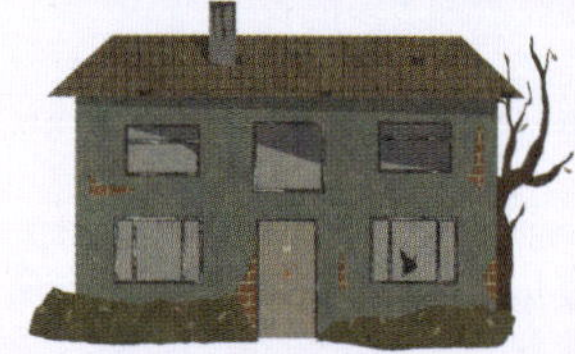

horrible

busy

quiet

small

big

25.3 REWRITE THE SENTENCES, PUTTING THE WORDS IN THE CORRECT ORDER

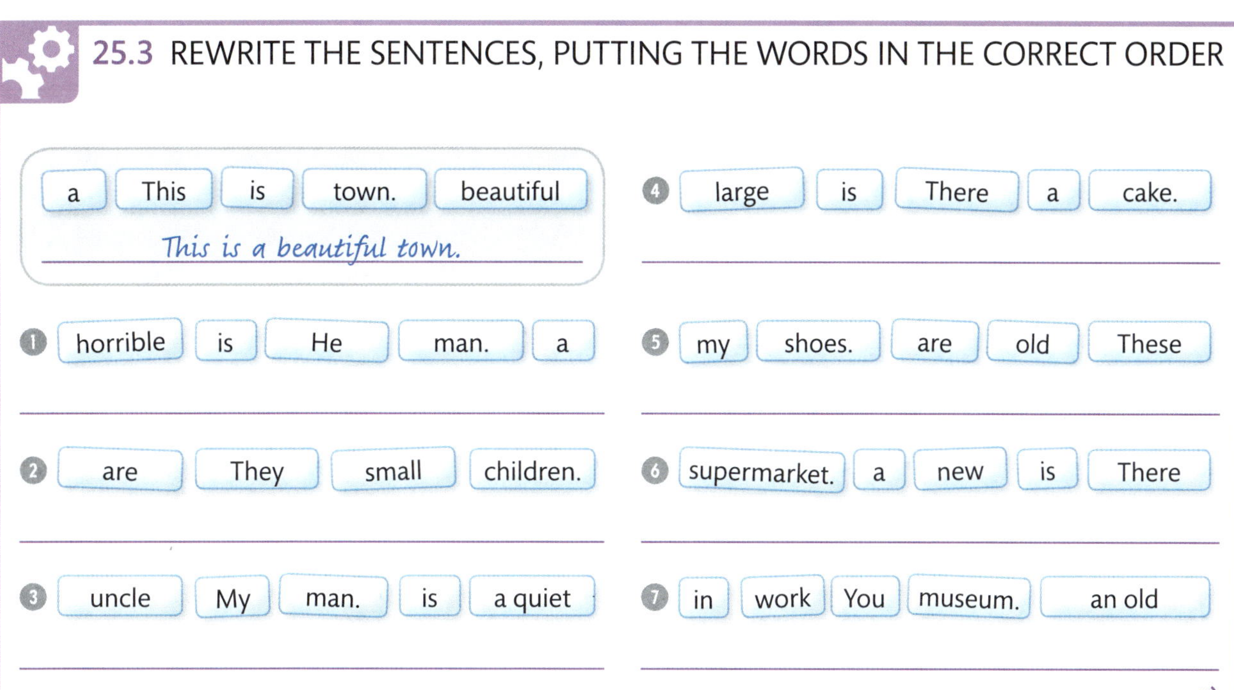

25.4 OTHER WAYS TO USE ADJECTIVES

Sometimes, adjectives can be put in different places in a sentence.

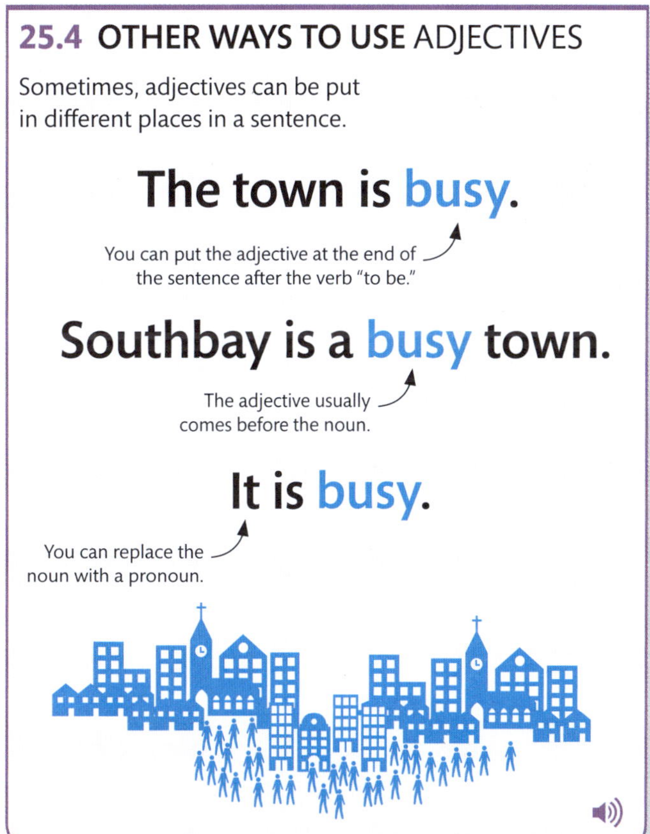

25.5 READ THE PASSAGE AND CIRCLE SEVEN ADJECTIVES

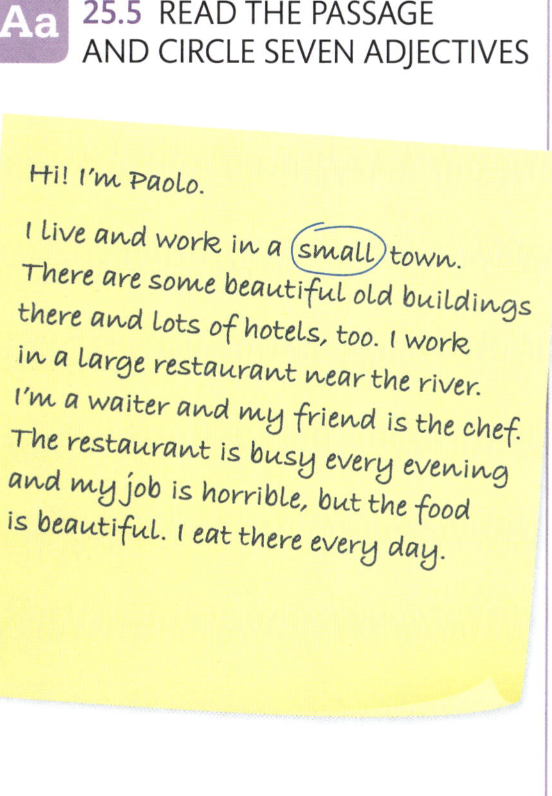

25.6 FILL IN THE GAPS TO WRITE EACH SENTENCE THREE DIFFERENT WAYS

	Rome is an **old** city.	The city is old.	It is old.
1	She is a **busy** nurse.		
2	He is a **quiet** dog.		
3	They are **new** patients.		
4	It is a **horrible** town.		
5	It is a **beautiful** car.		

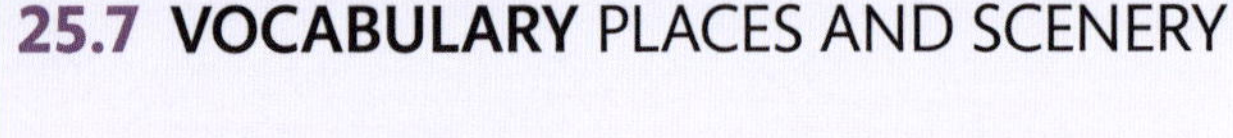

25.7 VOCABULARY PLACES AND SCENERY

beach

....

sea

....

sand

....

grass

....

countryside

....

tree

....

hill

....

river

....

mountain

....

lake

....

sky

....

cloud

....

25.8 READ THE POSTCARD AND CORRECT THE INCORRECTLY SPELLED WORDS

Hi Veronica,
We're in the **countyrsedi** this week on vacation. it's really **bauetiful**. The **leke** near the hotel is **lerge** but the water is cold. We walk in the **mountins** every day and eat at the **restartant** every night. Hope the **beech** is fun. Is it **bisy** or **qeuit**?
See you soon,
Tamara

countryside

1 ______
2 ______
3 ______
4 ______
5 ______
6 ______
7 ______
8 ______

25.9 SAY THE SENTENCES OUT LOUD, FILLING IN THE GAPS

The lakes *are* beautiful *and the* mountain *is* large.

1 ______ countryside ______ quiet ______ trees ______ beautiful.

2 ______ city ______ horrible ______ people ______ busy.

3 ______ hotel ______ new ______ swimming pool ______ large.

4 ______ beach ______ big ______ cafés ______ busy.

5 ______ city ______ old ______ buildings ______ beautiful.

25.10 KEY LANGUAGE USING QUANTITY PHRASES

English has many different phrases for quantities when the exact number is not known.

Use "some" when there is more than one, but you don't know exactly how many.

There are some buildings.

Use "a few" for a small number.

There are a few buildings.

Use "lots of" for a large number.

There are lots of buildings.

25.11 FURTHER EXAMPLES USING QUANTITY PHRASES

There are some trees.

There are lots of mountains.

There are lots of people.

There are a few cars.

25.12 LISTEN TO THE AUDIO, THEN NUMBER THE PICTURES IN THE ORDER THEY ARE DESCRIBED

A ☐

B ☐

C 1

D ☐

E ☐

F ☐

25.13 WRITE SENTENCES ABOUT THE IMAGE USING "A FEW," "SOME," OR "LOTS OF"

There are some trees.

1 ______________________ people.

2 ______________________ buildings.

3 ______________________ cars.

4 ______________________ parks.

25.14 LOOK AT THE TABLE, THEN SAY SENTENCES OUT LOUD USING "A FEW," "SOME," AND "LOTS OF"

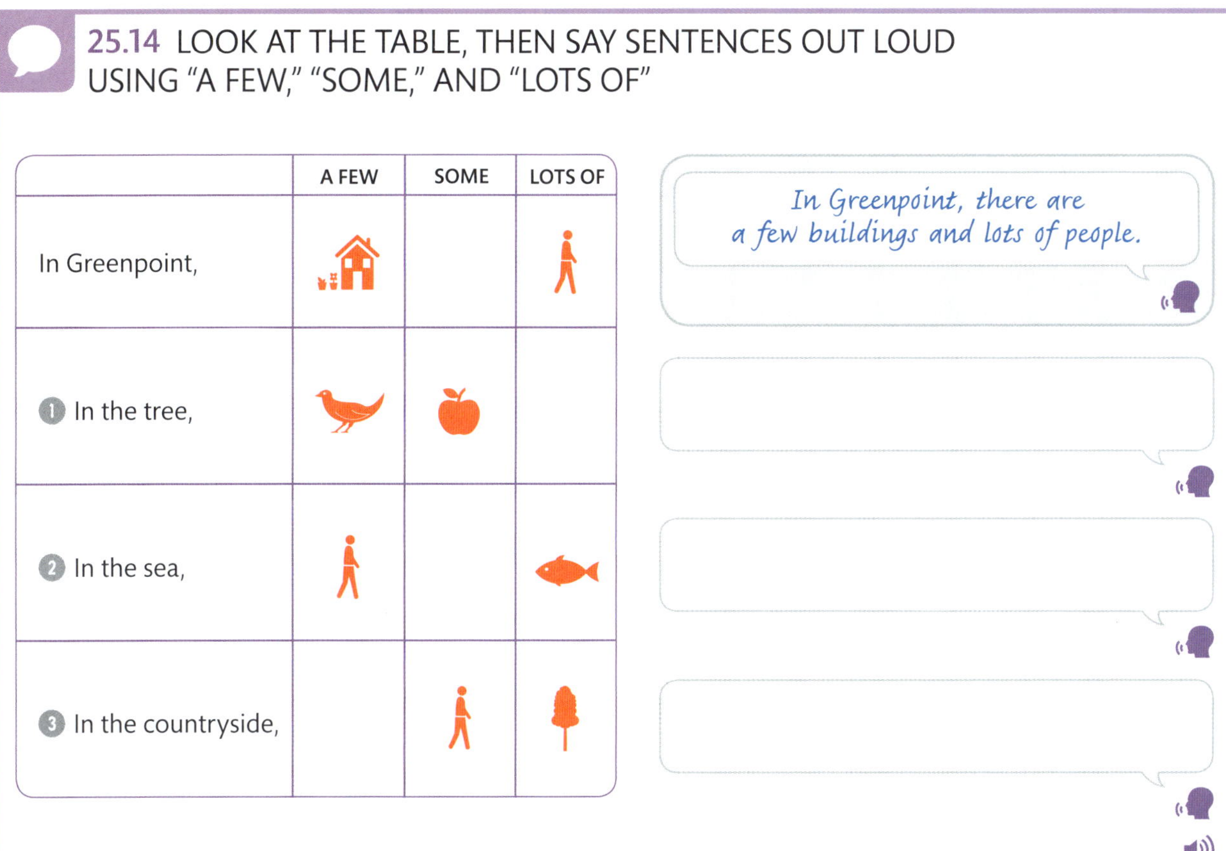

	A FEW	SOME	LOTS OF
In Greenpoint,			
1 In the tree,			
2 In the sea,			
3 In the countryside,			

25 CHECKLIST

Adjectives ☐ **Aa** Place adjectives and nouns ☐ Describing places ☐

26 Giving reasons

Use the conjunction "because" to give a reason for something. You can also use "because" to answer the question "Why?"

Key language "Because"
Vocabulary Places and jobs
New skill Giving reasons

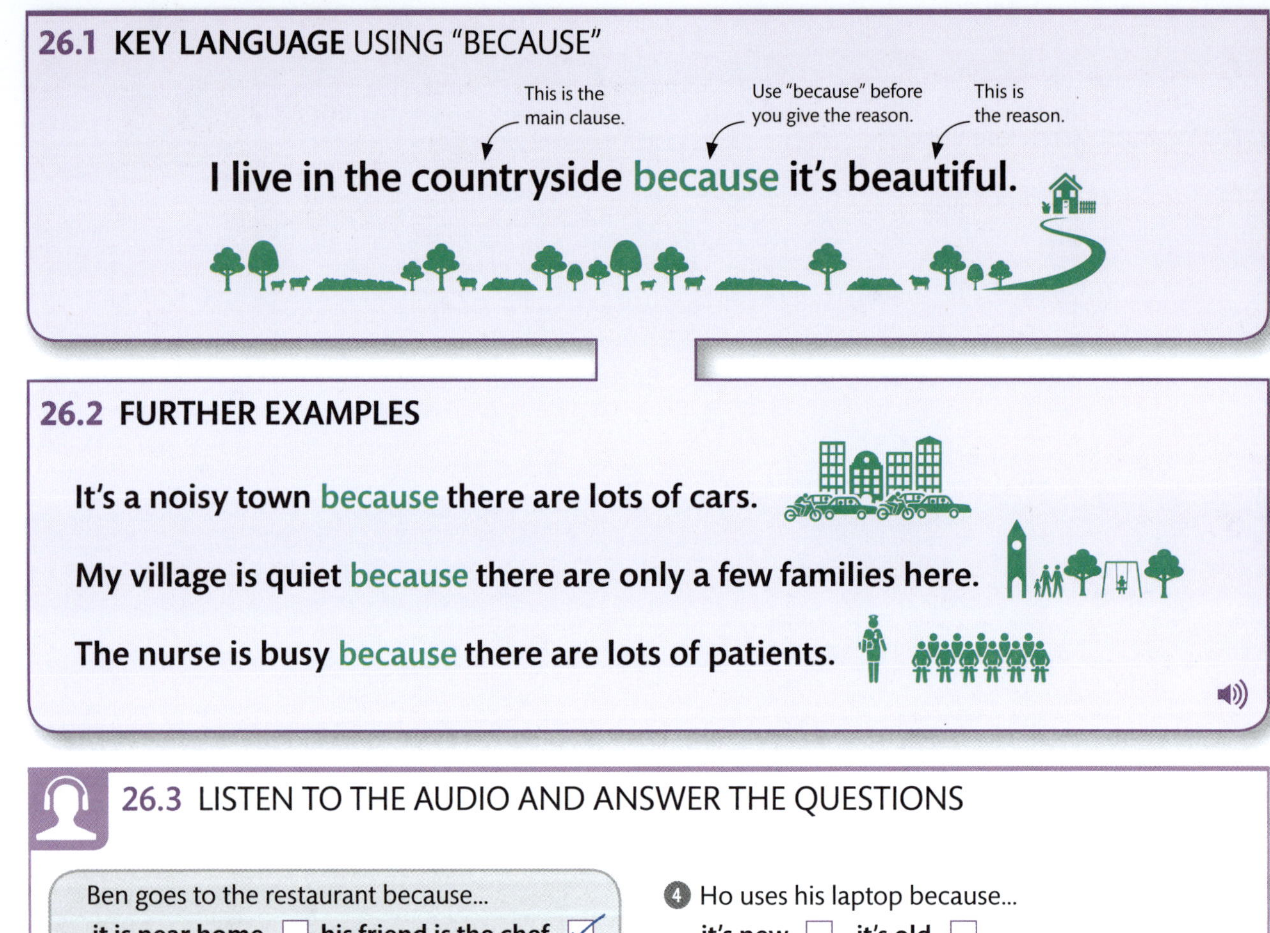

26.1 KEY LANGUAGE USING "BECAUSE"

This is the main clause. / Use "because" before you give the reason. / This is the reason.

I live in the countryside because it's beautiful.

26.2 FURTHER EXAMPLES

It's a noisy town because there are lots of cars.

My village is quiet because there are only a few families here.

The nurse is busy because there are lots of patients.

26.3 LISTEN TO THE AUDIO AND ANSWER THE QUESTIONS

Ben goes to the restaurant because...
it is near home. ☐ **his friend is the chef.** ☑

1. Jacob lives in Newport because his family...
   lives there. ☐ **lives far away.** ☐

2. Marina works outside because...
   she's a farmer. ☐ **she's a gardener.** ☐

3. Lin gets up at 6am because she...
   goes running. ☐ **goes swimming.** ☐

4. Ho uses his laptop because...
   it's new. ☐ **it's old.** ☐

5. Pablo is a doctor because he is good...
   with people. ☐ **with children.** ☐

6. Annie goes to Boston because...
   her aunt lives there. ☐ **she's a chef.** ☐

7. The countryside is quiet because there aren't...
   lots of people. ☐ **lots of animals.** ☐

26.4 FILL IN THE GAPS USING THE PHRASES IN THE PANEL

I work in a theater because *I'm an actor*.

1. She lives on a farm because ____________.
2. She works in a hotel because ____________.
3. They get up late because ____________.
4. We work with children because ____________.
5. You don't eat lunch because ____________.
6. I work outside because ____________.
7. My parents go to the countryside because ____________.

I'm a gardener
we're teachers
~~I'm an actor~~
you're busy
she's a farmer
they're students
it's quiet
she's a receptionist

26 CHECKLIST

"Because" ☐ Aa Places and jobs ☐ Giving reasons ☐

REVIEW THE ENGLISH YOU HAVE LEARNED IN UNITS 21–26

NEW LANGUAGE	SAMPLE SENTENCE	☑	UNIT
USING "THERE IS" AND "THERE ARE"	There is a hospital. There are three hospitals. There isn't a school. There aren't any schools.	☐	21.1, 21.6
ARTICLES	I work in a library. I work in the library on Main Street.	☐	22.1
USING "ANY" AND "SOME"	Are there any hotels? There are some hotels.	☐	22.8
IMPERATIVES	Stop! Be careful!	☐	23.1
JOINING SENTENCES	There's a library and a restaurant. There's a hotel, but there isn't a store.	☐	24.1, 24.7
USING ADJECTIVES	She is a busy woman. It is a busy town. The town is busy. It is busy.	☐	25.1, 25.4
USING "BECAUSE"	I live in the countryside because it's beautiful.	☐	26.1

27 Vocabulary

27.1 AROUND THE HOUSE

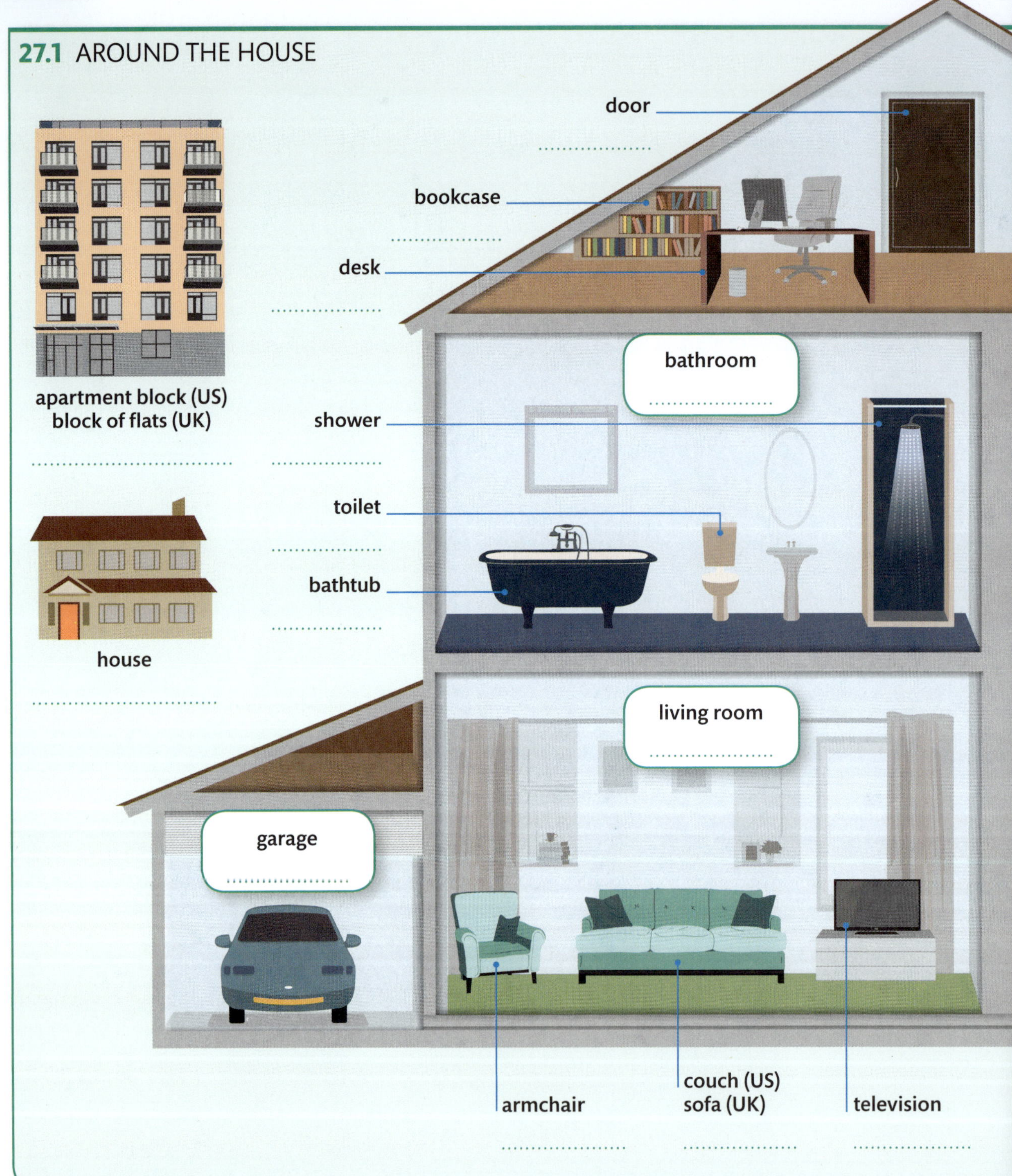

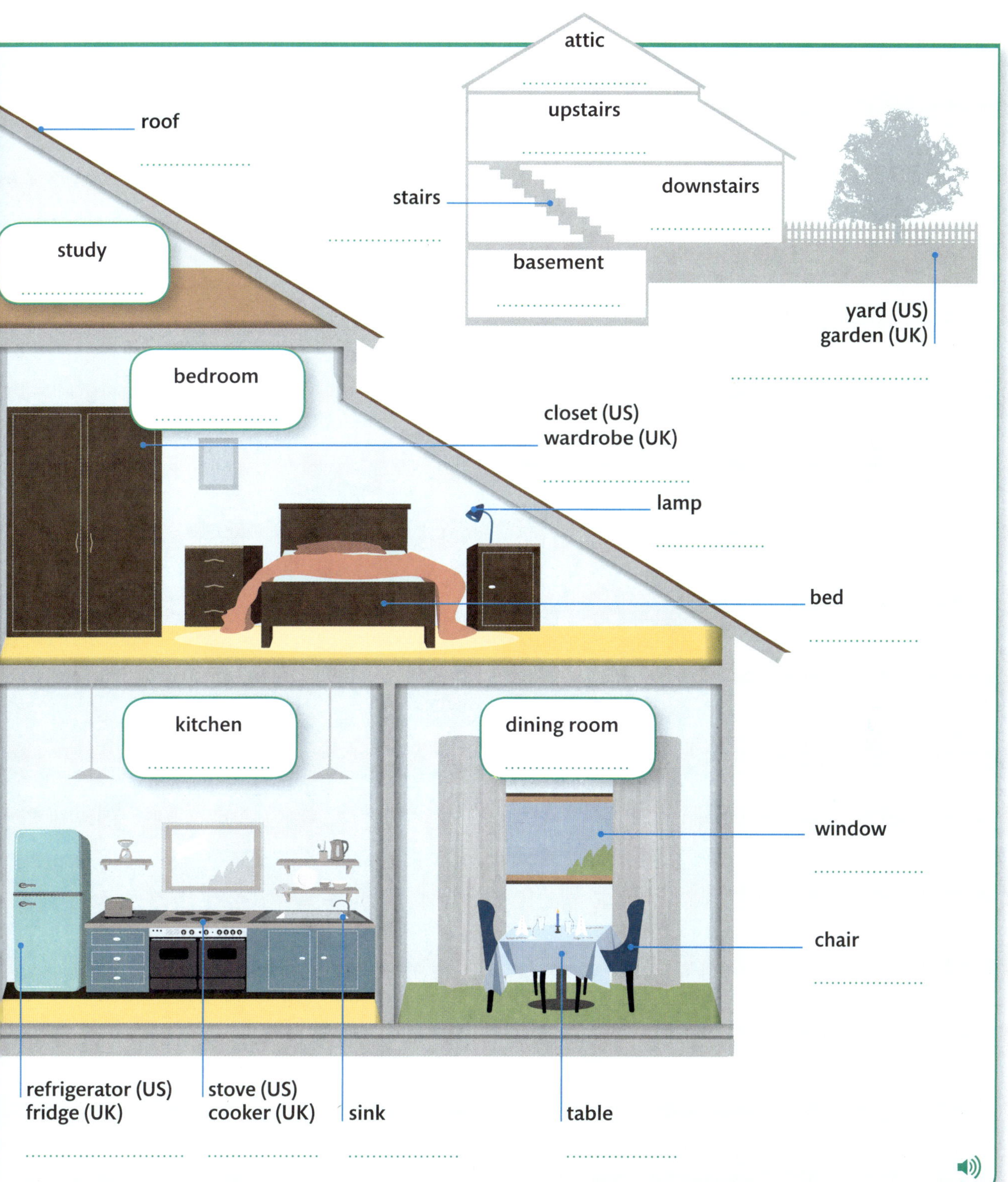
attic
upstairs
roof
stairs
downstairs
study
basement
yard (US)
garden (UK)
bedroom
closet (US)
wardrobe (UK)
lamp
bed
kitchen
dining room
window
chair
refrigerator (US)
fridge (UK)
stove (US)
cooker (UK)
sink
table

28 The things I have

When you talk about things you own, such as furniture or pets, you can use the verb "have." You can also use it to talk about your qualifications and the appliances and rooms in your home.

New language Using "have"
Vocabulary Household objects
New skill Talking about possessions

28.1 KEY LANGUAGE USING "HAVE"

"Have" is an irregular verb. The third person singular form is "has," not "haves."

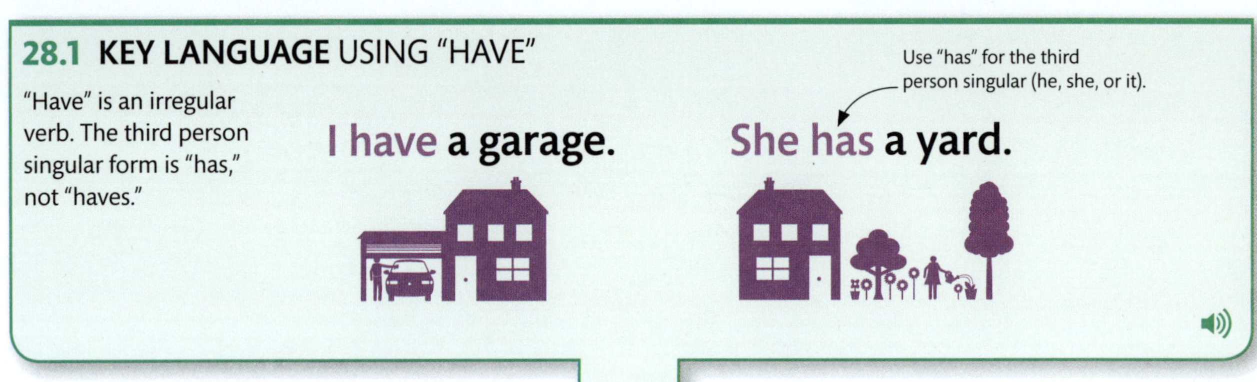

28.2 HOW TO FORM STATEMENTS USING "HAVE"

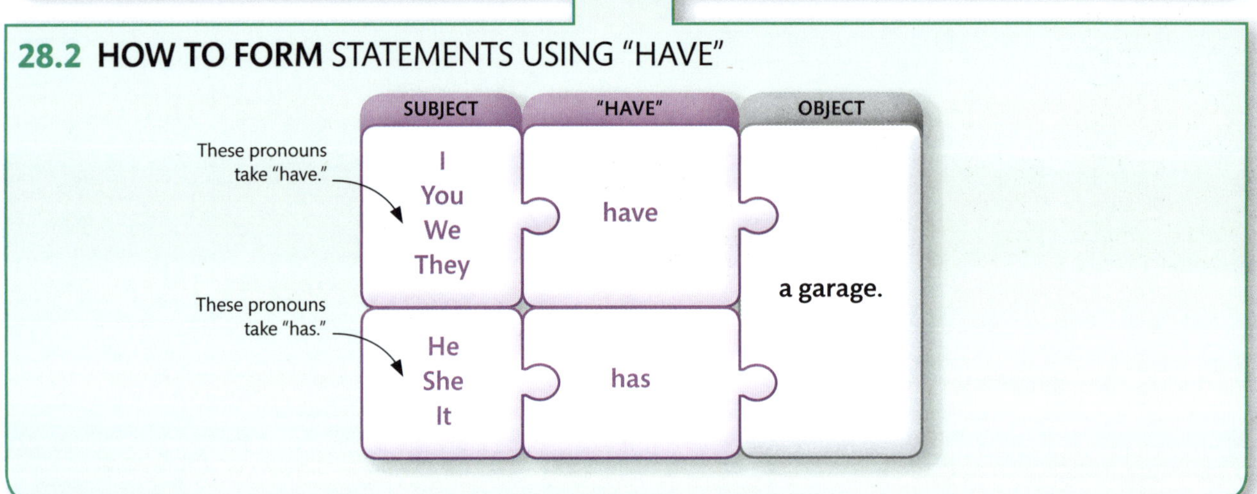

28.3 FILL IN THE GAPS USING "HAVE" OR "HAS"

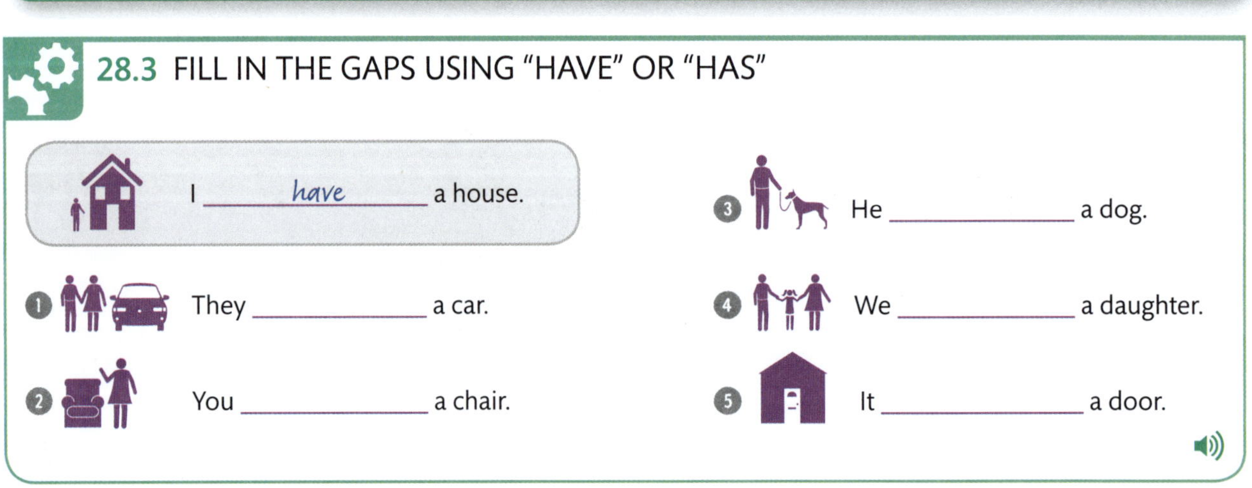

I ___have___ a house.

1. They ________ a car.
2. You ________ a chair.
3. He ________ a dog.
4. We ________ a daughter.
5. It ________ a door.

28.4 LISTEN TO THE AUDIO AND MARK WHO OWNS WHICH OBJECT

28.5 READ THE ADVERTISEMENTS AND ANSWER THE QUESTIONS

Riverside Apartment has four bedrooms.
True ☐ **False** ☑

1. Riverside Apartment has one bathroom.
   True ☐ **False** ☐
2. Lake View has a yard.
   True ☐ **False** ☐
3. Lake View has a garage.
   True ☐ **False** ☐
4. Stone Hill has five bedrooms.
   True ☐ **False** ☐
5. Stone Hill has a shower.
   True ☐ **False** ☐
6. Stone Hill has a kitchen.
   True ☐ **False** ☐

34 ACCOMMODATION

PROPERTIES TO RENT

Riverside Apartment **$800/month**
This old apartment is on the first floor of Riverside House. It has three bedrooms and two bathrooms. There's a beautiful park next door.

Lake View **$900/month**
This house is on a quiet street next to a lake. It has two bedrooms and a big kitchen in the basement. It also has a beautiful yard, but there is no garage.

Stone Hill **$1,500/month**
This house is in the old part of Bridgewater. It has four bedrooms and a bathroom with a bathtub and a shower. It also has a big kitchen. All the furniture is new and stylish.

28.6 KEY LANGUAGE "HAVE" NEGATIVES

Although "have" is irregular, its negative is formed in the usual way. The negative form can also be contracted as with other verbs.

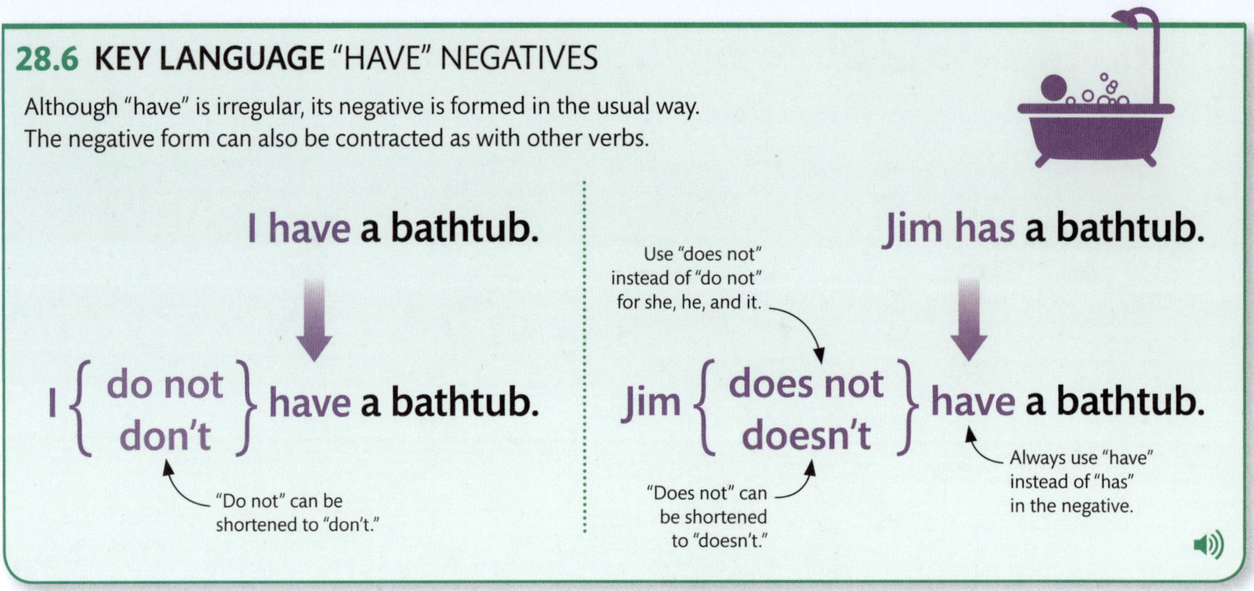

28.7 WRITE EACH SENTENCE IN ITS OTHER NEGATIVE FORM

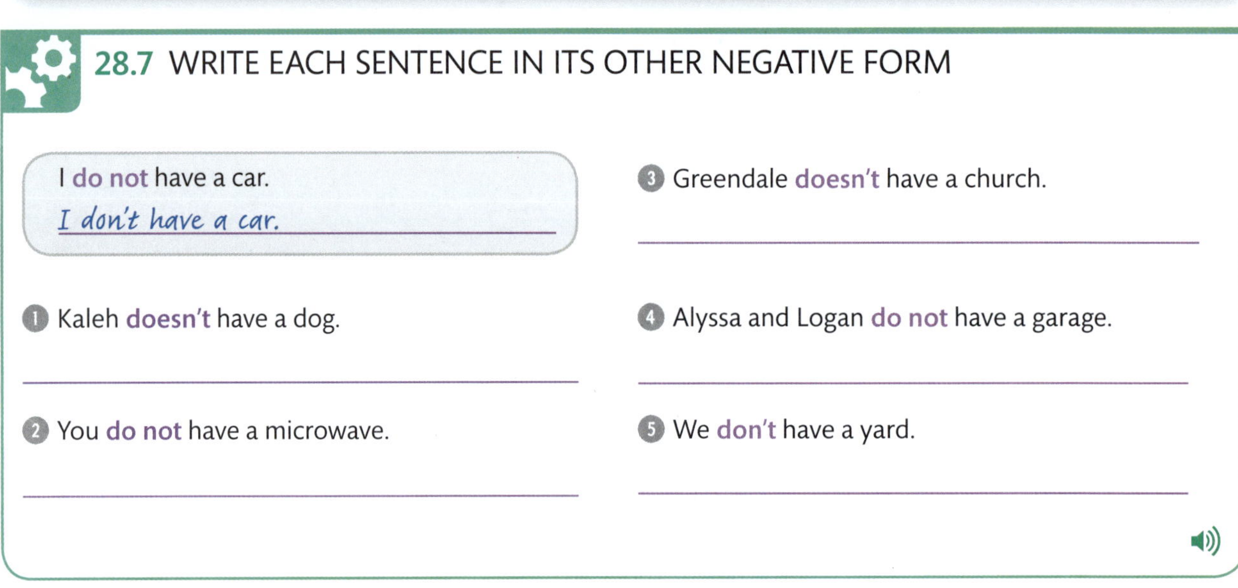

I do not have a car.
I don't have a car.

1. Kaleh doesn't have a dog.

2. You do not have a microwave.

3. Greendale doesn't have a church.

4. Alyssa and Logan do not have a garage.

5. We don't have a yard.

28.8 USE THE CHART TO CREATE 11 CORRECT SENTENCES AND SAY THEM OUT LOUD

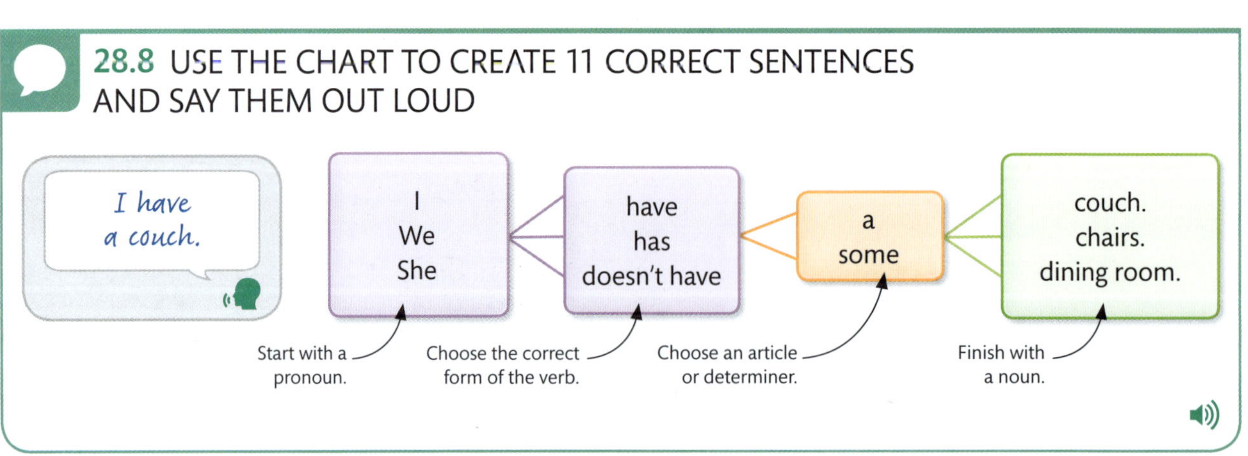

28.9 ANOTHER WAY TO SAY "HAVE"

Some English speakers, especially in the UK, use "have got" instead of "have." It means the same thing.

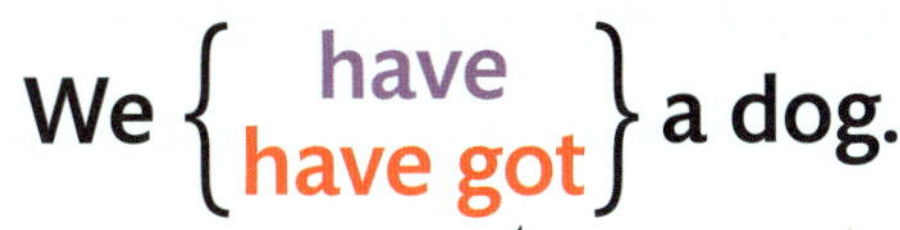

The only difference is the word "got."

28.10 HOW TO FORM "HAVE GOT"

POSITIVE	NEGATIVE
I have got a dog.	He has not got a dog.
I've got a dog.	He hasn't got a dog.

Only use this form when using "have" with "got." Don't shorten "I have" to "I've a dog."

"Has not got" can be shortened to "hasn't got."

28.11 WRITE EACH SENTENCE IN ITS OTHER TWO FORMS

	She has a computer.	*She has got a computer.*	*She's got a computer.*
1	They don't have a couch.		
2	He has three sisters.		
3	You don't have a bike.		
4	We have a microwave.		
5	It has a bathtub.		
6	They have a cat.		

28 CHECKLIST

- Using "have" ☐
- **Aa** Household objects ☐
- Talking about possessions ☐

29 What do you have?

Use questions with "have" to ask someone about the things they own. "Do" or "does" are used to form the question.

New language "Have" questions
Vocabulary House and furniture
New skill Asking about household objects

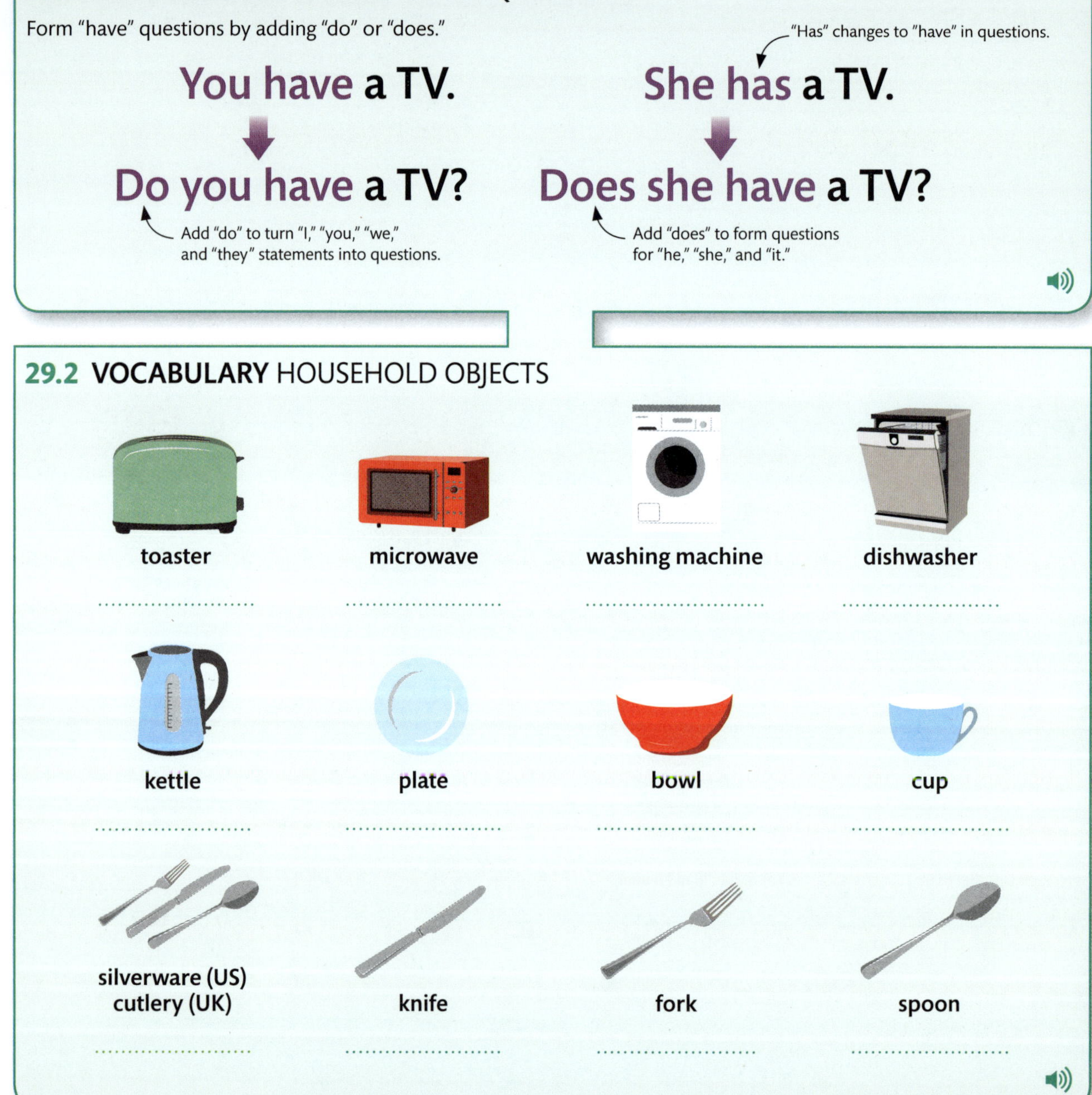

29.1 KEY LANGUAGE ASKING "HAVE" QUESTIONS

Form "have" questions by adding "do" or "does."

You have a TV. → **Do you have a TV?**

Add "do" to turn "I," "you," "we," and "they" statements into questions.

She has a TV. → **Does she have a TV?**

"Has" changes to "have" in questions.

Add "does" to form questions for "he," "she," and "it."

29.2 VOCABULARY HOUSEHOLD OBJECTS

toaster ....

microwave ....

washing machine ....

dishwasher ....

kettle ....

plate ....

bowl ....

cup ....

silverware (US)
cutlery (UK) ....

knife ....

fork ....

spoon ....

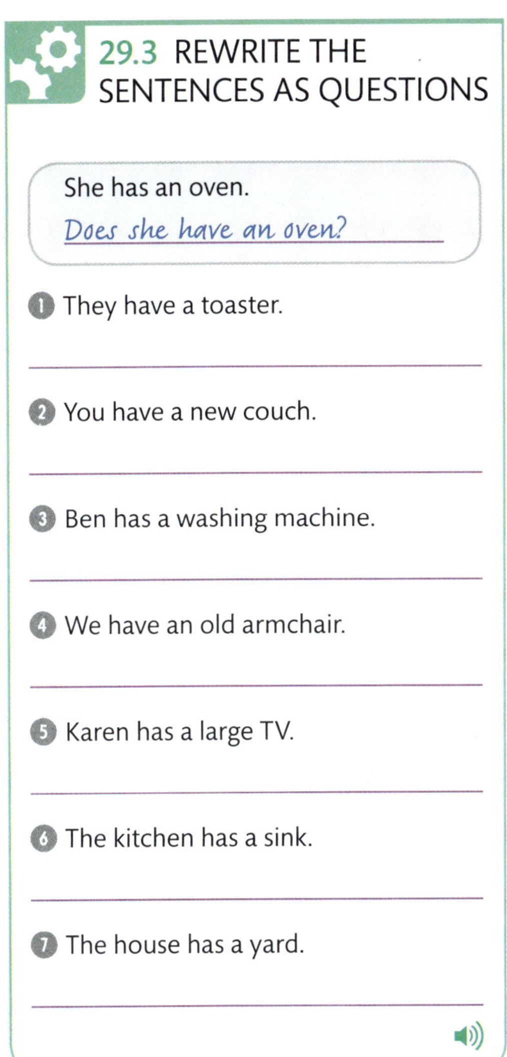

29.3 REWRITE THE SENTENCES AS QUESTIONS

She has an oven.
Does she have an oven?

1. They have a toaster.
2. You have a new couch.
3. Ben has a washing machine.
4. We have an old armchair.
5. Karen has a large TV.
6. The kitchen has a sink.
7. The house has a yard.

29.4 LISTEN AND MARK WHO OWNS WHICH OBJECTS

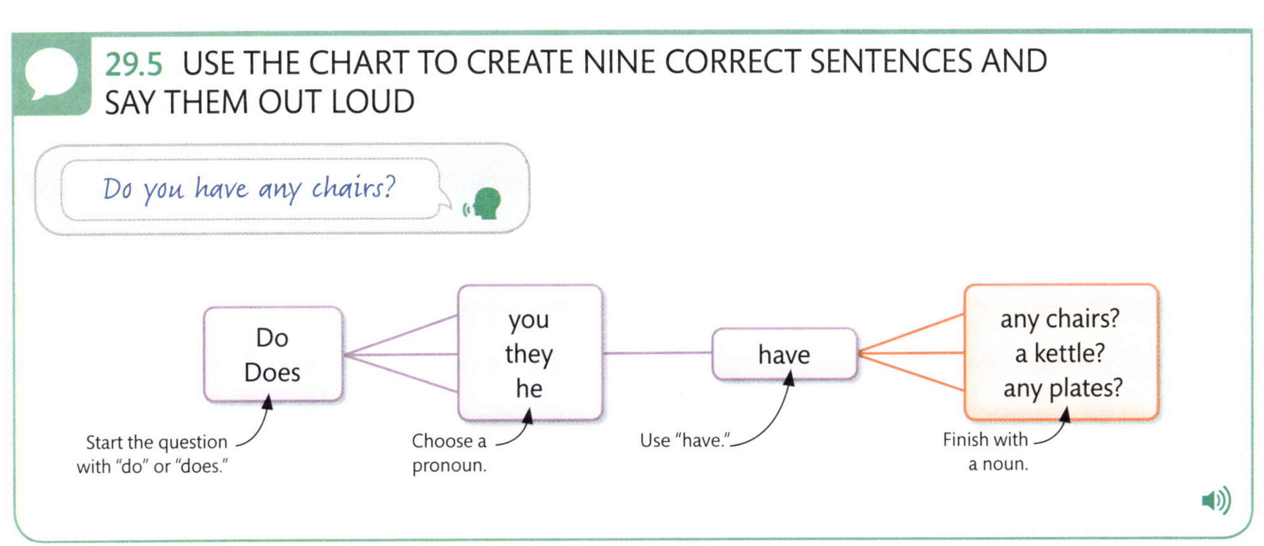

29.5 USE THE CHART TO CREATE NINE CORRECT SENTENCES AND SAY THEM OUT LOUD

Do you have any chairs?

29.6 KEY LANGUAGE SHORT ANSWERS TO "HAVE" QUESTIONS

You can give short answers to "have" questions using "do" and "don't."

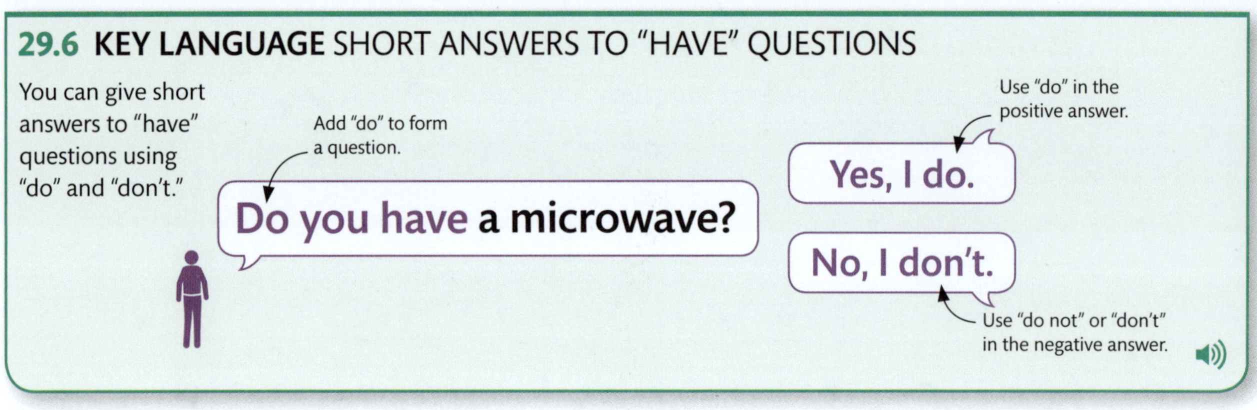

29.7 LOOK AT THE PICTURE AND WRITE SHORT ANSWERS TO THE QUESTIONS

Do you have a kettle?

Yes, I do.

1. Do you have a fork?

2. Do you have a spoon?

3. Do you have a toaster?

4. Do you have a microwave?

29.8 LOOK AT THE PICTURE, THEN ANSWER THE QUESTIONS OUT LOUD

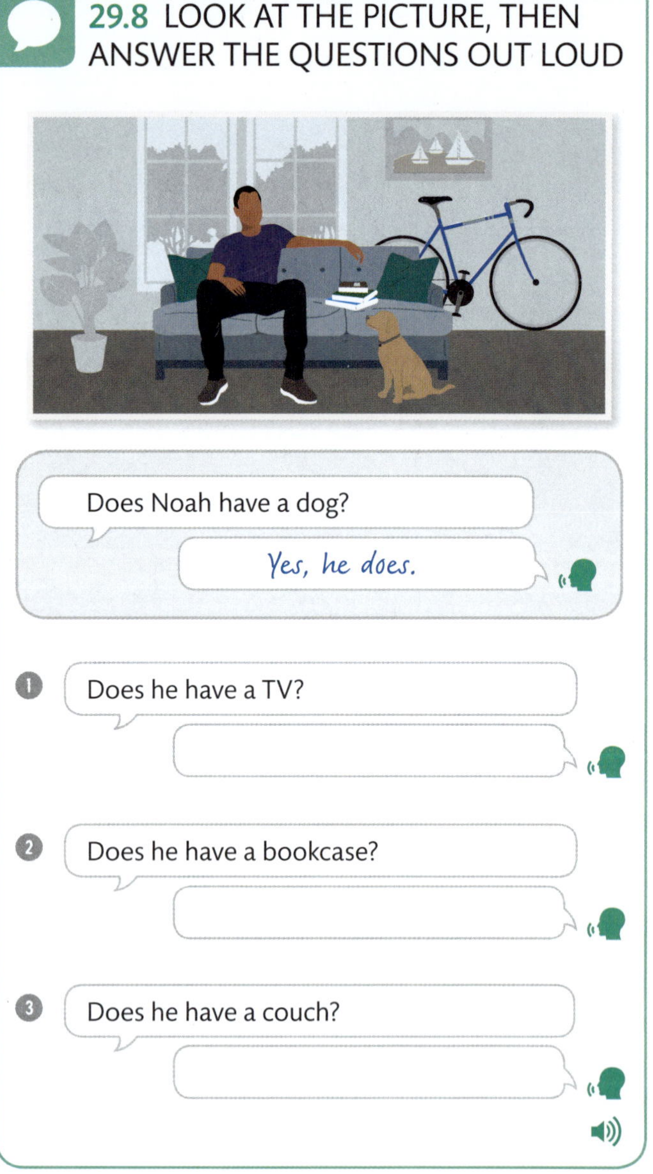

Does Noah have a dog?

Yes, he does.

1. Does he have a TV?

2. Does he have a bookcase?

3. Does he have a couch?

29.9 KEY LANGUAGE "HAVE GOT" QUESTIONS AND ANSWERS

Questions and answers using "have got" are formed differently. Remember, you mostly hear this in British English.

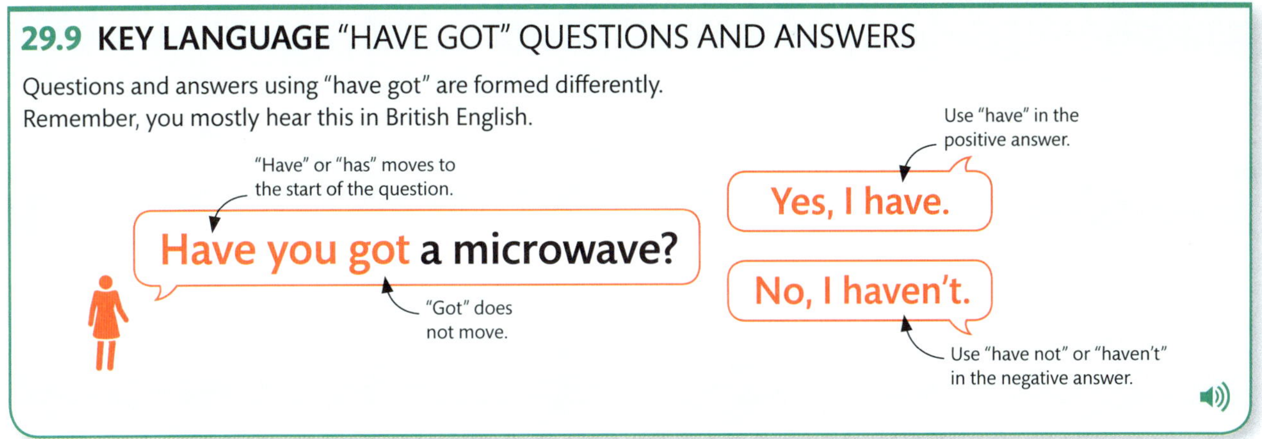

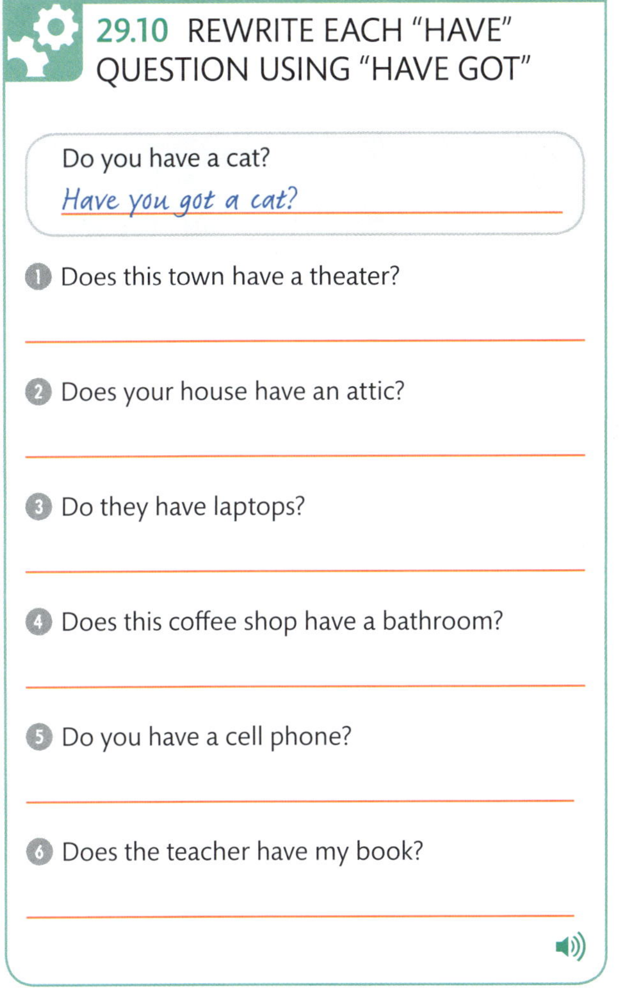

29.10 REWRITE EACH "HAVE" QUESTION USING "HAVE GOT"

Do you have a cat?
Have you got a cat?

1. Does this town have a theater?

2. Does your house have an attic?

3. Do they have laptops?

4. Does this coffee shop have a bathroom?

5. Do you have a cell phone?

6. Does the teacher have my book?

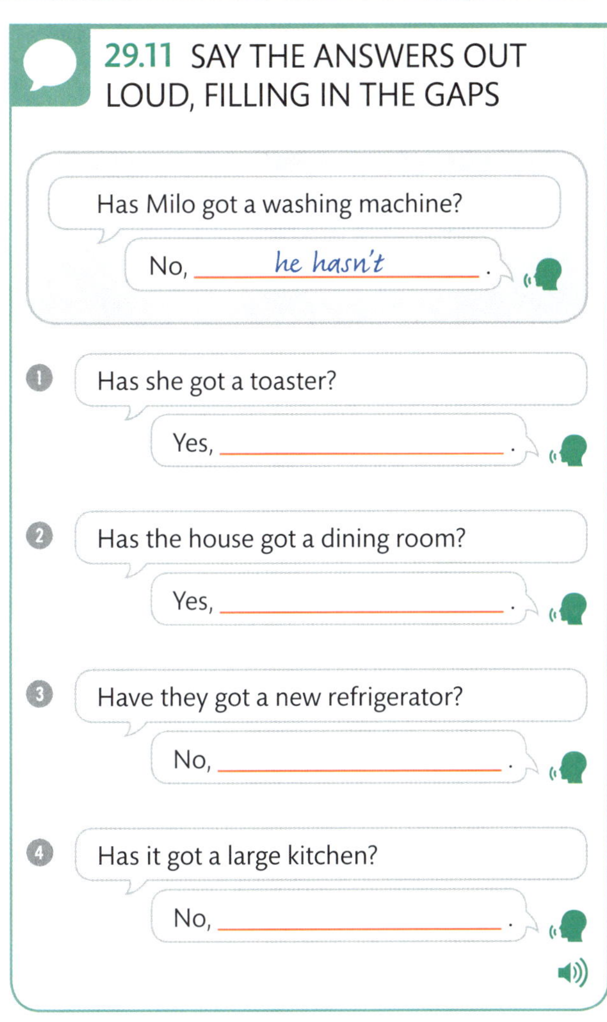

29.11 SAY THE ANSWERS OUT LOUD, FILLING IN THE GAPS

Has Milo got a washing machine?
No, *he hasn't*.

1. Has she got a toaster?
   Yes, ______.

2. Has the house got a dining room?
   Yes, ______.

3. Have they got a new refrigerator?
   No, ______.

4. Has it got a large kitchen?
   No, ______.

29 CHECKLIST

"Have" questions ☐ | Aa House and furniture ☐ | Asking about household objects ☐

30 Vocabulary

30.1 FOOD AND DRINK

food

drinks

breakfast

lunch

dinner

meat

fish

seafood

fruit

vegetables

bread

pasta

rice

noodles

potatoes

milk

cheese

butter

yogurt

eggs

sugar

cookie (US)
biscuit (UK)

chocolate

cake

cereal

orange

apple

banana

strawberry

mango

sandwich

burger

fries (US)
chips (UK)

spaghetti

salad

coffee

tea

juice

water

lemonade

31 Counting

In English, nouns can be countable or uncountable. Countable nouns can be individually counted. Objects that can't be separated and counted are uncountable.

New language Uncountable nouns
Aa Vocabulary Food containers
New skill Talking about food

31.1 KEY LANGUAGE COUNTABLE AND UNCOUNTABLE NOUNS

Use "a," "an," or a number to talk about countable nouns.
"Some" can be used for both countable and uncountable nouns.

COUNTABLE NOUNS

There is an egg.

There are four eggs.

There are some eggs.

Use "some" when there are more countable things than you can easily count.

UNCOUNTABLE NOUNS

Uncountable nouns are always paired with verbs in the singular.

There is some rice.

Always use "some" with uncountable nouns, not "a," "an," or a number.

31.2 FURTHER EXAMPLES COUNTABLE AND UNCOUNTABLE NOUNS

a sandwich
an apple
four bananas
two burgers

some milk
some water
some spaghetti
some sugar

31.3 CROSS OUT THE INCORRECT WORD IN EACH SENTENCE

Michael has ~~two~~ / some milk.

1. Jake has an / some apple.
2. There is a / some coffee.
3. Reena eats a / some spaghetti.
4. There are two / some eggs.
5. I've got a / some bananas.

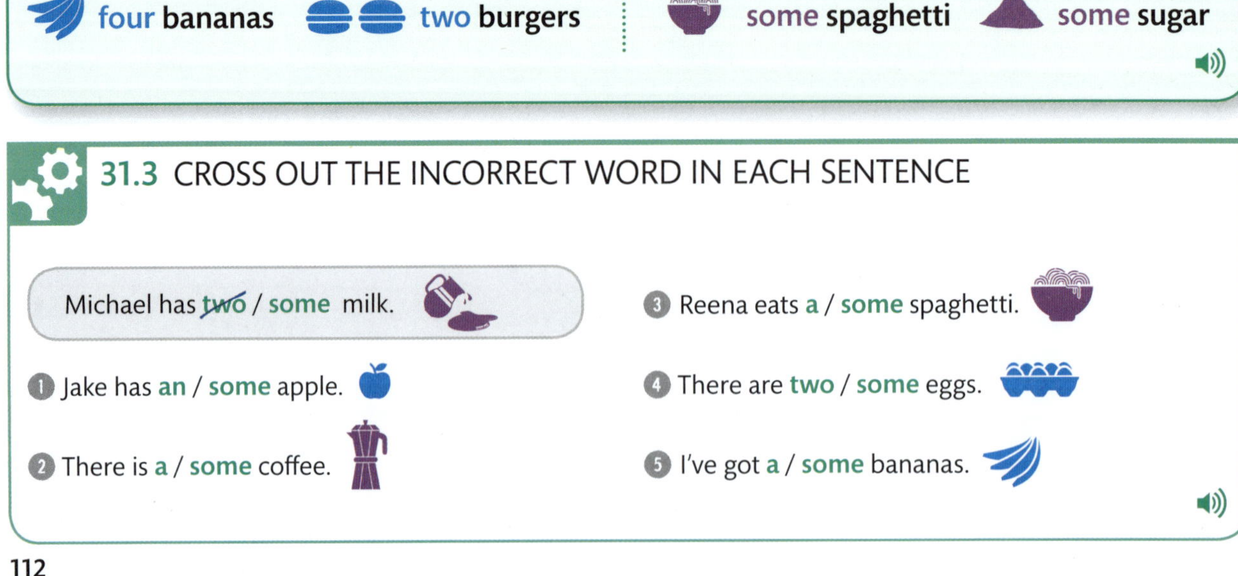

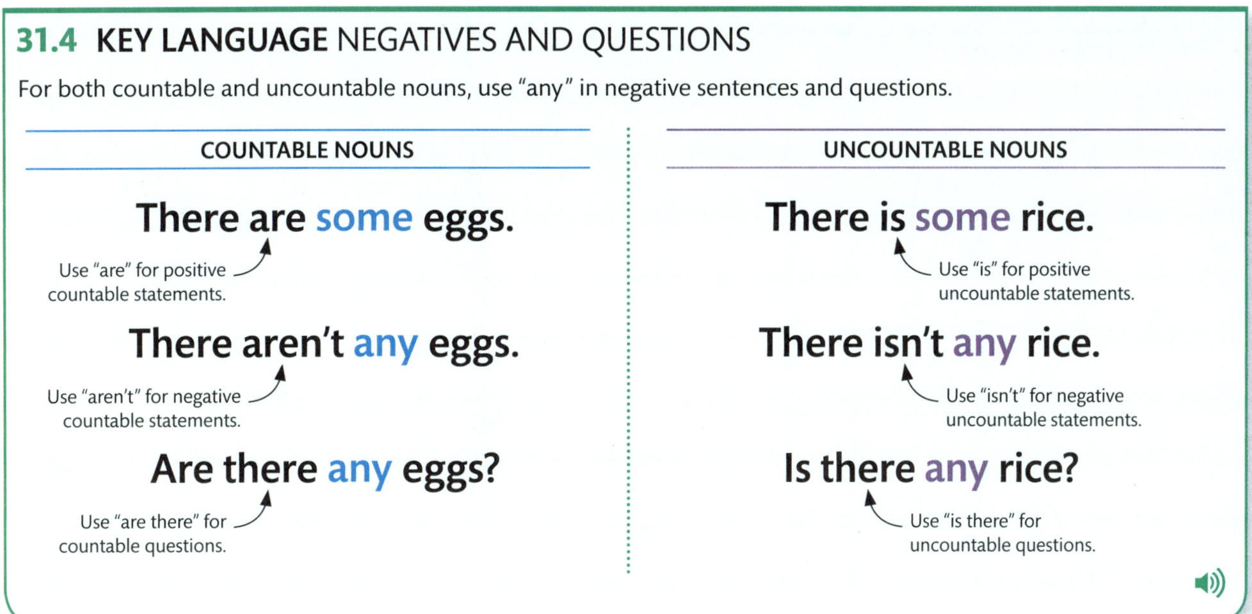

31.4 KEY LANGUAGE NEGATIVES AND QUESTIONS

For both countable and uncountable nouns, use "any" in negative sentences and questions.

COUNTABLE NOUNS	UNCOUNTABLE NOUNS
There are some eggs.	**There is some rice.**
Use "are" for positive countable statements.	Use "is" for positive uncountable statements.
There aren't any eggs.	**There isn't any rice.**
Use "aren't" for negative countable statements.	Use "isn't" for negative uncountable statements.
Are there any eggs?	**Is there any rice?**
Use "are there" for countable questions.	Use "is there" for uncountable questions.

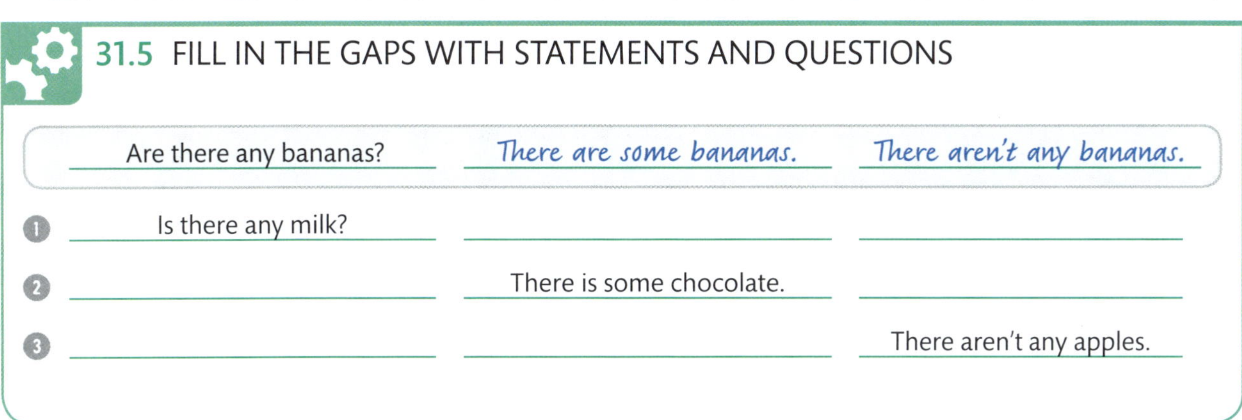

31.5 FILL IN THE GAPS WITH STATEMENTS AND QUESTIONS

	Are there any bananas?	*There are some bananas.*	*There aren't any bananas.*
1	Is there any milk?	______	______
2	______	There is some chocolate.	______
3	______	______	There aren't any apples.

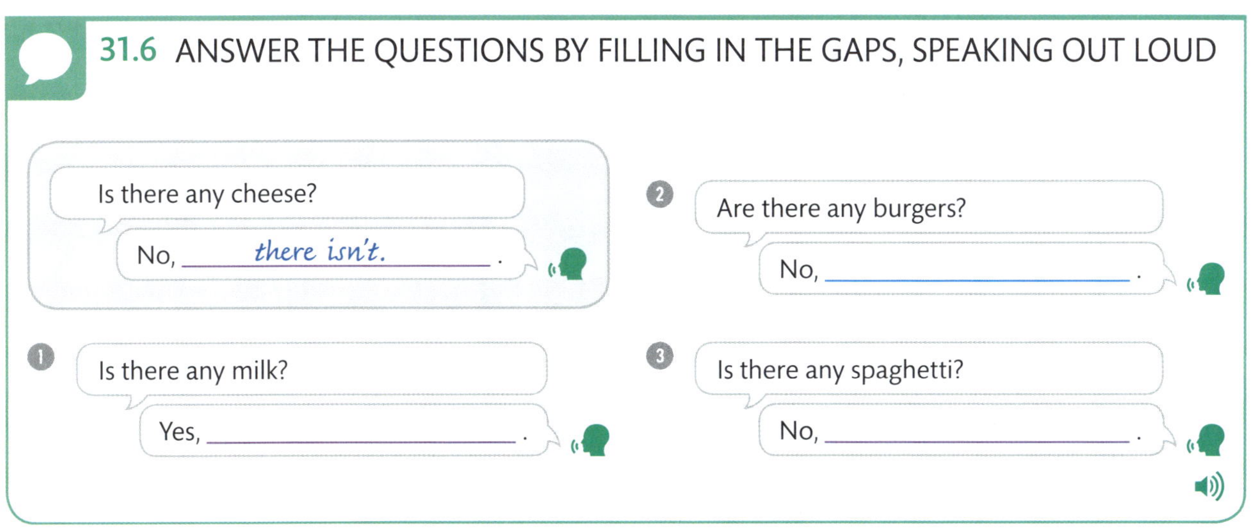

31.6 ANSWER THE QUESTIONS BY FILLING IN THE GAPS, SPEAKING OUT LOUD

Is there any cheese?
No, *there isn't.*

1 Is there any milk?
Yes, ______.

2 Are there any burgers?
No, ______.

3 Is there any spaghetti?
No, ______.

31.7 VOCABULARY FOOD CONTAINERS

box	bottle	bag	bar
....	....	....	....

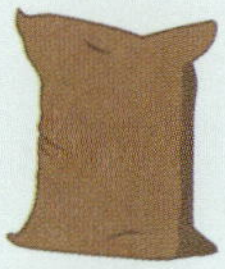

tube	glass	carton	jar
....	....	....	....

31.8 KEY LANGUAGE MAKING UNCOUNTABLE THINGS COUNTABLE

Uncountable nouns can be made countable if they are placed in containers.

some sugar → a **bag of** sugar

some water → three **bottles of** water

some cereal → a **bowl of** cereal

31.9 FILL IN THE GAPS TO COMPLETE THE SENTENCES

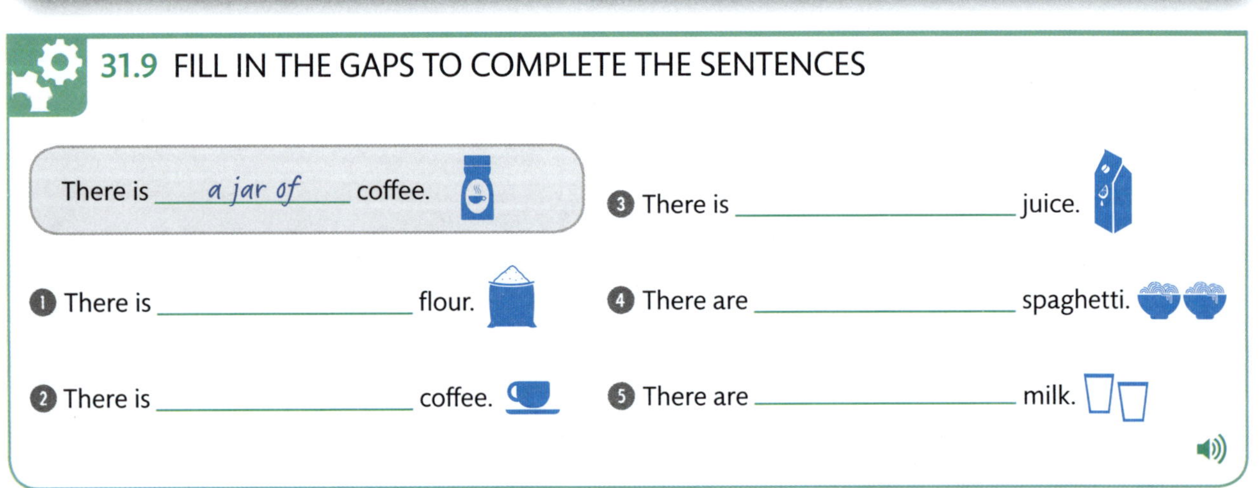

There is *a jar of* coffee.

1. There is ____________ flour.
2. There is ____________ coffee.
3. There is ____________ juice.
4. There are ____________ spaghetti.
5. There are ____________ milk.

31.10 KEY LANGUAGE QUESTIONS ABOUT QUANTITIES

You use "many" to ask questions about quantities of countable nouns, and "much" to ask questions about quantities of uncountable nouns.

How many eggs are there?

Use "many" for countable questions.

How much rice is there?

Use "much" for uncountable questions.

31.11 FURTHER EXAMPLES QUESTIONS ABOUT QUANTITIES

How many cupcakes are there?

How much pasta is there?

How many apples are there?

How much chocolate is there?

31.12 FILL IN THE GAPS USING "HOW MUCH" AND "HOW MANY"

How much pizza is there?

1. ______ glasses of juice are there?
2. ______ water is there?
3. ______ potatoes are there?
4. ______ bars of chocolate are there?
5. ______ pasta is there?
6. ______ cartons of juice are there?
7. ______ milk is there?

31.13 LISTEN TO THE AUDIO AND ANSWER THE QUESTIONS

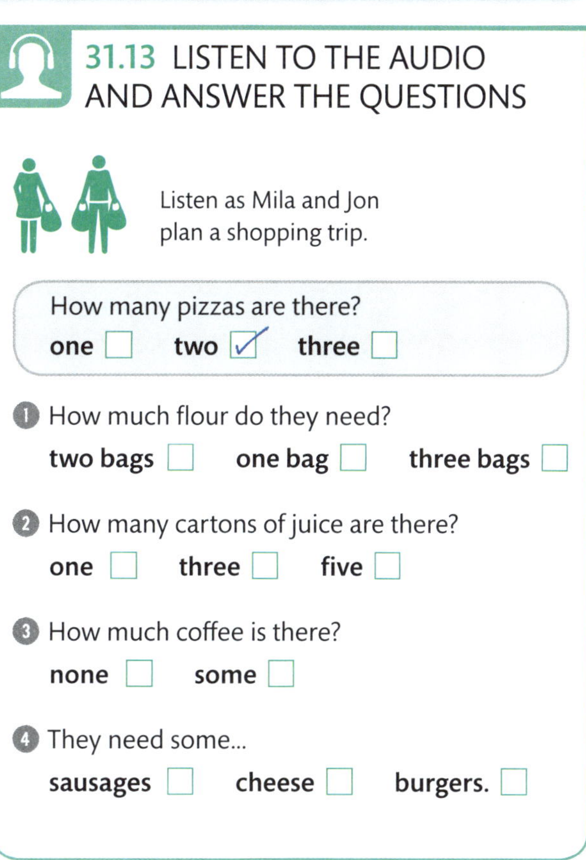

Listen as Mila and Jon plan a shopping trip.

How many pizzas are there?
one ☐ **two** ☑ **three** ☐

1. How much flour do they need?
two bags ☐ **one bag** ☐ **three bags** ☐
2. How many cartons of juice are there?
one ☐ **three** ☐ **five** ☐
3. How much coffee is there?
none ☐ **some** ☐
4. They need some...
sausages ☐ **cheese** ☐ **burgers.** ☐

31 CHECKLIST

Uncountable nouns ☐ **Aa** Food containers ☐ Talking about food ☐

32 Measuring

Use "enough" when you have the correct number or amount of something. Use "too many" or "too much" if you have more than enough.

New language Measurements
Aa Vocabulary Ingredients and quantities
New skill Talking about amounts

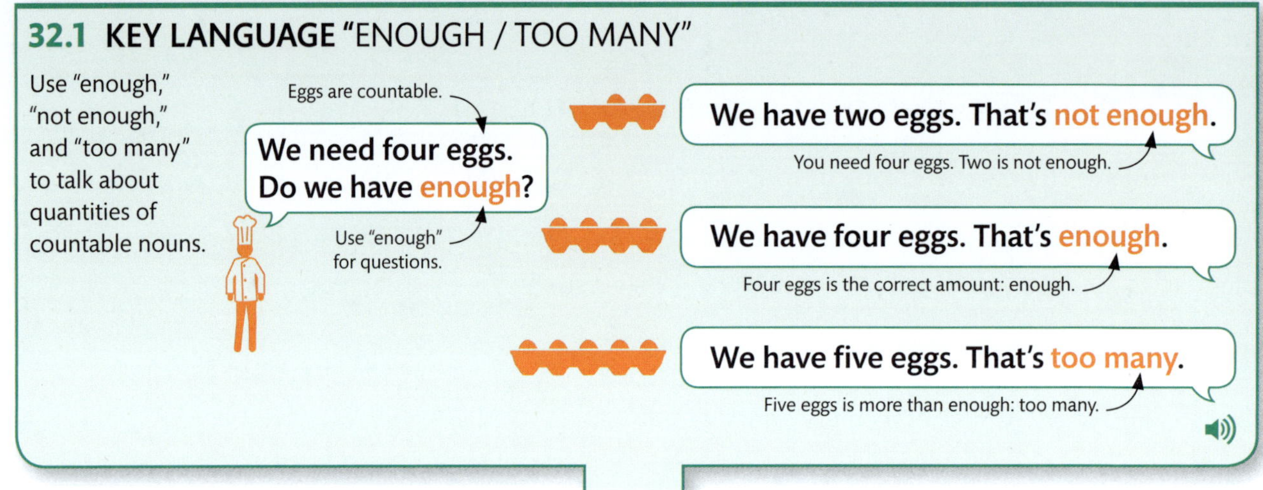

32.2 FURTHER EXAMPLES "ENOUGH / TOO MANY"

There are **enough** eggs.

You have **enough** eggs.

There **aren't enough** eggs.

You **don't** have **enough** eggs.

There are **too many** eggs.

You have **too many** eggs.

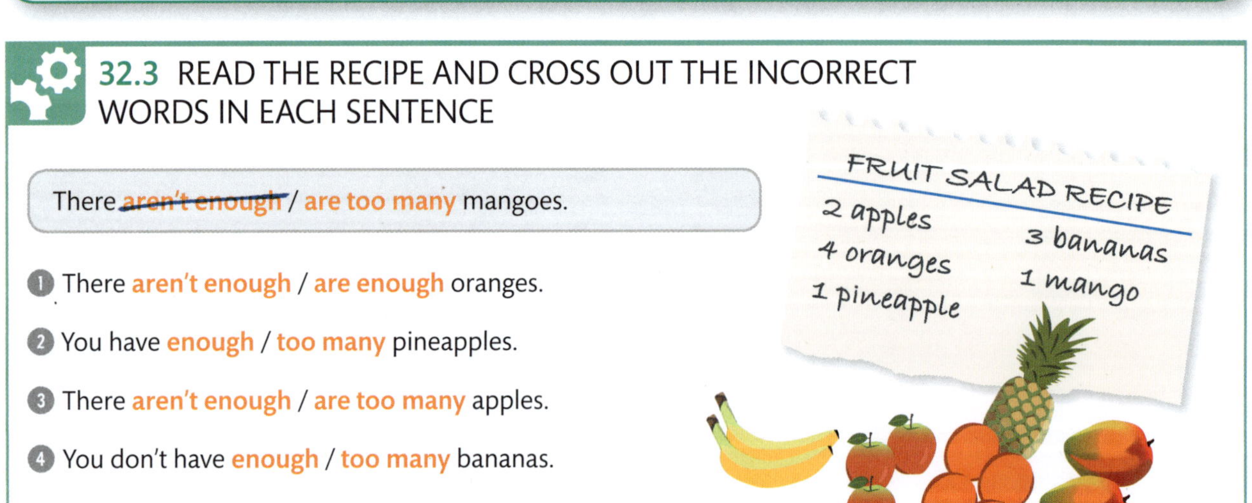

32.4 KEY LANGUAGE "ENOUGH / TOO MUCH"

Use "enough," "not enough," and "too much" to talk about quantities of uncountable nouns.

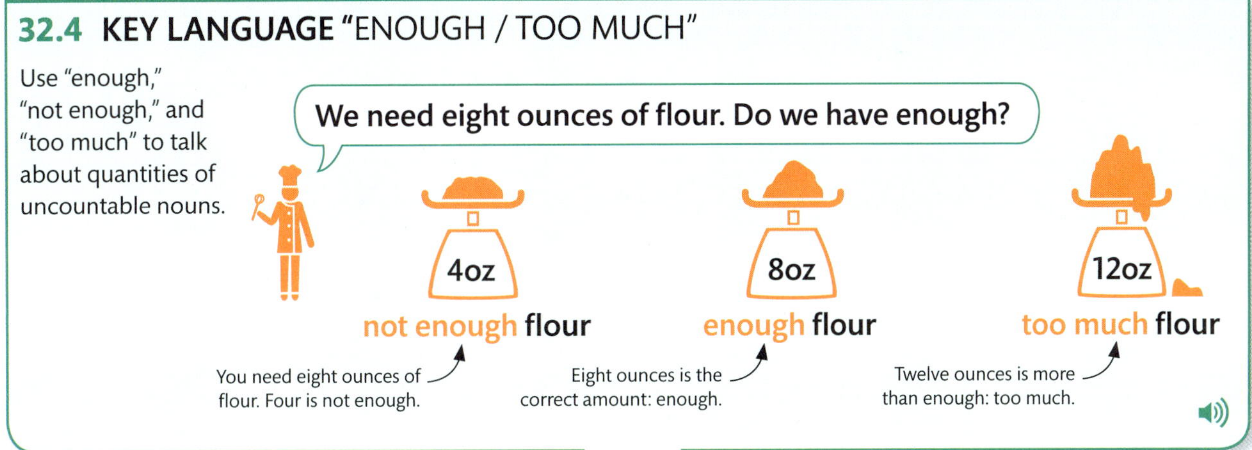

32.5 FURTHER EXAMPLES "ENOUGH / TOO MUCH"

There is enough flour.

They have enough flour.

There isn't enough flour.

They don't have enough flour.

There is too much flour.

They have too much flour.

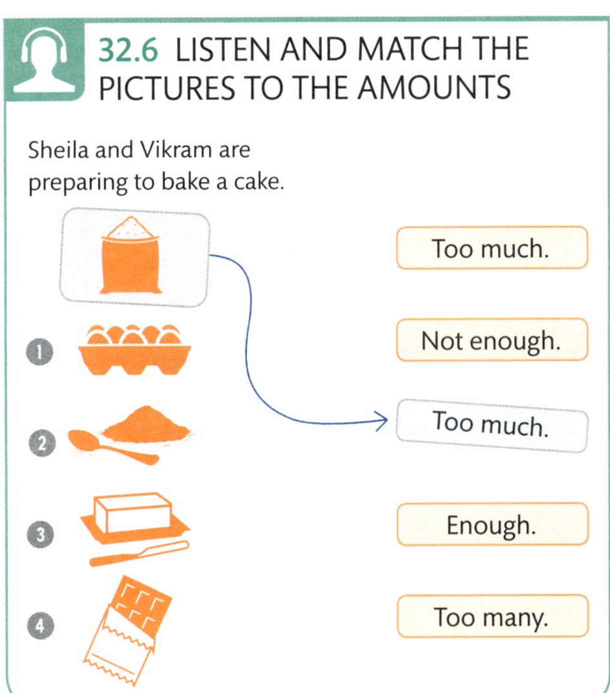

32.6 LISTEN AND MATCH THE PICTURES TO THE AMOUNTS

Sheila and Vikram are preparing to bake a cake.

Too much.

1 Not enough.

2 Too much.

3 Enough.

4 Too many.

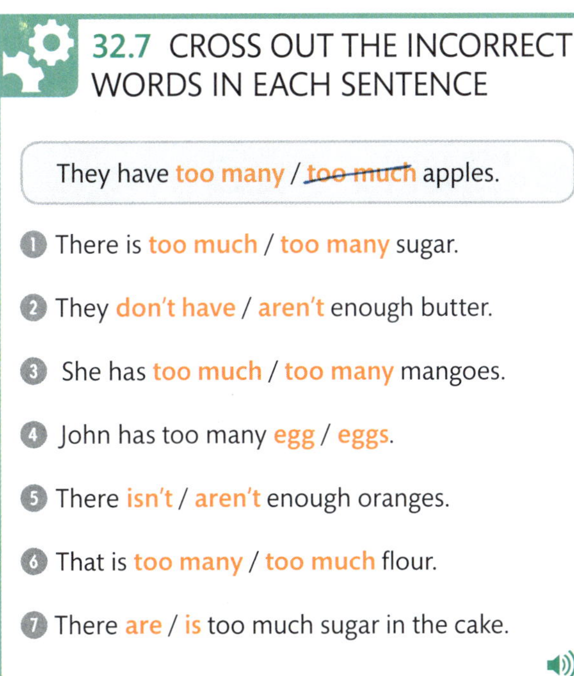

32.7 CROSS OUT THE INCORRECT WORDS IN EACH SENTENCE

They have too many / ~~too much~~ apples.

1. There is too much / too many sugar.
2. They don't have / aren't enough butter.
3. She has too much / too many mangoes.
4. John has too many egg / eggs.
5. There isn't / aren't enough oranges.
6. That is too many / too much flour.
7. There are / is too much sugar in the cake.

32 ✓ CHECKLIST

Measurements ☐ Aa Ingredients and quantities ☐ Talking about amounts ☐

33 Vocabulary

33.2 CLOTHING SIZES

extra small

small

medium

large

extra large

33.3 DESCRIBING CLOTHES

smart

casual

suit

uniform

short sleeves

long sleeves

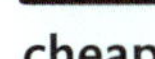

cheap

expensive

33.4 COLORS (US) / COLOURS (UK)

red

orange

yellow

green

blue

purple

pink

white

gray (US)
grey (UK)

black

34 At the shops

You can use many different verbs to talk about what happens when you are shopping. Use "too" and "enough" to describe how well clothes fit you.

New language Using "too" and "fit"
Aa Vocabulary Shopping and clothes
New skill Describing clothes

34.1 VOCABULARY SHOPPING VERBS

Ana **owns** a red hat.

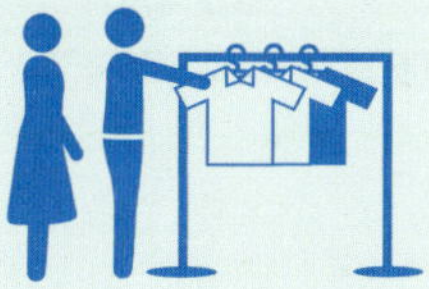

Choose a new shirt!

Luc **sells** old clothes.

They **want** new shoes.

The hat **fits** Jane.

Let's **buy** some hats!

34.2 CROSS OUT THE INCORRECT WORD IN EACH SENTENCE

Tsuru ~~want~~ / wants a green jumper.

1. Hannah choose / chooses a yellow skirt.
2. Elliot and Ruby buy / buys a new couch.
3. Sue own / owns an old winter coat.
4. Jess's dad buy / buys her a new bike.
5. Chris and Lisa own / owns a black sports car.
6. Gayle and Mike sell / sells shoes at the market.
7. Mia choose / chooses her red shoes.
8. The shoes fit / fits me.
9. We want / wants new white shirts.

34.3 REWRITE THE SENTENCES, PUTTING THE WORDS IN THE CORRECT ORDER

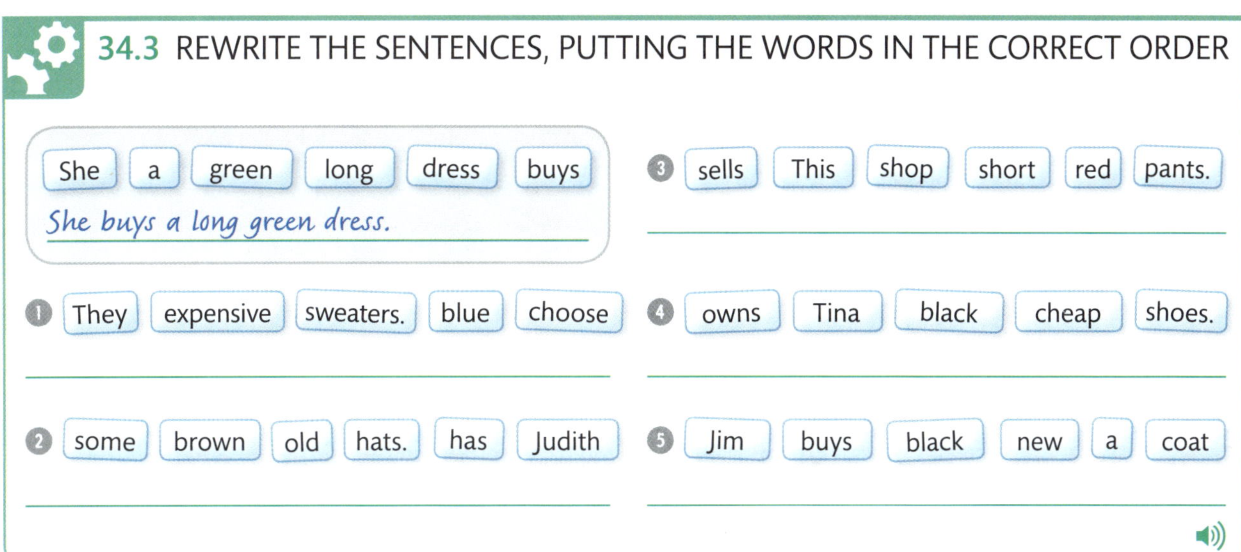

She | a | green | long | dress | buys

She buys a long green dress.

1. They | expensive | sweaters. | blue | choose

2. some | brown | old | hats. | has | Judith

3. sells | This | shop | short | red | pants.

4. owns | Tina | black | cheap | shoes.

5. Jim | buys | black | new | a | coat

34.4 READ THE MESSAGES AND CIRCLE 12 ADJECTIVES

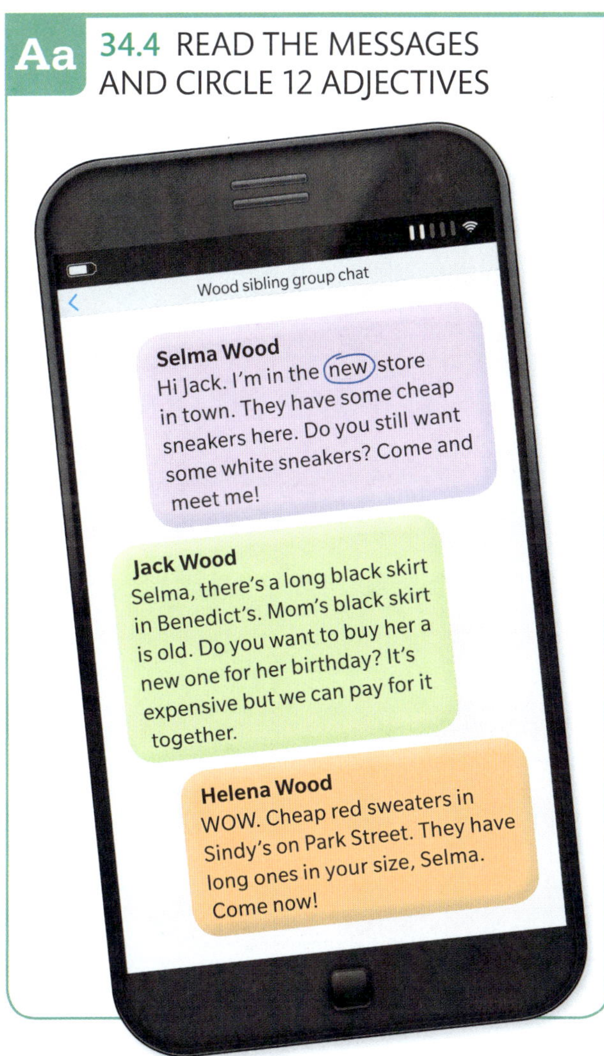

34.5 LISTEN TO THE AUDIO AND ANSWER THE QUESTIONS

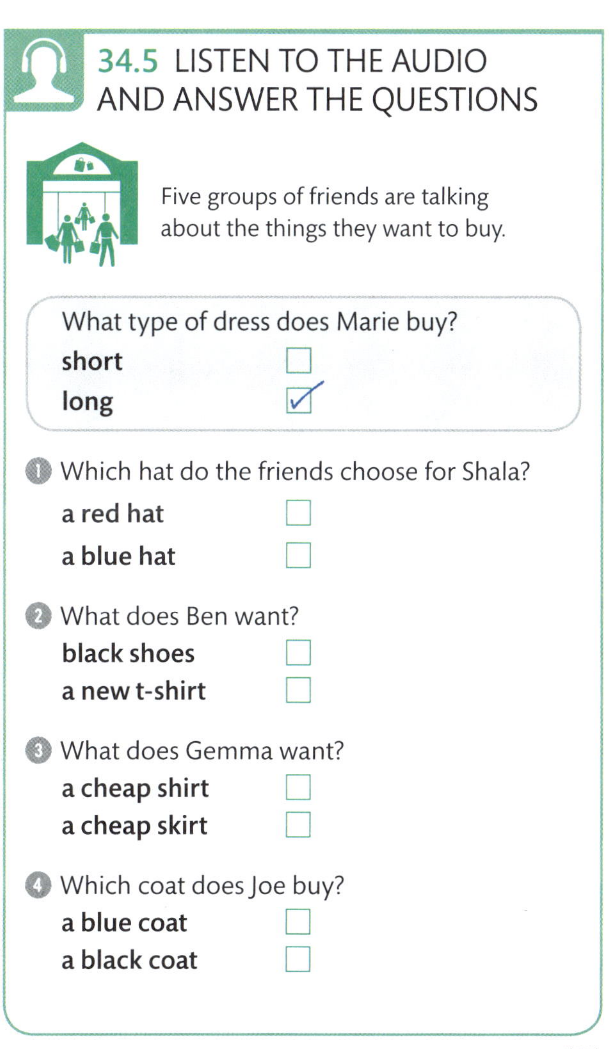

Five groups of friends are talking about the things they want to buy.

What type of dress does Marie buy?
short ☐
long ☑

1. Which hat do the friends choose for Shala?
   a red hat ☐
   a blue hat ☐

2. What does Ben want?
   black shoes ☐
   a new t-shirt ☐

3. What does Gemma want?
   a cheap shirt ☐
   a cheap skirt ☐

4. Which coat does Joe buy?
   a blue coat ☐
   a black coat ☐

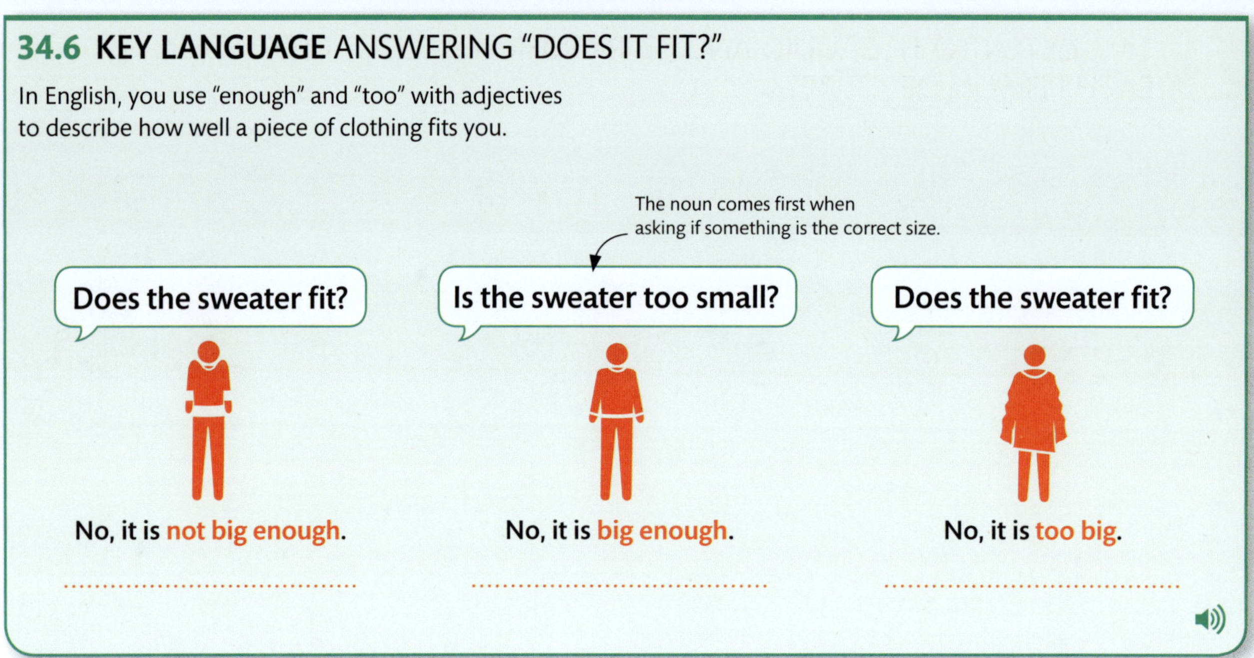

34.6 KEY LANGUAGE ANSWERING "DOES IT FIT?"

In English, you use "enough" and "too" with adjectives to describe how well a piece of clothing fits you.

The noun comes first when asking if something is the correct size.

Does the sweater fit?

No, it is not big enough.

Is the sweater too small?

No, it is big enough.

Does the sweater fit?

No, it is too big.

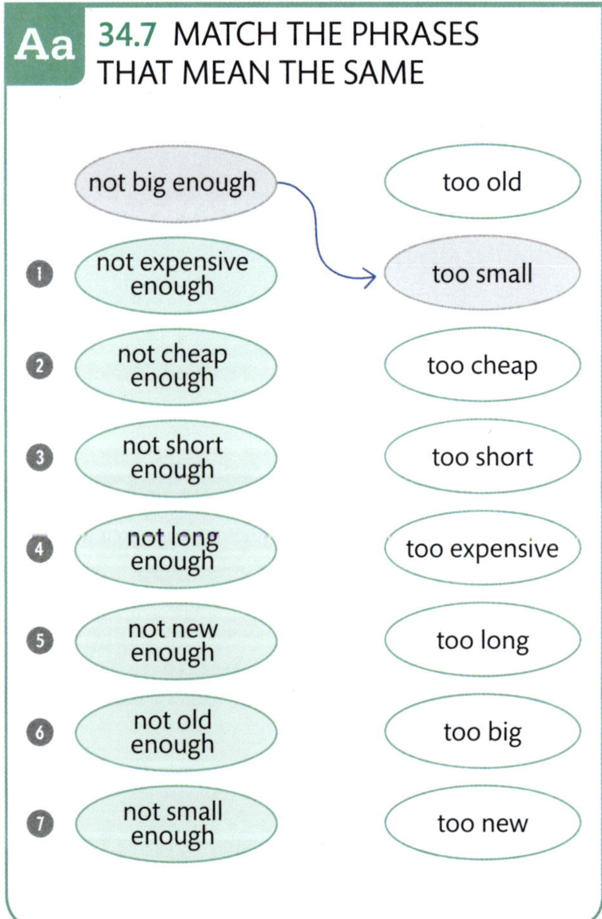

Aa 34.7 MATCH THE PHRASES THAT MEAN THE SAME

	not big enough	too old
1	not expensive enough	too small
2	not cheap enough	too cheap
3	not short enough	too short
4	not long enough	too expensive
5	not new enough	too long
6	not old enough	too big
7	not small enough	too new

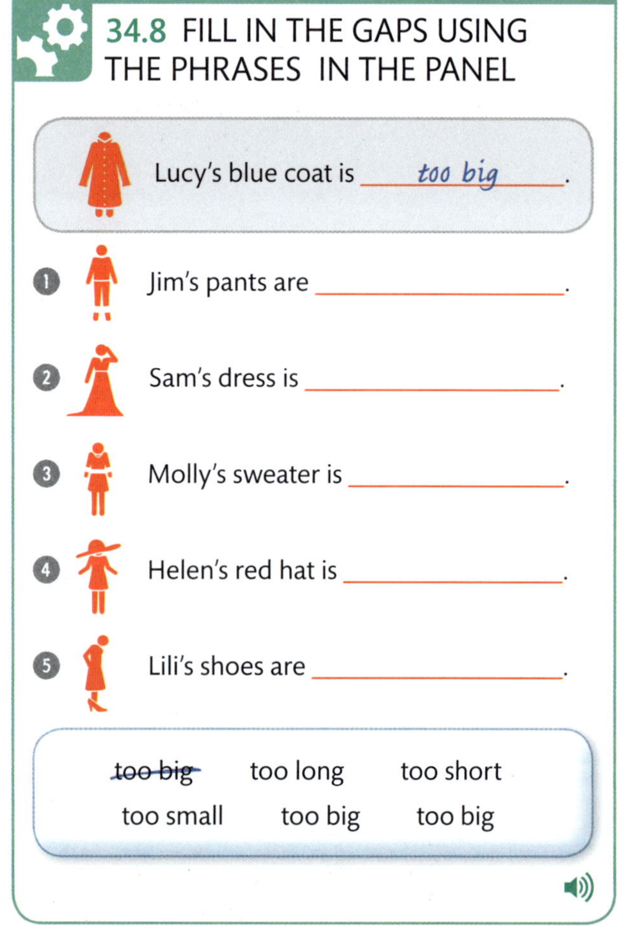

34.8 FILL IN THE GAPS USING THE PHRASES IN THE PANEL

Lucy's blue coat is *too big*.

1 Jim's pants are ______________.

2 Sam's dress is ______________.

3 Molly's sweater is ______________.

4 Helen's red hat is ______________.

5 Lili's shoes are ______________.

~~too big~~ too long too short
too small too big too big

34.9 LISTEN TO THE AUDIO AND MARK WHICH PIECE OF CLOTHING EACH PERSON DESCRIBES

A ✓ B

1 A B

2 A B

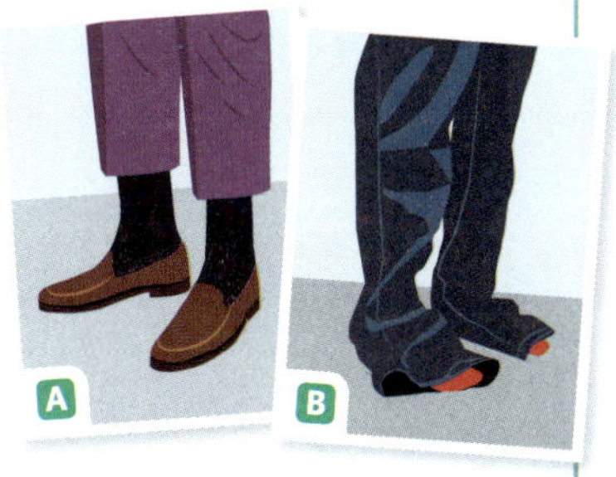

3 A B

4 A B

5 A B

34.10 USE THE CHART TO CREATE 12 CORRECT SENTENCES AND SAY THEM OUT LOUD

These black pants are too big.

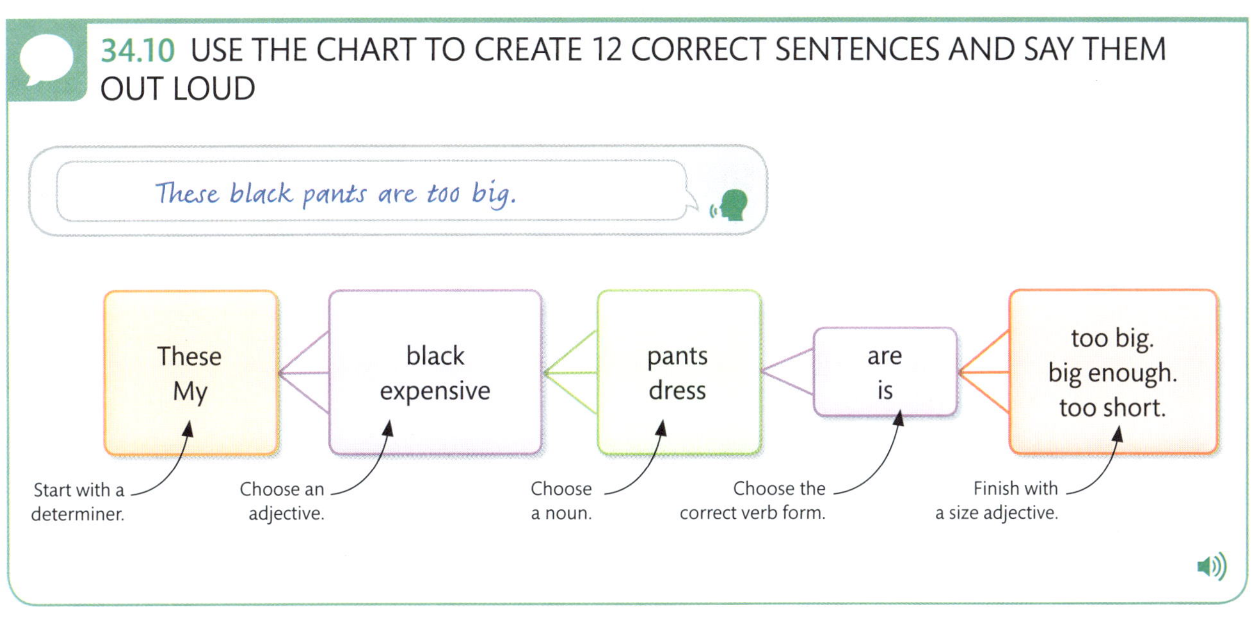

35 Describing things

You can use adjectives to give your opinion about things as well as to give factual information. You can use more than one adjective before a noun.

New language Opinion adjectives
Aa Vocabulary Shopping and materials
New skill Giving opinions

35.1 KEY LANGUAGE OPINION ADJECTIVES

Some adjectives give opinions, not facts.

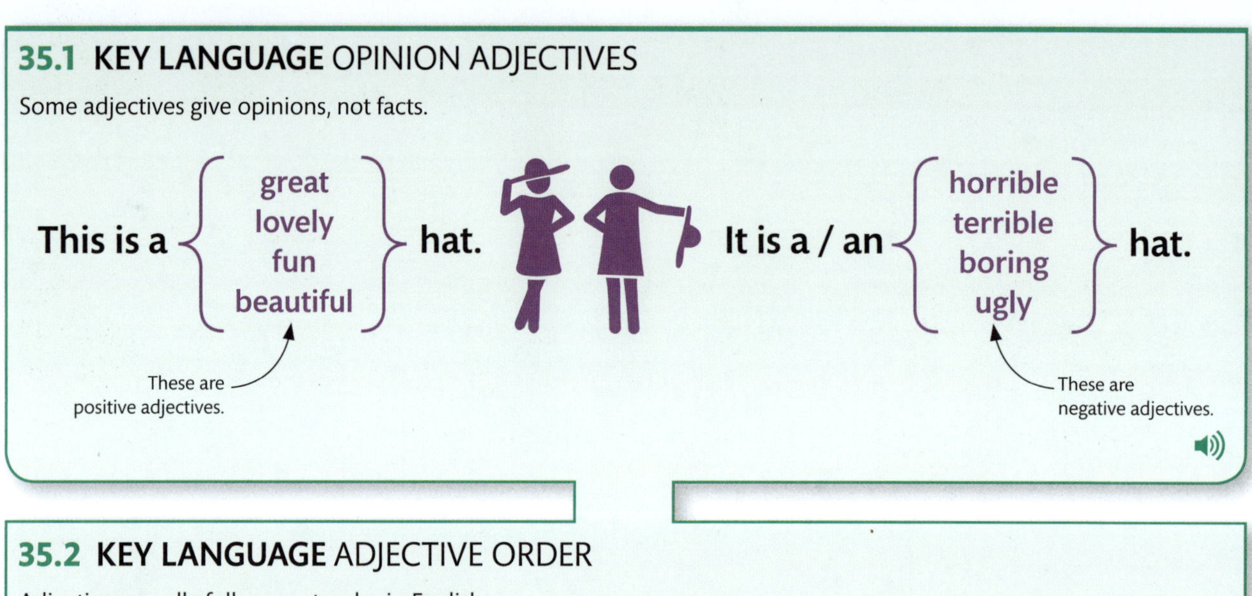

35.2 KEY LANGUAGE ADJECTIVE ORDER

Adjectives usually follow a set order in English.
Opinion adjectives come before fact adjectives.

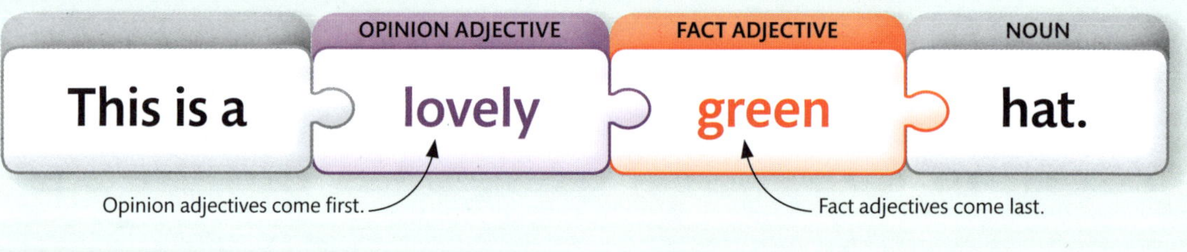

Opinion adjectives come first.

Fact adjectives come last.

35.3 FURTHER EXAMPLES ADJECTIVE ORDER

 It is a lovely big house.

 Natalie has a beautiful old cat.

 We have a horrible old car.

 They are ugly purple shoes.

 This is a great new book.

 He is a brilliant young actor.

35.4 CROSS OUT THE INCORRECT ADJECTIVE IN EACH SENTENCE

It is a good / ~~bad~~ young dog.

1. This is a lovely / horrible old t-shirt.

2. This is a boring / great movie.

3. I have a lovely / horrible long dress.

4. This is a beautiful / ugly bird.

5. This is a fun / boring party.

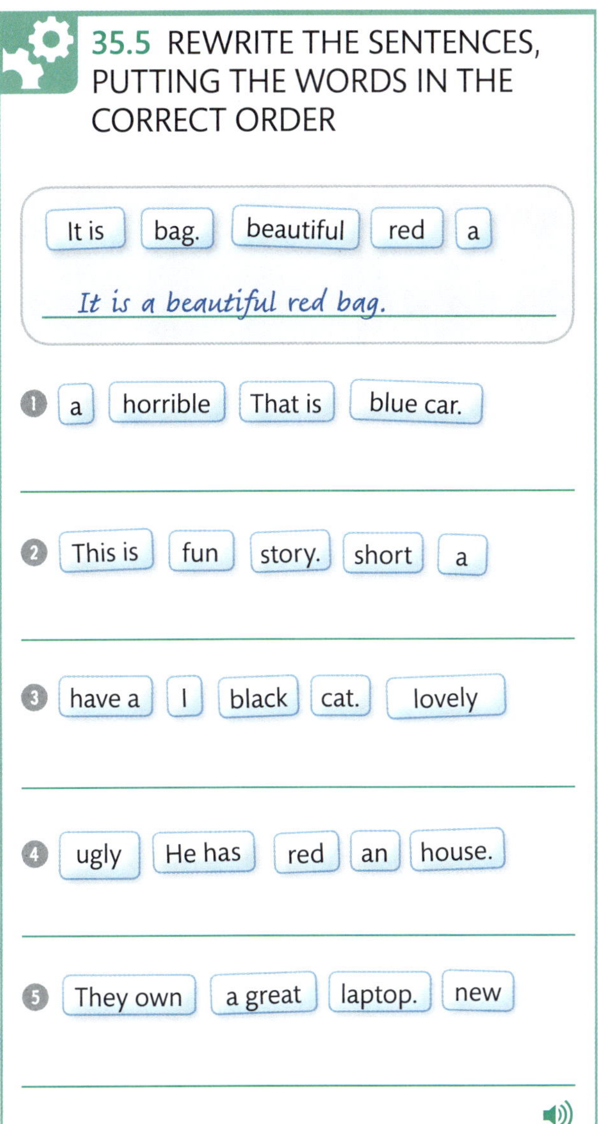

35.5 REWRITE THE SENTENCES, PUTTING THE WORDS IN THE CORRECT ORDER

It is | bag. | beautiful | red | a

It is a beautiful red bag.

1. a | horrible | That is | blue car.

2. This is | fun | story. | short | a

3. have a | I | black | cat. | lovely

4. ugly | He has | red | an | house.

5. They own | a great | laptop. | new

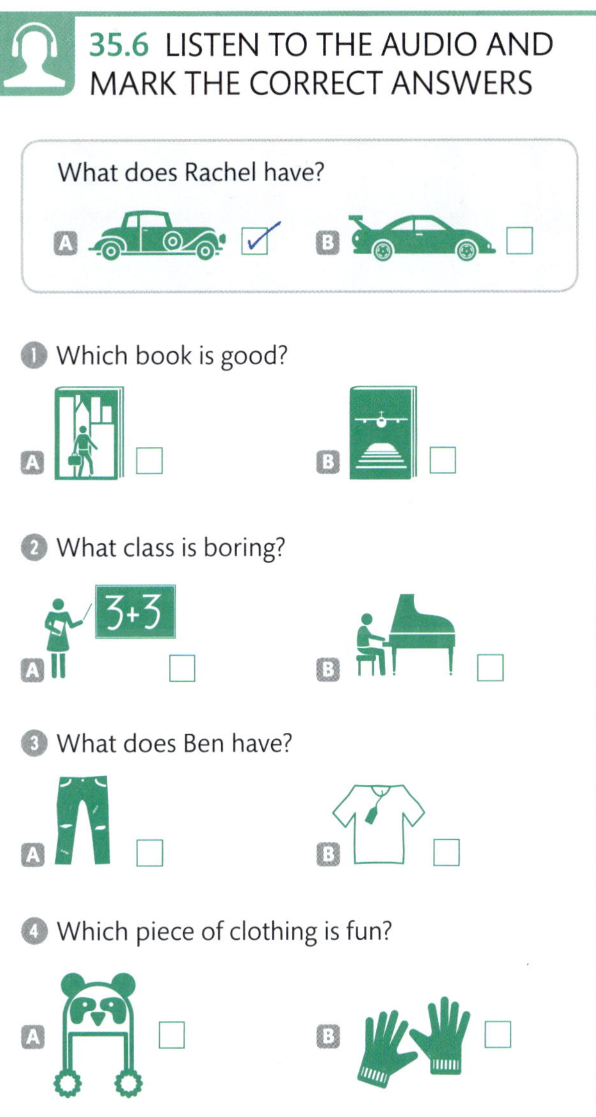

35.6 LISTEN TO THE AUDIO AND MARK THE CORRECT ANSWERS

What does Rachel have?

A ☑ B ☐

1. Which book is good?

A ☐ B ☐

2. What class is boring?

3+3

A ☐ B ☐

3. What does Ben have?

A ☐ B ☐

4. Which piece of clothing is fun?

A ☐ B ☐

35.7 VOCABULARY MATERIALS

Some words can be used both as nouns to name materials, and as adjectives to say what things are made of. Two of the nouns below change when they become adjectives: "wood" to "wooden", and "wool" to "woolen".

plastic ....

wood ....

glass ....

paper ....

wool ....

leather ....

metal ....

fabric ....

Aa 35.8 MATCH THE PICTURES TO THE CORRECT DESCRIPTIONS

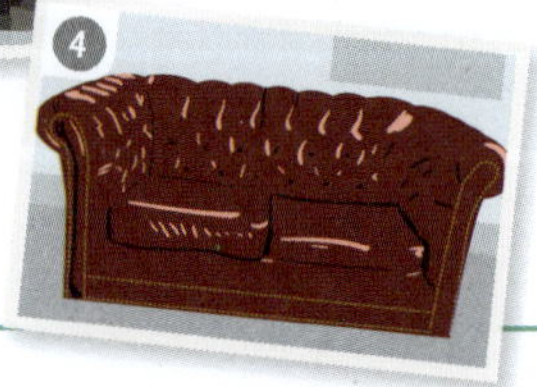

(Example: picture of table → This is a beautiful wooden table.)

1
2
3
4

Oh, no, the blue glass vase!

That's an expensive leather couch.

This is a beautiful wooden table.

What an interesting metal box!

We have two plastic chairs.

35.9 SAY THE SENTENCES OUT LOUD, CORRECTING THE WORD ORDER

We have lovely two purple couches.

We have two lovely purple couches.

1. She owns some wooden beautiful chairs.

2. We own don't those plastic plates horrible.

3. They have yellow an ugly car.

4. He wears a blue boring sweater.

5. She wants a metal lamp new.

6. He owns a fabric large bag.

7. Norah new a leather wants jacket.

35 CHECKLIST

Opinion adjectives ☐ **Aa** Shopping and materials ☐ Giving opinions ☐

REVIEW THE ENGLISH YOU HAVE LEARNED IN UNITS 28–35

NEW LANGUAGE	SAMPLE SENTENCE	☑	UNIT
USING "HAVE"	I have a garage. She has a yard. I do not have a bathtub.	☐	28.1, 28.6
ASKING "HAVE" QUESTIONS	Do you have a TV?	☐	29.1
COUNTABLE AND UNCOUNTABLE NOUNS	There are four eggs. There is some rice. Are there any eggs? Is there any rice?	☐	31.1, 31.4
USING "ENOUGH" AND "MANY"	We have enough eggs. We have too many eggs.	☐	32.1
SHOPPING VERBS	Ana owns a red hat. Luc sells old clothes. They want new shoes. The hat fits Jane.	☐	34.1
ADJECTIVE ORDER	This is a lovely green hat.	☐	35.1

36 Vocabulary

36.1 SPORTS

swimming

sailing

skateboarding

running

skiing

snowboarding

roller-skating

surfing

tennis

golf

badminton

baseball

basketball

soccer (US)
football (UK)

football (US)
American
football (UK)

rugby

volleyball

cycling

ice hockey

horse riding

36.2 EQUIPMENT

baseball bat

tennis racket

golf club

ball

skateboard

skis

surfboard

snowboard

36.3 VENUES

stadium

field (US)
pitch (UK)

tennis court

golf course

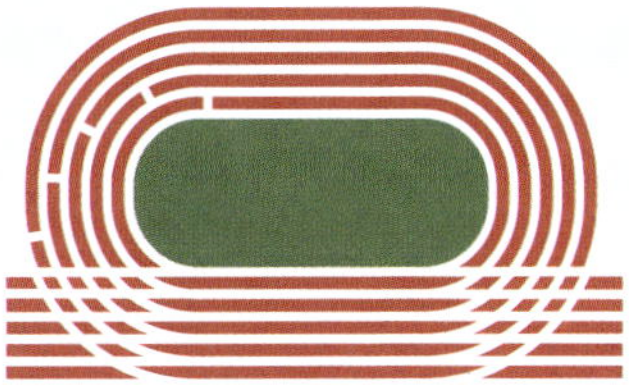

running track

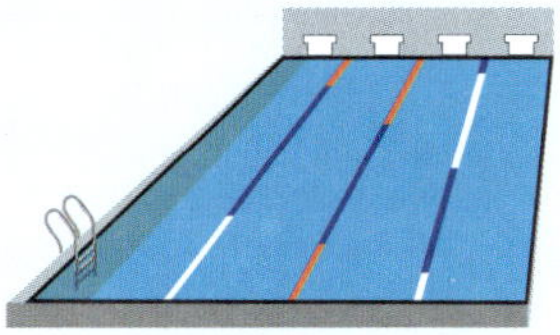

swimming pool

37 Talking about sports

To describe taking part in some sports, you use the verb "go" plus the gerund. For other sports, you use "play" plus the noun.

New language "Go" and "play"
Aa Vocabulary Sports
New skill Talking about sports

37.1 KEY LANGUAGE "GO" WITH A GERUND

You can make some verbs into nouns by adding "-ing" to their base forms. These are called gerunds.

"Go" changes with the subject.

She goes surfing on the weekend.

Add "-ing" to the base form of the verb.

37.2 FURTHER EXAMPLES "GO" WITH A GERUND

I go swimming once a week.

We don't go fishing at the lake.

He goes skateboarding twice a month.

He doesn't go cycling with his brothers.

Do they go dancing on Saturday nights?

Does she go sailing in the summer?

37.3 FILL IN THE GAPS TO COMPLETE THE SENTENCES

Tamara *goes* swimming in the sea.

1. We don't ______ surfing in the winter.
2. Do you ______ sailing on the weekend?
3. Tipo ______ cycling five times a week.
4. He ______ fishing on the river.
5. Sharon ______ dancing with her friend.
6. Do they ______ running every morning?
7. He doesn't ______ horse riding.

37.4 LISTEN TO THE AUDIO AND MATCH THE DAYS TO SAM'S SPORTS

1

2

3

4

Monday — Tuesday — Wednesday — Thursday — Friday

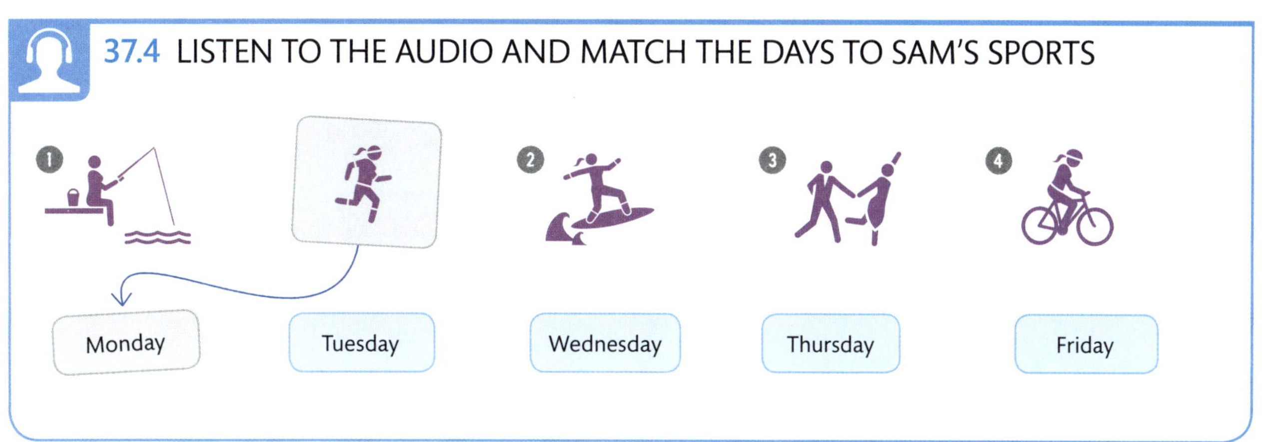

37.5 KEY LANGUAGE SPELLING GERUNDS

All gerunds end in "-ing" and are formed following these simple rules.

fish → go **fish**ing
For most verbs add "-ing."

For verbs that end in "e" delete the "e."
skate → go **skat**ing
Then add "-ing."

For single syllable verbs ending in a consonant + vowel + consonant...
swim → go **swim**ming
...double the final consonant and add "-ing."

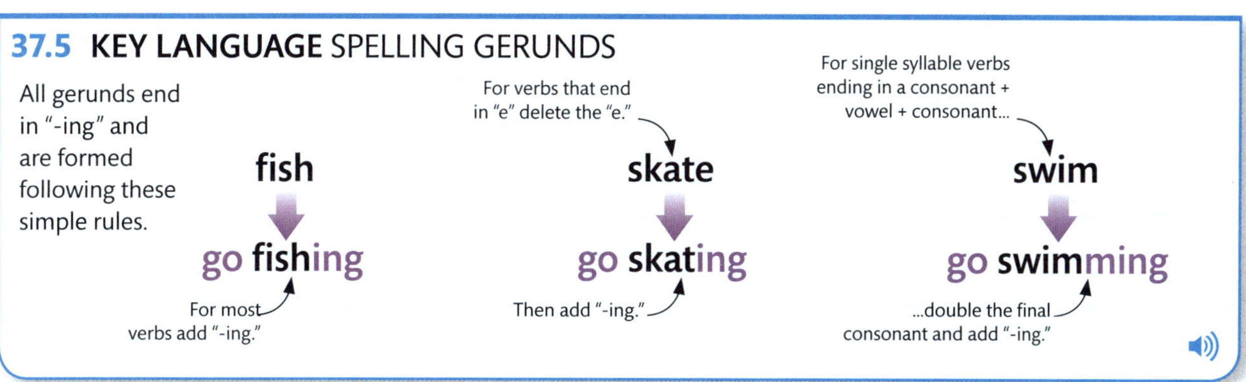

37.6 FIND NINE HIDDEN WORDS AND WRITE THEM IN THE CORRECT GROUP

G	L	G	P	A	O	Q	S	A	I	L	I	N	G	G	N	M	Y	L	F	I	C
M	F	S	K	A	T	I	N	G	O	F	I	F	N	B	Z	F	O	Y	W	M	Y
S	K	A	T	E	B	O	A	R	D	I	N	G	A	S	E	B	L	A	R	S	C
C	J	V	X	N	Y	A	S	N	O	W	B	O	A	R	D	I	N	G	F	L	L
A	L	M	H	J	H	I	B	I	S	H	O	R	S	E	R	I	D	I	N	G	I
W	V	S	Q	T	X	G	Z	X	G	N	S	R	U	N	N	I	N	G	O	B	N
Q	R	B	U	K	C	S	W	I	M	M	I	N	G	K	G	U	D	Q	S	S	G
S	H	O	P	P	I	N	G	X	B	A	C	Z	W	O	V	M	D	F	P	I	Y

REGULAR GERUNDS:

1. sailing
2. ______
3. ______

GERUNDS WITH DOUBLE CONSONANTS:

1. ______
2. ______
3. ______

GERUNDS WITH DROPPED "E":

1. ______
2. ______
3. ______

37.7 KEY LANGUAGE "PLAY" WITH A NOUN

For some sports, especially ball games and competitions, you use "play" with the noun.

"Play" changes, depending on the subject.

The noun is placed after the verb.

They play tennis on Sundays.

37.8 FURTHER EXAMPLES "PLAY" WITH A NOUN

I don't play tennis in winter.

Sala plays golf on Tuesday mornings.

He plays baseball for the town.

Do Ben and Si play chess together?

Does Dani play hockey on Mondays?

We don't play badminton any more.

37.9 CROSS OUT THE INCORRECT WORD IN EACH SENTENCE

I ~~plays~~ / play football in the park.

1. Shala don't / doesn't play tennis.
2. Mina plays / play golf at the club.
3. We plays / play squash on Mondays.
4. The dog plays / play with its ball.
5. Maria don't / doesn't play tennis.
6. The kids don't / doesn't play games at school.
7. They play / plays soccer at the park.

37.10 REWRITE THE SENTENCES, CORRECTING THE ERRORS

He don't play hockey in the summer.
He doesn't play hockey in the summer.

1. We plays tennis every Tuesday night.
2. They doesn't play golf during the week.
3. You doesn't play volleyball at the beach.
4. Do they plays together every Saturday?

37.11 READ THE ARTICLE AND ANSWER THE QUESTIONS

Who plays squash on Mondays and Fridays?
James ☑ Sara ☐ Chas ☐ Cassie ☐

1. Who plays golf?
James ☐ Sara ☐ Chas ☐ Cassie ☐

2. Who goes running in the park?
James ☐ Sara ☐ Chas ☐ Cassie ☐

3. Who goes swimming on Thursdays?
James ☐ Sara ☐ Chas ☐ Cassie ☐

4. Who plays badminton?
James ☐ Sara ☐ Chas ☐ Cassie ☐

YOUR SPORTS

Littleton's Sports Scene

Some local residents tell us about their sports routines

I go to Belgrade Sports. It's a great place to exercise. I play squash on Mondays and Fridays.
JAMES

I love Highfields Sports. I go swimming five days a week, from Monday to Friday. I play golf on Saturdays and I play tennis on Sundays. I really like it there!
SARA

Lots of my friends go to the park and some of them play football there. I go running there. It's great.
CHAS

I like badminton and skating. I can do both at Littleton Sports. I go swimming there on Tuesdays and Fridays because there's a nice pool, and I play football on Wednesdays.
CASSIE

37.12 SAY THE SENTENCES OUT LOUD, USING "GO" OR "PLAY" AND THE CORRECT FORMS OF THE VERBS IN BRACKETS

I *go dancing* (dance) with my friends on Mondays.

1. Milo and I ______________ (cycle) in the park on Saturdays.

2. The team ______________ (football) from 6pm to 7pm on Wednesdays.

3. Imelda ______________ (horse ride) once a month.

4. Luther ______________ (fish) during his vacation time.

5. Hannah ______________ (tennis) with her cousin on Monday evenings.

37 CHECKLIST

"Go" and "play" ☐ **Aa** Sports ☐ Talking about sports ☐

38 Vocabulary

38.1 HOBBIES AND PASTIMES

do puzzles

play cards

play chess

play board games

play computer games / play video games

read

draw

write

paint

take photos

play a musical instrument

walk / hike

cook

bake

sew

knit

watch television

watch a movie (US)
watch a film (UK)

see a play

play sport /
do exercise

go to the gym

do yoga

listen to music

go camping

go bird watching

go out for a meal

do the gardening

visit a museum /
art gallery

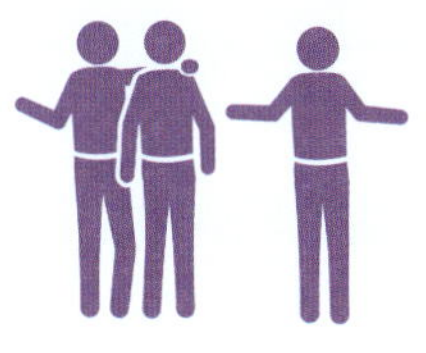

meet friends

go on vacation (US)
go on holiday (UK)

go sightseeing

go shopping

39 Free time

Adverbs of frequency show how often you do something, from something you do very frequently ("always") to something you don't do at all ("never").

New language Adverbs of frequency
Aa Vocabulary Pastimes
New skill Talking about your free time

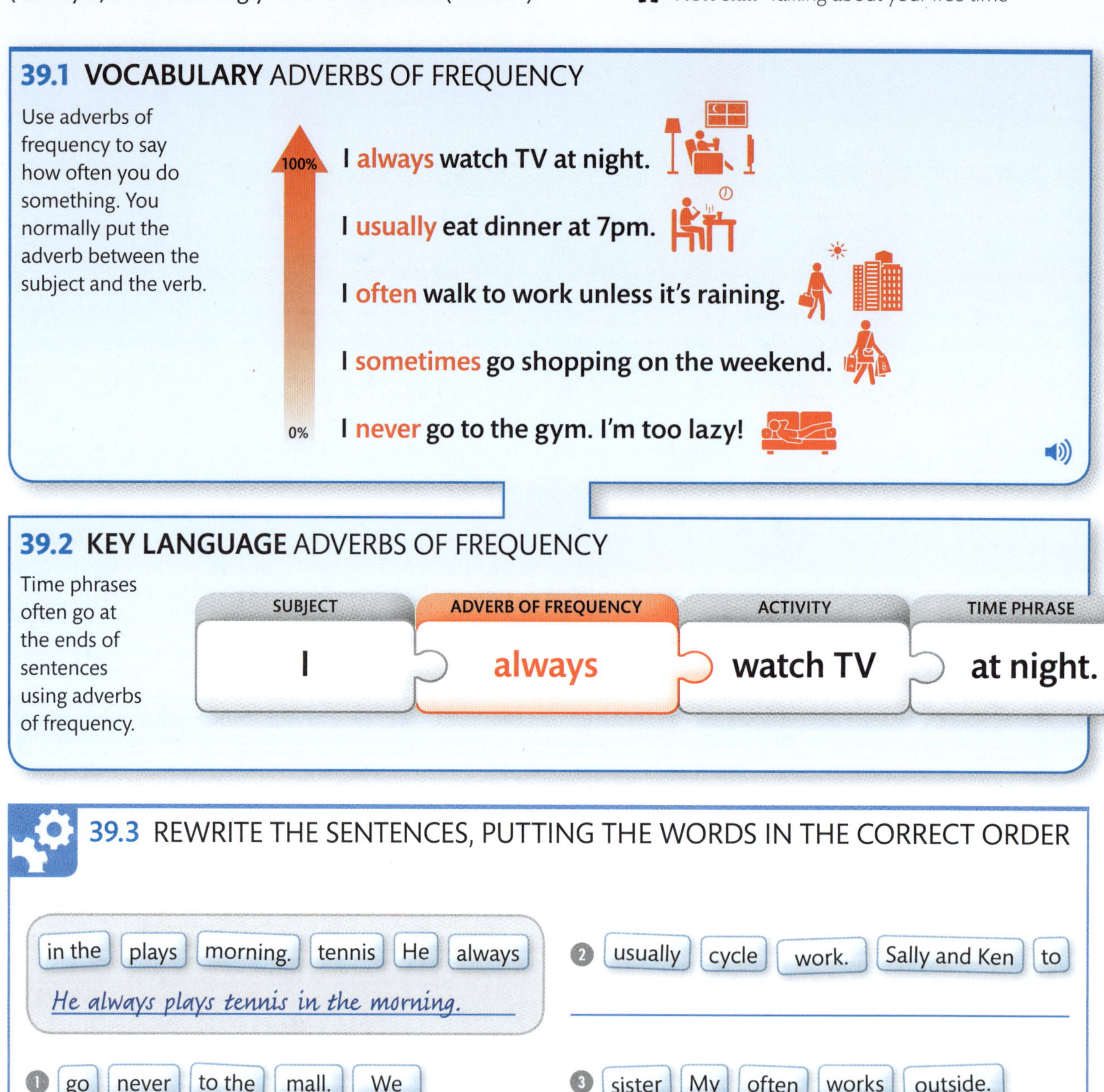

39.1 VOCABULARY ADVERBS OF FREQUENCY

Use adverbs of frequency to say how often you do something. You normally put the adverb between the subject and the verb.

100%

I **always** watch TV at night.

I **usually** eat dinner at 7pm.

I **often** walk to work unless it's raining.

I **sometimes** go shopping on the weekend.

I **never** go to the gym. I'm too lazy!

0%

39.2 KEY LANGUAGE ADVERBS OF FREQUENCY

Time phrases often go at the ends of sentences using adverbs of frequency.

SUBJECT	ADVERB OF FREQUENCY	ACTIVITY	TIME PHRASE
I	always	watch TV	at night.

39.3 REWRITE THE SENTENCES, PUTTING THE WORDS IN THE CORRECT ORDER

in the | plays | morning. | tennis | He | always

He always plays tennis in the morning.

1. go | never | to the | mall. | We

____

2. usually | cycle | work. | Sally and Ken | to

____

3. sister | My | often | works | outside.

____

39.4 LISTEN TO THE AUDIO AND MATCH THE PASTIME TO ITS FREQUENCY

Ben is taking part in a survey about how he spends his free time. Listen to his answers.

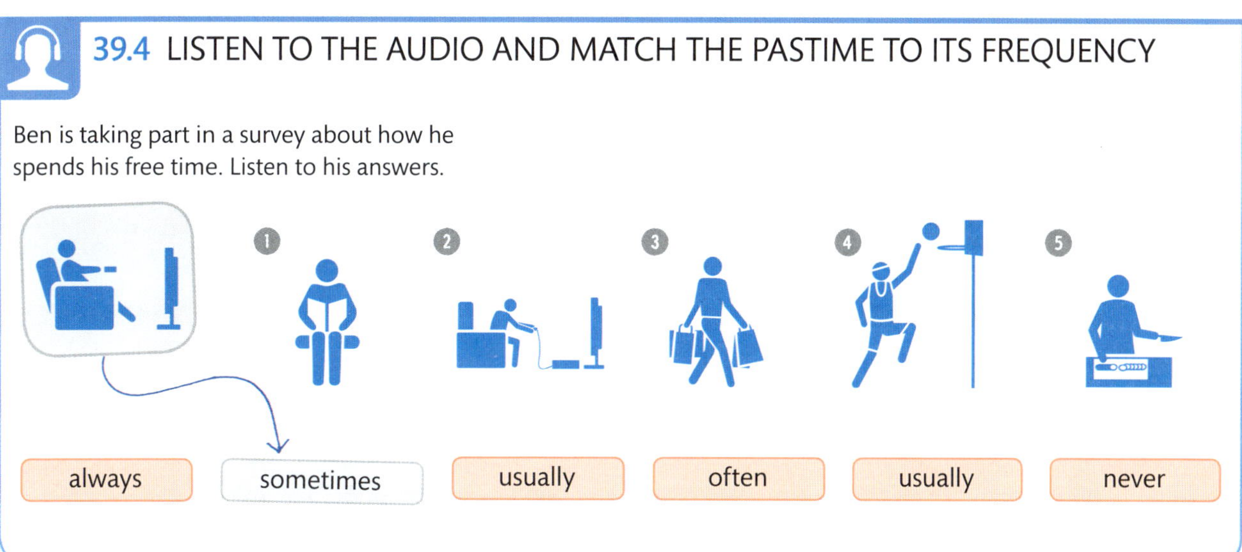

39.5 LOOK AT THE TABLE AND SAY THE SENTENCES OUT LOUD, FILLING IN THE GAPS

	ALWAYS	USUALLY	OFTEN	SOMETIMES	NEVER
SIMON	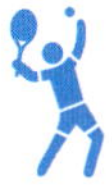			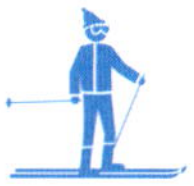	
NICO		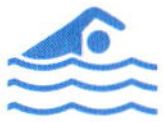			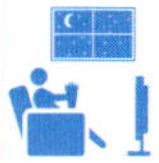
MEG			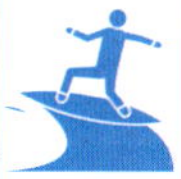	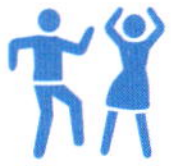	
ALMA	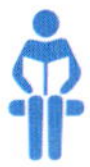			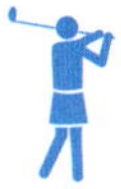	
CARRIE		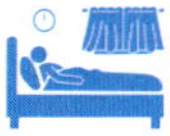			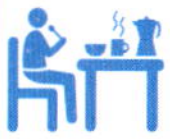

Simon *always* plays tennis on Fridays.
He *sometimes* goes skiing in the winter.

1. Nico ______________ swims after work.
   He ______________ watches TV on the weekend.

2. Meg ______________ goes surfing in Hawaii.
   She ______________ dances all night.

3. Alma ______________ reads on vacation.
   She ______________ plays golf on Sundays.

4. Carrie ______________ goes to bed late and
   she ______________ eats breakfast.

39.6 HOW TO FORM QUESTIONS ABOUT FREE TIME

Use different phrases to ask about the frequency with which someone does an activity and the specific time that they do something.

Use "how often" to ask about frequency.

How often do you go on vacation?

I usually go on vacation once a year.

Use "when" to ask about the day or time.

When do you go running?

I go on Thursday nights.

39.7 FURTHER EXAMPLES QUESTIONS ABOUT FREE TIME

How often do you go to the beach?

Not very often.

When do you go to the gym?

On Tuesdays and Fridays.

39.8 MARK THE CORRECT QUESTION FOR EACH ANSWER

About twice a week.
- [x] **How often** does Jack go running?
- [ ] **When** does Jack go running?

1. Five times a week.
   - [ ] **How often** do they go to work?
   - [ ] **When** do they go to work?

2. At 7:30am.
   - [ ] **How often** do you get up?
   - [ ] **When** do you get up?

3. About twice a year.
   - [ ] **How often** do you go on vacation?
   - [ ] **When** do you go on vacation?

4. At 7pm.
   - [ ] **How often** do they go shopping?
   - [ ] **When** do they go shopping?

5. Once a month.
   - [ ] **How often** do you visit Mischa?
   - [ ] **When** do you visit Mischa?

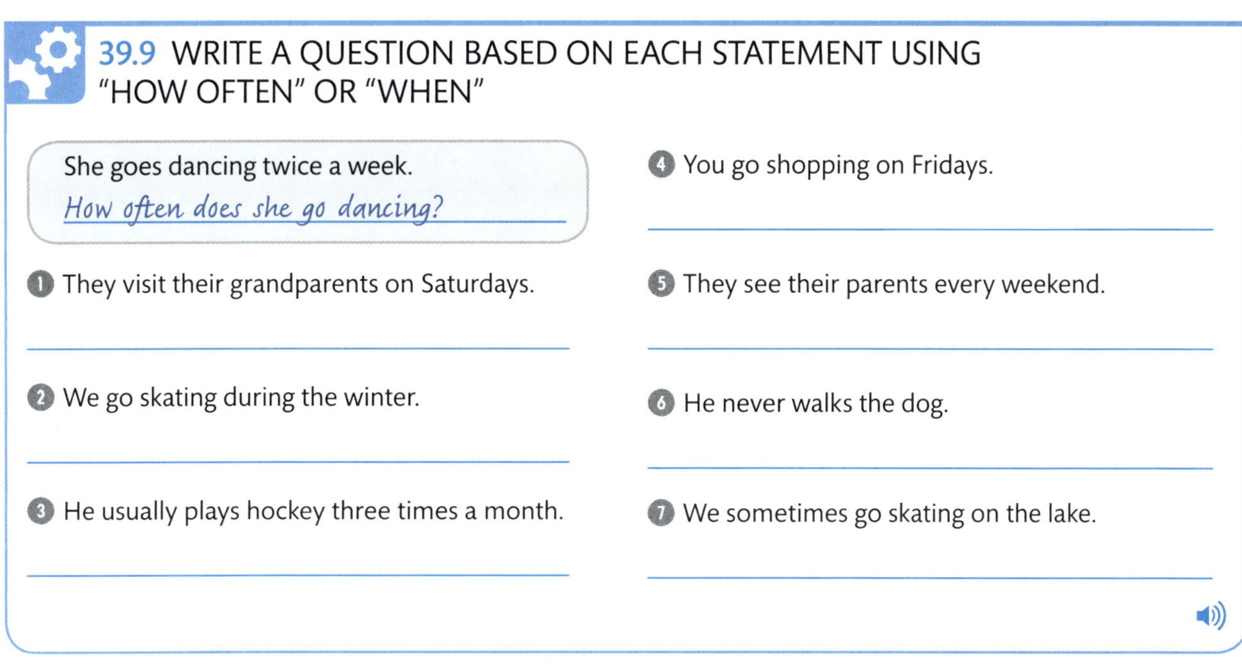

39.9 WRITE A QUESTION BASED ON EACH STATEMENT USING "HOW OFTEN" OR "WHEN"

She goes dancing twice a week.
How often does she go dancing?

1. They visit their grandparents on Saturdays.
2. We go skating during the winter.
3. He usually plays hockey three times a month.
4. You go shopping on Fridays.
5. They see their parents every weekend.
6. He never walks the dog.
7. We sometimes go skating on the lake.

39.10 SAY QUESTIONS OUT LOUD BASED ON THE STATEMENTS

How often do you listen to music?
I listen to music every night.

1. I do yoga on Monday nights.
2. I sometimes go to the movies.
3. I go skateboarding three times a month.
4. I arrive at work at 8am.
5. I usually go surfing once a week.

39 CHECKLIST

Adverbs of frequency ☐ **Aa** Pastimes ☐ Talking about your free time ☐

40 Likes and dislikes

Verbs such as "love," "like," and "hate" express your feelings about things. You can use these verbs with nouns or gerunds.

New language "Love," "like," and "hate"
Aa Vocabulary Food, sports, and pastimes
New skill Talking about what you like

40.1 KEY LANGUAGE LIKES AND DISLIKES WITH NOUNS

You can use these verbs to talk about nouns.

She likes tennis.

Use "do not" or "don't" and "does not" or "doesn't" to make negative statements.

Max doesn't like pizza.

I love chocolate.

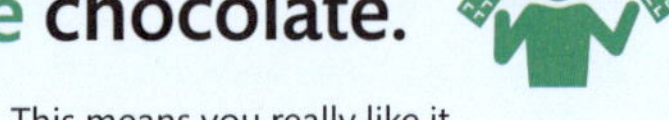

This means you really like it.

They hate coffee.

This is stronger than "don't like."

TIP
"Don't like" means "dislike," but people use "don't like" more often in spoken English.

40.2 FURTHER EXAMPLES LIKES AND DISLIKES WITH NOUNS

I love fries.

You don't like baseball.

The cat doesn't like its food.

Oliver hates board games.

40.3 MATCH THE PICTURES TO THE CORRECT SENTENCES

Shania hates mice.

Sam doesn't like TV.

Ava and Elsa love the mountains.

Cats don't like the rain.

Manuel likes his book.

40.4 WRITE THE NEGATIVE OF EACH SENTENCE USING "DOESN'T" OR "DON'T"

Jack likes London. — *Jack doesn't like London.*

1. Imelda hates pasta. ______
2. My dog loves steak. ______
3. Our grandfather likes coffee. ______
4. I love the sea. ______
5. Sam and Jen hate hockey. ______
6. You like the countryside. ______
7. We like our new cell phones. ______

40.5 LISTEN TO THE AUDIO AND MARK THE CORRECT ANSWERS

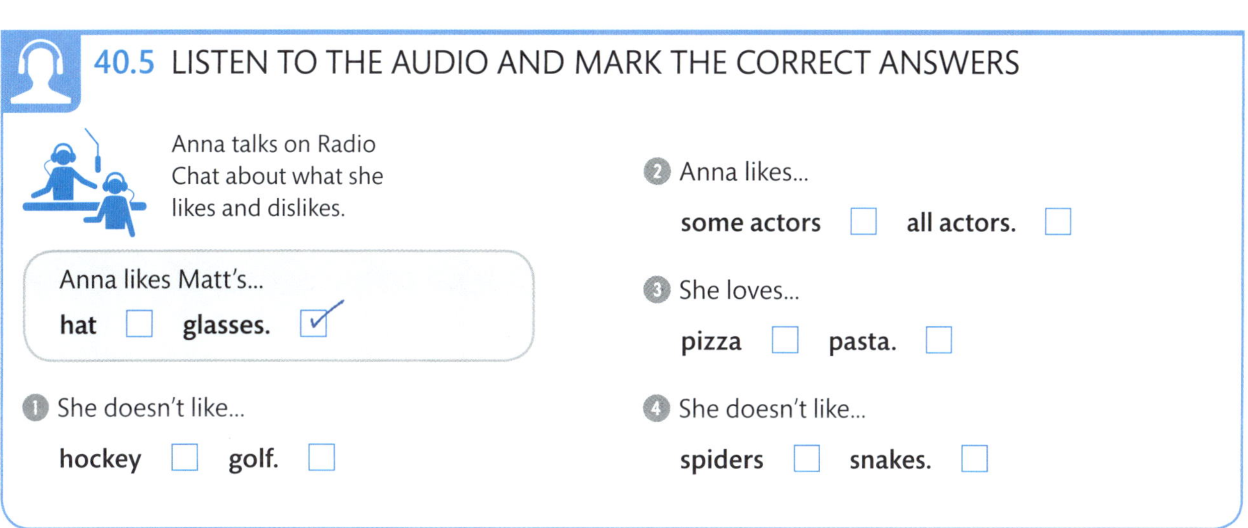

Anna talks on Radio Chat about what she likes and dislikes.

Anna likes Matt's...
hat ☐ **glasses.** ☑

1. She doesn't like...
hockey ☐ **golf.** ☐

2. Anna likes...
some actors ☐ **all actors.** ☐

3. She loves...
pizza ☐ **pasta.** ☐

4. She doesn't like...
spiders ☐ **snakes.** ☐

40.6 USE THE CHART TO CREATE NINE CORRECT SENTENCES AND SAY THEM OUT LOUD

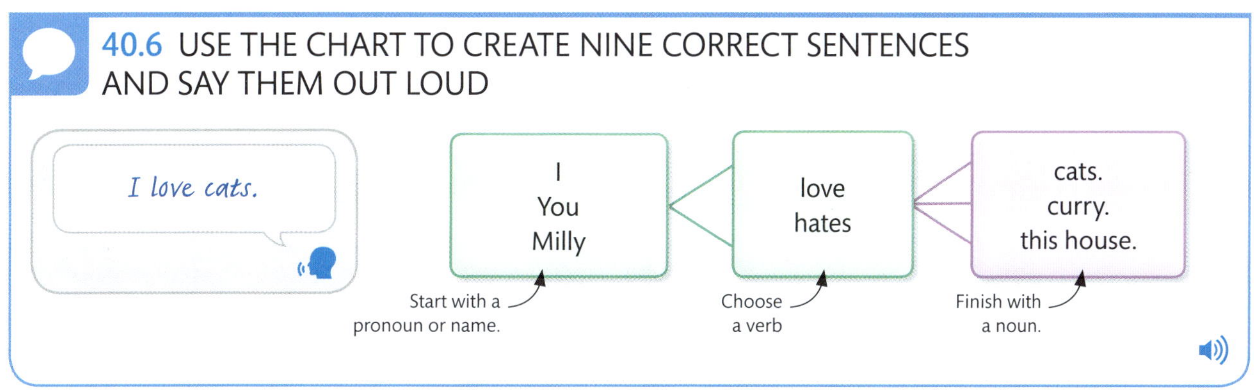

40.7 KEY LANGUAGE LIKES AND DISLIKES WITH GERUNDS

You can use verbs such as "like" and "hate" with gerunds to talk about activities.

They like **playing chess.** 

Ed doesn't like **cycling.** 

I love **swimming.** 

She hates **shopping.** 

40.8 FURTHER EXAMPLES LIKES AND DISLIKES WITH GERUNDS

Vi and Lu love **playing golf.** 

I don't like **working late.** 

Elliot loves **watching birds.** 

You like **drinking coffee.** 

40.9 LISTEN TO THE AUDIO AND MATCH THE LIKES AND DISLIKES WITH THE CORRECT ACTIVITIES

Jill loves... → [walking the dog]

1. Samuel hates...
2. Josh loves...
3. Davina doesn't like...
4. Daniella likes...

A

B

C

D

40.10 READ THE ARTICLE AND ANSWER THE QUESTIONS

48 OLDTON NEWS

CLUBS AND SOCIETIES

An Oldton student tells us about some local clubs

I am Mark Watson and I'm at Oldton University. This is the first week of classes and students are trying lots of activities. This is what I think of them…

Chocolate Club: Do you like chocolate? Well, the people in this club love it! I don't like chocolate, so this club is not for me. They make chocolate cakes and chocolate drinks.

Dancing Club: My girlfriend loves this club. She goes twice a week. It is great exercise, but I hate it because I am very clumsy.

Computer Gaming Club: I love playing computer games at home. I really like playing with other people, too, so I like this club. There are lots of players there every week.

Chess Club: I love playing chess. I go to this club because it's a lot of fun. The players are very good, so I don't win very often. It makes me a better player.

Skateboarding Club: This is a fantastic club where you can learn from great skateboarders. This club meets three times a week and it's a great place to make new friends. I love it!

Mark loves chocolate.
True ☐ False ☑

1. People make cakes at Chocolate Club.
True ☐ False ☐

2. Mark's girlfriend hates dancing.
True ☐ False ☐

3. Mark likes dancing.
True ☐ False ☐

4. He loves computer games.
True ☐ False ☐

5. He doesn't like the chess club.
True ☐ False ☐

6. The players are very good.
True ☐ False ☐

7. Skateboarding Club is horrible.
True ☐ False ☐

8. Skateboarding Club meets three times a week.
True ☐ False ☐

9. Mark loves three of the clubs.
True ☐ False ☐

40.11 VOCABULARY REASONS FOR LIKES AND DISLIKES

You can use these adjectives to talk about why you like something.

40.12 KEY LANGUAGE "DO" QUESTIONS ABOUT LIKES AND DISLIKES

Use "do" or "does" to ask if someone likes something.

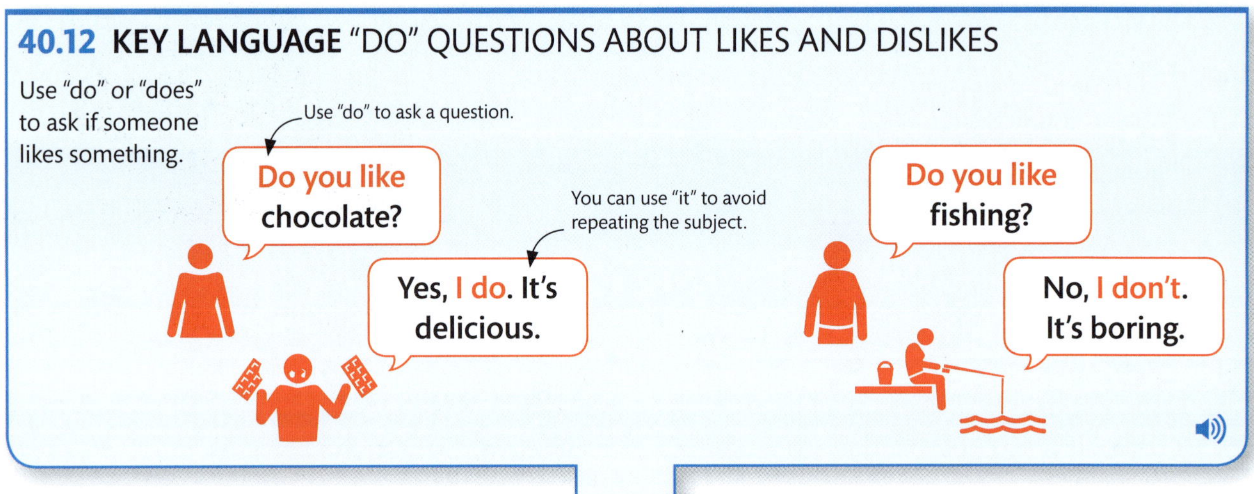

40.13 KEY LANGUAGE "WHY" QUESTIONS ABOUT LIKES AND DISLIKES

You can use "why" to find out the reasons why someone likes or dislikes something.

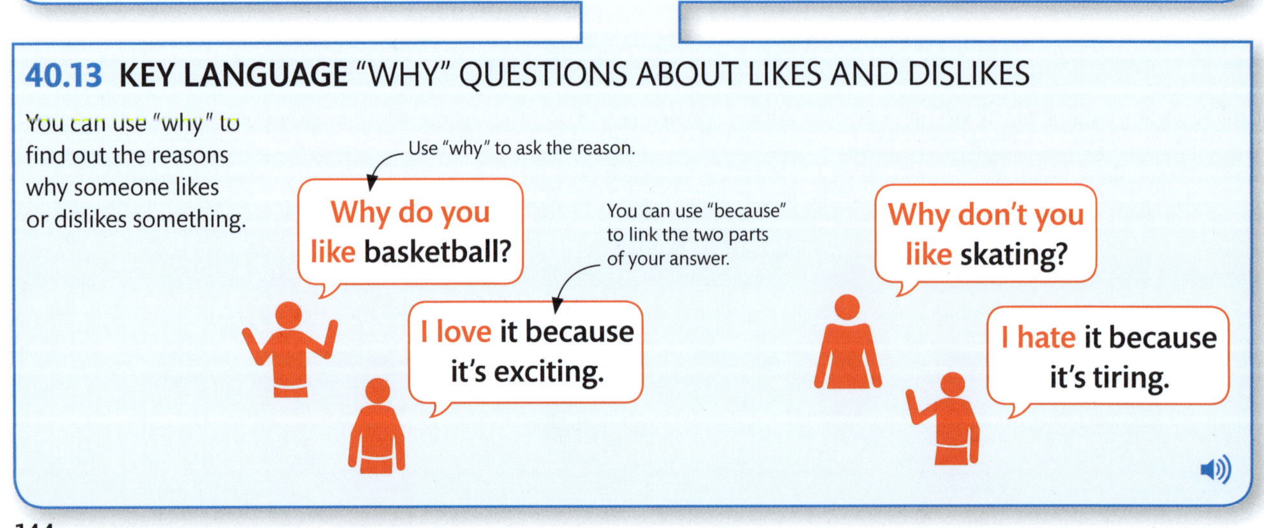

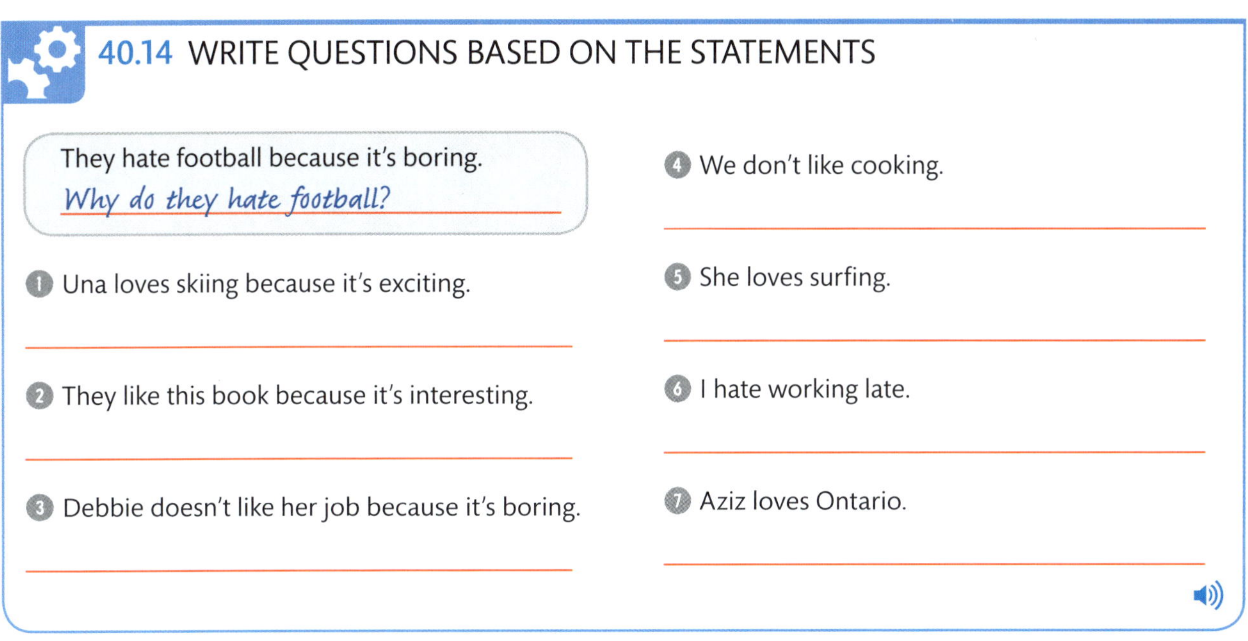

40.14 WRITE QUESTIONS BASED ON THE STATEMENTS

They hate football because it's boring.
Why do they hate football?

1. Una loves skiing because it's exciting.
____
2. They like this book because it's interesting.
____
3. Debbie doesn't like her job because it's boring.
____
4. We don't like cooking.
____
5. She loves surfing.
____
6. I hate working late.
____
7. Aziz loves Ontario.
____

40.15 ANSWER THE QUESTIONS OUT LOUD, USING THE WORDS IN THE PANEL

Why do they like pasta?
They like pasta because *it's delicious*.

1. Why do you like English class?
I like English class because ____________.
2. Why do you love skating?
We love skating because ____________.
3. Why does Luca hate cleaning?
He hates cleaning because ____________.

it's exciting
~~it's delicious~~
it's boring
it's interesting

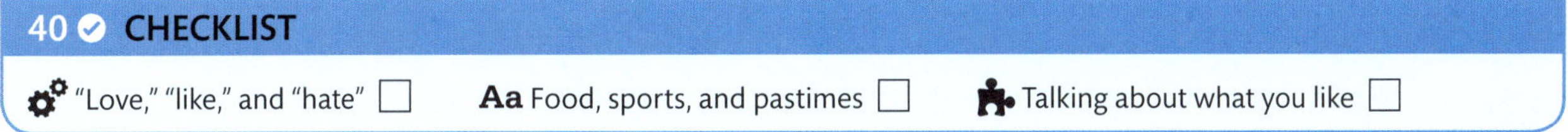

40 CHECKLIST

"Love," "like," and "hate" ☐ Aa Food, sports, and pastimes ☐ Talking about what you like ☐

41 Vocabulary

41.1 MUSIC

classical music

hip-hop

jazz

country

opera

soul

rap

rock

pop

Latin

orchestra

band /group

play the trumpet

guitar player

concert

festival

sing a song

singer

headphones

album

dance

microphone

conductor

audience

41.2 MUSICAL INSTRUMENTS

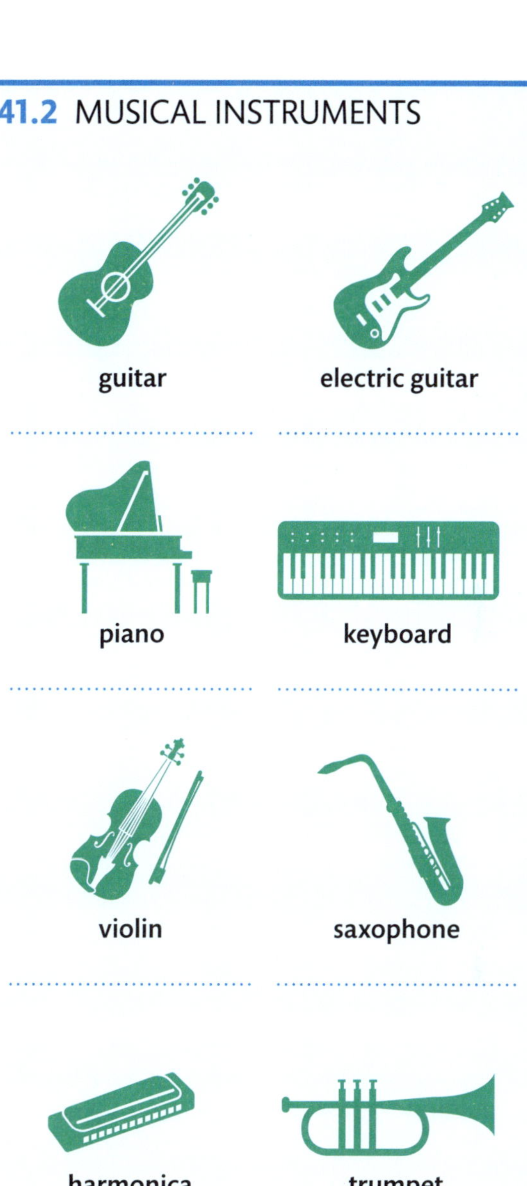

guitar

electric guitar

piano

keyboard

violin

saxophone

harmonica

trumpet

drum

flute

42 Expressing preference

You use "like" and "love" to show how much you enjoy something. "Favorite" is used to identify the thing you love most in a group.

New language Using "favorite"
Aa Vocabulary Food and music
New skill Talking about your favorite things

42.1 KEY LANGUAGE USING "FAVORITE"

"Like" and "love" are verbs, so they need subjects and objects. "Favorite" is an adjective, so it is always paired with a noun or gerund.

I like jazz and I love soul, but my favorite type of music is rock.

Remember, this verb is stronger than "like."

This shows you like this thing the most.

"Favorite" can be followed by a noun or the phrase "type of" and a noun.

42.2 FURTHER EXAMPLES USING "FAVORITE"

She likes salsa dancing.

Abdul loves sailing.

Her favorite type of food is Italian.

"Italian" is not a particular food, but a "type of" food.

Basketball is his favourite sport.

The UK spelling is "favourite".

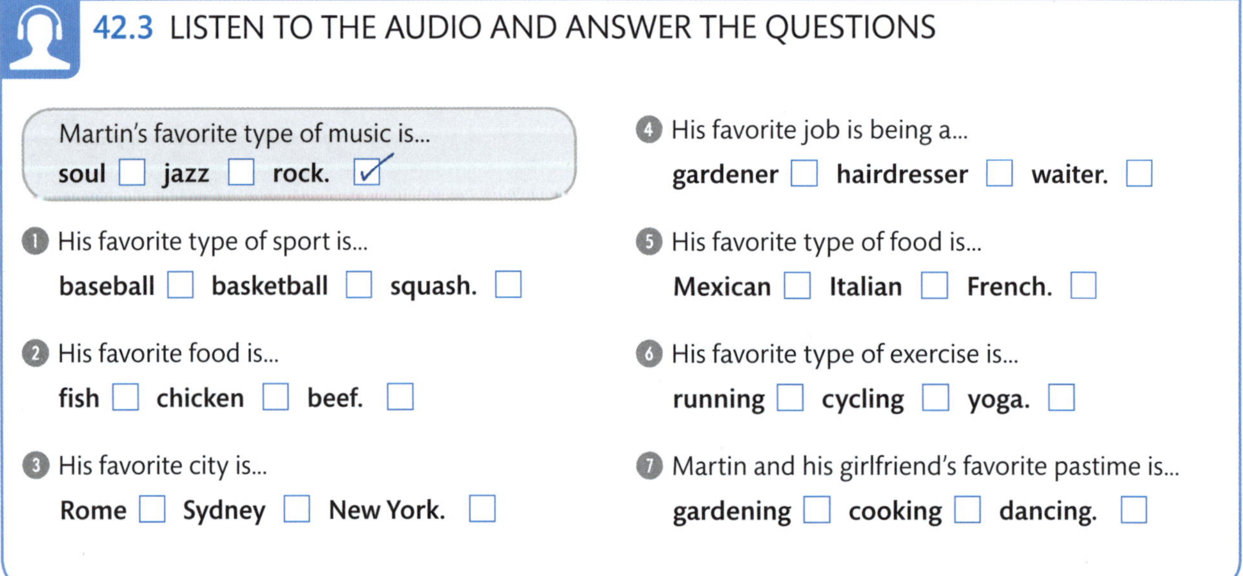

42.3 LISTEN TO THE AUDIO AND ANSWER THE QUESTIONS

Martin's favorite type of music is...
soul ☐ **jazz** ☐ **rock.** ☑

1. His favorite type of sport is...
baseball ☐ **basketball** ☐ **squash.** ☐

2. His favorite food is...
fish ☐ **chicken** ☐ **beef.** ☐

3. His favorite city is...
Rome ☐ **Sydney** ☐ **New York.** ☐

4. His favorite job is being a...
gardener ☐ **hairdresser** ☐ **waiter.** ☐

5. His favorite type of food is...
Mexican ☐ **Italian** ☐ **French.** ☐

6. His favorite type of exercise is...
running ☐ **cycling** ☐ **yoga.** ☐

7. Martin and his girlfriend's favorite pastime is...
gardening ☐ **cooking** ☐ **dancing.** ☐

Aa 42.4 MARK THE PICTURE THAT MATCHES EACH STATEMENT

Jack's **favorite** music is jazz.

A ☐ B ☑ C ☐

3 Aman's **favorite** sport is hockey.

A ☐ B ☐ C ☐

1 Ava's **favorite** thing is her new dress.

A ☐ B ☐ C ☐

4 Mo and Jamie's **favorite** food is chocolate.

A ☐ B ☐ C ☐

2 Deborah's **favorite** pet is her dog.

A ☐ B ☐ C ☐

5 Atif's **favorite** city is New York.

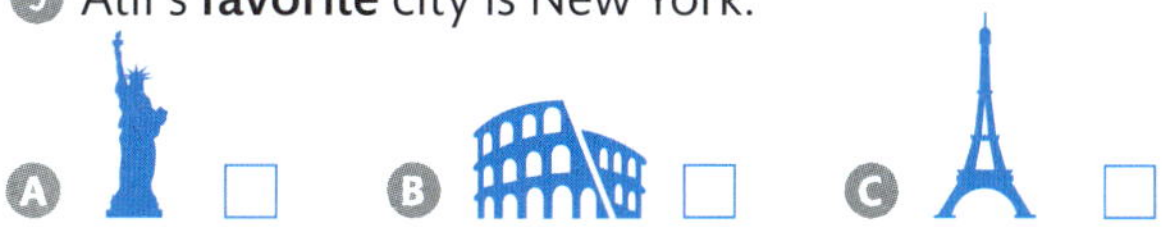

A ☐ B ☐ C ☐

Aa 42.5 FILL IN THE GAPS USING THE WORDS IN THE PANEL

Dana's favorite type of music is *opera*.

1 Grace's favorite food is ______________.

2 Poppy's favorite sport is ______________.

3 Dylan's favorite animal is his ______________.

4 Justin's favorite country is ______________.

5 Ling's favorite pastime is ______________.

6 Abdul's favorite color is ______________.

7 Mira's favorite number is ______________.

8 Jacob's favorite sweater is ______________.

9 Tori's favorite relative is her ______________.

surfing ~~opera~~ cousin horse pizza 10 Australia knitting purple woolen

42.6 LOOK AT THESE ONLINE PROFILES, THEN FILL IN THE GAPS AND SAY THE SENTENCES OUT LOUD

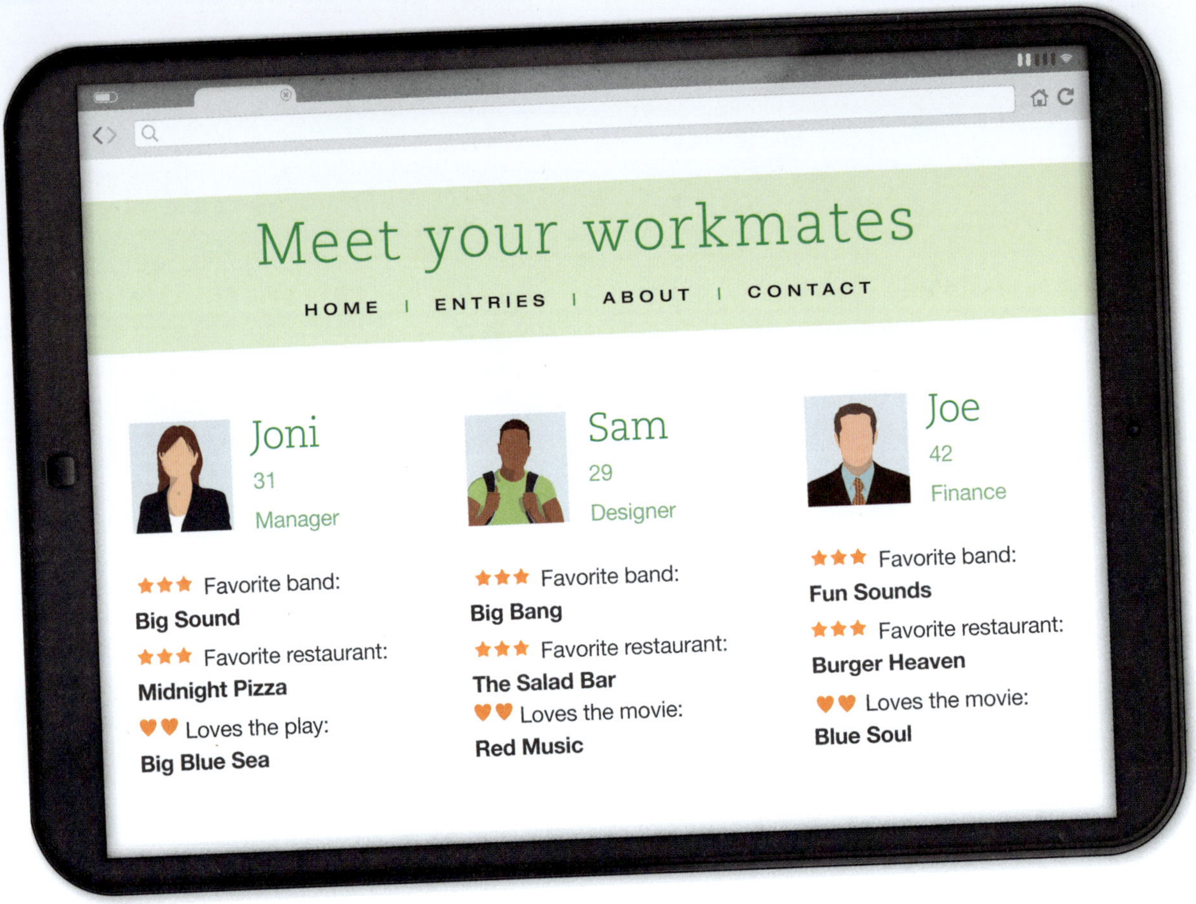

Meet your workmates

HOME | ENTRIES | ABOUT | CONTACT

Joni
31
Manager

Favorite band:
Big Sound
Favorite restaurant:
Midnight Pizza
Loves the play:
Big Blue Sea

Sam
29
Designer

Favorite band:
Big Bang
Favorite restaurant:
The Salad Bar
Loves the movie:
Red Music

Joe
42
Finance

Favorite band:
Fun Sounds
Favorite restaurant:
Burger Heaven
Loves the movie:
Blue Soul

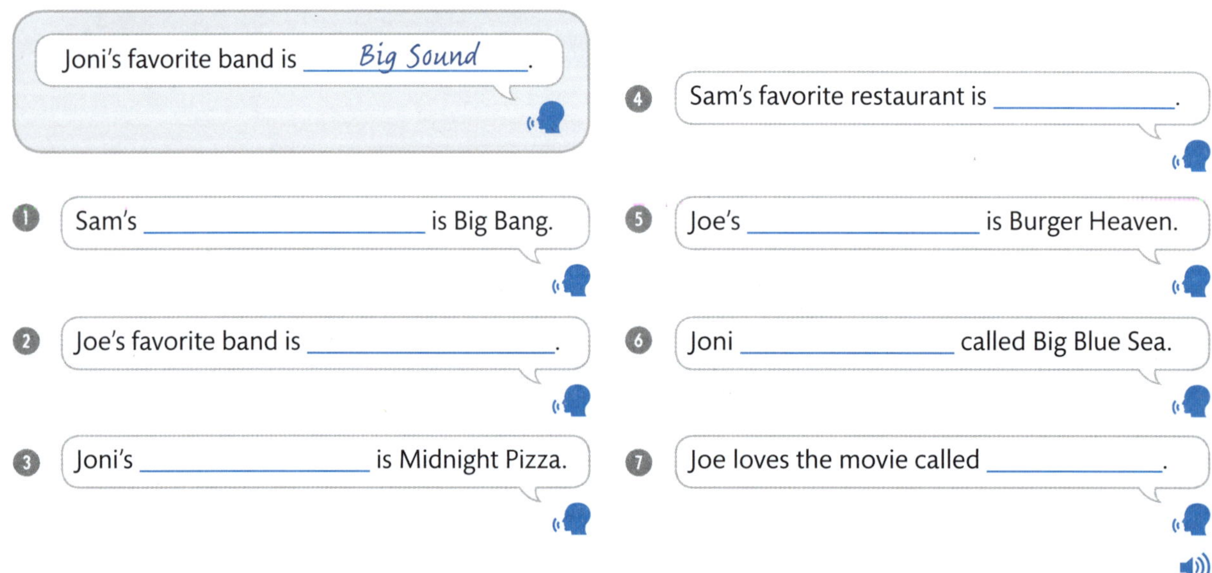

Joni's favorite band is *Big Sound*.

1. Sam's __________ is Big Bang.
2. Joe's favorite band is __________.
3. Joni's __________ is Midnight Pizza.
4. Sam's favorite restaurant is __________.
5. Joe's __________ is Burger Heaven.
6. Joni __________ called Big Blue Sea.
7. Joe loves the movie called __________.

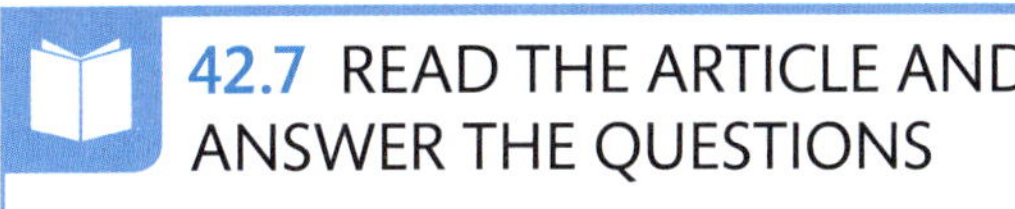

42.7 READ THE ARTICLE AND ANSWER THE QUESTIONS

What is the favorite time to exercise?
morning ☑ **afternoon** ☐ **evening** ☐

1. What type of exercise is their favorite?
   yoga ☐ **running** ☐ **swimming** ☐

2. What is Stanton people's favorite type of food?
   pizza ☐ **burgers** ☐ **ice cream** ☐

3. What is their favorite sport?
   golf ☐ **football** ☐ **surfing** ☐

4. Their favorite night out is going to...
   the movies ☐ **the theater** ☐ **a restaurant.** ☐

STANTON REVIEW

Town favorites

What's your favorite time to exercise? The morning, the afternoon, or the evening? In Stanton, people say it's the morning because there are too many other things to do in the evening. The favorite exercise is yoga: 20 classes take place each week.

Stanton townspeople like food. They eat lots of it: 4,000,000 burgers, 2,000,000 pizzas, and 3,000,000 ice cream cones every year.

And how about sports? In Stanton, there are hundreds of golfers and football players, but the favorite sport is surfing.

People like going out in the evening. Many love movies and the theater, but that's not their favorite night out. It's dinner in a restaurant. Food again. That's not a surprise!

42 ✓ CHECKLIST

Using "favorite" ☐ **Aa** Food and music ☐ Talking about your favorite things ☐

REVIEW THE ENGLISH YOU HAVE LEARNED IN UNITS 37–42

NEW LANGUAGE	SAMPLE SENTENCE	☑	UNIT
"GO" WITH GERUNDS, "PLAY" WITH NOUNS	I go swimming on Mondays and I play tennis with my brother on Fridays.	☐	37.1, 37.7
ADVERBS OF FREQUENCY	I always watch TV at night, and I sometimes go the the movies.	☐	39.1
QUESTIONS ABOUT FREE TIME	How often do you go on vacation? When does she go running?	☐	39.6
LIKES AND DISLIKES	She likes tennis. Max doesn't like pizza. I love swimming. She hates shopping.	☐	40.1, 40.7
QUESTIONS ABOUT LIKES AND DISLIKES	Do you like chocolate? Why do you like basketball?	☐	40.12, 40.13
USING "FAVORITE"	My favorite type of music is rock.	☐	42.1

43 Vocabulary

43.1 ABILITIES

jump

climb

fly

ride

drive

play

kick

throw

hit

catch

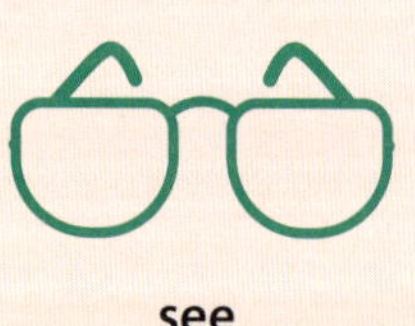
see

listen

whisper

talk

speak

shout

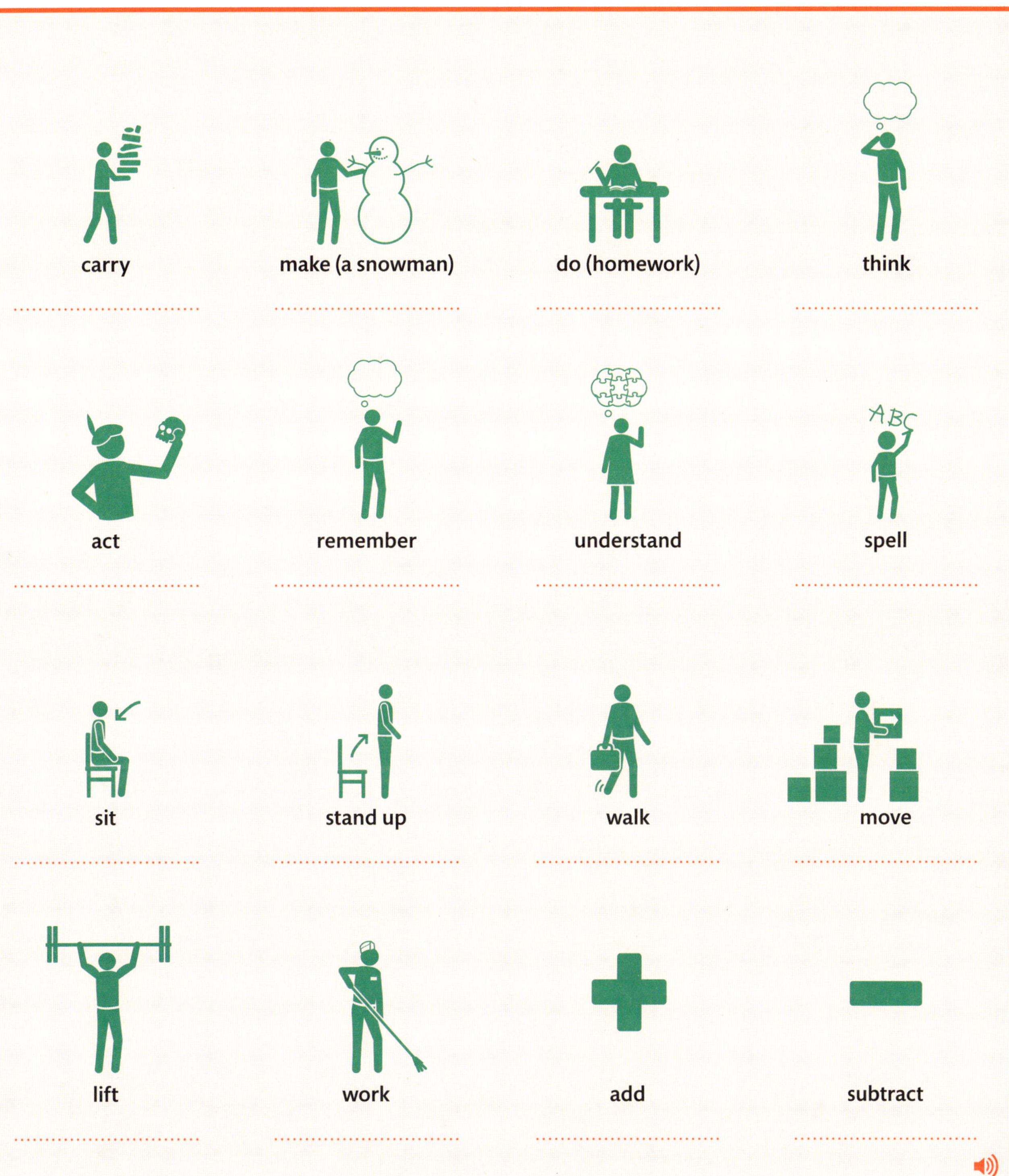

ABC
carry
make (a snowman)
do (homework)
think
act
remember
understand
spell
sit
stand up
walk
move
lift
work
add
subtract

44 What you can and can't do

Use "can" to talk about the things you are able to do, such as ride a bicycle or play the guitar. Use "cannot" or "can't" for things you are not able to do.

New language "Can," "can't," and "cannot"
Aa Vocabulary Talents and abilities
New skill Saying what you can and can't do

44.1 KEY LANGUAGE "CAN / CANNOT / CAN'T"

"Can" goes between the subject and the verb. The verb after "can" changes to its base form (the infinitive without "to").

I can ride a bicycle.

Base form of verb.

He can play the guitar.

"Can" is always the same. It doesn't change with the subject.

I {cannot / can't} sing jazz songs.

Short form of "cannot."

TIP
The long negative form "cannot" is always spelled as one word, not two words.

44.2 FURTHER EXAMPLES "CAN / CANNOT / CAN'T"

Janet can play tennis.

He cannot climb the tree.

Bob can swim well.

They can't lift the box.

44.3 HOW TO FORM "CAN / CANNOT / CAN'T"

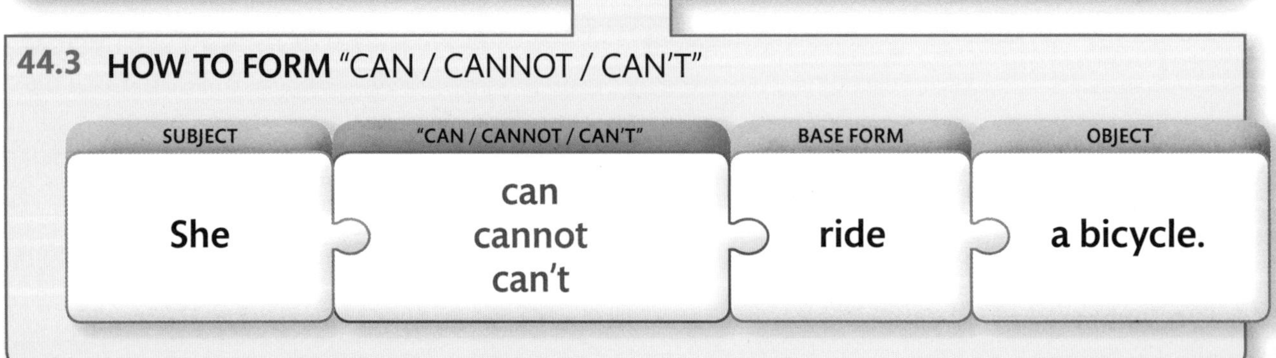

SUBJECT	"CAN / CANNOT / CAN'T"	BASE FORM	OBJECT
She	can cannot can't	ride	a bicycle.

44.4 REWRITE THE SENTENCES, PUTTING THE WORDS IN THE CORRECT ORDER

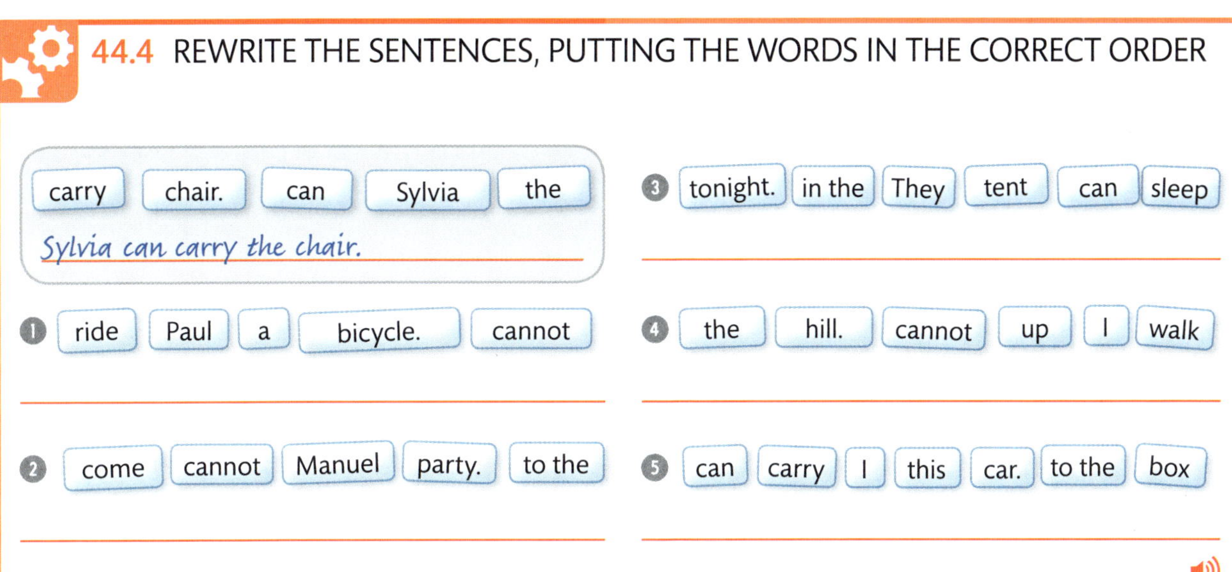

carry | chair. | can | Sylvia | the

Sylvia can carry the chair.

1. ride | Paul | a | bicycle. | cannot

2. come | cannot | Manuel | party. | to the

3. tonight. | in the | They | tent | can | sleep

4. the | hill. | cannot | up | I | walk

5. can | carry | I | this | car. | to the | box

44.5 CROSS OUT THE INCORRECT WORD IN EACH SENTENCE

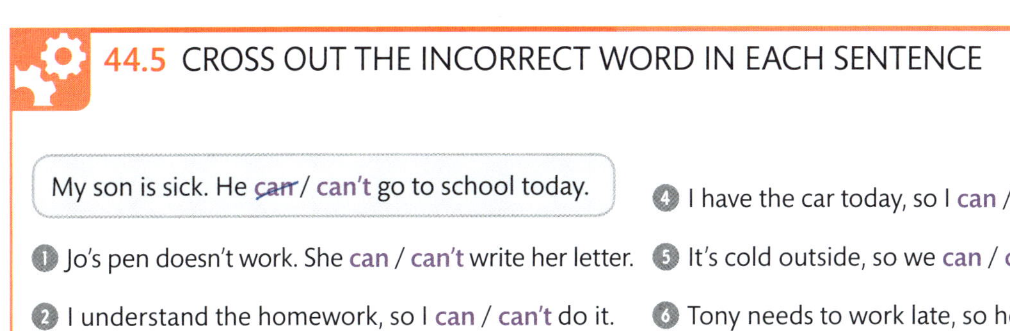

My son is sick. He ~~can~~ / can't go to school today.

1. Jo's pen doesn't work. She can / can't write her letter.
2. I understand the homework, so I can / can't do it.
3. The museum is closed. We can / can't get in.
4. I have the car today, so I can / can't drive you.
5. It's cold outside, so we can / can't have a picnic.
6. Tony needs to work late, so he can / can't come.
7. We can / can't play tennis. It's too dark.

44.6 FILL IN THE GAPS TO WRITE EACH SENTENCE THREE DIFFERENT WAYS

	I can read Russian.	*I cannot read Russian.*	*I can't read Russian.*
1		Shirley cannot drive a car.	
2	Ben and Julie can carry boxes.		
3			Ilaria can't spell English words.
4		He cannot go to work.	

44.7 KEY LANGUAGE QUESTIONS AND SHORT ANSWERS

To make a question using "can," put "can" before the subject. When you answer "can" questions, you don't need to repeat all the words from the question.

Can you ride a bicycle?

Yes, I can.

No, I can't.

44.8 FURTHER EXAMPLES QUESTIONS AND SHORT ANSWERS

Can she speak Japanese?

Yes, she can.

Can we climb that mountain?

No, we can't.

Can they swim?

No, they can't.

Can you move that chair?

Yes, I can.

44.9 SAY THE SENTENCES OUT LOUD, FILLING IN THE GAPS

Can you lift that heavy box?

Yes, *I can.*

1. Can he play the piano?

   No, ____________

2. Can they catch that big fish?

   Yes, ____________

3. Can you hit that ball over there?

   No, ____________

4. Can you spell "excited?"

   Yes, ____________

5. Can we lift this big table?

   No, ____________

6. Can she fly a kite in this weather?

   Yes, ____________

7. Can they cycle into town?

   No, ____________

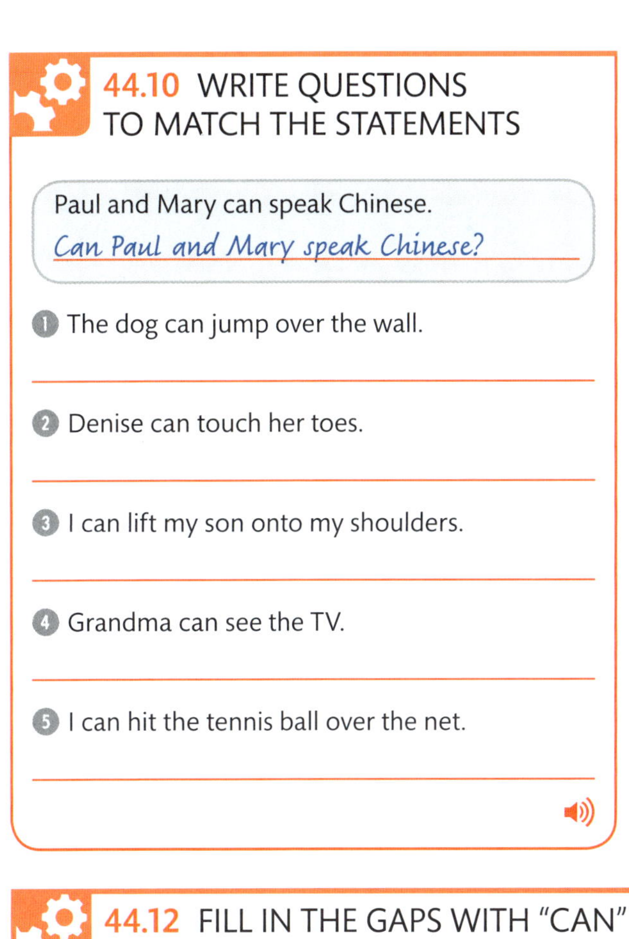

44.10 WRITE QUESTIONS TO MATCH THE STATEMENTS

Paul and Mary can speak Chinese.
Can Paul and Mary speak Chinese?

1. The dog can jump over the wall.
2. Denise can touch her toes.
3. I can lift my son onto my shoulders.
4. Grandma can see the TV.
5. I can hit the tennis ball over the net.

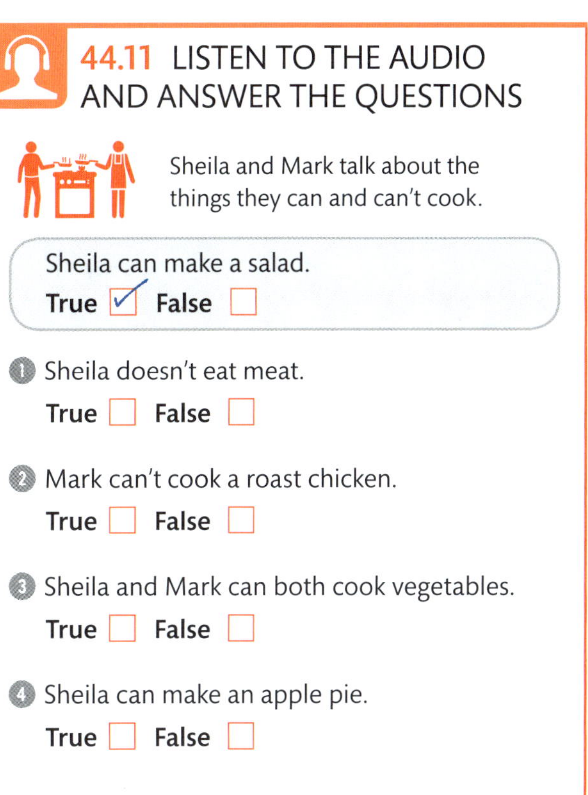

44.11 LISTEN TO THE AUDIO AND ANSWER THE QUESTIONS

Sheila and Mark talk about the things they can and can't cook.

Sheila can make a salad.
True ☑ **False** ☐

1. Sheila doesn't eat meat.
   True ☐ **False** ☐
2. Mark can't cook a roast chicken.
   True ☐ **False** ☐
3. Sheila and Mark can both cook vegetables.
   True ☐ **False** ☐
4. Sheila can make an apple pie.
   True ☐ **False** ☐

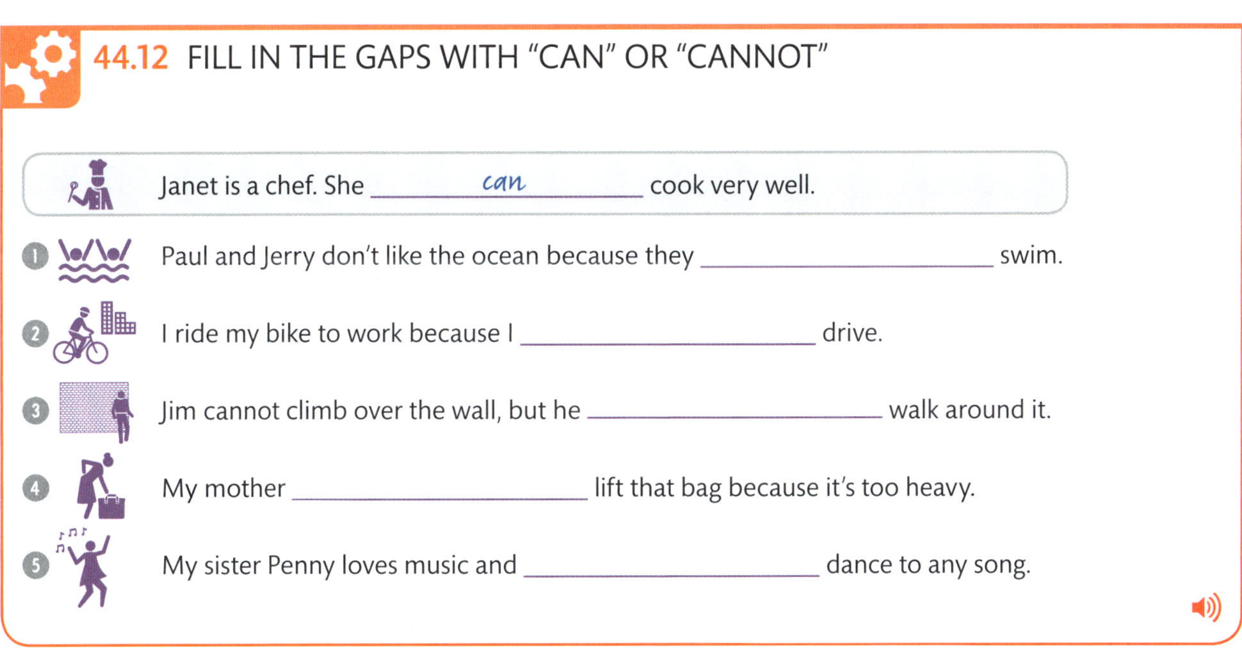

44.12 FILL IN THE GAPS WITH "CAN" OR "CANNOT"

Janet is a chef. She *can* cook very well.

1. Paul and Jerry don't like the ocean because they ______ swim.
2. I ride my bike to work because I ______ drive.
3. Jim cannot climb over the wall, but he ______ walk around it.
4. My mother ______ lift that bag because it's too heavy.
5. My sister Penny loves music and ______ dance to any song.

44 CHECKLIST

"Can," "can't," and "cannot" ☐ **Aa** Talents and abilities ☐ Saying what you can and can't do ☐

45 Describing actions

Words such as "quietly" and "loudly" are called adverbs. They give more information about verbs, so you can use them to describe how you do something.

New language Regular and irregular adverbs
Vocabulary Hobbies and activities
New skill Describing activities

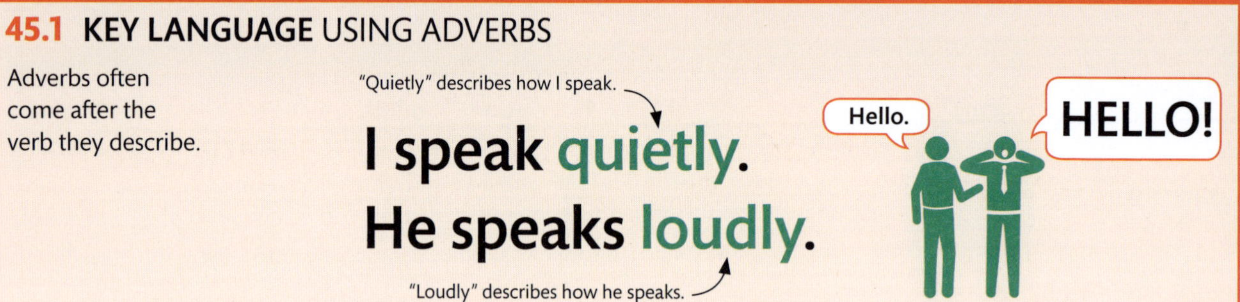

45.1 KEY LANGUAGE USING ADVERBS

Adverbs often come after the verb they describe.

"Quietly" describes how I speak.

I speak quietly.

He speaks loudly.

"Loudly" describes how he speaks.

45.2 FURTHER EXAMPLES USING ADVERBS

A tortoise moves slowly.

Horses can run quickly.

She sings beautifully.

I can play the piano badly.

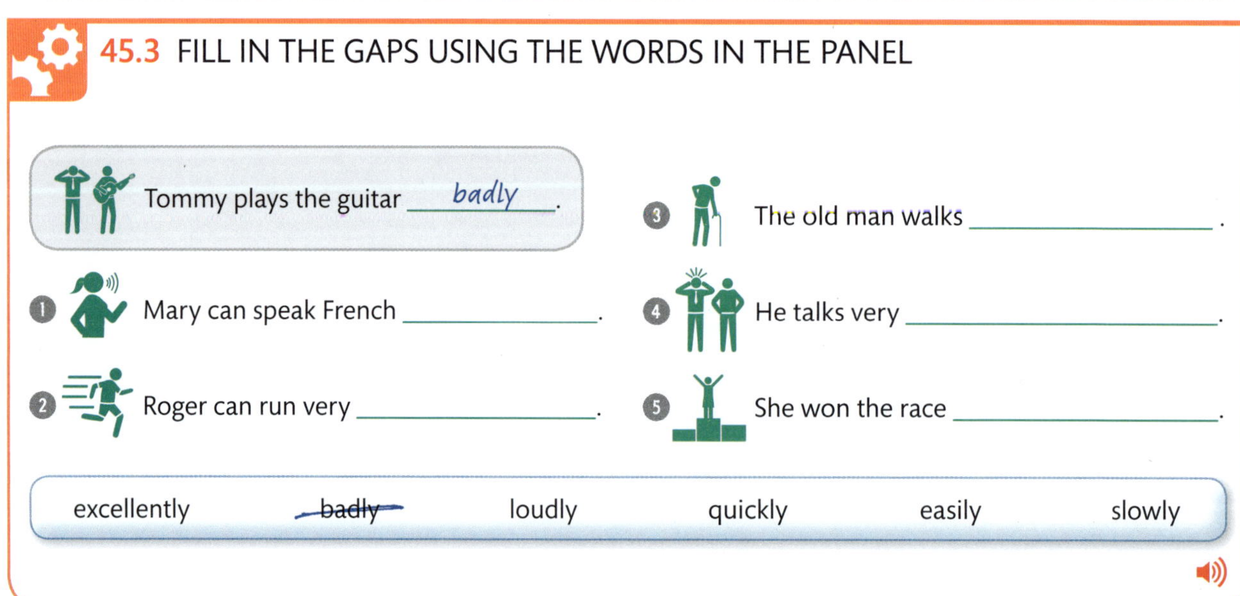

45.3 FILL IN THE GAPS USING THE WORDS IN THE PANEL

Tommy plays the guitar *badly*.

1. Mary can speak French ______.
2. Roger can run very ______.
3. The old man walks ______.
4. He talks very ______.
5. She won the race ______.

excellently | ~~badly~~ | loudly | quickly | easily | slowly

45.4 KEY LANGUAGE REGULAR AND IRREGULAR ADVERBS

REGULAR ADVERBS

To make most adverbs, just add "-ly" to the adjective. If the adjective ends in "y," leave out the "y" and add "-ily" to make the adverb.

bad → badly

careful → carefully

easy → easily

Drop the "y" and add "-ily."

IRREGULAR ADVERBS

Some adverbs are totally different to the adjective. Others are the same. These are called irregular adverbs.

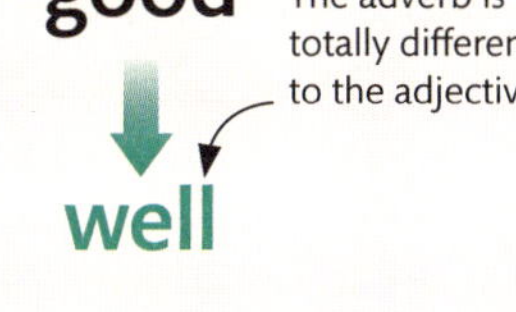

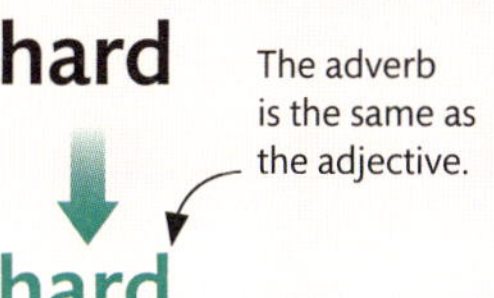

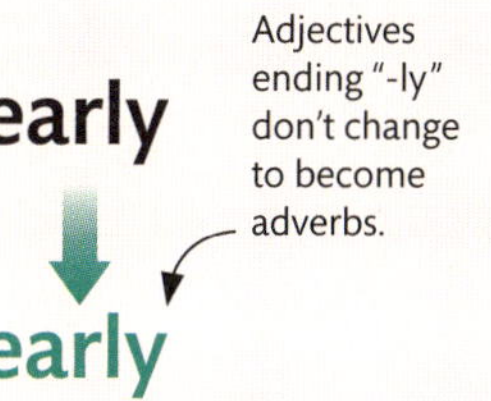

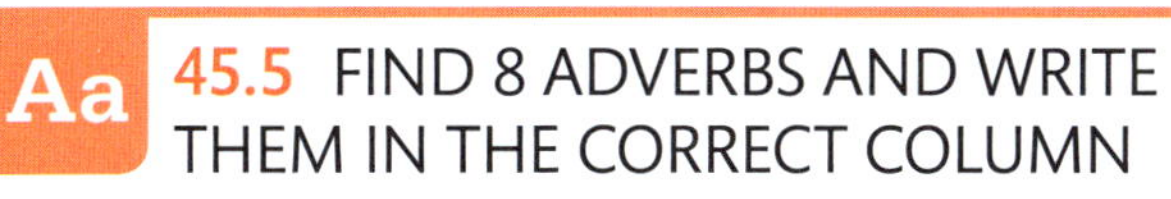

45.5 FIND 8 ADVERBS AND WRITE THEM IN THE CORRECT COLUMN

E A S I L Y W L K Q G
B N O Y U T E O A U R
A J S L O X L S G I W
D F L O U D L Y T C E
L F H A B L W H F K M
Y A G A R U E A R L Y
C S F U S Y Q R V Y W
I T R S L K A D B M S

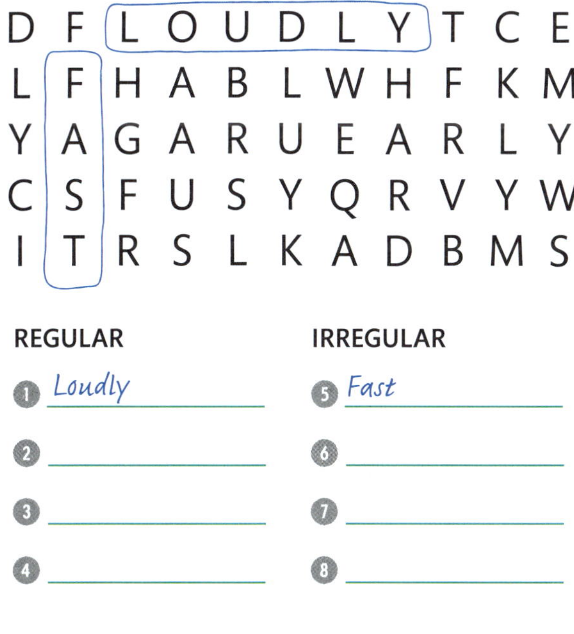

REGULAR	IRREGULAR
1 *Loudly*	5 *Fast*
2	6
3	7
4	8

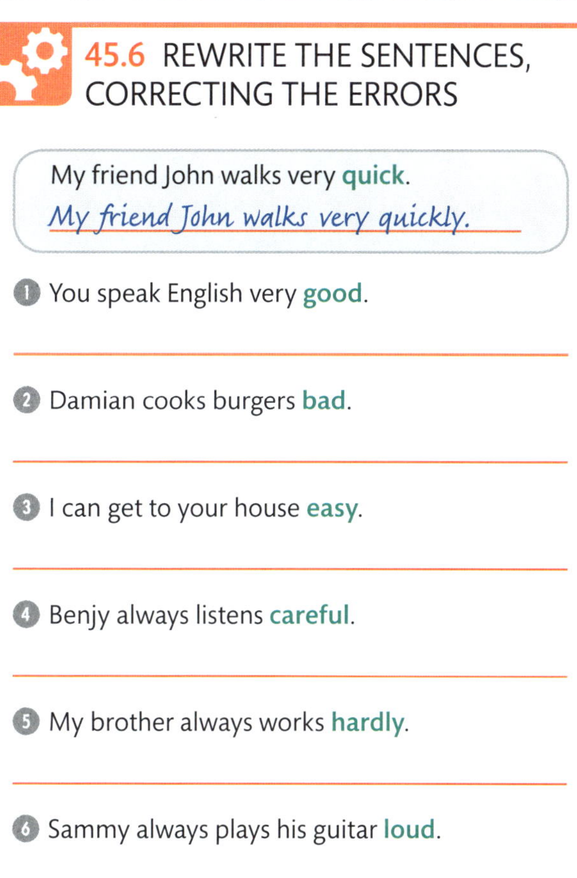

45.6 REWRITE THE SENTENCES, CORRECTING THE ERRORS

My friend John walks very quick.
My friend John walks very quickly.

1. You speak English very good.

2. Damian cooks burgers bad.

3. I can get to your house easy.

4. Benjy always listens careful.

5. My brother always works hardly.

6. Sammy always plays his guitar loud.

45.7 ANOTHER WAY TO SAY I DO SOMETHING WELL

If you're "good at" doing something, you do it well. Use a gerund or nouns after the phrase to say what you're "good at."

She can run well.

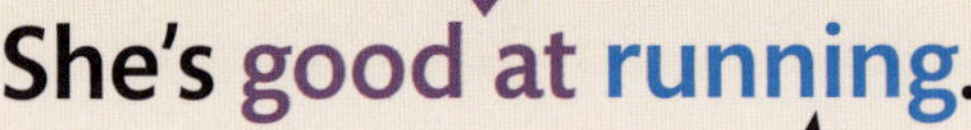

She's good at running.

You can use the gerund after "good at."

45.8 HOW TO FORM "GOOD AT / BAD AT"

The negative form of "good at" is "bad at."

SUBJECT + VERB	"GOOD AT / BAD AT"	GERUND / NOUN
She's	good at bad at	skiing. English.

45.9 FURTHER EXAMPLES "GOOD AT / BAD AT"

Aziz is good at climbing trees.

I am bad at making cakes.

Kate is good at soccer.

Harris is bad at chess.

45.10 REWRITE THE SENTENCES, PUTTING THE WORDS IN THE CORRECT ORDER

the guitar. | good at | playing | Pablo is

Pablo is good at playing the guitar.

1. is | at | good | My horse | jumping.

2. bad at | early. | getting up | I am

3. writing | Mary is | bad at | German.

4. good | swimming. | at | are | Jo and Bob

5. cleaning. | is | Millie | bad at

45.11 REWRITE EACH SENTENCE IN ITS OTHER FORM

She can play the piano well.
She's good at playing the piano.

1. Conchita can play basketball well.

2. You're good at driving a van.

3. Shania and Dave can surf well.

4. My father is bad at speaking English.

5. Manu can't write stories well.

45.12 LISTEN TO THE AUDIO AND MARK WHO IS GOOD AT OR BAD AT EACH ACTIVITY

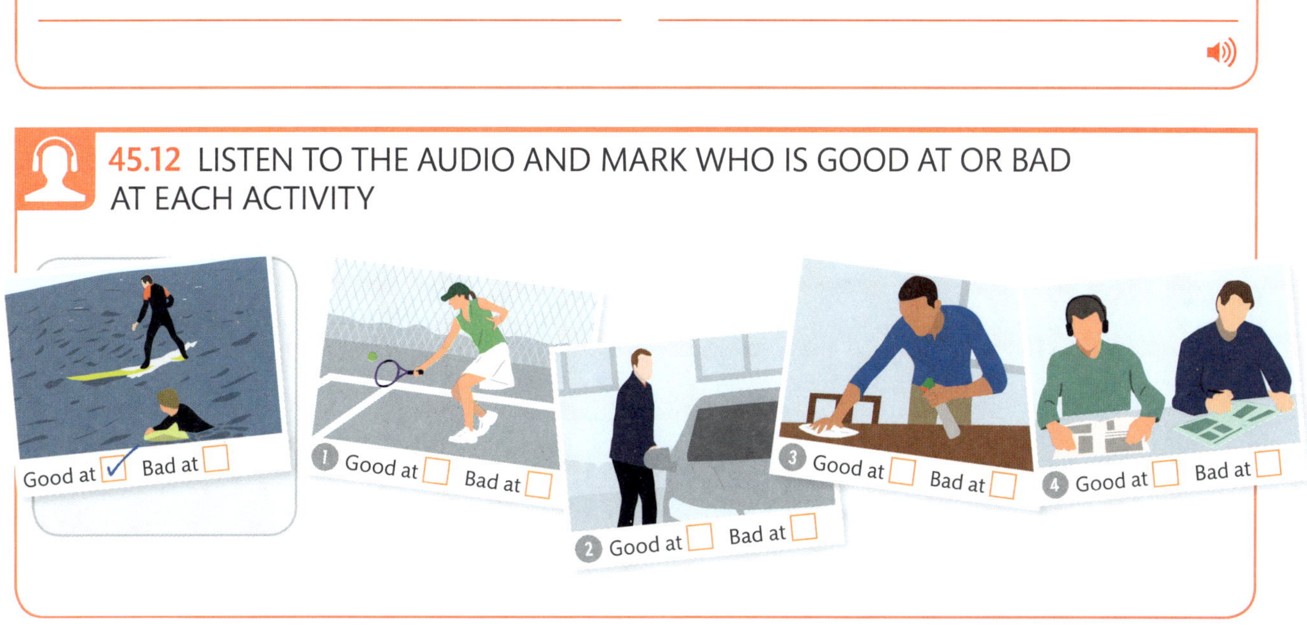

45.13 USE THE CHART TO CREATE 12 CORRECT SENTENCES AND SAY THEM OUT LOUD

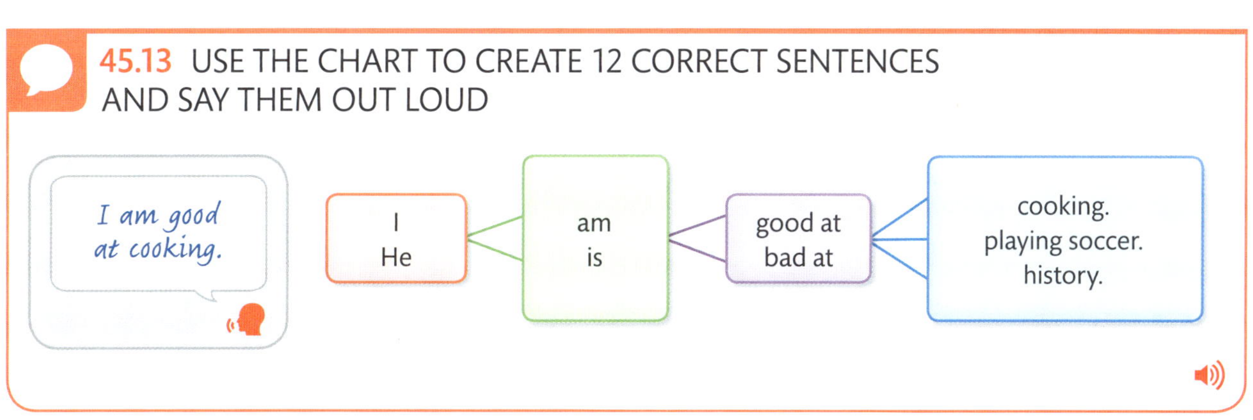

45 CHECKLIST

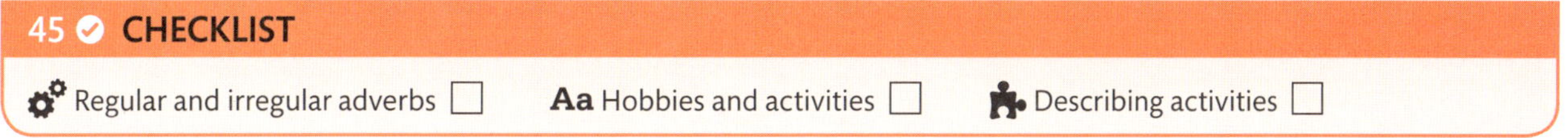

46 Describing ability

Words such as "quite" and "very" are modifying adverbs. You can use them before other adverbs to give more information about how you do something.

New language Modifying adverbs
Aa Vocabulary Skills and abilities
New skill Saying how well you do things

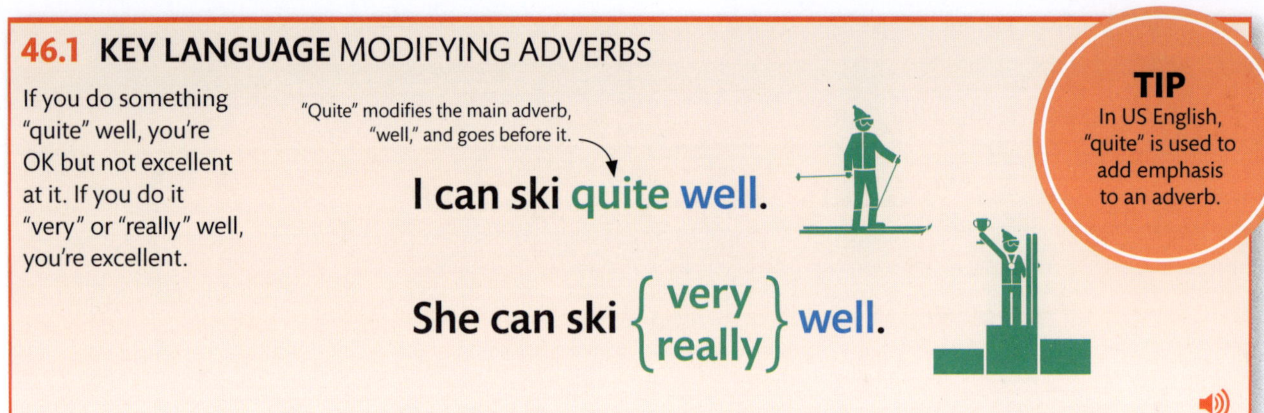

46.1 KEY LANGUAGE MODIFYING ADVERBS

If you do something "quite" well, you're OK but not excellent at it. If you do it "very" or "really" well, you're excellent.

"Quite" modifies the main adverb, "well," and goes before it.

I can ski quite well.

She can ski {very / really} well.

TIP
In US English, "quite" is used to add emphasis to an adverb.

46.2 FURTHER EXAMPLES MODIFYING ADVERBS

Ben can climb really high.

My dad dances quite well.

Jenny can swim very well.

I speak Spanish quite well.

Aa 46.3 MATCH THE BEGINNING OF THE SENTENCES TO THE CORRECT ENDINGS

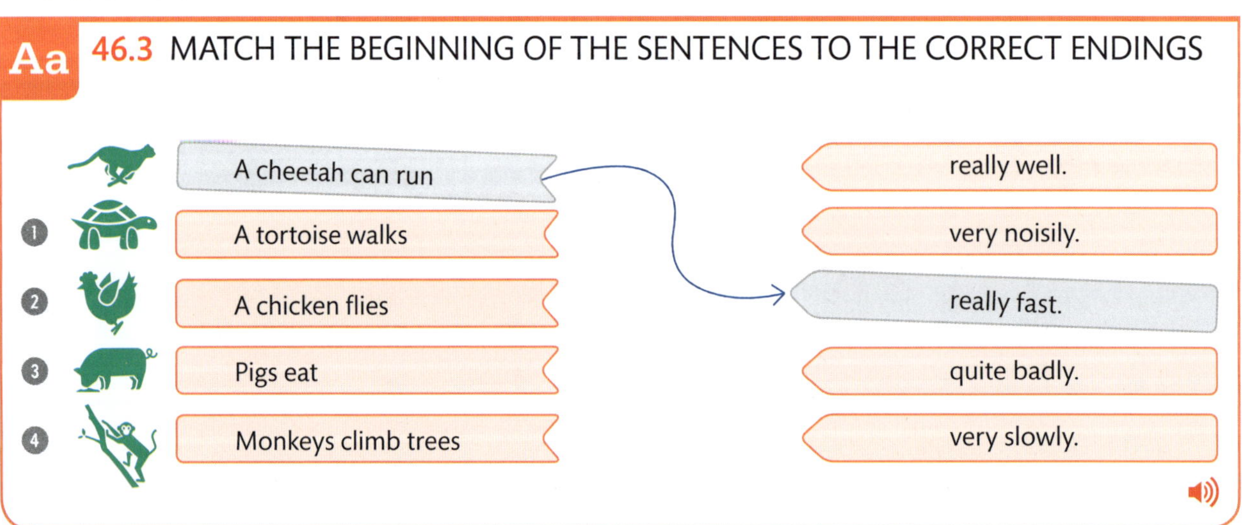

A cheetah can run → really fast.

1. A tortoise walks
2. A chicken flies
3. Pigs eat
4. Monkeys climb trees

really well.
very noisily.
really fast.
quite badly.
very slowly.

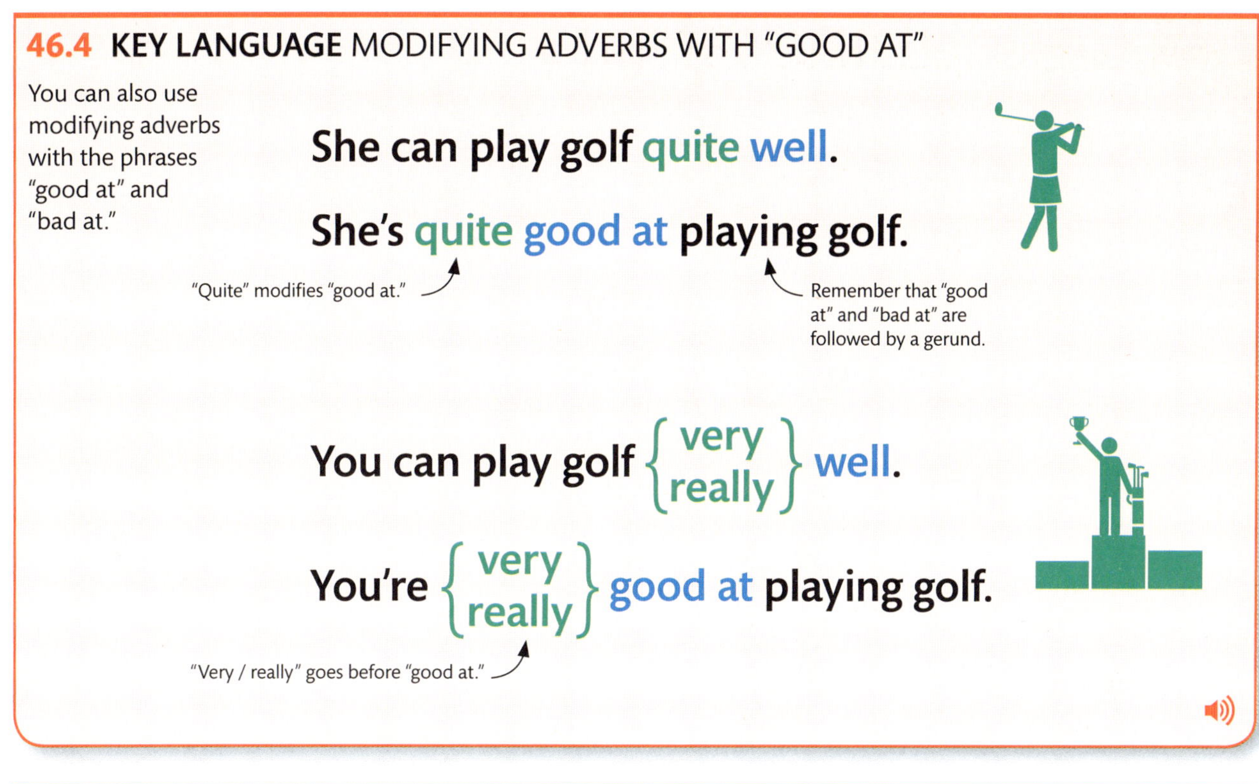

46.5 READ THE REPORT AND ANSWER THE QUESTIONS

How good is Juan at learning vocabulary?
Quite good ☑ **Really good** ☐

1. How good is he at speaking English?
   Quite good ☐ **Really good** ☐
2. How good is Juan at reading?
   Quite good ☐ **Really good** ☐
3. How good is he at listening to English?
   Quite good ☐ **Really good** ☐
4. How good is Juan at writing English?
   Quite good ☐ **Really good** ☐

English report: Juan Ramirez

Writing 99%	Excellent.
Vocabulary 65%	Ok, but you need to study more.
Speaking 95%	Well done.
Listening 66%	Better. Try watching more English movies to improve.
Reading 63%	Ok. You need to read more English texts to improve.

46 ✓ CHECKLIST

Modifying adverbs ☐ **Aa** Skills and abilities ☐ Saying how well you do things ☐

47 Wishes and desires

You can use "I want" and "I would like" to talk about things you want to do. You can also use their negative form to say what you would not like to do.

New language "Would" and "want"
Vocabulary Leisure activities
New skill Talking about ambitions

47.1 KEY LANGUAGE "I WOULD LIKE / I WANT"

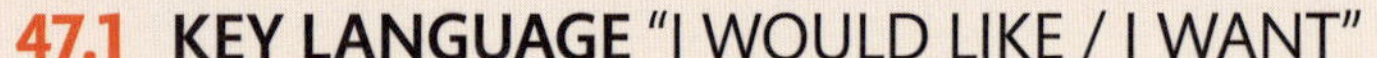

"I would like" is similar to "I want," but "I want" is stronger.

He wants to write a book.

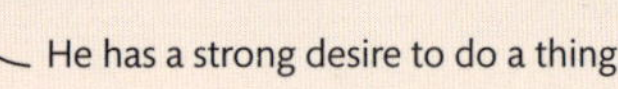

He has a strong desire to do a thing.

I would like to climb a mountain.

I'd like to go scuba diving.

The contracted form of "I would."

47.2 HOW TO FORM "I WOULD LIKE / I'D LIKE"

"Would" is a modal verb, so its form doesn't change.

SUBJECT	MODAL VERB	VERB	INFINITIVE + OBJECT
I / You / He / She	would	like	to go cycling.
We / You / They			

47.3 FURTHER EXAMPLES "I'D LIKE / I WANT"

She'd like to go to Bali.

He wants to go surfing in Hawaii.

We'd like to cook dinner.

We want to go on a boat.

I'd like to drive a sports car.

The dog wants to jump in the river.

47.4 FILL IN THE GAPS TO WRITE EACH SENTENCE THREE DIFFERENT WAYS

	I want to buy a house.	*I would like to buy a house.*	*I'd like to buy a house.*
1			He'd like to get a dog.
2		You would like to work in Turkey.	
3	We want to learn Chinese.		
4			They'd like to start a rock band.

47.5 MATCH THE PICTURES TO THE DESCRIPTIONS

He'd like to travel around Asia.

He'd like to act in a musical.

He wants to be in the Olympics.

She wants to work with lions in Africa.

She'd like to sail a boat.

47.6 USE THE CHART TO CREATE 12 CORRECT SENTENCES AND SAY THEM OUT LOUD

I'd like to climb this tree.

I'd like I want She wants	to climb to read	this tree. that mountain. a newspaper. another book.

47.7 KEY LANGUAGE "I WOULD LIKE / I WANT" NEGATIVES

Use "not" after "would" to make the negative. "Don't" and "doesn't" go before "want."

I would not like to go snowboarding.

I wouldn't like to go shopping.

The contracted form of "would not."

They don't want to go fishing.

"Don't" goes before "want."

47.8 FURTHER EXAMPLES "I WOULD LIKE / I WANT" NEGATIVES

They wouldn't like to go swimming.

We don't want to eat dinner.

She wouldn't like to be a hairdresser.

He doesn't want to go shopping.

47.9 FILL IN THE GAPS TO WRITE EACH SENTENCE THREE DIFFERENT WAYS

	I would not like to go skiing.	*I wouldn't like to go skiing.*	*I don't want to go skiing.*
1	______	______	He doesn't want to play tennis.
2	______	She wouldn't like to study science.	______
3	______	______	They don't want to go to work.
4	You would not like to sing.	______	______
5	______	We wouldn't like to go diving.	______

47.10 KEY LANGUAGE QUESTIONS AND SHORT ANSWERS

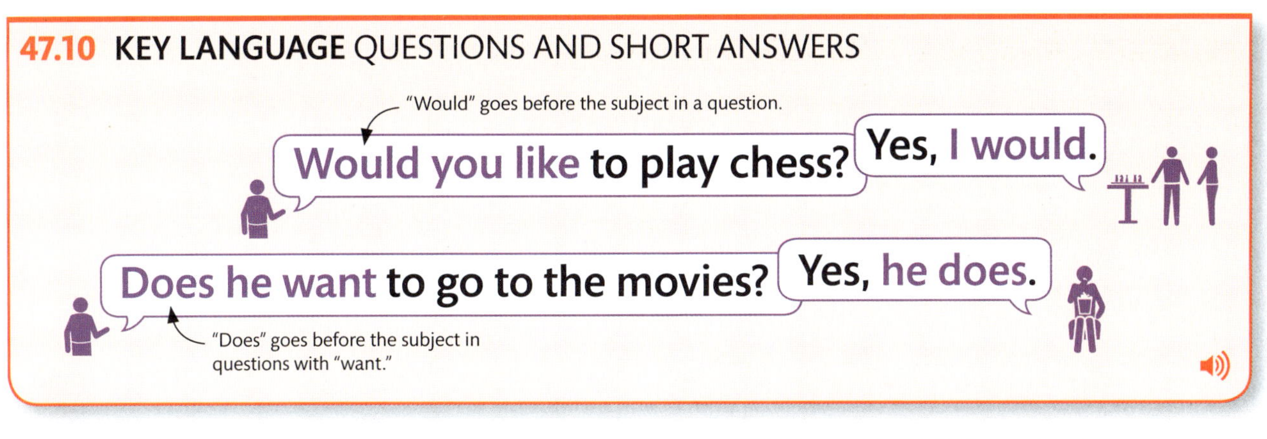

47.11 LISTEN TO THE AUDIO AND ANSWER THE QUESTIONS

Does Mark want to play tennis later?
Yes, he does. ☑ **No, he doesn't.** ☐

1. Would Sarah like to go to a restaurant today?
   Yes, she would. ☐ **No, she wouldn't.** ☐
2. Does Vangelis want to make the dinner?
   Yes, he does. ☐ **No, he doesn't.** ☐
3. Would Lee like to work on Saturday?
   Yes, he would. ☐ **No, he wouldn't.** ☐
4. Does Mary want to skateboard tonight?
   Yes, she does. ☐ **No, she doesn't.** ☐
5. Would Anoushka like to go bowling?
   Yes, she would. ☐ **No, she wouldn't.** ☐

47.12 REWRITE THE SENTENCES, CORRECTING THE ERRORS

Would you **want** to go home?
Would you like to go home?

1. He **don't** want to climb that hill.
2. I wouldn't **likes** to be a judge.
3. They **doesn't** want to go to work today.
4. She would **want** to play tennis tonight.
5. I **wants** to climb that tree.

47 CHECKLIST

"Would" and "want" ☐ **Aa** Leisure activities ☐ Talking about ambitions ☐

48 Studying

When talking about your studies you can use "I would" and "I want" to say which subjects you would like to learn. Use adverbs to say how much you want to do them.

New language Adverbs and articles
Vocabulary Academic subjects
New skill Talking about your studies

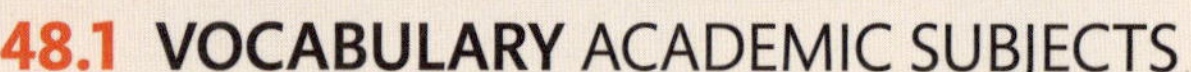

48.1 VOCABULARY ACADEMIC SUBJECTS

 art and design	  drama	 physical education	 English	 music	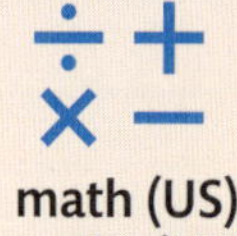 math (US) maths (UK)
 science	 chemistry	 biology	 physics	 geography	 history

48.2 KEY LANGUAGE "REALLY / QUITE"

The adverb "really" means you want to do something a lot. "Quite" is less strong.

I love music. I'd really like to study it next term.

You have a strong desire to do it.

I like biology. I'd quite like to study it next year.

Your desire is not as strong.

48.3 FURTHER EXAMPLES "REALLY / QUITE"

Bella is good at science, and she'd really like to study it at college.

Richard loves jazz, so he'd really like to go to that music festival.

This band is OK. I'd quite like to listen to their new CD.

48.5 REWRITE THE SENTENCES, PUTTING THE WORDS IN THE CORRECT ORDER

to do | quite | an English degree. | like | Sheila | would

Sheila would quite like to do an English degree.

1. his driving test. | Jerry | really | would | to pass | like

2. would | an IELTS test. | like | Ben and Sam | to take | really

3. like | Helen | her English. | would | to practice | quite

4. the piano | like | quite | to play | tonight. | I'd

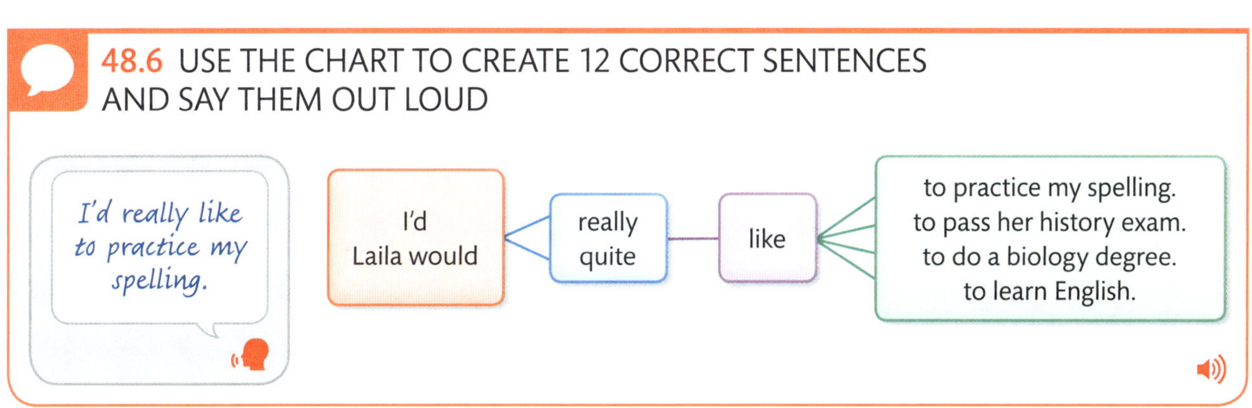

48.7 KEY LANGUAGE THE ZERO ARTICLE

You don't use an article ("a" or "the") with some places and institutions when you are talking about what they are used for.

She goes there to study, which is the purpose of schools, so don't use the article.

Liz is seven. She goes to school now.

Larry works at the school in Park Street.

Use the article to talk about the specific building where he works.

48.8 FURTHER EXAMPLES THE ZERO ARTICLE

ZERO ARTICLE	ARTICLE
I am at university in Chicago. 	The University of Chicago is good. 
Pierre is in hospital. 	The hospital is far away. 
Liz goes to church on Sundays. 	St. Mary's is an old church. 
Go to bed, Tom! 	Your shirt is on the bed. 
Sue is in town this afternoon. 	Hancock is a nice town. 
Sarah studies at home. 	This dog hasn't got a home. 

48.9 CROSS OUT THE INCORRECT WORDS IN EACH SENTENCE

Sheila works at ~~school~~ / the school near here.

1. Emily has lovely home / a lovely home.
2. Sue always takes her lunch to office / the office.
3. Can you see where church / the church is?
4. Jim went to bed / the bed hours ago.
5. Can you drive me into town / a town later?
6. I live next to university / the university.
7. I leave home / a home at 8am every weekday.

48.10 LISTEN TO THE AUDIO AND MATCH THE PICTURES TO THE NAMES

Maureen talks about what her family are doing and where they are.

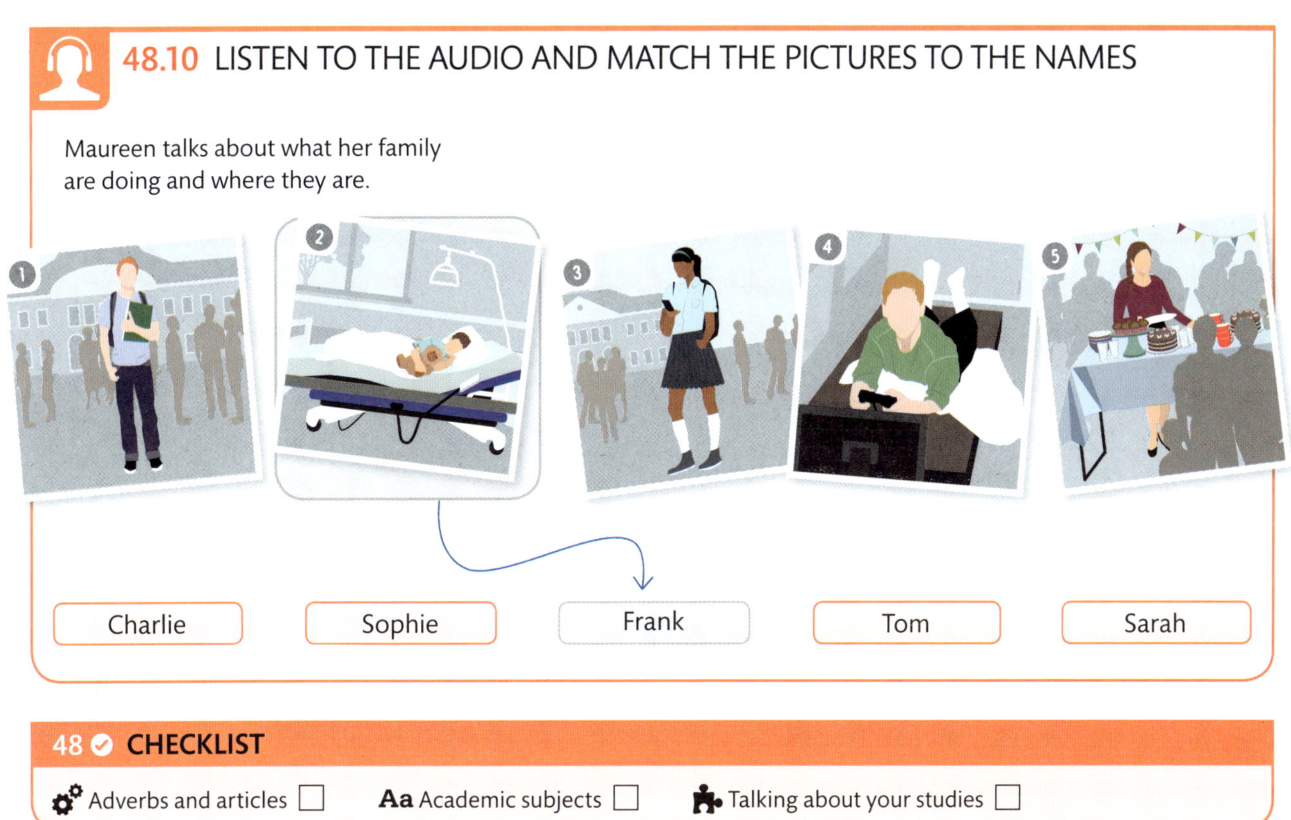

48 ✓ CHECKLIST

Adverbs and articles ☐ **Aa** Academic subjects ☐ Talking about your studies ☐

REVIEW THE ENGLISH YOU HAVE LEARNED IN UNITS 44-48

NEW LANGUAGE	SAMPLE SENTENCE	☑	UNIT
"CAN," "CANNOT," AND "CAN'T"	I can ride a bicycle. He can play guitar. I cannot / can't sing jazz songs.	☐	44.1, 44.3, 44.7
USING ADVERBS	I speak quietly. He speaks loudly.	☐	45.1, 45.4
"GOOD AT" AND "BAD AT"	She's good at running. I am bad at making cakes.	☐	45.7, 45.8
MODIFYING ADVERBS	I can ski quite well. She can ski very well. She can ski really well.	☐	46.1, 46.4
"I WOULD LIKE" AND "I WANT"	He wants to write a book. I would like to climb a mountain.	☐	47.1, 47.7
"REALLY" AND "QUITE"	I love music. I'd really like to study it this term. I like biology. I'd quite like to study it next year.	☐	48.2, 48.3
THE ZERO ARTICLE	My daughter goes to school now.	☐	48.7, 48.8

R Reference

R1 THE ALPHABET

The **English alphabet** has 26 letters. "A," "E," "I," "O," and "U" are vowels, and the rest are consonants.

Aa Bb Cc Dd Ee Ff Gg Hh Ii Jj Kk
Ll Mm Nn Oo Pp Qq Rr Ss Tt Uu
Vv Ww Xx Yy Zz

R2 PARTS OF SPEECH

The different types of words that make up sentences are called **parts of speech.** Pronouns, nouns, and verbs are essential elements of a sentence, but other parts of speech, such as adjectives and adverbs, can make a sentence more descriptive.

PART OF SPEECH	DEFINITION	EXAMPLES
noun	a name, object, concept, or person	**cat**, **Maria**, **girl**, **house**, **water**, **happiness**
adjective	describes a noun or pronoun	**big**, **funny**, **light**, **red**, **young**
verb	shows an action or a state of being	**be**, **go**, **read**, **speak**, **swim**, **walk**
adverb	describes verbs, adjectives, and other adverbs, giving information on how, where, when, or how much	**briskly**, **easily**, **happily**, **here**, **loudly**, **quite**, **rather**, **soon**, **together**, **very**
pronoun	takes the place of a noun	**he**, **she**, **you**, **we**, **them**, **it**
preposition	describes the relationship between a noun or pronoun and another word in the sentence	**about**, **above**, **from**, **in**
conjunction	a joining word, used to link words, phrases, or clauses	**and**, **because**, **but**, **while**, **yet**
interjection	an exclamation or remark	**ah**, **hey**, **hi**, **hmm**, **wow**, **yes**
article	used with a noun to specify whether the noun is a particular person or thing, or something general	**a**, **an**, **the**
determiner	precedes a noun and puts the noun in context	**all**, **her**, **my**, **their**, **your**

R3 PUNCTUATION

English uses various **punctuation marks** to separate and join different clauses, and to make sentences clearer.

PUNCTUATION MARK	NAME	USE
.	**period (US)** **full stop (UK)**	• marks the end of a complete statement • marks the end of an abbreviated word
...	**ellipsis**	• marks where text has been omitted or a sentence is unfinished
,	**comma**	• follows an introductory word, phrase, or clause • can separate a non-essential part of a sentence • can be used with a conjunction to join two main clauses • separates words or phrases in a list • represents omitted words to avoid repetition in a sentence • can be used between an introduction to speech and direct speech
;	**semi-colon**	• separates two main clauses that are closely related • separates items in a complex list
:	**colon**	• connects a main clause to a clause, phrase, or word that is an explanation of the main clause, or that emphasizes a point in the main clause • introduces a list after a complete statement • introduces quoted text
'	**apostrophe**	• marks missing letters • indicates possession
-	**hyphen**	• links two words in compound modifiers and some compound nouns • can be used in fractions and in numbers from twenty-one to ninety-nine • can join certain prefixes to other words
" "	**inverted commas**	• can be used before and after direct speech and quoted text • can be used to pick out a word or phrase in a sentence • can be used around titles of short works
?	**question mark**	• marks the end of a sentence that is a question
!	**exclamation mark**	• marks the end of a sentence that expresses strong emotions • can be used at the end of an interruption to add emphasis
()	**parentheses (US)** **brackets (UK)**	• can be used around non-essential information in a sentence • can be used around information that provides clarification
–	**dash**	• can be used in pairs around interruptions • marks a range of numbers (5–6 hours) • indicates start and end of a route (Paris–Dover rally)
•	**bullet point**	• indicates a point in a list
/	**slash**	• can be used to show an alternative instead of using the word "or"

R4 PRONOUNS AND POSSESSIVE ADJECTIVES

Pronouns can be used to replace nouns and noun phrases. There are different types of pronouns, which can refer to the subject or object of a sentence, or indicate ownership of something. **Possessive adjectives** are also used to indicate possession.

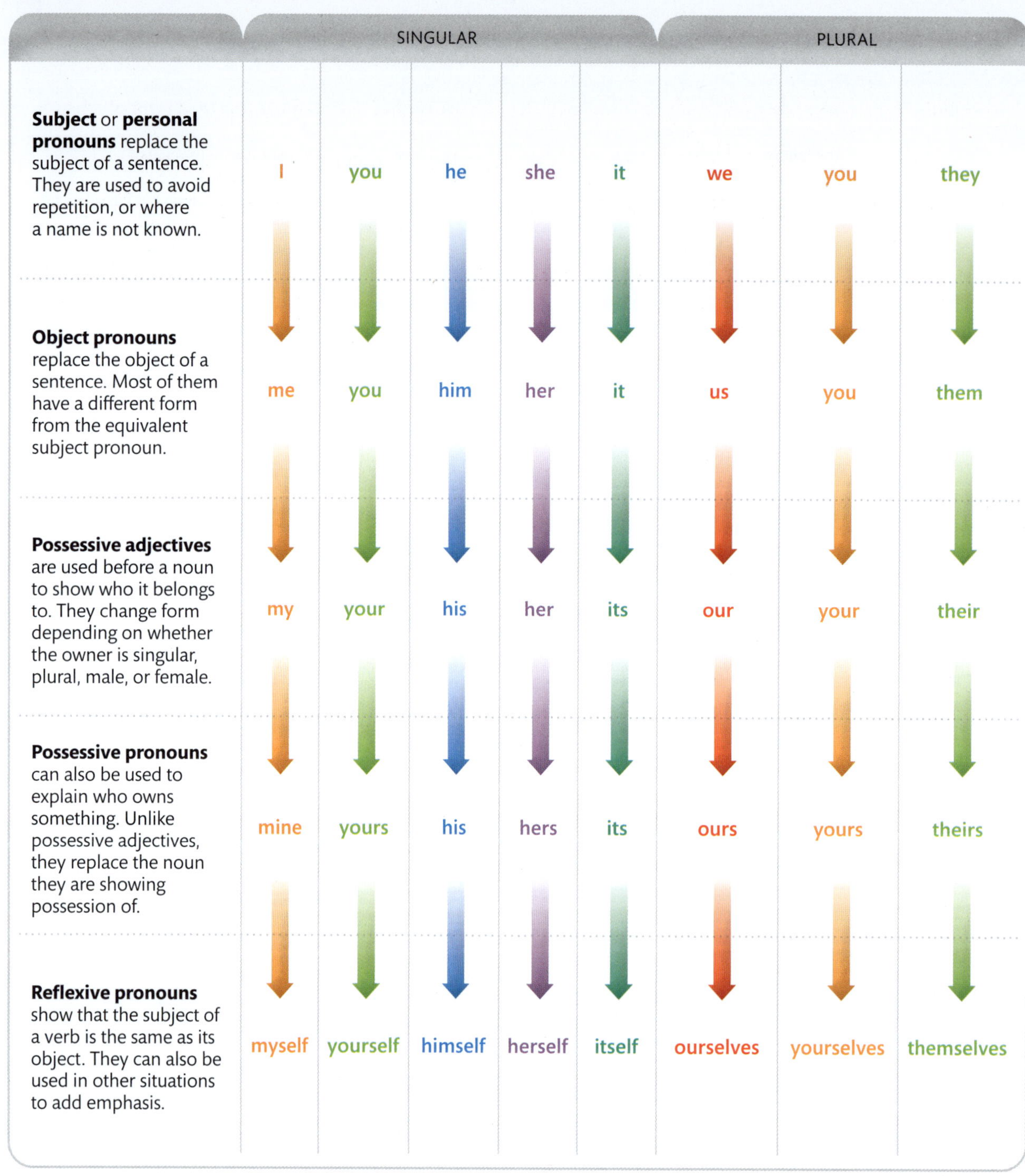

	SINGULAR					PLURAL		
Subject or **personal pronouns** replace the subject of a sentence. They are used to avoid repetition, or where a name is not known.	I	you	he	she	it	we	you	they
Object pronouns replace the object of a sentence. Most of them have a different form from the equivalent subject pronoun.	me	you	him	her	it	us	you	them
Possessive adjectives are used before a noun to show who it belongs to. They change form depending on whether the owner is singular, plural, male, or female.	my	your	his	her	its	our	your	their
Possessive pronouns can also be used to explain who owns something. Unlike possessive adjectives, they replace the noun they are showing possession of.	mine	yours	his	hers	its	ours	yours	theirs
Reflexive pronouns show that the subject of a verb is the same as its object. They can also be used in other situations to add emphasis.	myself	yourself	himself	herself	itself	ourselves	yourselves	themselves

R5 PREPOSITIONS

Prepositions are words that are used to create or show relationships between different parts of a clause, for example time, place, or reason. They can only be followed by a noun, noun phrase, pronoun, or gerund. You will come across some of these prepositions in other books in the *English for Everyone* series.

PREPOSITION	SAMPLE SENTENCE
about	Today's lecture is **about** the Cold War.
above	The balloon flew **above** the city.
after	We can go to the park **after** lunch.
against	I'm **against** building new houses here.
among	The document is **among** these papers.
at	Let's meet **at** the bus stop later.
because of	I'm late **because of** the trains delays.
before	Could you get here **before** lunchtime?
behind	The park is **behind** that hedge.
below	He lives in the apartment **below** mine.
beneath	Potatoes grow **beneath** the ground.
between	I live **between** Vancouver and Calgary.
between... and	They'll arrive **between** 7pm **and** 8pm.
by	Please pay **by** the end of the month.
despite	The café is busy **despite** the high prices.
due to	**Due to** the rain, the game was delayed.
during	Turn off your phone **during** the show.
except (for)	I like all fruit **except (for)** apples.
following	**Following** losses, the store closed down.
for	I haven't been back to Delhi **for** years.
from	Our new colleague is **from** Lithuania.
from... to	I work **from** 9am **to** 5pm.
in	There's plenty of food **in** the cupboard.

PREPOSITION	SAMPLE SENTENCE
in front of	Don't stand **in front of** the television!
instead of	Can we have pizza **instead of** pasta?
like	This tastes **like** butter, but it has less fat.
near	We live quite **near** the airport.
next to	The supermarket is **next to** the bank.
on	I have piano lessons **on** Tuesdays.
on top of	Put the vase **on top of** the bookcase.
out of	Don't let the cat **out of** her box yet.
over	Lots of planes fly **over** my village.
past	It's ten **past** nine. You're late!
regarding	Let's talk **regarding** your new job.
since	I haven't been to Las Vegas **since** 2007.
thanks to	**Thanks to** your efforts, we won a prize.
through	Shall we walk **through** the park?
throughout	I laughed **throughout** the whole movie.
to	When are you going **to** Canada?
toward	The child just ran **toward** his mother.
unlike	It's **unlike** Karen to be so rude.
until	We'll be in Portugal **until** Friday.
under(neath)	I think the ball's **under(neath)** the bush.
with	Will you come **with** us to the concert?
within	I ran the marathon **within** four hours.
without	I've come out **without** my phone.

R6 CONJUNCTIONS

Conjunctions are words used to link or show a relationship between two or more words, phrases, clauses, or sentences. This can be cause, effect, emphasis, contrast, or comparison. You will come across more conjunctions in other books in the *English for Everyone* series.

CONJUNCTION	USE	EXAMPLE
after	Shows that something happens later than another action	I have dinner **after** I come home from work.
and	Joins two sentences together to avoid repetition and to link ideas	My cousin lives **and** works in the city.
as	Gives a reason for an action or decision	We didn't go fishing **as** it was raining.
because	Gives a reason for an action or decision	I like living in the countryside **because** it's quiet.
before	Shows that something happens earlier than another action	I need to go shopping **before** I make dinner.
but	Joins a positive statement to a negative one, or shows a contrast between two clauses	There is a supermarket **but** there isn't a post office.
if	Refers to the result of an action, or what might happen when something else happens	**If** it's sunny, we will go to the beach.
or	Lists two or more choices. Can also be used to talk about the consequences of an action, which are usually negative	Do you want to go swimming **or** sailing?
so	Shows that something happens because of something else	The café was too busy, **so** I went home.
than	Compares two or more things. It is used with comparative adjectives and adverbs	This car is smaller **than** my previous one.
when	Refers to actions in the future that must happen before another action can take place	**When** it stops raining, I will go outside.

R7 GERUNDS

Gerunds are verbs that are used as nouns. They are sometimes known as verbal nouns. Gerunds are formed by adding "-ing" to the base form of the verb.

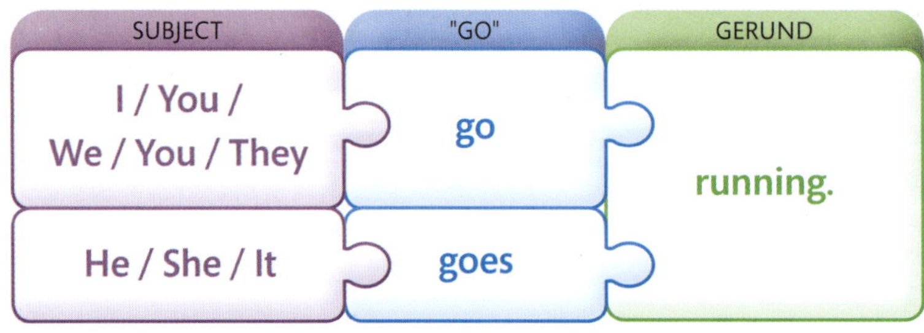

R8 ADVERBS

Adverbs describe and give more information about verbs, adjectives, phrases, and other adverbs. They can be used to give further information regarding the following qualities:

Time These adverbs give more information about when something happens.

See you **soon**!

Place Like prepositions, these adverbs can describe location or distance.

We were born **there**.

Frequency These adverbs show how often something is done.

They **usually** read at night.

Manner These adverbs describe the way something is done.

She can play the guitar **well**.

Degree These adverbs come before adjectives or verbs to strengthen their meaning.

I **really** like studying!

R9 IMPERATIVES

Imperatives are used to make requests or give commands. They are formed using the base form of the verb. To make an instruction or request negative, add "do not" or "don't" before the verb. Some instructions use the base form of the verb on its own.

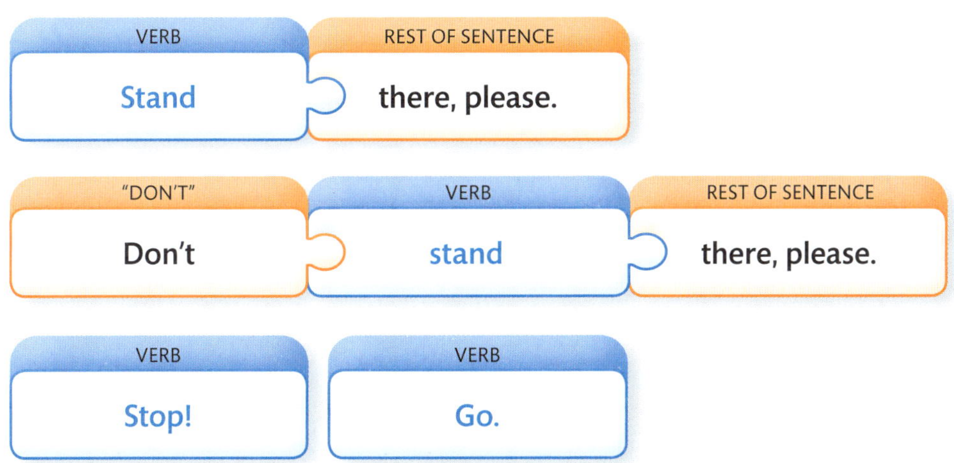

R10 THE PRESENT SIMPLE: REGULAR VERBS

The **present simple** is used to talk about things that happen repeatedly or as part of your daily routine.
It can also be used to make simple statements of fact and to describe things that are always true.

POSITIVE	NEGATIVE	QUESTION
I work	I do not / I don't work	Do I work...?
You work	You do not / You don't work	Do you work...?
He works	He does not / He doesn't work	Does he work...?
She works	She does not / She doesn't work	Does she work...?
It works	It does not / It doesn't work	Does it work...?
We work	We do not / We don't work	Do we work...?
You work	You do not / You don't work	Do you work...?
They work	They do not / They don't work	Do they work...?

R11 THE PRESENT SIMPLE: "TO BE"

"To be" is a common verb in English that has an irregular present simple form.
It is used to describe the characteristics of something or someone.

POSITIVE	NEGATIVE	QUESTION
I am / I'm	I'm not	Am I...?
You are / You're	You're not / You aren't	Are you...?
He is / He's	He's not / He isn't	Is he...?
She is / She's	She's not / She isn't	Is she...?
It is / It's	It's not / It isn't	Is it...?
We are / We're	We're not / We aren't	Are we...?
You are / You're	You're not / You aren't	Are you...?
They are / They're	They're not / They aren't	Are they...?

R12 THE PRESENT SIMPLE: "TO DO"

"To do" is a common verb in English that has an irregular present simple form in the third person. It is used to form questions and negative phrases when paired with another verb.

POSITIVE	NEGATIVE	QUESTION
I do	I do not / I don't	Do I..?
You do	You do not / You don't	Do you...?
He does	He does not / He doesn't	Does he...?
She does	She does not / She doesn't	Does she...?
It does	It does not / It doesn't	Does it...?
We do	We do not / We don't	Do we...?
You do	You do not / You don't	Do you...?
They do	They do not / They don't	Do they...?

R13 THE PRESENT SIMPLE: "TO HAVE"

"To have" is a common verb in English that has an irregular present simple form in the third person. It is used to describe ownership or possession.

POSITIVE	NEGATIVE	QUESTION
I have / I've	I've not / I haven't	Do I have...?
You have / You've	You've not / You haven't	Do you have...?
He has / He's	He's not / He hasn't	Does he have...?
She has / She's	She's not / She hasn't	Does she have...?
It has / It's	It's not / It hasn't	Does it have...?
We have / We've	We've not / We haven't	Do we have...?
You have / You've	You've not / You haven't	Do you have...?
They have / They've	They've not / They haven't	Do they have...?

Transcripts of listening exercises

UNIT 1

1.5.1 Hi. I'm Katherine.

1.5.2 Hello. My name's Joseph. Some people call me Joe.

1.5.3 Hi. I'm Ruby.

1.5.4 My name's Oliver, or Oli for short.

1.5.5 My name's Charlotte, but my friends call me Charlie.

1.5.6 I'm Elliot.

1.9 ex: My name's Jack Lord. That's Jack... J-A-C-K... Lord... L-O-R-D.

1.9.1 My name's Belinda.
That's B-E-L-I-N-D-A.

1.9.2
A: What's your name?
B: Lewis.
A: How do you spell that?
B: L-E-W-I-S.

1.9.3
A: My name's Jessica Adams.
B: How do you spell your last name?
A: It's A-D-A-M-S.

1.9.4 My name's Bob. That's B-O-B.

1.9.5
A: My name's Alice Spencer.
B: How do you spell your last name?
A: It's S-P-E-N-C-E-R.

1.9.6
A: My name's Kate Wallace.
B: How do you spell that?
A: It's Kate... K-A-T-E... Wallace... W-A-L-L-A-C-E.

1.9.7 I'm Saul Jackson. That's Saul... S-A-U-L and Jackson... J-A-C-K-S-O-N.

1.9.8
A: What's your full name?
B: It's Natalie Lau.
A: How do you spell that?
B: Natalie... N-A-T-A-L-I-E... Lau... L-A-U.

1.9.9 I'm Chris Boyle.
That's C-H-R-I-S B-O-Y-L-E.

UNIT 3

3.8 ex: My name's Tamar and I'm 50 years old.

3.8.1 I'm Bobby and I'm 40.

3.8.2 My brother's called Carl and he's 30.

3.8.3 Lia is 19 years old.

3.8.4 My name's Sam and I'm 60.

3.8.5 My grandma is called Molly and she's 80.

3.8.6 Hi, I'm Justin and I'm 17.

3.8.7 I have a daughter called Ada. She's 13.

UNIT 5

5.10.1 This is my cat. Her name's Priscilla and she's five years old.

5.10.2 That is our dog. His name's Rex and he's a labrador.

5.10.3 This is our parrot. His name's Boris and he speaks English.

5.10.4 That snake in the zoo comes from Mexico. It's a python and its name is Luis.

5.10.5 That is Blaze, our horse. She lives in our field.

UNIT 6

6.4
A: Look at these. Are they Ben's photos?
B: Yes, they're photos of his family.
A: Who's this? I don't know her.
B: It's Edith. She's Ben's grandmother.
A: Oh, and this is Ben's father?
B: Yes, that's right. It's Lucas.
A: Here's Lily. I know her.
B: Oh, Ben's mother. Yes, that's a good photo of her.
A: And this is Noah.
B: He's Ben's son. He's 14 now.
A: Wow.
B: Here's a photo of Grace.
A: Ben's sister. You're right.
B: They're great photos. Oh, and here's an old picture of Alex.
A: Isn't he Ben's brother?
B: Yes. He looks very young in the photo.

UNIT 8

8.10
Sarah: Hurry up, Tom. We're late for work.
Tom: Oh, all right. Let's get our things.
Sarah: So this purse is mine, but these sandwiches are yours.

Tom: Yeah, they're my lunch. And this is my cell phone.
Sarah: OK. And your ID card is here, too.
Tom: These are your books.
Sarah: Oh yes... and this is your chocolate bar...
Tom: ...and that brush is yours...
Sarah: ...and this is my notebook. Great. Well, I think that's it. Have a nice day.
Tom: You, too. See you later.

UNIT 10

10.9.1 I'm Levi and I work outside all day. I work on construction sites, building houses.

10.9.2 I'm Violet and I work in the kitchen of a busy restaurant. I cook the food and I work with waiters and waitresses.

10.9.3 My name's Tina and I'm 23 years old. I work outside on a farm. I work with animals every day.

10.9.4 My name's Diego and I work in a school. I teach children English and music.

10.9.5 My name's Theo and I work in a hospital. I work with nurses and I see patients every day.

10.9.6 I'm Isabella and I work outside in gardens every day. I work with plants and trees. It's a great job. I love working outside.

10.13
Friend: Hi, Noah. How are you?
Noah: I'm well, thanks. I've got a new job. I'm a mechanic in the new garage in town.
Friend: Wow, that's great news.
Noah: Yes... and my sister is still a nurse at the hospital. She works with patients there.
Friend: What about your brother?
Noah: He's a scientist. He works in a laboratory in the city.
Friend: That's interesting.
Noah: I know. And my mother works from home. She's an artist. She's really good!
Friend: And what about your dad?
Noah: He's a farmer. He works on our farm.
Friend: With lots of animals?
Noah: Yes. He works with cows and sheep every day. It's a tiring job.

UNIT 11

11.4 ex:
A: What time is it, please?
B: It's a quarter to six. It's five forty-five.

11.4.1
A: Excuse me. What time is it?
B: It's half past eleven. It's eleven thirty.

11.4.2
A: Excuse me. What's the time, please?
B: It's seven o'clock. It's seven.

11.4.3
A: What's the time?
B: It's a quarter past four. It's four fifteen.

11.4.4
A: Excuse me. What is the time?
B: It's half past nine. It's nine thirty.

11.4.5
A: What's the time, please?
B: It's a quarter past two. It's two fifteen.

UNIT 13

13.12
Friend: So, what time do you start work, Joan?
Joan: 4am.
Friend: 4am? You start work at 4 o'clock in the morning?
Joan: Yes.
Friend: Wow!
Joan: Yes, but I finish work at noon.
Friend: OK. That's better.
Joan: Yes. I go home and eat lunch at 1pm, and then I take it easy.
Friend: When do you eat dinner?
Joan: Early. At 6pm.
Friend: And then what? What do you do in the evening?
Joan: I watch TV.
Friend: Do you play video games?
Joan: No, but I go on the computer for an hour.
Friend: What time do you go to bed?
Joan: I go to bed at 8:30pm.
Friend: Wow!

UNIT 14

14.10 ex: I'm Angela. I'm a farmer, so I get up early every day. I wake up at 5am and get up at quarter past five to feed the animals.

14.10.1 My name is Fred. I'm a businessman and I work in an office in London. I work from 8am to 6pm five days a week. I don't work on weekends.

14.10.2 I'm Scott. I'm a nurse in a hospital and I work at night. I start work at 7pm and finish at 5am. I have dinner at 6am, then go to bed at 8am.

14.10.3 I'm Linda. I'm a chef and I work in a busy restaurant every day. I start work at 4pm and finish at 11pm. It's hot in the kitchen, so I have a shower every night when I get home.

14.10.4 I'm Jennifer, and I'm a student. I study during the day and I work in the evenings to pay for my studies. I'm busy every night, so on the weekend I just watch TV. It's the only time I get to relax.

14.10.5 My name is Tim. My daughter is only two years old, so she has a bath and goes to bed at 6:30pm from Monday to Saturday. On Sundays, we go out for the day, so she goes to bed at 7pm.

UNIT 15

15.6.1 My name's Mark and I'm 35 years old. I'm not a doctor. I'm a vet. It's a great job, because I work with animals every day.

15.6.2 I'm Elsa and I'm 70 years old. I've got eight grandchildren and they visit me every week. I read stories to them, but I'm not a writer. I'm an artist.

15.6.3 My name's Josh and I'm a police officer. I live and work in Canada, but I'm not Canadian. I'm from the US.

15.6.4 My name is Alain and I am a farmer in France. I am not married. I live by myself on my farm.

15.6.5 I'm from Spain and I'm called Nuria. During the day, I'm a waitress and I work in a restaurant. But I'm not a waitress in the evenings. I'm an actor in the evenings.

UNIT 16

16.5

Frank: Hi. My name's Frank and I'm 25 years old. I work in a store on Queen Street. It's in the middle of town, near the train station. I get up early every day. I don't get up at 5am or anything. No, I get up at 7 during the week and at 9 on the weekends. I have lunch at 1 every day and I usually buy a sandwich from the café next to my work. I go swimming three times a week. I always go on Mondays, Thursdays, and Saturdays. I go in the evening, after work. Another thing I do in the evening is watch TV, but I don't watch it every night.

UNIT 17

17.5 ex: A: Is Sue an actor?
B: No. She's a doctor.

17.5.1
A: Is David French?
B: No. He's American.

17.5.2
A: Is Tigger a dog?
B: Yes, he is.

17.5.3
A: Is Dawn at the airport?
B: No. She's at the train station.

17.5.4
A: Is Pat a man?
B: No. She's a woman.

17.5.5
A: Are you in your office?
B: No. I'm outside, in the country.

17.5.6
A: Is the key in your shopping bag?
B: No. It's in my purse.

UNIT 18

18.3

Maria: Hello.
Receptionist: Oh, hello. Are you Maria Kowalski?
Maria: Yes. I'm here for my job interview.
Receptionist: OK. I need some information from you before your interview. Your name sounds Polish. Are you from Poland?
Maria: No, I'm not. I'm from Germany, but my father's Polish.
Receptionist: So, are you a receptionist at the moment?
Maria: Yes, I am.
Receptionist: And do you work in an office?
Maria: No, I don't. I work in a surgery near here.
Receptionist: Do you like your job?
Maria: Yes, I love it, but it's time to move on.
Receptionist: We start work at 8am. Do you start work at that time?
Maria: No, I don't. I start work at 9am.
Receptionist: And do you work five days a week?
Maria: No. I work three days a week. I study English on the other two days.
Receptionist: Thank you, Maria. Please wait here for your interview.

UNIT 19

19.13

Marie: Hi, Ben. How are you?
Ben: I'm fine, thanks, Marie.
Marie: Are you happy at college?
Ben: Yes, it's great.
Marie: How is the food?
Ben: It's not good.
Marie: Oh, no. Where do you eat dinner?
Ben: I usually go home to eat. I like to have dinner with my family.
Marie: That's nice. Do your classes start early in the morning, then?
Ben: Yes. Too early. They start at 8am.
Marie: Oh, no. When do you eat breakfast?
Ben: I have it at 7am, before class.
Marie: You must be tired. What do you study, Ben?

Ben: I study English. The classes are hard and expensive.
Marie: That's too bad. Do you have a job in town?
Ben: Yes.
Marie: Where do you work now?
Ben: I work at the supermarket three days a week: on Mondays, Wednesdays, and Fridays. I work from 2 to 7pm, and I go to class in the morning.
Marie: Oh... that woman in the café wants to talk to you. Who is she?
Ben: Oh, that's Mrs. Donaldson. She's my new professor.
Marie: OK. I've got to go now anyway. Nice to see you, Ben.
Ben: Good to see you, too, Marie. Bye.

UNIT 21

21.11.1 I live in a big town. There are three factories and two supermarkets. There isn't a town hall, but there's a bus station and an airport.

21.11.2 It's a big city. There's a big airport and four hotels. There are three restaurants and there's a bus station. There aren't any theaters or movie theaters, so it's a bit boring.

21.11.3 In my town there's a big supermarket, but there aren't any other stores. There's a castle near my house. I work there on the weekends. There is a mosque here, too. There's a café, but there isn't a theater.

21.11.4 There is a movie theater and a theater in my town, but no museum or library. There are three bars here. My brother works in a really nice restaurant.

UNIT 23

23.11 ex: A: Excuse me. Where's the Hotel Bel Air?
B: No problem. Go straight ahead at the first intersection and then turn left. Take the next right and the hotel is on the left.

23.11.1
A: Is there a movie theater in this town?
B: Yes, there is. Take the first right, then turn left at the next intersection. The movie theater is on the left.

23.11.2
A: Excuse me. Could you tell me where the swimming pool is?
B: Sure. That's easy. Go straight on. The swimming pool is on the right, before the third intersection.

23.11.3
A: Excuse me. How do I get to the science museum?
B: Sure. Go straight... no, wait. That's not it. Instead, take the first right, then turn left. Go straight ahead and the science museum is on the left, after the next intersection.

23.11.4
A: Excuse me. Is the library near here?
B: Of course, I go there all the time. Go straight ahead and turn left at the second intersection. The library is on the right.

UNIT 24

24.4 ex: Every Saturday morning I go to the swimming pool and the gym before breakfast.

24.4.1 There is a train station and a clothing store near Jane's house.

24.4.2 I work in two places. On Mondays and Tuesdays, I work at the movie theater and on Wednesdays and Fridays, I work in an office.

24.4.3 There is a school and a hospital in Greenway.

24.4.4 My grandfather goes to the post office and the supermarket once a week.

UNIT 25

25.12.1 This is a big city. There are lots of buildings and people.

25.12.2 This beach is so quiet. I love coming here with the children. The sand is beautiful and there are only a few people.

25.12.3 This part of the countryside is wonderful – very quiet. There are only a few cows. There are some hills. They are beautiful.

25.12.4 This town is old and quiet. There are some stores, but it's never noisy.

25.12.5 The Canadian countryside is amazing. There are lots and lots of lakes and mountains, so many sports to do, and so much nature to see.

25.12.6 This beautiful village has some old trees in the main street. There are a few stores, but not a lot of tourists, so it's really quiet.

UNIT 26

26.3 ex: I'm Ben. There is a restaurant near my office. I go there once a week because my friend is the chef. The food is really good.

26.3.1 I'm Jacob. I live in Newport. It's a busy town and there are lots of beautiful houses, but I live there because that's where my family is.

26.3.2 My name's Marina. I don't work inside in an office. I work outside every day. I work with animals on a farm.

26.3.3 I'm Lin. I get up early, at 6am, every day because I go swimming at the pool. It's so early that I see the sun rise every morning.

26.3.4 My name's Ho. I'm a businessman. I have two computers. My desktop computer has a large screen, but I use my laptop now because it is new.

26.3.5 My son Pablo is a doctor because he's very good with people. My daughter, Lucia, is a teacher. She works with children.

26.3.6 My name's Annie. I go to Boston on the weekends because my aunt lives there. She's a lawyer, and her husband is a chef.

26 3.7 The countryside is beautiful and quiet because not a lot of people live there. There are lots of animals and trees.

UNIT 28

28.4

Maya: Hi, I'm Maya. I live in an apartment. The bedroom is upstairs. The living room is downstairs. It has a couch and a dining table. The kitchen doesn't have a stove, but it has a microwave and a toaster. The bathroom has a toilet and a shower.

Ben: Hello, I'm Ben. I live at Number 36, Park Street. I live in a house with my brother and sister. I work at home, so I have a desk in my bedroom. The bathroom has a bathtub, but there's no shower. In the living room, we have a big TV. We all watch TV together every evening.

UNIT 29

29.4

Lucy: We get the keys to our apartment next month, Tim. Do you have any things we can take with us? I have some.
Tim: I can't wait, Lucy! Well, I have a washing machine.
Lucy: Great, and I have a new refrigerator, so we can use that. Do you have any plates? I have lots of cups and bowls, too.
Tim: Yes, I have some new, white plates.
Lucy: And I have an old couch. Do you have a TV?
Tim: Yes, I do. We can put them both in the living room.
Lucy: Perfect!

UNIT 31

31.13

Mila: OK. We need to get some things for the weekend. Are there any pizzas in the fridge? We need three.
Jon: Well, there are two, so we need one more.
Mila: And how much flour is there?
Jon: There are two small bags of flour in the cupboard.
Mila: I only need one bag for the cake, so that's great.
Jon: What about drinks? Do we need more juice?
Mila: How many cartons do we have?
Jon: There are three here.
Mila: So we need three more then. And is there any coffee?
Jon: There is some, but not much.
Mila: OK, so let's get another jar.
Jon: Now we've got lots of burgers and sausages for the barbecue, but we need some cheese.
Mila: Do we have any?
Jon: None at all.
Mila: OK. Is that everything?
Jon: Yes, great. Let's go!

UNIT 32

32.6

Vikram: OK! Let's make a cake. Where's the recipe?
Sheila: Here it is.
Vikram: Great. So, we need flour. Let me measure some. There's ten ounces of flour. Is that enough?
Sheila: It's too much. We only need eight ounces.
Vikram: Oops. OK.
Sheila: Errr... And how about eggs?
Vikram: Erm... We have four.
Sheila: Well, that's too many because we only need three.
Vikram: That's all right.
Sheila: We also need sugar. How much sugar do we have?
Vikram: Seven ounces.
Sheila: Really? Oh, OK. Well, we need eight ounces.
Vikram: Hmm, there isn't enough. Oh well. What about butter? How much do we need?
Sheila: Eight ounces, too.
Vikram: Ha. Easy to remember. OK, well, we've got eight ounces.
Sheila: Great! That's perfect. Do we want chocolate in it?
Vikram: Why not? How much do we need?
Sheila: Three and a half ounces.
Vikram: Right, so there's... four ounces here. That's too much.

Sheila: Never mind, let's put it all in. I like chocolatey cakes.
Vikram: Yum. OK, what's next? Mix the flour and the sugar together...

UNIT 34

34.5 ex: Friend: Look, Marie. There are long dresses over here.
Marie: Oh yes, but I don't want an orange one.
Friend: They have a red one. Here!
Marie: That's perfect.

34.5.1
A: Shala wants a new hat for her birthday.
B: Which colors does she have?
A: She has a black one and a red one.
B: OK, so let's get her a blue hat.
A: Great, let's buy that!

34.5.2
Friend: So, Ben, we have your new shoes. Do you want to buy any clothes today?
Ben: Well, all my t-shirts are old, so I want a new one. I want a blue t-shirt.

34.5.3
Friend: Look, Gemma. They have some great skirts here.
Gemma: Some are really expensive. I don't have much money.
Friend: This one isn't expensive.
Gemma: Oh, no, it's cheap and beautiful. This is a great skirt. Thanks!

34.5.4
Joe: I own a blue coat, but I need a new coat.
Friend: This black one is cool. Does it fit?
Joe: I think it's too long.
Friend: No, it looks great on you. Buy it!

34.9 ex: These pants are too long.

34.9.1 This black shirt is too big. It doesn't fit me!

34.9.2 Wow, I can't buy these purple pants. They are too short!

34.9.3 Oh, no! This hat is too small to wear to the wedding.

34.9.4 This long, brown coat is great. I want it for my birthday.

34.9.5 What a bargain! These shoes are cheap! I want the pink pair.

UNIT 35

35.6 ex: Friend: Hi, Rachel. Is that your car?
Rachel: Yes.
Friend: It's great. Is it new?
Rachel: Well, it's new to me, but it's about 80 years old!

35.6.1
A: This book is terrible. It's called *In the Sky*.
B: Read this instead. It's great. It's called *In the City*.

35.6.2
A: Oh! It's English next.
B: Is it a good class?
A: Yeah, it's great. I like Professor Lewis. But my music class is terrible. Professor Chang is boring.

35.6.3
Friend: Ben, those pants are old. They are horrible!
Ben: Well, I'm a gardener so I don't wear new pants. I wear my old pants and sweaters.

35.6.4
A: I want something fun to wear with my new gloves.
B: How about this hat?
A: Yeah, great. It's fun!

UNIT 37

37.4
Friend: Hi, Sam. How are you?
Sam: Fine, thanks.
Friend: You look great!
Sam: Thanks. I do sports every weekday at the moment.
Friend: That's great. Well, I exercise on Mondays. I go swimming then.
Sam: I go running with my brother then. We go to the park.
Friend: Great. How about Tuesdays?
Sam: Well, I go salsa dancing with my friend Alison. It's a really good class.
Friend: Awesome. And how about Wednesdays?
Sam: I go fishing. That's not exercise, really.
Friend: No, it's not.
Sam: But then on Thursdays, I go cycling with my friends. We do about 20 miles in the evening.
Friend: That's good.
Sam: And on Fridays after work I go surfing at the beach. I do it every Friday. It's a great way to finish the week.
Friend: Sounds amazing!

UNIT 39

39.4
Friend: So, Ben. How do you spend your free time?
Ben: OK, well, I do different things. I don't watch TV every day. I sometimes watch TV on the weekend.
Friend: And do you read books? »

Ben: Of course. I read one or two books every week. I go to work by bus so I usually read books then.
Friend: And how about computer games? Do you play those?
Ben: No, I don't. I never play them. I haven't got any.
Friend: Ah... interesting. Do you go shopping?
Ben: Yes. I work downtown so I usually go shopping at lunchtime. I don't go shopping every day.
Friend: And what about sports?
Ben: Well, I often play basketball with my friends.
Friend: Anything else you enjoy doing?
Ben: I love cooking. I always cook dinner at home.

UNIT 40

40.5

Matt D: I'm Matt D and this is Radio Chat. Today in the studio, we have the Hollywood actress, Anna Thompson. Hello, Anna!
Anna: Hi there.
Matt D: So, Anna, this show is called *Love It or Hate It*. So, to start with: do you like my hat?
Anna: I'm sorry, I don't, but I like your glasses!
Matt D: Thanks! Anna, do you like hockey?
Anna: No, I don't. I never watch it. I like golf. It's a good game.
Matt D: OK, Anna, next question. Do you like actors?
Anna: Hmm. That's a difficult question. Do I love them or hate them? Well, I like some of them, but not all of them.
Matt D: Great... any names?
Anna: No!
Matt D: Pizza, do you love it or hate it, Anna?
Anna: I love it, especially in Italy. I always eat pizza in Rome. It's amazing.
Matt D: Do you love or hate snakes?
Anna: I like them. They're OK. I don't like spiders.
Matt D: Great! Thanks for joining us today, Anna.

40.9 ex: Hi, I'm Jill. My likes and dislikes? Hmm, well, I don't like getting up early in the morning, but I love walking my dog. It's great exercise.

40.9.1 I'm Samuel. I love riding my bike. I do it about three times a week. But my bike gets dirty a lot because I ride it in the countryside and I hate cleaning it.

40.9.2 Hello, I'm Josh. I don't like going to college because the teachers aren't very interesting. But I love playing my guitar. I do that in the evenings at home.

40.9.3 Hi there, I'm Davina. I like making cakes. I make them for all my friends' birthday parties. But I don't like eating them. There's too much sugar in them.

40.9.4 Hello, I'm Daniella. I'm not sure about my likes and dislikes. I like drinking tea and I don't like doing exercise. How's that?

UNIT 42

42.3

Martin: I listen to music all the time. Rock music is my favorite, but I like jazz, too.

I like lots of sports. I love baseball, but my favorite sport is basketball. It's a fast game and a lot of fun, too!

I like food and I do a lot of cooking. I love beef, but fish is my favorite. I eat it three times a week. I love visiting lots of cities around the world. Sydney in Australia is great. I love New York, too. There are so many things to see there. Rome is my favorite city, though. I have two jobs. I'm a gardener on the weekend. That's my favorite job, but I love working in a hairdresser's salon, too.

I love going to restaurants. My favorite type of food is Italian. I love the Italian restaurant on Main Street.

I do a lot of exercise, some every day. I go cycling three times a week. I love it. My favorite is running. I do it every day.

My girlfriend and I share a lot of pastimes. We play computer games together, go dancing, and we cook a lot. I think that's our favorite, cooking.

UNIT 44

44.11

Sheila: Hi, Mark. You look unhappy. What's wrong?
Mark: Hi, Sheila. There's a big dinner at my house this weekend and I don't know what to make. Can you help?
Sheila: Well... I can make a good salad. Does that help?
Mark: Great. Thanks, Sheila. What else can you make?
Sheila: I don't eat or cook meat, but I know a lot of recipes for fish. I can make one for you.
Mark: Thanks, Sheila. I don't know how to cook fish, so that would help a lot. But I can cook a good roast chicken.
Sheila: Brilliant. Do you want me to cook some vegetables to go with it?
Mark: Thanks, but I can cook the vegetables. Can you bring dessert?
Sheila: Sure. I can make a great apple pie.
Mark: Perfect. Thanks, Sheila.
Sheila: No problem. See you there.

UNIT 45

45.12 ex: I'm Andrew and I live by the ocean. I love my life here because I can surf every day. I'm really good at surfing. I go fishing, too, but I'm very bad at it. I never catch anything.

45.12.1 My name's Karen and I work in a gym. I love sports. I play a lot of soccer, and I play well. I'm in a college team. I love tennis, too, but I'm bad at it.

45.12.2 I'm Matthew and I work in London. The traffic is very busy here and I'm bad at driving, so I cycle to work. I'm good at cycling because I do it every day, and it's now my favorite sport.

45.12.3 Hi. I'm Richard and I'm a doctor. I love dancing, and I do it well. I love to dance around my house on the weekends. But I'm bad at cleaning, so my house is quite dirty.

45.12.4 My name's Charlie and I'm a student. I read a lot, and I'm good at studying. But I'm bad at getting up early because I always go to bed after midnight.

UNIT 47

47.11 ex: Friend: Hey, Mark. Would you like to play tennis later?
Mark: What time?
Friend: 6pm at the court in Eastville Park.
Mark: OK, see you later.

47.11.1
Friend: Hi, Sarah. Do you want to come to that new restaurant?
Sarah: Oh, not today. I'm very tired.
Friend: Oh well, another time.

47.11.2
Sophie: Vangelis! How are you?
Vangelis: I'm fine, thanks, Sophie. Actually, I want to cook a meal for some friends tonight. I love cooking and I can't wait! Do you want to come?
Sophie: That's great. I'd love to. Thanks.

47.11.3
Friend: Hey, Lee. We want some people to work on Saturday at the music festival. Can you do it?
Lee: Is it the big festival at the park?
Friend: That's right.
Lee: Great. There are some really good bands playing. What time do you want me to come?

47.11.4
Friend: Hello, Mary. How are you?
Mary: I'm fine. What are you up to?
Friend: I want to skateboard at the park this evening. Do you want to come?
Mary: At what time?
Friend: About 8pm?
Mary: Sorry, no. I want to stay home and watch TV tonight.
Friend: That's a shame. Oh well.

47.11.5
Friend: Hello, Anoushka. I want to go bowling tonight. Would you like to come with me?
Anoushka: Is it at the mall?
Friend: Yeah, at 6 o'clock.
Anoushka: Great. I'll be there.

UNIT 48

48.10
Maureen: Hello?
Alan: Hi, Maureen. It's Alan. I'm in Tokyo now. How are you?
Maureen: I'm good, Alan.
Alan: How are the kids? Are they OK?
Maureen: Frank hurt his leg at football today. It's not too bad, but he's in the hospital, just in case.
Alan: Oh, no! Give him a hug from me. Is Tom home from college?
Maureen: No, he has a lot to study this week. He's still at college.
Alan: Oh yes. I remember. How about Sophie, Charlie, and Sarah?
Maureen: Sophie is at school. She got an "A" on her English exam.
Alan: That's great. Tell her that I'm very happy.
Maureen: Charlie is in his bedroom, with his video games. He didn't go to school because he's sick.
Alan: Oh, poor boy. How about Sarah?
Maureen: She's at the town hall. There's a party there today.
Alan: Oh, that's nice. Well, give them all a hug from me...

Answers

01

1.4

1. I'm Charlotte.
2. My name's Una.
3. My name's Simone.
4. I'm Carlos.
5. I'm Juan.
6. My name's Miriam.
7. I'm Sarah.

1.5

A 5
B 1
C 2
D 3
E 6
F 4

1.6

1. Hi! My name is Linda.
2. Hi! My name is Abdul.
3. Hi! My name is Paolo.
4. Hello! My name is Linda.
5. Hello! My name is Abdul.
6. Hello! My name is Paolo.
7. Hi! I am Linda.
8. Hi! I am Abdul.
9. Hi! I am Paolo.
10. Hello! I am Linda.
11. Hello! I am Abdul.
12. Hello! I am Paolo.

1.9

1. B-E-L-I-N-D-A
2. L-E-W-I-S
3. A-D-A-M-S
4. B-O-B
5. S-P-E-N-C-E-R
6. K-A-T-E W-A-L-L-A-C-E
7. S-A-U-L J-A-C-K-S-O-N
8. N-A-T-A-L-I-E L-A-U
9. C-H-R-I-S B-O-Y-L-E

1.10

1. B-A-S-H-I-R
2. B-E-N J-A-M-E-S
3. M-O-L-L-Y
4. L-O-P-E-Z
5. N-A-D-I-Y-A L-A-T-I-F

03

3.5

1. eleven
2. seventeen
3. thirty-four
4. fifty-nine
5. eighty-five

3.6

1. Theo **is** 45 years old.
2. Madison **is** 27 years old.
3. Jeremy and Tanya **are** 90 years old.
4. We **are** 29 years old.
5. I **am** 34 years old.

3.8

1. 40
2. 30
3. 19
4. 60
5. 80
6. 17
7. 13

3.12

1. Japan
2. US
3. France

3.13

1. Spanish
2. German
3. Canadian
4. American
5. Australian
6. Chinese

3.14

1. I am Australian.
2. I am English.
3. I am from Italy.
4. I am from France.
5. You are Australian.
6. You are English.
7. You are from Italy.
8. You are from France.
9. They are Australian.
10. They are English.
11. They are from Italy.
12. They are from France.

05

5.3

1. your horse
2. their sheep
3. our fish
4. its bone
5. his dog

5.4

1. Bingo is **my** dog.
2. **Her** aunt is called Goldie.
3. **My** cat eats fish.
4. **Their** rabbit lives in the backyard.
5. **Our** parrot is from Colombia.
6. **His** wife is called Henrietta.
7. **Their** dog is 10 years old.
8. **Our** aunt lives on a farm in Ohio.
9. Here is **its** ball.

5.5

1. Farida **is** their sister.
2. Duke **is** our dog.
3. Daisy **is** her mother.
4. They **are** his grandparents.
5. It **is** our horse.
6. John **is** our cousin.
7. I **am** Daisy's daughter.
8. You **are** my friend.

5.8

1. **This** is her horse.
2. **That** is our rabbit.
3. **That** is their pig.
4. **This** is his cow.
5. **This** is your fish.

5.9

1. Lily is their sister.
2. Our son is 12 years old.
3. That is their cow.
4. This is your ball.
5. Her father is called Caspar.

5.10

A 2
B 1
C 5
D 3
E 4

5.11

1. This is my cat.
2. This is my parrot.
3. This is her cat.
4. This is her parrot.
5. This is their cat.
6. This is their parrot.
7. That is my cat.
8. That is my parrot.
9. That is her cat.
10. That is her parrot.
11. That is their cat.
12. That is their parrot.

06

6.3

1. Ben's son
2. Sam and Ayshah's cat
3. Debbie's house
4. Marco and Kate's car
5. Elsa's grandchild
6. Beth's parrot

6.4

1. Lucas is Ben's father.
2. Lily is Ben's mother.
3. Noah is Ben's son.
4. Grace is Ben's sister.
5. Alex is Ben's brother.

6.7

1. Angela is Skanda's wife.
2. That is my cousins' snake.
3. Sue is Ella and Mark's aunt.
4. Ginger is John's cat.

6.8

1. Kathy is **Dave's** aunt.
2. Rex is **Noah and Pat's** dog.
3. This is **her cousins'** house.
4. Felix is **the children's** cat.

08

8.2

1. **These** are Diego's keys.
2. **This** is Olivia's purse.
3. **Those** are my books.
4. **These** are my pencils.
5. **That** is Anna's sandwich.
6. **That** is Malik's phone.

8.3

1. That is his apple.
2. Those are her pens.
3. That is my ring.
4. These are our keys.
5. That is his brother.
6. These are my pencils.

8.5

"s" PLURALS:
1. apples 2. bottles 3. necklaces
"es" PLURALS:
4. sandwiches 5. brushes 6. watches
"ies" PLURALS:
7. dictionaries 8. diaries

8.6

1. watches
2. books
3. sandwiches
4. toothbrushes
5. necklaces
6. apples
7. keys
8. cell phones

8.9

1. This is her laptop. This laptop is hers.
2. Those are their keys. Those keys are theirs.
3. These are our passports. These passports are ours.
4. That is his brush. That brush is his.

8.10

TOM'S BAG:
sandwiches, cell phone, ID card, chocolate bar.
SARAH'S BAG:
purse, books, brush, notebook.

8.11

1. Those are my books.
2. Those are my dogs.
3. That is my brother.
4. These are my books.
5. These are my dogs.
6. This is my brother.
7. Those are Bruno's books.
8. Those are Bruno's dogs.
9. That is Bruno's brother.
10. These are Bruno's books.
11. These are Bruno's dogs.
12. This is Bruno's brother.

10

10.2

1. You **are a** doctor.
2. She **is a** farmer.
3. They **are** teachers.
4. We **are** nurses.
5. I **am an** actor.
6. She **is a** chef.

10.3

1. You **are** a driver.
2. I **am** a mechanic.
3. He **is** a vet.
4. We **are** sales assistants.
5. They **are** businesswomen.
6. She **is** a waitress.
7. We **are** receptionists.
8. She **is** a gardener.

10.5

1. hospital
2. farm
3. laboratory
4. restaurant
5. school
6. construction site
7. hospital
8. theater
9. restaurant

10.7

1. False 2. False 3. True 4. True

10.9

A. 3
B. 4
C. 1
D. 6
E. 5
F. 2

10.10

1. She **is a builder. She works on a construction site.**
2. We **are scientists. We work in a laboratory.**
3. You **are an actor. You work in a theater.**
4. He **is a waiter. He works in a restaurant.**
5. Chloe **is a nurse. She works in a hospital.**

10.13

1. Noah's mother
2. Noah's sister
3. Noah's father
4. Noah's brother

10.14

1. Selma **is a** chef. **She works with** food.
2. Max **is a** nurse. **He works with** patients.
3. Mat **is a** mechanic. **He works with** cars.
4. Ana **is a** vet. **She works with** animals.
5. Jazmin **is a** judge. **She works with** people.

11

11.3

1. It's midnight.
2. It's half past three.
3. It's quarter to twelve.
4. It's two thirty.
5. It's a quarter past nine.
6. It's ten thirty.

11.4

1. 11:30
2. 7:00
3. 4:15
4. 9:30
5. 2:15

11.5

1. 9:00
2. 1:15
3. 3:25
4. 2:30
5. 12:15

11.6

1. It's half past five. / It's five thirty.
2. It's a quarter to seven. / It's six forty-five.
3. It's twenty-five to twelve. / It's eleven thirty-five.
4. It's a quarter past eight. / It's eight fifteen.
5. It's twenty-two past ten. / It's ten twenty-two.

13

13.4

1. He **wakes** up at 7 o'clock.
2. You **leave** home at 8:30am.
3. I **start** work at 10am.
4. Ellen **gets** up at 5 o'clock.
5. My wife **takes** a shower in the evening.
6. I **take** a shower in the morning.
7. My parents **eat** lunch at 2pm.
8. We **leave** work at 4pm.
9. My brother **works** with animals.

13.5

1. I **leave** work at 5:30pm.
2. Phil **eats** lunch at 12:30pm.
3. We **get** up at 8am.
4. His son **starts** work at 5am.
5. My sister **leaves** work at 7pm.
6. They **eat** dinner at 10pm.

13.6

1. My son **wakes** up at 5am.
2. I **leave** work at 6:30pm.
3. We **eat** breakfast at 8am.
4. Paula **works** outside.
5. My wife **starts** work at 7am.
6. He **eats** lunch at noon.

13.9

1. washes
2. watches
3. wakes
4. goes
5. finishes
6. leaves

13.10

1. Lucia **wakes** up at 7am.
2. I **get** up at 7:30am.
3. Ethan **goes** to work at 5am.
4. You **leave** work at 5pm.
5. Shona **watches** TV in the evening.

13.11

1. My mother **watches** TV in the morning.
2. We **go** to bed at midnight.
3. My husband **finishes** work at 6:30pm.
4. Rob **goes** to work at 8:30am.
5. I **take** a shower in the morning.
6. I **leave** work at 6 o'clock in the evening.

13.12

1. True
2. True
3. False
4. False
5. True
6. True

13.13

1. I start work at noon.
2. I finish work at noon.
3. My brother starts work at noon.
4. My brother finishes work at noon.
5. They start work at noon.
6. They finish work at noon.
7. I start work at 2:30pm.
8. I finish work at 2:30pm.
9. My brother starts work at 2:30pm.
10. My brother finishes work at 2:30pm.
11. They start work at 2:30pm.
12. They finish work at 2:30pm.

14

14.3

1. We eat lunch at 3pm **on** the weekend / **at** the weekend.
2. She goes to bed at 1am **on** the weekend / **at** the weekend.
3. I go to work **from** Monday **to** Wednesday.
4. They eat dinner at 9pm **on** the weekend / **at** the weekend.
5. We finish work at 3pm **on** Fridays.
6. I eat breakfast at work **on** Mondays.

14.5

1. He **goes to the gym** on Tuesdays and Fridays.
2. They **go swimming** on Thursdays.
3. He **plays soccer** on Wednesdays.
4. I **take a bath** on the weekend.
5. You **read the newspaper** on Saturdays.

14.6

1. I watch TV **on** Sundays.
2. I take a bath **at** 7pm every day.
3. I go to bed **at** 10 o'clock **on** Sundays.
4. I get up **at** 8am **from** Monday to Friday.

14.10

1. True 2. True 3. False 4. True
5. False

14.11

1. I get up at 6am five days a week.
2. They go to bed at 11pm every day.
3. Sarah plays soccer twice a week.
4. Jamie washes his clothes once a week.

14.12

1. We get up **at** 7am five times a week
2. They go to work **from** Monday to Friday.
3. Linda washes her face **every** day.
4. Colin sleeps **from** 11pm **to** 6am.

15

15.4

1. She is not my sister.
2. That is not her car.
3. I am not 35 years old.
4. We are not Spanish.
5. Chad is not a vet.

15.5

1. He **is not** in the office.
2. She **is not** a businesswoman.
3. I **am not** 18 years old.
4. This **is not** a snake.
5. We **are not** artists.
6. You **are not** at work.
7. Dexter **is not** a cat.

15.6

A. 3
B. 1
C. 5
D. 2
E. 4

15.9

1. It **is not** 10 o'clock in the morning.
2. You **aren't** 35 years old.
3. I **am not** Australian.
4. My brother **isn't** married.
5. Tom and Angela **aren't** construction workers.

15.10

1. True
2. True
3. False
4. True
5. False
6. True
7. False

15.11

1. I am not at work.
2. I am not tired.
3. I am not 24 years old.
4. You aren't at work.
5. You aren't tired.
6. You aren't 24 years old.

7. He isn't at work.
8. He isn't tired.
9. He isn't 24 years old.
10. They aren't at work.
11. They aren't tired.
12. They aren't 24 years old.

16

16.4

1. I **do not** read the papers on Saturday.
2. The dog **does not** eat fish.
3. They **do not** go to the theater often.
4. Ben and I **do not** live on a farm now.
5. Theo **does not** cycle to work.
6. You **do not** work at Fabio's café.
7. Claire **does not** watch TV in the evening.
8. We **do not** play football at home.
9. Pierre **does not** wake up before noon.

16.5

1. False
2. True
3. False
4. False

16.8

1. We go to work every day. We do not go to work every day.
2. He watches TV in the evening. He doesn't watch TV in the evening.
3. You do not work in an office. You don't work in an office.
4. They play tennis. They do not play tennis.
5. She works with children. She doesn't work with children.

16.9

1. We don't work with animals.
2. I don't eat chocolate.
3. Sandy doesn't work in a hairdresser's.
4. Melanie and Cris don't have a car.
5. They don't live in Park Road now.
6. We don't watch Hollywood movies.
7. She doesn't drive a taxi.

16.10

1. I don't work outside.
2. I don't have a bicycle.
3. I don't play tennis.
4. You don't work outside.
5. You don't have a bicycle.
6. You don't play tennis.
7. We don't work outside.
8. We don't have a bicycle.
9. We don't play tennis.
10. Meg doesn't work outside.
11. Meg doesn't have a bicycle.
12. Meg doesn't play tennis.

16.11

1. Kim
2. Selma
3. Chiyo
4. Maria
5. Selma

17

17.4

1. Is Brad a nurse?
2. Are these my keys?
3. Are Ruby and Farid actors?
4. Is this his laptop?
5. Is Valeria his sister?

17.5

1. A
2. B
3. B
4. A
5. A
6. B

17.7

1. **Is** Holly your mother?
2. **Are** they from Argentina?
3. **Are** you a teacher?
4. **Is** this your dog?
5. **Is** there a post office?

17.11

1. **Do** you get up at 7am?
2. **Do** they live at number 59?
3. **Do** we finish work at 6pm today?
4. **Does** the parrot talk all day?
5. **Do** you work in a lab?

17.12

1. Do you live in New York?
2. Does she work on a farm?
3. Does he get up at 5am every day?
4. Do they come from Peru?
5. Does Brad work in the post office?

17.13

1. Do they live in New York City?
2. Does he work in a restaurant?
3. Does Lewis go swimming on Fridays?
4. Does Marisha work with animals?

17.14

1. **Does** she go swimming on Tuesdays?
2. **Do** you read the paper on Sundays?
3. **Does** she work with animals?
4. **Do** they work on a construction site?

18

18.3

1. True
2. False
3. False
4. True
5. False

18.4

1. No, it isn't.
2. Yes, it is.
3. Yes, she does.
4. No, I don't.
5. No, it isn't.

18.5

1. No, **I'm not**
2. Yes, **they do.**
3. No, **it isn't.**
4. Yes, **she does.**
5. No, **she isn't.**
6. Yes, **they do.**
7. No, **he isn't.**

19

19.3

1. What **are** their names?
2. What **is** the time?
3. What **are** my favorite colors?
4. What **is** the hotel next to?
5. What **are** they?
6. What **is** your uncle's name?
7. What **is** my name?

19.6

1. What is the time? It's 5 o'clock.
2. When is your birthday? July 23.
3. Which is your car? The red Ferrari.
4. Why are you here? For a meeting.
5. How old are you? I'm 25.
6. Who is there? It's me, Marcus.

19.7

1. **Where** are your parents from?
2. **How** old are you?
3. **When** is breakfast?
4. **Who** is your friend talking to?
5. **Why** is it cold in here?
6. **Which** person is your teacher?

19.11

1. When **does** she eat lunch?
2. Where **do** they live?
3. Which bag **do** you want?
4. Where **does** he come from?
5. When **does** the movie end?

19.12

1. Where does he play football?
2. When do you clean the car?
3. What time does the party start?
4. Which days do you play tennis?

19.13

1. When do you eat breakfast?
2. What do you study?
3. Where do you work?
4. Who is she?

19.14

1. **Where** do you work in the city?
2. **When** do you start work?
3. **What** time does it open?
4. **How** many people do you work with?
5. **Who** do you work with?

19.15

1. Her brother
2. Two
3. At 7am
4. Goes swimming
5. By the pool
6. Tomorrow

19.16

1. Where does Kate play golf?
2. Where do they play golf
3. Where do you play golf?
4. Where does Kate go to the gym?
5. Where do they go to the gym?
6. Where do you go to the gym?
7. When does Kate play golf?
8. When do they play golf?
9. When do you play golf?
10. When does Kate go to the gym?
11. When do they go to the gym?
12. When do you go to the gym?

19.17

1. How often **do** they play tennis?
2. Which office **does** he work in?
3. Where **is** the party?
4. What **do** you do?

19.18

1. What **is her cat called**?
2. Who **is your English teacher**?
3. Where **does Ben work**?
4. How **is your grandmother**?

21

21.3

1. **There are** two churches.
2. **There is** a swimming pool.
3. **There is** a library.
4. **There are** two castles.

21.4

1. airports
2. theaters
3. schools
4. hospitals
5. bars
6. churches
7. factories
8. offices

21.5

1. There are two schools.
2. There are two cafés.
3. There is a hospital.
4. There is a restaurant.
5. There are three stores.

21.7

1. There **isn't** a theater.
2. There **aren't** any factories.
3. There **isn't** a bus station.
4. There **aren't** any airports.
5. There **aren't** any churches.

21.10

1. There **are** no castles.
2. There **aren't** any factories.
3. There **are** no hospitals.
4. There **aren't** any churches.
5. There **are** no swimming pools.
6. There **are** no airports.

21.11

A. 3
B. 1
C. 2
D. 4

21.12

1. True
2. False
3. False
4. True

21.13

1. **There isn't** a park.
2. **There is** a hotel.
3. **There are** no cafés.
4. **There isn't** an airport.
5. **There are** two stores.
6. **There isn't** a train station.
7. **There are** two theaters.

22

22.3

1. **The** new teacher is called Miss Jones.
2. There is **a** good café in the park.
3. I work at **the** hotel next to the library.
4. There is **a** swimming pool near my office.
5. It is **the** dog's favorite toy.
6. Janie is **an** artist at the gallery.
7. See you at **the** café at the bus station.

22.6

1. There are **some** stores on Broad Street.
2. There is **a** café next to the castle.
3. There are **some** cakes on the table.
4. There is **a** phone here.
5. There are **some** factories downtown.

22.7

1. There **are** some supermarkets in town.
2. There **is** an office near the river.
3. There **are** some chocolate bars in my bag.
4. There **is** a hospital near the bus station.

22.10

1. Are there **any** stores on your street?
2. Is there **an** airport near Littleton?
3. Are there **any** mosques in the city?
4. Is there **a** swimming pool downtown?
5. Are there **any** offices in that building?

22.11

1. Is there a supermarket near here?
2. Are there any cafés on Elm Road?
3. Are there any hotels near your house?
4. Is there a café near your office?
5. Is there a bar next to the bank?

22.13

1. Yes, **there is**.
2. Yes, **there are**.
3. No, **there isn't**.
4. Yes, **there are**.
5. No, **there isn't**.
6. No, **there aren't**.

22.14

1. Yes, there are.
2. No, there isn't.
3. No, there aren't.
4. Yes, there is.

23

23.3

1. Wake up
2. Do
3. Start
4. Have
5. Wait
6. Stop
7. Work

23.5

1. Take the second right. The station is on the left.
2. Take the first left, then turn right. The restaurant is on the right.
3. Take the second left, and the hospital is on the right.

4. Take the first left, then go straight ahead. The hotel is on the right.
5. Take the first left, then turn left. The castle is on the right.

23.7

1. The supermarket is **next to** the post office.
2. The museum is **behind** the café.
3. The station is **in front of** the church.
4. The cinema is on the **corner** of the intersection.
5. The post office is **between** the café and the supermarket.

23.10

1. Don't read that book.
2. Don't go past the hotel.
3. Don't give that to the cat.
4. Don't have a shower.
5. Don't drive to the mall.

23.11

1. Library
2. Swimming pool
3. Movie theater
4. Science museum

24

24.3

1. There are two hotels and three shops.
2. Hilda works in a school and a theater.
3. My uncle is a scientist and my aunt is a doctor.
4. Sue watches TV and she reads books.
5. The store opens at night and Jan starts work.

24.4

A 3
C 1
D 4
E 2

24.6

1. There are hotels, bars, and stores.
2. Sam eats breakfast, lunch, and dinner.
3. I play tennis, soccer, and chess.
4. Teo plays with his car, train, and bus.
5. There is a pencil, a bag, and a cell phone.
6. My friends, girlfriend, and aunt are here.
7. Ling works on Monday, Thursday, and Friday.

24.8

1. This is my car, but these aren't my car keys.
2. We eat a small breakfast, but we eat a big lunch.
3. I work from Monday to Friday, but not on the weekend.
4. The bathroom has a shower, but it doesn't have a bathtub.

24.9

1. There isn't a bathtub, but there is a shower.
2. There isn't a bar, but there is a café.
3. The bag is Maya's, but that laptop isn't hers.
4. Si doesn't have any dogs, but he has two cats.
5. Sally reads books, but she never watches TV.

24.10

1. Lu reads books **and** magazines.
2. I work every weekday, **but** not on weekends.
3. Jim is a husband **and** a father.
4. There is a cinema, **but** no theater.
5. There isn't a gym, **but** there is a pool.

24.11

1. There is a cat and a rabbit, but there isn't a snake.
2. There is a doctor and a builder, but not a chef.
3. There is a laptop and a newspaper, but there isn't a cell phone.
4. There is a movie theater and a restaurant, but not a theater.

25

25.3

1. He is a horrible man.
2. They are small children.
3. My uncle is a quiet man.
4. There is a large cake.
5. These are my old shoes.
6. There is a new supermarket.
7. You work in an old museum.

25.5

1. **small** 2. **beautiful** 3. **old** 4. **large** 5. **busy** 6. **horrible** 7. **beautiful**

25.6

1. The nurse is busy. She is busy.
2. The dog is quiet. He is quiet.
3. The patients are new. They are new.
4. The town is horrible. It is horrible.
5. The car is beautiful. It is beautiful.

25.8

1. beautiful
2. lake
3. large
4. mountains
5. restaurant
6. beach
7. busy
8. quiet

25.9

1. **The** countryside **is** quiet **and the** trees **are** beautiful.
2. **The** city **is** horrible **and the** people **are** busy.
3. **The** hotel **is** new **and the** swimming pool **is** large.
4. **The** beach **is** big **and the** cafés **are** busy.
5. **The** city **is** old **and the** buildings **are** beautiful.

25.12

A 2
B 5
C 1
D 4
E 3
F 6

25.13

1. There are **lots of** people.
2. There are **some** buildings.
3. There are **a few** cars.
4. There are **a few** parks.

25.14

1. In the tree, there are a few birds and some apples.
2. In the sea, there are a few people and lots of fish.
3. In the countryside, there are some people and lots of trees.

26.3

1. lives there.
2. she's a farmer.
3. goes swimming.
4. it's new.
5. with people.
6. her aunt lives there.
7. lots of people.

26.4

1. She lives on a farm because **she's a farmer**.
2. She works in a hotel because **she's a receptionist**.
3. They get up late because **they're students**.
4. We work with children because **we're teachers**.
5. You don't eat lunch because **you're busy**.
6. I work outside because **I'm a gardener**.
7. My parents go to the country because **it's quiet**.

28

28.3

1. They **have** a car.
2. You **have** a chair.
3. He **has** a dog.
4. We **have** a daughter.
5. It **has** a door.

28.4

1 Maya 2 Ben 3 Ben 4 Ben

28.5
1. False
2. True
3. False
4. False
5. True
6. True

28.7
1. Kaleh does not have a dog.
2. You don't have a microwave.
3. Greendale does not have a church.
4. Alyssa and Logan don't have a garage.
5. We do not have a yard.

28.8
1. I have a couch.
2. I have some chairs.
3. I have a dining room.
4. We have a couch.
5. We have some chairs.
6. We have a dining room.
7. She has a couch.
8. She has some chairs.
9. She has a dining room.
10. She doesn't have a couch.
11. She doesn't have a dining room.

28.11
1. They have not got a couch. They haven't got a couch.
2. He has got three sisters. He's got three sisters.
3. You have not got a bike. You haven't got a bike.
4. We have got a microwave. We've got a microwave.
5. It has got a bathtub. It's got a bathtub.
6. They have got a cat. They've got a cat.

29

29.3
1. Do they have a toaster?
2. Do you have a new couch?
3. Does Ben have a washing machine?
4. Do we have an old armchair?
5. Does Karen have a large TV?
6. Does the kitchen have a sink?
7. Does the house have a yard?

29.4
1. Lucy
2. Lucy
3. Lucy
4. Tim
5. Tim

29.5
1. Do you have any chairs?
2. Do you have a kettle?
3. Do you have any plates?
4. Do they have any chairs?
5. Do they have a kettle?
6. Do they have any plates?
7. Does he have any chairs?
8. Does he have a kettle?
9. Does he have any plates?

29.7
1. No, I don't.
2. Yes, I do.
3. Yes, I do.
4. No, I don't.

29.8
1. No, he doesn't.
2. No, he doesn't.
3. Yes, he does.

29.10
1. Has this town got a theater?
2. Has your house got an attic?
3. Have they got laptops?
4. Has this coffee shop got a bathroom?
5. Have you got a cell phone?
6. Has the teacher got my book?

29.11
1. Yes, **she has**.
2. Yes, **it has**.
3. No, **they haven't.**
4. No, **it hasn't.**

31

31.3
1. Jake has **an** apple.
2. There is **some** coffee.
3. Reena eats **some** spaghetti.
4. There are **some** eggs.
5. I've got **some** bananas.

31.5
1. There is some milk. There isn't any milk.
2. Is there any chocolate? There isn't any chocolate.
3. Are there any apples? There are some apples.

31.6
1. Yes, **there is**.
2. No, **there aren't**.
3. No, **there isn't**.

31.9
1. There is **a bag of** flour.
2. There is **a cup of** coffee.
3. There is **a carton of** juice.
4. There are **two bowls of** spaghetti.
5. There are **two glasses of** milk.

31.12
1. **How many** glasses of juice are there?
2. **How much** water is there?
3. **How many** potatoes are there?
4. **How many** bars of chocolate are there?
5. **How much** pasta is there?
6. **How many** cartons of juice are there?
7. **How much** milk is there?

31.13
1. one bag
2. three
3. some
4. cheese

32

32.3
1. There **are enough** oranges.
2. You have **enough** pineapples.
3. There **are too many** apples.
4. You don't have **enough** bananas.

32.6
1. Too many
2. Not enough
3. Enough
4. Too much

32.7
1. There is **too much** sugar.
2. They **don't have** enough butter.
3. She has **too many** mangoes.
4. John has too many **eggs**.
5. There **aren't** enough oranges.
6. That is **too much** flour.
7. There **is** too much sugar in the cake.

34

34.2
1. Hannah **chooses** a yellow skirt.
2. Elliot and Ruby **buy** a new couch.
3. Sue **owns** an old winter coat.
4. Jess's dad **buys** her a new bike.
5. Chris and Lisa **own** a black sports car.
6. Gayle and Mike **sell** shoes at the market.
7. Mia **chooses** her red shoes.
8. The shoes **fit** me.
9. We **want** new white shirts.

34.3
1. They choose expensive blue sweaters.
2. Judith has some old brown hats.
3. This shop sells short red pants.
4. Tina owns cheap black shoes.
5. Jim buys a new black coat.

34.4
1. **new** 2. **cheap** 3. **white** 4. **long** 5. **black** 6. **black** 7. **old** 8. **new** 9. **expensive** 10. **cheap** 11. **red** 12. **long**

34.5
1. a blue hat
2. a new t-shirt
3. a cheap skirt
4. a black coat

34.7
1. too cheap
2. too expensive
3. too long
4. too short
5. too old
6. too new
7. too big

34.8
1. Jim's pants are **too short**.
2. Sam's dress is **too long**.
3. Molly's sweater is **too small**.
4. Helen's red hat is **too big**.
5. Lili's shoes are **too big**.

34.9
1. B
2. A
3. B
4. A
5. A

34.10
1. These black pants are too big.
2. These black pants are big enough.
3. These black pants are too short.
4. My expensive pants are too big.
5. My expensive pants are big enough.
6. My expensive pants are too short.
7. My black dress is too big.
8. My black dress is big enough.
9. My black dress is too short.
10. My expensive dress is too big.
11. My expensive dress is big enough.
12. My expensive dress is too short.

35

35.4
1. This is a **horrible** old t-shirt.
2. This is a **boring** movie.
3. I have a **lovely** long dress.
4. This is a **beautiful** bird.
5. This is a **fun** party.

35.5
1. That is a horrible blue car.
2. This is a fun short story.
3. I have a lovely black cat.
4. He has an ugly red house.
5. They own a great new laptop.

35.6
1. A
2. B
3. A
4. A

35.8
1. Oh, no, the blue glass vase!
2. We have two plastic chairs.
3. What an interesting metal box!
4. That's an expensive leather couch.

35.9
1. She owns some beautiful wooden chairs.
2. We don't own those horrible plastic plates.
3. They have an ugly yellow car.
4. He wears a boring blue sweater.
5. She wants a new metal lamp.
6. He owns a large fabric bag.
7. Norah wants a new leather jacket.

37

37.3
1. We don't **go surfing** in the winter.
2. Do you **go sailing** on the weekend?
3. Tipo **goes cycling** five times a week.
4. He **goes fishing** on the river.
5. Sharon **goes dancing** with her friend.
6. Do they **go running** every morning?
7. He doesn't **go horse riding**.

37.4
1. Wednesday
2. Friday
3. Tuesday
4. Thursday

37.6
REGULAR GERUNDS:
sailing, **snowboarding**, **skateboarding**
GERUNDS WITH DOUBLE CONSONANTS:
swimming, **running**, **shopping**
GERUNDS WITH A DROPPED "E":
skating, **horse riding**, **cycling**

37.9
1. Shala **doesn't play** tennis.
2. Mina **plays** golf at the club.
3. We **play** squash on Mondays.
4. The dog **plays** with its ball.
5. Maria **doesn't play** tennis.
6. The kids **don't play** games at school.
7. They **play** soccer at the park.

37.10
1. We **play** tennis every Tuesday night.
2. They **don't play** golf during the week.
3. You **don't play** volleyball at the beach.
4. Do they **play** together every Saturday?

37.11
1. Sara
2. Chas
3. Sara
4. Cassie

37.12
1. Milo and I **go cycling** in the park on Saturdays.
2. The team **plays /play football** from 6pm to 7pm on Wednesdays.
3. Imelda **goes horse riding** once a month.
4. Luther **goes fishing** during his vacation time.
5. Hannah **plays tennis** with her cousin on Monday evenings.

39

39.3
1. We never go to the mall.
2. Sally and Ken usually cycle to work.
3. My sister often works outside.

39.4
1. usually
2. never
3. usually
4. often
5. always

39.5
1. Nico **usually** swims after work. He **never** watches TV on the weekend.
2. Meg **often** goes surfing in Hawaii. She **sometimes** dances all night.
3. Alma **always** reads on vacation. She **sometimes** plays golf on Sundays.
4. Carrie **usually** goes to bed late and she **never** eats breakfast.

39.8
1. How often do they go to work?
2. When do you get up?
3. How often do you go on vacation?
4. When do they go shopping?
5. How often do you visit Mischa?

39.9
1. When do they visit their grandparents?
2. When do we go skating?
3. How often does he play hockey?
4. When do you go shopping?
5. How often do they see their parents?
6. How often does he walk the dog?
7. How often do we go skating on the lake?

39.10

1. When do you do yoga?
2. How often do you go to the movies?
3. How often do you go skateboarding?
4. When do you arrive at work?
5. How often do you go surfing?

40

40.3

1. Ava and Elsa love the mountains.
2. Shania hates mice.
3. Manuel likes his book.
4. Cats don't like the rain.

40.4

1. Imelda doesn't hate pasta.
2. My dog doesn't love steak.
3. Our grandfather doesn't like coffee.
4. I don't love the sea.
5. Sam and Jen don't hate hockey.
6. You don't like the countryside.
7. We don't like our new cell phones.

40.5

1. hockey
2. some actors
3. pizza
4. spiders

40.6

1. I love cats.
2. I love curry.
3. I love this house.
4. You love cats.
5. You love curry.
6. You love this house.
7. Milly hates cats.
8. Milly hates curry.
9. Milly hates this house.

40.9

1. D
2. B
3. C
4. A

40.10

1. True
2. False
3. False
4. True
5. False
6. True
7. False
8. True
9. True

40.14

1. Why does Una love skiing?
2. Why do they like this book?
3. Why doesn't Debbie like her job?
4. Do we like cooking?
5. Does she love surfing?
6. Do I hate working late?
7. Does Aziz love Ontario?

40.15

1. I like English class because it's interesting.
2. We love skating because it's exciting.
3. He hates cleaning because it's boring.

42

42.3

1. basketball
2. fish
3. Rome
4. gardener
5. Italian
6. running
7. cooking

42.4

1. A
2. B
3. A
4. C
5. A

42.5

1. Grace's favorite food is pizza.
2. Poppy's favorite sport is surfing.
3. Dylan's favorite animal is his horse.
4. Justin's favorite country is Australia.
5. Ling's favorite pastime is knitting.
6. Abdul's favorite color is purple.
7. Mira's favorite number is 10.
8. Jacob's favorite sweater is woolen.
9. Tori's favorite relative is her cousin.

42.6

1. Sam's **favorite band** is Big Bang.
2. Joe's favorite band is **Fun Sounds**.
3. Joni's **favorite restaurant** is Midnight Pizza.
4. Sam's favorite restaurant is **The Salad Bar**.
5. Joe's **favorite restaurant** is Burger Heaven.
6. Joni **loves the play** called Big Blue Sea.
7. Joe loves the movie called **Blue Soul**.

42.7

1. yoga
2. burgers
3. surfing
4. a restaurant

44

44.4

1. Paul cannot ride a bicycle.
2. Manuel cannot come to the party.
3. They can sleep in the tent tonight.
4. I cannot walk up the hill.
5. I can carry this box to the car.

44.5

1. Jo's pen doesn't work. She **can't** write her letter.
2. I understand the homework, so I **can** do it.
3. The museum is closed. We **can't** get in.
4. I have the car today, so I **can** drive you.
5. It's cold outside, so we **can't** have a picnic.
6. Tony needs to work late, so he **can't** come.
7. We **can't** play tennis. It's too dark.

44.6

1. Shirley can drive a car. Shirley can't drive a car.
2. Ben and Julie cannot carry boxes. Ben and Julie can't carry boxes.
3. Ilaria can spell English words. Ilaria cannot spell English words.
4. He can go to work. He can't go to work.

44.9

1. No, **he can't**.
2. Yes, **they can**.
3. No, **I can't**.
4. Yes, **I can**.
5. No, **we can't**.
6. Yes, **she can**.
7. No, **they can't**.

44.10

1. Can the dog jump over the wall?
2. Can Denise touch her toes?
3. Can I lift my son onto my shoulders?
4. Can Grandma see the TV?
5. Can I hit the tennis ball over the net?

44.11

1. True
2. False
3. True
4. True

44.12

1. Paul and Jerry don't like the ocean because they **cannot** swim.
2. I ride my bike to work because I **cannot** drive.
3. Jim cannot climb over the wall, but he **can** walk around it.
4. My mother **cannot** lift that bag because it's too heavy.
5. My sister Penny loves music and **can** dance to any song.

45

45.3

1. Mary can speak French **excellently**.
2. Roger can run very **quickly**.
3. The old man walks **slowly**.
4. He talks very **loudly**.
5. She won the race **easily**.

45.5

REGULAR
loudly, quickly, badly, easily
IRREGULAR
fast, well, hard, early

45.6

1. You speak English very **well**.
2. Damian cooks burgers **badly**.
3. I can get to your house **easily**.
4. Benjy always listens **carefully**.
5. My brother always works **hard**.
6. Sammy always plays his guitar **loudly**.

45.10

1. My horse is good at jumping.
2. I am bad at getting up early.
3. Mary is bad at writing German.
4. Jo and Bob are good at swimming.
5. Millie is bad at cleaning.

45.11

1. Conchita is good at playing basketball.
2. You can drive a van well.
3. Shania and Dave are good at surfing.
4. My father can't speak English well.
5. Manu is bad at writing stories.

45.12

1. Bad at
2. Bad at
3. Bad at
4. Good at

45.13

1. I am good at cooking.
2. I am bad at cooking.
3. I am good at playing soccer.
4. I am bad at playing soccer.
5. I am good at history.
6. I am bad at history.
7. He is good at cooking.
8. He is bad at cooking.
9. He is good at playing soccer.
10. He is bad at playing soccer.
11. He is good at history.
12. He is bad at history.

46

46.3

1. A tortoise walks very slowly.
2. A chicken flies quite badly.
3. Pigs eat very noisily.
4. Monkeys climb trees really well.

46.5

1. Really good
2. Quite good
3. Quite good
4. Really good

47

47.4

1. He wants to get a dog.
He would like to get a dog.
2. You want to work in Turkey.
You'd like to work in Turkey.
3. We would like to learn Chinese.
We'd like to learn Chinese.
4. They want to start a rock band.
They would like to start a rock band.

47.5

1. He'd like to act in a musical.
2. He wants to be in the Olympics.
3. He'd like to travel around Asia.
4. She'd like to sail a boat.
5. She wants to work with lions in Africa.

47.6

1. I'd like to climb this tree.
2. I'd like to climb that mountain.
3. I'd like to read a newspaper.
4. I'd like to read another book.
5. I want to climb this tree.
6. I want to climb that mountain.
7. I want to read a newspaper.
8. I want to read another book.
9. She wants to climb this tree.
10. She wants to climb that mountain.
11. She wants to read a newspaper.
12. She wants to read another book.

47.9

1. He would not like to play tennis.
He wouldn't like to play tennis.
2. She would not like to study science.
She doesn't want to study science.
3. They would not like to go to work.
They wouldn't like to go to work.
4. You wouldn't like to sing.
You don't want to sing.
5. We would not like to go diving.
We don't want to go diving.

47.11

1. No, she wouldn't.
2. Yes, he does.
3. Yes, he would.
4. No, she doesn't.
5. Yes, she would.

47.12

1. He doesn't want to climb that hill.
2. I wouldn't like to be a judge.
3. They don't want to go to work today.
4. She would like to play tennis tonight.
5. I want to climb that tree.

48

48.5

1. Jerry would really like to pass his driving test.
2. Ben and Sam would really like to take an IELTS test.
3. Helen would quite like to practice her English.
4. I'd quite like to play the piano tonight.

48.6

1. I'd really like to practice my spelling.
2. I'd really like to do a biology degree.
3. I'd really like to learn English.
4. I'd quite like to practice my spelling.
5. I'd quite like to do a biology degree.
6. I'd quite like to learn English.
7. Laila would really like to pass her history exam.
8. Laila would really like to do a biology degree.
9. Laila would really like to learn English.
10. Laila would quite like to pass her history exam.
11. Laila would quite like to do a biology degree.
12. Laila would quite like to learn English.

48.9

1. Emily has **a lovely home**.
2. Sue always takes her lunch to **the office**.
3. Can you see where **the church** is?
4. Jim went to **bed** hours ago.
5. Can you drive me into **town** later?
6. I live next to **the university**.
7. I leave **home** at 8am every weekday.

48.10

1. Tom
2. Frank
3. Sophie
4. Charlie
5. Sarah

Index

All entries are indexed by unit number. Unit numbers for main entries are in **bold**. Unit numbers with the prefix R, for example R1, refer to information in the reference section.

A

B

C

DE

F

GH

I

Acknowledgments

The publisher would like to thank:
Jo Kent, Trish Burrow, and Emma Watkins for additional text; Thomas Booth, Helen Fanthorpe, Helen Leech, Carrie Lewis, and Vicky Richards for editorial assistance; Stephen Bere, Sarah Hilder, Amy Child, Fiona Macdonald, and Simon Murrell for additional design work; Simon Mumford for maps and national flags; Peter Chrisp for fact checking; Penny Hands, Amanda Learmonth, and Carrie Lewis for proofreading; Elizabeth Wise for indexing; Tatiana Boyko, Rory Farrell, Clare Joyce, and Viola Wang for additional illustrations; Liz Hammond for editing audio scripts and managing audio recordings; Hannah Bowen and Scarlett O'Hara for compiling audio scripts; George Flamouridis for mixing and mastering audio recordings; Heather Hughes, Tommy Callan, Tom Morse, Gillian Reid, and Sonia Charbonnier for creative technical support; Vishal Bhatia, Kartik Gera, Sachin Gupta, Shipra Jain, Deepak Mittal, Nehal Verma, Roohi Rais, Jaileen Kaur, Anita Yadav, Manish Upreti, Nisha Shaw, Ankita Yadav, and Priyanka Kharbanda for technical assistance.